Scientific Temperaments

Three Lives in Contemporary Science

Philip J. Hilts

A TOUCHSTONE BOOK
Published by Simon & Schuster, Inc.
New York

10 9 8 7 6 5 4 3 2 1
10 9 8 7 6 5 4 3 2 1 Pbk.
Library of Congress Cataloging in Publication Data
Hilts, Philip J.
   Scientific temperaments.
   Includes bibliographical references and index.
   1. Wilson, Robert R., 1914-   2. Ptashne, Mark
3. McCarthy, John, 1927-   . 4. Scientists—United
States—Biography. 5. Fermi National Accelerator
Laboratory—History. 6. Biological research—History.
7. Artificial intelligence—History. I. Title.
QC16.W56H54   1982   509'.2'2[B]   82-10694
ISBN 0-671-22533-2
ISBN 0-671-50590-4 Pbk.

Acknowledgments

Some thanks ought to be committed to print. The patient and always enthusiastic Nan Talese carried the project, without flagging, through more than four years. E. L. and K. B. Hilts, Richard and LaVerne McKeown, Arnold and Nancy Bennett, Juergen and Mary Haber, and Rebecca Leet all provided funds at desperate moments, as well as continuing supplies of cheeriness. The Cornell University Library provided me access to the Robert Wilson papers. The extraordinary collection on recombinant DNA at the Massachusetts Institute of Technology was a godsend.

TO DONNA.
A dedication is no recompense,
but merely an IOU taken in public.

Contents

Preface

An expert, says the American proverb, is only a damned fool who happens to be a long way from home. In the spirit of that thought, I believe we take scientists too seriously. We forget they are people of ordinary habits and passions and that this is one of the most important facts necessary to an understanding of science.

In my ten years or so of spending time among scientists while not being one of them, I have found that the best are those who speak plain English, have a sense of humor, and do not make glorified claims for their craft. I recall one eminent physicist who said he had no special interest in physics when he went to college but, in his freshman physics class, found one or two people he liked a great deal. He enjoyed their humor, their sense of the outrageous, their willingness to think about things in odd and interesting ways. He wanted to be around them. So he studied physics.

In all human activities, it is not ideas or machines that dominate; it is people. I have heard people speak of "the effect of personality on science." But this is a backward thought. Rather, we should talk about the effect of science on personalities. Science is not the dispassionate analysis of impartial data. It is the human, and thus passionate, exercise of skill and sense on such data. Science is not an exercise in objectivity but, more accurately, an exercise in which objectivity is prized.

To find evidence for these facts, we need only look at science journals and science grants. Several sociologists recently studied the way that the National Science Foundation gives out grants, and whether they are distributed by merit alone. The group could not escape the conclusion that at least half, and possibly more, of what's involved is pure dumb luck. Grant applications are carefully screened by panels of eminent scientists, yes. But things other than ideational merit, including simple prejudice, entered into the judgment. Is your mentor someone we know? How like our ideas are yours? Is this type of research in fashion? Another study looked at the other end of scientific work, publishing work already done. The authors of this study took already-published work, changed the author's name and home institution, and resubmitted the papers. It is interesting that the journals did not recognize papers they had already published. But more important, when these already-accepted papers were resubmitted with the names of unfamiliar authors and small or unknown schools, the papers were rejected for publication. In this and other things, science is not different from any other profession.

But we know science less well. When I conceived this book, it was with this thought in mind: we have read in detail, especially through the "new journalists" such as Gay Talese, of the lives of Mafia figures, businessmen, drug dealers, reporters, politicians, and more. But we have not read such tales about scientists. It has been my purpose to go to scientific laboratories and learn something about the lives and the craft of the people working there. These three profiles are the result.

I think a clear play between science and personality is shown in these profiles. And it is interesting that the single strongest trait in common among the scientists I met is not dispassion. It is passion, even obsession. I heard one wife of a physics genius say that physicists do not become human until they are fifty. Before that, they are so morbidly absorbed in the competition to do something important that they have little time for novels and concerts, art and conversation. She added, though, that once they do come out of the cocoon, they are incomparably colorful people.

Not by reason alone, but by the combustive chemistry of idea and temperament mixed, do scientists carry on. Here then, with that thought in mind, are three lives in science.

One

The Main Ring
Robert Wilson and the
Building of Fermilab

1

THE leather was cold and stiff as we pulled the saddles from their pegs and hauled them toward the stalls. It was dawn without the sun, thirty-seven degrees. Gray clouds pitched and reached in the wind. The snow had just melted in this part of the Illinois farmland, but the edge of winter had not yet gone. That morning, Dr. Robert Wilson, a particle physicist, wore a fedora that was black as jet and made of fur. He wore a quilted nylon jacket and a baggy pair of jeans. The jeans rode Western style, below his center of gravity, as low as was conceivable for a pair of trousers. The black boots he wore had pointed toes, and angled heels, and whorls of fancy stitching.

Wilson spoke to an attractive woman as he led his horse out of the barn. "This is how we used to mount a bucking bronco," he said with a grin. He hooked the rein with his elbow, and pulled it so the horse had to turn its head around to the saddle. "If her head's back this way, she can't start bucking so easily," he said, nodding toward the horse's hindquarters. He mounted with a single, easy arc of his foot.

His horse was a gray Arabian called Star. He walked her around the white fence of a pasture and then trotted her across the flat Illinois prairie, straight toward an odd geographic feature about a quarter of a mile away. There, the ground rose up in a twenty-foot welt. In this prairie, where the ground might not rise more than a few feet in a mile, the object ahead clearly was made by man. It was a long, earthen mound that stretched off to the right and left, curving out of sight. Larger than human scale, the whole mound cannot be discerned from horseback, but maps of the area show that it continues curving around for four miles. The curve meets itself directly opposite where we ride, completing the circle. The clearest sense of its size comes from photographs of northern Illinois taken from a satellite about three hundred miles up in space. They show the spreading towns and suburbs of the region as ragged blotches. Against this background appears one sharp and seemingly perfect circle. It is the only feature on earth of such size and regularity; it stands out against the Midwestern landscape like a dandelion in short grass.

Building the ring of tall earth was Robert Wilson's idea. It is a feature of the Fermi National Accelerator Laboratory, where he was the director from its inception in 1967 until 1978. Fermilab is among the largest of the world's laboratories, and all of its more than a hundred buildings, fifteen hundred workers, perhaps a million tons of equipment were created as support for a single great piece of machinery. The Fermilab machine is circular, a great four-mile loop, buried directly below the earthwork circle toward which we were riding. Physicists call the ring-shaped machine a particle accelerator; in newspaper stories it is called an atom smasher. There are only a few dozen of these machines in the world, and the one at Fermilab is the most powerful of its kind. Fermilab and its European twin, called CERN, are possibly the largest machines of any kind in the world.

It is unusual as machinery goes, not only for its great size, but because it has no practical purpose. It manufactures nothing and makes no profit. "Our work here is primarily spiritual," says Wilson. "We are concerned with the ultimate nature of matter." Congressmen and others asked him, frequently, what are the practical applications of the physics that go on in this machine? There are none, he says. No more, at least, than there are applications for literature, for theater, for poetry or painting. "Scientific understanding has inherent cultural value," he once explained to the Joint Committee on Atomic Energy. "It has great beauty. It adds to the satisfaction of our lives."

Since Wilson has some political as well as artistic sense, he usually adds as an aside the more practical answer of another scientist when put on the spot by a politician. When Faraday had found that electricity might be induced to flow in a trickling current, he hadn't any idea where this arcane fact might lead. But when Gladstone asked him, "What's the use of it?" Faraday replied boldly, "Sir, someday you will tax it."

We rode through the wheat-colored grass, which was still matted from the winter's weight of snow, toward the tall earth-work mound. Though the particle machine beneath it was on, there was no sound.

I had met Wilson in his role as laboratory director, and listened to Wilson in the role of physicist, in a comfortable office the day before. But there is a small revelation in watching him ride a horse. It is like watching the gears and levers of a machine, which seemed angled and awkward at rest, become all at once a thing of fine balance as it reaches speed. On the ground, Robert Wilson walks with an oddly rigid posture, which becomes exaggerated by his emphatic gestures. His hair is wild, like gray porcupine spikes. But once on horseback, everything begins to fit. The gestures and attitudes of body are not the habits of a physicist with too many years of lecturing, but natural parts of the deportment of a cowboy. Trotting, cantering, and running, he sits on his horse as comfortably as if he were relaxing against a fence. Walking or riding, his back is straight as a rod, and his limbs pivot from it with a floppy, cowhand's grace.

As the horses approached the twenty-foot-high hill on that cold March morning, they slowed to a walk. A few drops of freezing rain bit our faces as Wilson, with a turn of his wrist, reined his horse to walk her parallel to the long earth mound. The particle accelerator lies in a tunnel that is twenty feet below the bottom of the mound and forty feet below the fawn-colored tufts of grass that grow on the top. We walked the horses near what looks like a cement blockhouse sitting up against the mound. Here, and in several other places around the ring, there is a door and a deep stairwell leading down under the mound to the accelerator tunnel. If the machine were off and the doorway open, a visitor might climb down the stairway to the tunnel, which is ten feet wide, and constructed like a large cement sewer pipe. The actual accelerating machine runs on the inside curve of the cement tunnel, and consists mainly of rectangular iron boxes strung together like two-foot-high boxcars of a miniature freight train. There are about one thousand of the iron boxes in the four-mile length of tunnel, each hitched to its neighbor and the last completing the circle by connecting with the first. Each iron box, twenty feet long and weighing twenty thousand pounds, contains one huge, elongated magnet, and is surrounded by pipes feeding it water and electricity while retrieving from it electronic data. But the heart of this great ring-shaped machine is a thin pipe of stainless steel. It is only a few inches in diameter, it is all one piece, and it runs through the entire four-mile train of boxes just as a thread runs through the beads of a necklace. The stainless-steel pipe is vacuum-sealed and completely airtight. The pipe is like the inner tube of a tire four miles around. Protons enter the tube from a bulb of gas much as air enters an inner tube—through the stem of a valve. The stem of Fermilab's tube is one third of a mile long.

Protons are sent into the airless, frictionless space within the tube, and the resulting stream of particles is pulled by the magnets around the four-mile circumference about four hundred thousand times, gaining speed with each successive circling. The beam of particles has about the thickness of a flower stem or a piece of taut twine. As the particles circle, they reach 99.999 percent of the speed of light. The snake of protons is then extracted from the four-mile tube, guided down another tube, and aimed at a small aluminum rod. When the protons hit, a small portion of the rod is annihilated. The atoms of aluminum are destroyed, transformed into a smear of pure energy. The energy quickly congeals again, becoming a spray of matter. Among the array of hundreds of particles created this way, most do not exist freely on earth. They cannot be found in the rest of the universe either. The only other place, and time, in which such matter was formed was at the Creation and (in the billions of years since the Creation) during the sudden, immense stellar explosions which reprise the Creation. The particle accelerator thus reenacts, in the small chamber of a human machine, the beginning of the universe.

A simple scale of energy for physical events has been sketched by physicist Alfred K. Mann in a lecture he gave at Fermilab: Strike a match and the particles in that flare carry an energy of a few electron volts. Inside the furnace of the sun, each particle has an energy of millions of electron volts. And in the explosion of Creation, each particle raced apart from the others with an energy of billions of electron volts. The Fermilab's particles are accelerated to that same range, four hundred to five hundred billion electron volts.

For the past forty years, the foremost occupation of physics has been to read, like a star map, the arcs and angles and trajectories which emerge from the flash of energy in particle accelerators. From this the elementary structure of matter may be deduced. The method is indirect, and a little obscure, but it is the only way to see the skeleton of the universe, the particles which underlie and support the flesh of all appearance.

Alongside the great machine of physics, the physicists move in daily routines like priests repeating rituals of transubstantiation. If physics may be pictured as a single corpus of belief—as one work with no author and thousands of successive editors—then the bright flash at the accelerator target is perhaps the best symbol, the summary in a single action, of the whole achievement of physics.

The string of iron boxes, the tubes and pipes in the cement tunnel, and the circular mound above them, together make up a bundle of concentric rings. And there are more aboveground. There is a ring of road around the inside of the four-mile mound and a ring of ponds and fountains used for cooling the machine. The workers here refer to all the bands, above- and belowground, in a single phrase—"the main ring."

2

We rode out along the curve of the main ring for more than an hour—Wilson, myself, and Rich Orr, the owner of the horses and a physicist who was serving as the Fermilab's business manager. Under the violent clouds, the accelerator site looked more like fresh prairie than a federal laboratory facility. The landscape was a study in two plain colors, brown and gray. But present in a dozen contrasting shades, each color was animated by play against itself. The vertical stripes of the trees were carbon black, smoky gray, bluish gray, and silver. The grasses were white gold, fawn brown, reddish sienna, and dark umber brown.

Wilson has kept the Fermilab site as wild as possible. In fact, it is wilder than it was in 1967, when the land was owned by farmers. There are 1800 acres of the site devoted to corn, 650 acres left to pasture, 250 for hay, and some thousand still open, including the one and a quarter square miles in the center of the ring. There have been four-pound bass caught in Fermilab ponds and eight-pound catfish. During an Audubon bird count one year there were about forty different sorts of birds spotted at the lab, including about five hundred mallard ducks, a pair of the rarer canvasbacks seen floating in the cooling ponds, five rufous-sided towhees, about a score of hawks, a score of ring-necked pheasant, five purple finches, a dozen woodpeckers, and sixty-four common crows. There are deer, fox, raccoon, mink, and several lodges of beaver. When the accelerator suddenly overheated and shut down one afternoon some time ago, there was bewilderment in the control room. The cooling system had failed, but not for any apparent mechanical reason. Some time passed before it was found that muskrats, which like to make burrows in the main-ring bunker, had dug too close to the edge of a cooling pond. The side collapsed, the water emptied, and one segment of the machine quickly heated up.

Not long after Wilson completed the design and construction of Fermilab, an odd article about the lab appeared in *The New Republic* magazine. It was an art review of the place by critic Kenneth Evett, who began his review saying, "While advocates of the marriage of art and technology go marching down the aisle . . . whom should they meet coming in the opposite direction but Robert R. Wilson, designer and director of the Fermi National Laboratory at Batavia, Illinois, offering his creation— one of the largest, most complex, and sophisticated instruments of scientific research on earth—as his version of that improbable consummation in which technology has become one with art. The inadvertent beauty of functional machines has long been widely noted, but Wilson, while responding to the rigorous necessities of efficiency and experimental precision, has, in addition, consciously designed his laboratory in every particular and on a gigantic scale to satisfy his own esthetic predilections. The rare combination of artistic and scientific aspiration . . . has produced a hybrid creation unprecedented in the history of art or science . . . the ensemble sits there, an island of intense Celebration and high Civilization amidst the suburban semi-rural expanses of northern Illinois." In addition to making the Fermilab artful, Wilson managed to build it within a tight budget, and give it double the experimental power planned for it.

In at least one respect, particle physics in the twentieth century is like astronomy in the seventeenth. In that time, just after the invention of telescopes, there was a race to create newer and bigger telescopes because each larger size practically guaranteed new discoveries through new depths of vision. Each telescope was superseded by another, and so astronomy advanced in leapfrog fashion. It has been the same with particle accelerators from the 1930s to today. There are some physicists who say that without Fermilab, and without Wilson's successful schedule and budget for the machine, accelerators around the world would not have reached such high experimental energies for another two or three decades. And when those energies finally came, they would not have been in American machines, but in European or Soviet ones. After Nobelist Ernest Lawrence, inventor of the circular particle accelerators, Robert Wilson has been the chief figure in physics always ready to build a newer, bigger machine—even when it seemed impossible, even at the expense of current experiments.

Wilson, who left the directorship of Fermilab in 1978, is still helping to build Fermilab's newest and most powerful accelerator, called the Tevatron because it is expected to produce beam energies of a trillion electron volts. Wilson, who is now sixty-eight years old, has also lived some length of time in Beijing, helping the Chinese to build their first large accelerator. He was pleased, he said, to find that the site chosen for the Chinese machine is an aesthetically fine one, within sight of the hallowed Ming Tombs.

As Wilson and I rode back toward the barn, a pair of Canadian geese flew up from the tall grass near one of the ponds; the birds bleated noisily as they joined a small squadron of geese flying over the main ring. We rode on, touring the borders of a thick stand of trees that ran right up to the edge of the main-ring bunker. During the building of the laboratory, after the site for the ring had been picked, Wilson noticed that the ring was going to cut through this stand of trees. Changing the plans at that point would have meant thousands of dollars in extra cost, and taking certain risks in placing the particle machine on the uncertain ground of a bog. Without hesitation Wilson moved the machine; the trees stood.

Since 1967, this land has reclaimed some of its past. The land by now would certainly be under several housing tracts, but it has been held open and is used as a public park. Some of the original Illinois prairie grass, which in the past two hundred years has been nearly choked off by strains of European grass, has been replanted, and large patches of it are seeded inside the main ring. At Fermilab there are also about thirty-five buffalo, which have not flourished here for about eight hundred years. At that time tribes living by the Fox River would send bands of hunters up to the site in the summer. They would make camp by the ponds, take their kill, and bring it back to the larger river settlement. The habit of hunting at this site goes back probably nine thousand years, perhaps more. Arrowheads, which not long ago littered the ground, have been collected and preserved.

The grounds of Fermilab are a patched quilt of sculpture, buildings, and equipment of Robert Wilson's design. So much is Wilson's that the display seems nearly indecent. Driving into Fermilab from the west, the first noticeable influence of Wilson's hand is at the front gate—or at the lack of a front gate. There is a token guardhouse by the road, but no guard, no barrier. Other similar federal facilities are so fierce about their privacy, one feels a flash of guilt passing through Fermilab's open entrance.

Wilson and assistant director Ned Goldwasser fought for the openness against constant demands by the government and Fermilab's own security forces. During the emotional storm of the 1960s, especially after a laboratory at the University of Wisconsin was bombed, the Atomic Energy Commission told Wilson to come up with a plan for handling activists should they appear at the National Accelerator Laboratory. Wilson wrote in response that he would face the students alone, "armed with the most potent student-stopper yet devised—a lecture on physics. I have found that when exposed to such strong verbal radiations strong men waver, brave men weep. A touch of Newton or a dose of quantum mechanics causes the eyes to glaze over, unconsciousness to set in. The fact is, I rather hesitate to use this weapon of overkill. . . ."

Far more than most physicists, Robert Wilson is aware of the aesthetic dimensions of physics. The giant particle accelerator might not have been built at all without Wilson, but it was designed and constructed with a sense of art as well as science. Before Wilson, the machines of physics were made with a chaos of wires and tubes and metal bars. They were the color of the parts, modified by dirt and grease. But the main body of the accelerator, the circular string of magnets resembling a four-mile-long freight train, is painted in bright colors. In this machine, as in others by Wilson, the magnets are bright blue, with every fourth one painted bright red. The magnets sit on yellow

metal stands, which Wilson designed with decorative corners
and scalloped edges. The wires and other paraphernalia he
tucked neatly into steel tubes. Wilson's machines are gorgeous.

At one moment during our morning ride at the Fermilab,
Wilson was trotting Star not far from the ring of tall earth
under which the proton machine was working. He looked over
and gauged the height of the mound, or "berm" as the physicists call it.

"What exactly is the purpose of the berm?" I asked him.
Since the machine was already buried underground, I was uncertain just why this mound of dirt should also be piled on
top of it. "Is it to absorb the extra radiation from the machine?"

"No, not really," he said. "Mostly we put it there to accentu-
ate the ring. When we were building it, we looked out and saw
that the ring just wasn't very visible. I was really disappointed.
You could see where the cooling ponds were all right, but not
the ring itself. So when we dug out the ponds, I had them pile
the dirt up here. . . ." Wilson gestured toward the immense
circle of dirt.

I looked at him, and thought of the view from three hundred
miles up in space. "The berm is for aesthetic reasons?"

"Yes."

3

THE cold drizzle had stopped by the time we led the horses back into the barn. As we hung our tack and brushed the horses, I asked Wilson about his reputation as a cowboy.

It had probably served him best in 1942, when the atomic bomb project was beginning. He and other scientists had been dragged out of their ivy-covered buildings in the colonies, and sent to the strange Western landscapes near Los Alamos, New Mexico. The other scientists were greenhorns, awkward in their tweedy suits and street shoes. But Wilson surprised his colleagues. He had boots. He could recall Western folklore and stories old cowhands had passed on to him. He could ride horseback. He could mount his spotted pony with a single step and a leap. He could tell about roping steer at a full gallop, or the time he rode a hundred miles in a single day. His cowboy skill made him something of a star then, adding immeasurably to his reputation as a bright young man of physics.

Now it is still a source of humor, and, when other physicists are angry with him, it is also put into the shape of a profanity: "Wilson doesn't understand. He's nothing but a damn cowboy!" We led the horses to their stalls, and we talked about the skill of using a lariat. Wilson said he would show me.

"You have a lariat with you?" I asked.

"Sure. I always carry it with me, in the trunk of my car."

I was surprised. "You do?"

"Yes," he said with a grin. "It doubles as a towrope."

Outside the barn, he pulled the Mexican rope from his trunk. He showed me the special slipknot used to rope a steer—if your throw is precise, one firm yank will close the loop around the animal's feet and pull him down; if your throw misses, a flip of the wrist, a shiver of the rope, and the knot comes untied, preventing the cowboy from inadvertently roping his own horse's feet or some stray cactus.

In a moment, Wilson made what looked like an immense loop in the rope, maybe four feet long, and began swinging it in the air. Briefly he threatened to bring down Rich Orr who was walking to his car, but then settled for the capture of a couple of tall pipes near the barn.

The sun was now up, its rise still concealed in an angry display of clouds. Soon the working day would begin. Robert Wilson stepped into his long black car and started toward home to exchange his jeans and boots for his laboratory director's outfit, a plain suit and dark tie. The black car glided along the narrow road running beside the mound of earth and the huge machine which lay beneath it. The machine was on, had been on all night, spraying protons like water beads into the webs of waiting experiments.

The physicists who had spent the night with their experiments, their logbooks, and the fluttering digits on dozens of animated machines would now be putting on their coats and slipping into the cold morning air. In return, crews of freshly washed faces would appear, blinking, ready for another watch among the particles.

Back at the central laboratory building, Robert Wilson's office is on the second floor. There are no formalities in getting to see him, none of the usual secretarial tic-tac-toe—"Do you have an appointment? I'll buzz him and see if he's ready to see you yet. . . ." There is no secretarial guard post outside the director's door. In fact, there is no door. There is no wall in which to place a door. His office, like most in the building, is open. The outside wall is all glass, overlooking the main-ring berm. The other three sides of the office are screens or simply a few tall plants. Because his office doesn't have walls, and because the rest of the building has either no walls or glass walls, it is possible to stand on the fifth floor, three floors higher and entirely on the other side of the building from Wilson's office, and look down across the atrium to see the director slumped in his chair, reading.

When I first met him in his Fermilab office, he greeted me with a big grin, a vigorous handshake, and large gestures: "Come on in. Come in. Sit down. Take a chair." Then I had the curious sensation of watching a pond freeze over. Wilson has no repertoire whatsoever of small talk. "He is a shy man," said his secretary, Judy Ward. "After the first few words, you can always hear that pause. You can see the wheels going around, him trying to think of something to say." But he can't. "He also has a good deal of trouble talking to women," she says. "I know that when I first came here, for quite a long time he couldn't look me in the eye." Mrs. Ward is a striking woman, a blonde, with a friendly and outgoing manner. "He would just look at the ground or somewhere else when he was talking to me. He was embarrassed."

Robert Wilson, personally, is a difficult and shy man. But as a public figure in physics, he is not only not shy, he has a reputation for boldness. He conducted his affairs and those of the lab as a dramatist, or a conjurer, might.

When Fermilab was being built, an architect once brought him a set of plans to approve even though they were not the cost and design Wilson had outlined. Wilson bellowed. He took the architect's drawings and ripped them up. He threw them on the floor. He jumped on them. He gesticulated madly before throwing the man out of his office. In this manner, Wilson ruled Fermilab. He is aware of the value of aggressive display when he wants something done his way. The plans for the Fermilab cafeteria called for a freight elevator to move all the dishes from the dining area to the kitchen. When Wilson found out what the cost of the elevator was, he thought it outrageously high. He quickly called up the cafeteria manager. "How much does a place setting cost? How many meals would you serve in a year?" When he hung up the phone he flatly told the architect: "Forget the elevator. Build me a chute from the cafeteria straight into the Dempsey Dumpster. We can get twenty years of dishes for the price of one elevator!"

"Wilson can be very enthusiastic," reports former colleague John DeWire of Cornell, "and some say that he can be cruel.

He gets an idea and he decides he is going to do it no matter what. He walks over you." As another physicist commented, "As for the line of command here, there is none. He makes every decision, big or small. He does not work through the heads of the divisions at all." There was at least one moment, and perhaps more than one, during which open mutiny at Fermilab was possible. Not long ago a prominent physicist emerged beet red from a meeting with Wilson. Wilson had asked him to do a job, the man had apparently accepted but not carried out the work as Wilson had intended. "I have never been spoken to in such a way before," the physicist said. "I felt like a child being reprimanded by his parent. If Wilson weren't such an old man, I would have punched him in the mouth!" Another physicist who was asked to keep to a tough Wilson schedule refused. After an angry exchange, the man departed permanently. It has been suggested that Fermilab at one time did not attract the best technicians, even though it should be able to because of its prominence as the most powerful facility in the world. The reason cited was that Wilson is a strong leader who did not accept opposition well.

Wilson has some understanding of his own ferocity; he jokes about it when he can. He once recalled a story about his designing an accelerator some years earlier at Cornell University. Wilson had set his mind on a specific site for the building, a site which involved extra work and a large retaining wall to hold back the soil of an embankment. Over difficulties and objections, Wilson ordered the architect to carry on with the plan. Deep into the project, Wilson reversed his decision. He wrote, "Although I had insisted on the particular location of the building, I now innocently suggested moving the building away from the bank by about forty feet, which meant that their fine wall was no longer necessary. Now it turns out that architects are funny people and are not at all like ordinary people such as physicists, who are only pleased to think about this kind of helpful suggestion. Instead, the architects turned absolutely green—arose in a body and stomped out of the room. After fifteen minutes had elapsed, one of them came back. He had torn the list of architects from the yellow pages of the telephone book. 'Here,' he said, handing it to me with obvious disgust. 'We'll help you get one of these.' "

When he was at the Cornell lab, he ran the small facility with purposely unstated lines of hierarchy. He disliked administrative detail and hated organization charts. When he was asked to produce an official organization chart for the lab, he ignored the request. He was asked again, and he refused. When he was pressed, he ended the matter by making what he called Organization Chart. It was a vertical stand of wire, with a piece of metal placed across the top of it. The metal piece moved like a balance. At one end was a jar with nuts and bolts and money. Balanced against it on the other side were some of the prettier parts he found around the lab meant to suggest people. He presented it as his final word on the subject.

Leading a laboratory with a cowboy's ornery confidence, as Wilson led Fermilab, has its value. When work had to be contracted for outside the laboratory, Wilson did not simply select a contractor. He selected two. He gave each of them one third of the job. The last third, the most profitable after both companies had tooled up to do the work, was awarded to the quickest and best work. The result of this sort of gimmick was good work, cheaply done.

There was no telephone in Robert Wilson's office. He did have one for a few days when he first moved into a temporary office at Fermilab. But he could not stand it for long. The damned device, he said, kept intruding on his thought and his conversations. So in a moment of anger one day he tore the phone out of the wall and threw it into the hallway. Later when he moved into his permanent quarters, a new phone lay in wait for him. Not long afterward, when his secretary Judy Ward wanted to put a call through to him, she went into his office, noticed that there seemed to be no phone, and began to look for it. She finally found the cord, which led to a large potted plant in the corner. Wilson had taken the phone and buried it in the moss and dirt.

"If you don't have a phone, you take a whole level of trivia out of your life," he says. "A whole level of frustration disappears. The best situation would be if there was one pay phone on the floor, a nickel pay phone, so you had to go down the hall to make the call. When you have a phone in your office, people will call you up to say a lot of trivial things; you get all kinds of meaningless interruptions. But if they have to come up and make a special trip to see you, nine times out of ten they'll get along fine without it."

Wilson learned early in his career the importance of social inventions, and now believes strongly in their importance. He had made physical inventions since he was a child. But physics does not move by ideas and machines alone. Physics is a social endeavor. The withdrawn and socially inept Wilson first realized this in 1941 when he had an idea which seemed like the idea of a lifetime. It was the beginning of World War Two, when Wilson was at Princeton, and the single thing standing between scientists and an atomic bomb was the great difficulty of making enough of the rare and unstable uranium 235. The solution to the problem came to Wilson all at once. He swiftly worked out the idea on paper, and he raced to build a staff to build his uranium isotope device. The shy Wilson was feeling a swell of confidence, almost light-headedness, such as he had never felt. He was given some workers by Princeton, but he still needed more people. Boldly he went asking. He approached the great physicist I. I. Rabi, at the radiation laboratory in Cambridge, Massachusetts, who was even then a giant in physics. Wilson was only twenty-seven years old, but was completely confident as he went to visit the great man. He laid out the idea to Rabi, asked for the loan of a researcher or two, and began to expand on the importance of his idea. But as he spoke, Wilson became dismayed. Rabi seemed uninterested, even cynical. "I could see I was losing him," Wilson says. "So, I don't know why, I started talking louder and started waving my arms. He seemed to look more interested and I started to jump up and down. In a minute I was really jumping high up off the floor and pounding on the desk. To my amazement, it worked. He said all right, he would lend me one man for the project. . . ." That experience, and its lesson, have remained with him.

4

From the time of the first philosophers, it has been recognized that the hazard and perhaps the charm of consciousness is that it is susceptible to illusion. What appears immediately to our senses is only conjury, a thin film of false images spread over the surface of things. It has been the work of physics to discover the hidden motions and props of the conjury.

From the beginning it was believed that there must be a simple substance, a universal material, out of which the motley forms of the world were magicked. And, for twenty-five hundred years, it has been believed by many that the universal material comes in granules. Particles. For that long they have been objects (conceived only, never seen) of puzzlement, excitement, study, and obsession. For two and a half thousand years, the ideas about atoms, about particles, remained practically unchanged. It was only thirty years before Robert Wilson arrived at Berkeley that the picture of particles shifted suddenly.

The first disturbing news, gained by the use of primitive accelerators, was that the atom was not a single, solid grain. It had parts. And these parts were given to spontaneously bursting. The word atom had been used up to that time because it meant indivisible. But the atom turned out not only to be divisible, but unstable, gyrating wildly. Fragments had been found flying off in hundreds of different directions.

Still it was assumed that the little atomic parts packed together to form a little sphere. The English physicist J. J. Thompson compared that sphere to a plum pudding, with raisins of negative charge spread evenly in a cake of positive charge.

But then came the surprise which turned out to be only one of several shocks for the physicists before 1930. The great Lord Rutherford, already winner of a Nobel Prize, decided to make a routine test of Thompson's pudding. He set a graduate student on the job, firing particles at a target atom. It was expected that the particles would pass through the target, deflected only a little by the spots of charge within. But the actual results of the experiment showed that the particles often veered off at wide angles, and many of them even bounced straight back in the direction they came from.

When a new picture of the atom was finally sketched out, many found it difficult to believe. The bits of negative charge, the electrons, were found to make up an immaterial, cloudlike outer shell, and a tiny yet heavy nucleus of matter lay within. And the sizes were bizarre: if the cloud of electrons were blown up to the size of the Notre Dame Cathedral, the nucleus would still be practically invisible, a fly in the vast space under the vaulted roof.

The atom is practically all empty space. Worse, the tiny nucleus is immensely heavy. It accounts for practically the entire weight of the cathedral, while all the pillars, walls, and vaults are light as vapor.

After twenty-five hundred years, physicists had finally begun to pry up the floorboards of reality, and the first glimpses beneath were rather unsettling. There was no foundation.

"In removing our illusion, we have removed the substance," wrote astronomer and physicist Arthur Eddington. "For indeed we have seen that substance is one of our greatest illusions." He explained the magician's gimmicks behind the conjury. "The sparsely spread nuclei of electrical forces become to us a tangible solid; their restless agitation becomes the warmth of summer; the octave of ethereal vibration becomes a gorgeous rainbow." The endearing objects of our world are merely casual groupings of atoms. Solids are crowds packed in geometric arrays like the restless, confined crowd at a football stadium. Liquids are more casual crowds, like the loose stream of cars that moves along freeways and collects in the pools of parking lots.

As atoms were found to be empty, particle accelerators have shown that even the particles within the atoms—the protons of the nucleus, the electrons of the shell—have been found to be without substance. They are merely forces reaching out from a central point. The mathematical description of a particle is a description of fields of force, entities with practically no existence other than the pull they exert on the space around them. We encounter such a field when we hold two magnets apart and our hands feel the pull. Particles are only this—pull with a center.

These particles are permanently stable and cannot be destroyed unless they are caught in the caldrons of stars or the target chambers of human particle accelerators. This unusual destruction, or change of state, is in its way spectacular. There are only a few kinds of particles in the ordinary way of things, but some three hundred may burst into life temporarily when two particles collide with enough force. In the collision, particles appear in one form, then change to another as they spray forward. The entire display occurs in a time measured in pico-seconds, or even atto-seconds, billion-billion-billionths of a second. It ends with energy dissipated, with the particles slipping back into the cooler sobriety of the stable forms—the proton, the electron, the neutron, and the photon.

It is the brief cascades of action, occurring in the jump from a stable particle, through the shifting intermediate shapes, to another of the stable particles, which holds the physicists' attention. These showers of matter are created within equipment endowed with an electronic nervous system which can perceive the passage of particles. The physicists cannot watch the action directly in most cases, but speak to one another of "taking data" when they have an experiment in progress.

The daily product of the Fermilab, besides the fresh stream of particles, is a torrent of black digits on computer paper. There is an abstract, colorless quality to the actual moments of experimentation. In the early years of experiments with particles, physicists could watch the flashes of light when a particle struck a screen, they could shoot a particle beam out into the air and watch it create its eerie blue glow. But now they sit in monitoring trailers and watch only the ticking red numbers in a dozen readout windows; they hear the beeps and whirs of machines speaking to one another. They often cannot tell the results of an experiment for days, as they must wait for a computer analysis.

But still, the experiments excite the physicists, excite them as much as apparitions would stir a cloister of monks. What they watch, track, and tabulate are the permanent characteristics of the particles, the few things that should remain unchanged during the flash and confusion of particle interaction. When the property remains constant through many experiments, it is said to be conserved. Particles are simple objects—there are only about eight sorts of behavior which are conserved. These completely identify each particle, and are called quantum numbers. (They include such characteristics as the amount of electric charge, the amount of spin, the amount of energy, and other items of behavior such as "charm" and "strangeness." As an example of conservation, if two particles collide, and each has a charge of $+1$, then among all the resulting particles the total charge must still add up to the same total, $1 + 1$, or $+2$.)

A group of physicists who worked at Fermilab once wrote that "Quantum numbers describe the properties of a particle in the same way that a list of facial features might describe a person. The complete list of quantum numbers defines the particle uniquely; together with its mass, such a list represents all one can possibly know about the particle." This suggests how elementary the elementary particles are; with a person or even a simpler object of nature, there is practically no limit to the description which could be given—endless words could be expended in telling about the appearance, behavior, and nature of each detail. But with particles, only eight things need be said, eight numbers given, and nothing else.

This raises a curious problem among physicists. If particles are so utterly without attributes, how is a physicist to think about them? When he works with "massless" particles, he is simply working with a particle that has in its mathematics, quite simply, a zero where the term for mass should be. The math is neutral, and does not suggest how we should imagine what "massless" means.

In public, physicists speak in formalisms which are careful

and limited. But privately physicists grapple with the particles
in just the way that the rest of us do. They try to picture them,
they try to imagine them as things acting in thing-filled ter-
rains. Each physicist has his own vision of the things he studies.
Asking a physicist to disclose his private way of imagining
particles is, perhaps, like asking a theologian to disclose his
private way of imagining God. Does the theologian picture God
as he prays to Him? Is the image a man, perhaps with a beard?
It would probably embarrass theologians to confess their private pictures of God because their intellectual descriptions seem
so sophisticated and abstract. Their pictures of God might seem
childlike by comparison.

The trouble is a natural one. God and particles by definition
have no description. They haven't got the attributes we call
"appearance," even though our minds by habitual necessity try
to put particles and everything else into simple images. Particles
have no possible appearance. Our organs of seeing require vast
numbers of light particles to register at all, so there are no
conceivable means by which a single particle could "appear."
Particles lack all the properties by which we usually describe
things; they are so utterly simple that they are indescribable.

So when a physicist is asked for his personal view of the
unimaginable, he is understandably reluctant, perhaps a little
embarrassed. He would not like his colleagues to hear him talking about little flying balls. But privately, the physicists *do* see
little spheres for particles, just as Democritus and Newton did.

The image a physicist conjures up for the particle depends on
the problem, Wilson says. Some time ago when the problem was
the internal composition of the atomic nucleus, he says, Wilson
imagined the nucleus as a hornet's nest, inside which a cloud of
mad protons, neutrons, pions, and other things buzzed. Now
that the nucleus is better known and the problem is the activity
inside the proton, the proton has become a hornet's nest with
quarks buzzing within.

Very few particles are actually counted as structureless, and
truly elementary, particles—among them the electron, the neutrino, and the celebrated but uncertain quark. All the rest of
the three hundred known particles are composed of these few
elementary ones.

The electron is the particle which people have known the

longest. The source of its name is the Greek word for "bright and shining." The Greeks used the word to describe the yellow mineral amber, which first acquainted mankind with electric charge by its ready crackling with static electricity when it is rubbed. The electron as we now imagine it has no measurable size and is treated by physicists as that classical entity of mathematics, the dimensionless point.

The neutrino is also a dimensionless point, but in addition it has no mass. It has no charge. It forgoes all the traits of other particles, excepting only spin. The neutrino is practically nothing but disembodied spin. It is the most abundant of all particles, yet it almost wholly shuns contact with them. Neutrinos are a white flood, drenching every centimeter of the universe without touching any of it. Trillions of neutrinos pass through each human body every second, yet none collides with another particle; neutrinos pass through the earth with the same ease. They are pumped into the universe constantly from the fusion in stars: the sun rains them down upon us during the day, and up through our feet an invisible "neutrino shine" comes at night.

The neutrino is a strange particle, and by the articles of physical law should be an impossible particle. There should be no such thing as a particle without mass, since nothing may travel faster than the speed of light, and everything slower than the speed of light has mass. The neutrino circumvents the problem by traveling at exactly the speed of light, never faster, never slower. It escapes in a loophole of relativity theory.

Fermilab creates huge quantities of neutrinos every day, and they appear as ghosts in the photographs from the bubble chamber. In this chamber, the tracks of passing particles can be seen as razor-thin white lines and arcs and spirals. A neutrino's passage may be recognized where white figures of disturbed particles blossom out of apparently nothing in the black background of the picture.

The proton, as particles go, is elephantine. It has two thousand times the bulk of the electron and it is, strictly speaking, not an elementary particle. The proton is composed of three quarks, and it is the quark which is now chief object of interest and speculation in physics.

Beginning with the naming of the quark, there has been a

burst of whimsy in the naming of particles during the past fifteen years. Murray Gell-Mann, a Nobel-winning theorist, named the quark in 1963. He theorized that the confusing array of particles found inside the nucleus could be explained in a simple way by inventing an underlying particle which could combine in twos or threes and create all the known particles.

When Gell-Mann came up with the idea, he didn't immediately give his particles a name, but he did have a nonverbal barking sort of sound which he whimsically associated with them. Then, a short time later, he was leafing through *Finnegans Wake* by James Joyce. He had studied and enjoyed the linguistic invention of the book for some years, and on this skimming he came across the phrase, "Three quarks for Muster Mark!" The word sounded like his sound, and in addition, his theory called for three of them. So the particles became quarks.

There are now believed to be six sorts of quark, and following Gell-Mann's lead, they have been given whimsical designations: the up quark, the down quark, the strange quark, the charmed quark, the top quark, and the bottom quark. (For these last two, some have suggested calling them truth and beauty rather than top and bottom.) The force which theoretically holds the quarks together in pairs and trios is called gluon.

Two up quarks and one down quark, spinning around each other in a tight little system, make a proton. Two down quarks and one up quark make a neutron, a particle which is nearly identical to the proton except that the proton is positively charged and the neutron is neutral. Each random combination of the quarks makes a new particle: if the quarks were a deck of cards and they were shuffled and dealt out in piles of two and three, each pile would be a recognizable particle.

Nearly all of this knowledge has come to us suddenly, within the past one hundred years. First, atoms were found to underlie the many phenomena of the world. Then, in a second era of modern understanding which began in the 1920s, the nucleus of the atom was penetrated and found to contain new forces and still more minute particle-structures than the atom. In the third modern era of physics, now passing, our knowledge is penetrating yet smaller structures within those nuclear structures.

Most of Robert Wilson's experiments over the years, and his building of a series of particle-accelerating machines, helped

urge forward the second era, the nuclear era in physical understanding. But beginning with some experiments in the 1950s
and early 1960s, and later with the building and directing of
the Fermilab, Wilson has helped open the third era, the era of
elementary particles. His work, particularly his experiments
which were part of the first deciphering of proton structure, led
through several steps to the edge of the discovery of quarks.
Some physicists will spend their lives with the neutrino and
some, like Robert Wilson, pry the bulk of the familiar proton.
Working in this way physicists have given us not our broadest,
but our most deeply penetrating glimpses of existence.

Still, with our newly acquired knowledge, we have difficulty
imagining that the solid objects of a substantial world are made
mostly of empty space and rioting particles. How is it that my
writing paper does not fall through my table and my pen not
sink into my paper? How do insubstantial things act as solids?
For the physicist, as Arthur Eddington has said, every object in
the world has a duplicate. There is the commonplace object
with which we are all familiar. A common table—it has extension, it is comparatively permanent, it is colored, and above all
it is substantial. But Eddington's table has a duplicate—a scientific table which he knows is mostly emptiness. Sparsely scattered in the emptiness are particles rushing about with great
speed. "Notwithstanding its strange construction," writes Eddington, "it turns out to be an entirely efficient table. It supports my writing paper as satisfactorily as table no. 1, for when
I lay the paper on it, the little electrical particles with their
headlong speed keep on hitting the underside, so that the paper
is maintained in shuttlecock fashion at a nearly steady level. If I
lean upon this table I shall not go through; or, to be strictly
accurate, the chance of my scientific elbow going through my
scientific table is so excessively small that it can be neglected in
practical life. . . .

"I need hardly tell you," Eddington goes on, "that modern
physics has by delicate test and remorseless logic assured me
that my second, scientific table is the only one which is really
there—wherever 'there' may be. On the other hand, I need not
tell you that modern physics will never succeed in exorcising
that first table—strange compound of external nature, mental
imagery, and inherited prejudice. . . ."

5

ROBERT Rathbun Wilson was born in the town of Frontier, Wyoming. The romantic sound of the town's name should not be taken seriously, according to Jane Wilson. Having spent some time in the place with her husband, she comments, "Romantic Wyoming it ain't. It's more like an extension of Nebraska—one of those nasty little towns with lots of bars, and culture zero. The winds blow and the climate is frightful. They cannot grow a flower there. . . ."

Wilson was a lonely child whose parents divorced when he was eight years old. He attended seven grammar schools in four different states as he moved around with his mother, then stayed with his father, then back again with his mother. But always in the summers he would return to Wyoming to the ranches of relatives, particularly Uncle Dan Rathbun's ranch. Perhaps because of the ranch life, Wilson started to show some mechanical interests while at Todd School, the Illinois private school he attended. Classmates called him "the inventor" because of his ability with erector-set mechanics and his bright ideas. One of his popular childish inventions was the freezing of apples. He discovered that the taste of apples changed greatly when they were frozen. "They tasted great—more like ice cream," he says. "I have no idea why, or how I discovered that."

In the summers when he worked the ranch, he absorbed some

of the cowboy's sense about the way of things: the work was quite hard, and sometimes lonely, but the cowboys were self-sufficient. They knew enough about the behavior of horses, and weather, and machinery to get what they wanted out of them.

"I suppose in looking back on it there were at least a couple of things important to my physics," Wilson says. "There was the blacksmith's shop. If the mowing machine broke down, we would go in and hammer out a piece that would replace the broken piece. The equipment for stacking hay was all home-made. We'd go up and cut logs and make devices for stacking. We made the big box rakes for collecting the hay. . . . It was all made from iron and odd parts lying around. The assumption was that we could do anything in the blacksmith shop. And generally we could."

The nearest town from the ranch was forty miles. When the truck broke down, it was fixed with parts fashioned in the shop before a trip to town was attempted. Whenever Wilson went fishing near the ranch, he had to build himself a raft. Some parts were chopped and sawed, while some, like the pieces to hold and steer the rudder, were cut and formed over a high flame. He found himself in the blacksmith shop a lot, and he would linger there over the things he was making. "Whenever I made anything in the blacksmith shop, I tried to make it pretty. After you have worked on anything half an hour, it becomes a matter of feeling. You think about whether you've done a good job, whether you are pleased. Part of what you are doing is pleasure, even though you are making a practical thing." The smoothness of the curves, the angles, the tidiness of the thing he was making had a value.

There were parts of the ranch life he loathed. The strain of mowing and raking hay, the hard and empty physical labor day after day. The sun was hot, and he rode the lurching mower under a cloud of stinging mosquitoes. The nastiest horses—those which could run away with the lighter farm equipment—were always put on the mowers. The horses would jerk and run at the wrong time, would stop at the wrong time, and would ruin a man's work and his mood.

"But thank God," says Wilson, "every so often it would rain. You couldn't put up any hay. So you would take the chance to go up in the mountains on horseback. You would ride for strays, or push the cattle from one place to another." One summer which he remembers fondly, when he was sixteen or seventeen years old, he did no haying at all, but stayed by himself in the mountains tending cattle. There was a bunk in his small cabin and a bedroll for the nights out on the range. He rode a circuit of fifty or sixty miles a day. He cooked his food, shod his horse, and whatever broke down, he repaired. He was alone and in charge of the world.

It was at this impressionable time of his childhood that Wilson read Sinclair Lewis' *Arrowsmith*, a romantic novel which followed the struggle of one scientific researcher. "That romantic idealization of a man dedicated to research made a deep impression upon me. As I remember it," Wilson says, "Lewis portrays in his novel a young and devoted medical scientist who, working long hours in solitude, finally experiences the ultimate exaltation that comes to any creative person. I was a lonely boy in Wyoming, and for some reason it was natural for me to relate to Lewis' hero. . . . My job, when I wasn't in school, was riding the range for cattle. It, too, was an isolated life, but one of delightful independence. I felt I had something in common with and could empathize with Arrowsmith on his lonely research frontier."

Wilson had already learned a little about physics in high school, perhaps because it was not much different than work in the blacksmith shop, perhaps because of Arrowsmith. For twenty-five cents he once bought a thick book on scientific instruments. He had no hope of understanding most of it, but he was curious. He flipped through its contents, which were mathematical derivations for complex machinery. He stopped at a simple one, one which measured a kind of electric current. There was a small patch of algebra about the distance the needle would swing for a given current; the angle of the swing was proportional to the power of the current. He was amazed. He understood it. "It hit me like a bombshell. Here was a thick tome on scientific equipment, a professional book, and I could follow the math. I had thought you had to be pretty good to understand this stuff and to use mathematics as a way of understanding. But I looked at this: 'Gee, this is easy!' "

Wilson read more physics, and he began tinkering. His room at home in California was a large, unfinished attic, with exposed beams in some places and the plain wallboard showing in others. At one end of his room the floor jutted upward to table height: this was his workbench.

One of the things the young Wilson made in the attic could have made him rich. He was looking for an easy way to create a vacuum in a bottle. He took a rubber hose, inserted one end in the bottle and made a loop with the other end. He put a metal collar completely around the loop, took a small wheel, and with it pinched the hose against the inside of the metal collar. As the wheel moved, it pinched the hose and moved air ahead of it. The wheel raced around the inside of the collar. Ahead of it, it pushed air out the exhaust end of the loop. Behind it, air rushed up into the hose from the bottle. The air in the bottle, always seeking an even distribution of itself, got thinner and thinner, creating the needed vacuum. Wilson never tried to patent the device which he thought up in 1931, when he was seventeen. Manufacturers later invented the device for themselves, or borrowed it, and it is still being made and sold today.

More exciting to him, but with less practical value, was the palm-sized particle accelerator he made. After forty-five years in physics, Wilson still seems a little surprised at what he did. "Making that thing was one of the hardest things I ever did in my life. Especially making the mercury pump that I had to have for it. . . ."

The little accelerator, called a gaseous discharge tube, was made of glass. It is, fundamentally, much like the great particle-accelerating machines which followed. Both depend upon the action between particles of opposite charge. At one end of the discharge tube is a negative pole, and the other end is a positive pole. Electrons on the negative side are pulled across the vacuum toward the positive side, and they speed up as they move across the gap. The existence of the electron and the proton were discovered with just such simple tubes.

At the time Wilson made his, making a discharge tube did not begin with the purchase of the glass tube. He had to *make* the glass parts, and that meant learning to blow glass. It was an unusually delicate process in which a tube of brittle lead-glass had to be heated very slowly over a gasoline flame—first to singe it gently at some distance, then moving it closer and closer until it was molten. It had to be kept spinning in his fingers the whole time. When he blew the air into the soft glass, he tilted and twirled it. When he removed it from the fire it had to come away with an excruciating slowness, perhaps a full two minutes to move it just out of the flame. Glass blowing is a difficult craft, as Wilson found with one tube after another shattered or mis-shapen, and the mercury pump he made was a complex glass instrument with tubes and bulbs of many difficult shapes.

When he was finished, the little machine sent electrons shoot-ing from one end of the tube to the other. The tube was a closed bulb of glass, with a wire running in at each end. Be-tween the wires was a gap. The air would be pumped out of the tube by a mercury pump together with the pump of his own design. Then electric current would be put into the wires. The electrons from the current reached one end of the wire in the tube, shot off into the vacuum, and crossed the gap over to the other, positively charged, wire. Wilson would sit in his dark-ened attic, turn on the power, and flip on the vacuum pump. The electrons raced across, and since there was still air in the tube, they collided with the molecules of air. The result was a bright reddish glow at first, and as the air pumped down, the glow changed color and began to shift its shape within the tube.

"I wasn't doing any experiments," says Wilson. "I wasn't learning anything. I would just sit there in the dark, I would turn up the radio. I would stare into the tube, and look deep into those colors. I wanted to understand them just by looking. . . . It was red, and then as it pumped down there was less air and proportionally more mercury floating in there from the mercury pump. It was beautiful, changing to a greenish color with glowing bands jumping around. . . ."

Wilson's solitary work in the attic and his fantasies were im-portant to him. Outside them, he seemed a failure. His father was a gregarious man whom he wanted very much to please, but could not. Platt Wilson was a politician, dean of the Wyoming State Senate for a time, but he had no spare praise or affection for his son. His letters to Robert were funny and full of gossip, but empty of personal remarks. At the bottom of letters to his son there was no complimentary close, just a formal signature: "Platt Wilson."

"I recall once that my father took me to a luncheon of some

kind, a father and son thing," Wilson says. "It may have been a Kiwanis affair. I remember the other boys would get up and make little speeches, they would all be very good and very adult. They were able to say appropriate things to the group. Of course, my father was very good at this sort of thing, at speaking in public. But I couldn't compete with the other boys. I just sat there. I couldn't get up and make a speech or be at all articulate. My father was disappointed. He didn't *make* me do it, but I knew he was very unhappy that I couldn't do it.

"I didn't fit with those kids who were all going to be successful like my father. So failure was a factor in my doing other things. I could make things on my own, and it seemed to me I could be quite loquacious when I was with some old cowhands who were telling stories. . . ."

At the end of high school, Robert wanted to go on to college. His father said no. It would be a damn fool thing to do, wasting your years on more school, he said. He pointed out that his own education as a civil engineer hadn't done him any good. He was one of the first automobile dealers in the West—he started a Chevy dealership in 1915—and he later went into politics. But his schooling was useless. Robert insisted, and the two argued bitterly. Finally against his father's strong feelings, he left for school.

There was one day from his first year in college which Wilson recalls with vivid detail. It was 1932, he was eighteen years old, and he was walking across the campus at Berkeley toward his freshman chemistry lab. He had to pass an old building on the way, and he recalls stopping there and peering in the window. He had stopped before, and he remembered "the whining noise of the generators, the crackling of the sparks, the brilliant and beautiful glow of mercury-arc rectifiers, strange shiny instruments, the fevered activity of men in laboratory coats moving rapidly in and out of the deep shadows caused by the eerie light. . . ."

It was pouring rain, Wilson was drenched, but he couldn't take his eyes off the scene and the particle accelerators inside. "It just seemed like a heaven, with its sights and sounds and smells and flashing lights—it was very appealing. I was in the middle of the rainstorm and I had my nose plastered up against the window, completely entranced. Somebody came to the door

—a medical doctor by the name of Exner—he looked out and said, 'My God! What are you standing in the rain for, you idiot! Come in and get out of the rain!' "

The doctor brought him in, and they talked for a time about a little particle accelerator called the Sloan Tube. It was being used to test the completely new idea of destroying diseased human tissue by pencil-thin beams of fast particles. They looked at the particle-making machinery for some time, and the doctor invited Wilson to come back. Wilson was not studying physics at Berkeley. He had wanted to major in philosophy, which was his first love at that time, but he had given in to practicality. It was the bottom of the Depression years, and he was studying electrical engineering. He took one physics course, and he was almost flunking it. But the actual *machinery* of physics, like the Sloan Tube, stirred an excitement in him which he could not suppress.

Standing that day in the rain by the window of the radiation laboratory, events, accidents, and dreams seemed to mix. They seemed suddenly to precipitate a solid bead of resolution. Wilson returned to the radiation lab again. Then he decided to change his major to physics. His teachers and advisers howled; it was madness to turn his worst subject—he was still nearly failing his one physics course—into his full-time pursuit. He would sink like a stone out of the university. Wilson ignored the warnings. Within two years, before even finishing his undergraduate work, Wilson had done some physics that was acceptable as a Ph.D. thesis. "Never take the advice of professionals," he says.

6

WILSON sat in his Fermilab office, swiveling in a black chair. He was recalling his entry into physics, in the 1930s, at the Berkeley Radiation Laboratory of the famous Ernest O. Lawrence. Physics was different before the war, before the bomb, he said. It was obscure, it was without government money. "When I went into physics nobody even knew what a physicist was. No one in my family ever heard of a physicist. I always had to explain that I wasn't a druggist."

He once recalled visiting home from Berkeley, and standing beside a campfire "with the neighboring 'men folks' at the ranch of my Uncle Dan Rathbun up on North Piney River near Big Piney. The mountains around us, the range talk, the smell of the sage brush brought back happy memories of riding for cattle. . . . One of the Budd boys asked about my work. I described the research I would do as an instructor of physics. . . . My old friend, Billy Gauss, looked at me startled, 'Instructor, teaching?' he asked. 'Yes, partly teaching, partly research. . . .' Billy looked me over very slowly from head to toe, then back. 'Fust goddamned Rathbun ever to be a school teacher,' he muttered, and walked away in utter disgust. I never saw him again."

There was no glamour then in physics and certainly no money.

There are times, Wilson says, when a physicist senses that he inhabits a terrain that is shared by few others. To the mind's eye it is a lunar continent, airless and etched in sharp relief. The view is exciting but lonely. Leaving the laboratory at dawn after a night's pressed labor, he watches the world stir with the sun and go to work, passing him going in the opposite direction. He feels himself singular, gliding against the current, and it is exhilarating.

Although the cyclotron was the most important physics of its day, there were a number of other pieces of equipment at the Berkeley lab—such as the Sloan Tube—on which research was carried out. The cyclotron was a physically dominating piece of machinery. One of several versions of the machine, built in 1938, had a magnet shaped like a great iron doorway. The magnet was so huge that all twenty-seven men of the radiation lab could stand inside its arch to have their picture taken. (That group picture contains many important physicists of the era, including three Nobelists, J. Robert Oppenheimer, and a young, cocky-looking Robert Wilson.) Attached to the great magnet was a far smaller piece of equipment. It was a vacuum chamber, in which the protons raced, and it was shaped like a five-foot metal pillbox.

When Wilson first arrived at the radiation lab, he worked with a smaller version of the cyclotron. Its vacuum chamber was a rather makeshift box little more than two feet across. "The vacuum chamber," Wilson recalled once, "was a joy to behold. It was made by screwing brass sides to the poletips of the magnet. The whole thing was then made vacuum tight by heating the metal with a gas torch and painting a hot, smelly, smoking mixture of beeswax and rosin over the surface. . . ."

The radiation laboratory at Berkeley, with the cyclotron and other instruments made by hand, was both Wilson's blacksmith shop and Arrowsmith's laboratory. "Nearly everything was secondhand or had been scrounged from some factory or dump yard," Wilson recalls. "The electronic equipment was obtained by taking discarded radios apart. Most of the mechanical parts were handmade in the small shop, and usually the physicists themselves turned out the parts on an old lathe."

There was some small titillation of danger about physics. Experimental physicists make machines of dangerous power whose operations are only incompletely understood. Wilson recalled one time years later at Cornell when he and his colleagues were getting ready to turn on an electric accelerator after they had done some work on it. They decided to turn it on at a safe one hundred volts.

"On closing the switch there was a woof and a thump and then a spiral of smoke rising above the machine—all that was left of various wires. For some reason I decided to inspect the fuses in the condenser room. To be perfectly safe, even though the voltage had been only one hundred volts, I took a grounding hook along with me as I entered this terrifying room. . . . As I touched the grounding bar to the main bus bar, a tremendous flash blinded me, my eyebrows were singed, a great bang rendered me deaf, and I nearly maimed three graduate students by the force of my sudden withdrawal from the room. . . .

"The trouble had been that the third harmonic of a generator becomes important when it is connected directly across a condenser bank . . . thus, instead of one hundred volts, there were many thousands of volts on the condensers and magnet before the switch tripped open. It was in this way that we became sophisticated about the third harmonic self-excitation of a generator. Probably there is an easier way."

Wilson also recalls the numerous and subtle methods by which the Berkeley physicists would sniff out leaks in the circular vacuum chamber of the machine. One method included the use of a gauge that was sensitive only to the presence of hydrogen; the vacuum chamber would be squirted from the outside with hydrogen, and if hydrogen was sucked into the chamber it would register on the gauge near the vacuum pump. On occasion, however, larger amounts of hydrogen were sucked in. At these times all care and subtlety in leak detection became unnecessary. The tiny fluctuation of a needle detecting a leak was replaced by rather more obvious indications: "The hydrogen would explode. . . . One could not only hear the explosion, but since the pump was right under the wooden floor of the pit [work area], one could also detect the leak by being thrown a few inches into the air . . . probably the only really kinesthetic leak detector ever developed," Wilson wrote. When looking for leaks, the physicists had to descend into this pit in the center of the magnet. "The noise was terrific in this pit when the magnet was on, but even worse were the visual effects of the alternating magnetic field. . . . Descending into the magnetic field region, you at first became aware that the externally received light was being modulated on and off (mentally) at sixty cycles per second. Descending further though, even with your eyes closed, you were aware of the beautiful optical effects not unlike fireworks, evidently due to currents induced in the optic nerve. When a calculation showed that the currents induced in the brain were comparable to or even greater than those used in shock therapy, we decided to turn off the magnet before going down into the pit."

First aid and resuscitation were studied by the workers at the radiation laboratory. To protect the lab workers against the power of neutrons coming out of the target area, thick layers of paraffin were used like screens around the machine. But eventually so much of it got so hot that the paraffin shield itself was a fire hazard. Then, cans of water were stacked three feet thick and seven feet high around the area as barriers to absorb the particle energy.

There were no gauges which could test the amount of voltage in the high-powered machinery, so radiation lab workers would take a stick with a nail on the end of it and watch how close they could come to the hot machine before a spark cracked across to the nail. The farther the spark leaped, the higher the voltage. Once, a man standing on a ladder was testing the voltage this way when some sixteen thousand volts of power shot past the nail down to his hand; it smashed through the right side of his body, down through the nails in his shoes, and threw him violently off the ladder. The man's hand and foot burns did not heal for six months, but the electricity had fortunately missed his heart. Another radiation lab man was applying the beeswax and rosin mixture against vacuum leaks in the cyclotron when the gooey mixture burst into flame. He quickly put the mixture under a faucet of running water; the water exploded into hot steam and shot the wax into his face like a shotgun blast. He survived, but several physicists of that time were killed in their interrogations of nature.

It took and it gave self-assurance to make physics in this way —with one's own hands, from scavenged equipment and the spare parts of courage and obsession. The mental qualities of cowboys and experimental physicists are different in many things, but alike in at least a few particulars. Wilson learned from cowboys the feeling that he could do almost anything with his hands. The world was not just an arrangement of technical black boxes whose workings were unknown, but was instead mechanically transparent.

When he entered Berkeley and began to work at the radiation laboratory, Wilson found he worked best at night, when he was alone and had all the machinery to himself. He became possessed only with his work; for him, people were difficult. He met the woman who would be his wife, Jane Scheyer, during those years at Berkeley. "It is hard to realize what a devoted person he was," she says, "and what a bum kind of boyfriend. It was past anything you can imagine. He wouldn't go to my senior prom. Nothing like that. He worked desperately hard during the days, and then about eleven-thirty at night, the phone would ring; we'd go out and have a hamburger together. The comical thing about this rather innocent courtship, and rather boring one, was that because I went out so late I was constantly getting on the 'late return' list. It was one of those places where, if you didn't come in *at all,* you were not on the list. I was always on it. . . . Anyway, Bobby was always kind of a lone wolf. He didn't have many friends. He was very quiet. Very introverted."

One of the afflictions of physics, like any other art, is this lonely passion. Working in the lab, he ignored his health and it failed often. Once, he pressed on without rest, ignoring the pain in his body until he collapsed. After a stern lecture from Ernest Lawrence, Wilson was taken to the hospital, and Lawrence got the best surgeon in the area to perform the emergency surgery. Wilson's appendix had burst inside him several days before.

7

ALL accelerators, including the first cyclotron and all the
machines which have evolved out of it, depend on a single
principle for their operation—the attraction of opposites. Using
this attraction between positive and negative, a particle can be
pulled to greater speeds, from attraction to attraction, in a
long pipe. The speed and energy achieved depend on how long
the pipe is. The longer the pipe, the more attracting electrodes
can be placed along it to pull the passing particle. Achieving
very high energies would thus require extremely long machines
—tens or hundreds or thousands of miles long.

Lawrence's idea came to him in a single stroke of genius,
which he spent the rest of his life working out in detail. He
realized that the straight path through the long string of electrodes was unnecessary. If the particles could be made to travel
in a *circle* then they would pass through the same electrode
system again and again. The same voltage can be applied to the
particles every time around the city, for thousands of trips
around.

Before Lawrence's cyclotron, several attempts had been made
to create a beacon of high-energy particles. But making fast
particles meant making either very long machines or very high
electric voltages. One group tried to use the enormous natural
voltage of lightning to accelerate particles. An insulated cable
was hung between two mountain peaks in the Alps; during

storms; charges as high as fifteen million volts were on the line. When the physicists tried to apply the electricity to the particle-accelerating tube, the power was too much. The jolt of electricity burst through and killed one of the men. In England, a large machine was built by stringing together a number of smaller accelerators. The charge in this machine was also dangerously large. When the voltage rose too high, over a half million volts, a huge spark cracked against the wall near the machine, leaving what looked like a bullet hole in the concrete.

Lawrence's circular machine was a great simplification, and its working had a special mechanical beauty. There is a grace in the neatness of particle motions within it. Two complementary motions are imparted to the particle—one to accelerate it and the other to curve its path and make it travel in a circle.

The path of particles in the cyclotron is not the same as the path of particles in the Fermilab machine, but they resemble one another as an embryo resembles the grown child. The cyclotron was small, and the chamber in which the particles flew was a round, undivided pillbox. The particles within it described a spiral. Particles were squirted into the center of the machine as a gas. The milling particles were slow, and made a small circle at the center of the machine. As the particles moved faster, they swung in wider and wider circles. They reached to break free of the magnetic field, just as the ball on the end of a string pulls harder and harder to break the string as it is swung faster and faster in a circle. So the particles made a spiral from the slow circles in the middle of the machine to the fast circles at the outer edge of the machine. Finally, at the largest orbit the machine will allow, the particles were released from their magnetic bonds to fly at a target.

During acceleration, particles were pulled from one half of the circular machine to the other. As the positive particles were pulled toward the half of the machine that was negative, their movement quickened. But suddenly, just as the protons reached the appointed place, the charge was reversed. A plus appeared in place of the minus. The deceived protons continued on, pulled forcibly around toward the other side of the machine where the minus now lay.

It was a game of mirrors for the particles; they always chased a phantom, from one side of the machine to the other and back again. The protons were attracted, disappointed, and drawn on again. The small excitations added up each time around the circle, and the particles continued gaining in speed. The end was collision at the target and penetration into subnuclear space.

While the cyclotron was a single, small accelerating machine, the Fermilab complex which evolved from it is actually composed of several accelerators, which give particles an initial boost of speed before they are injected into the main ring. There is first a small accelerator of 1930s design, to get the protons going, then a linear accelerator 475 feet long. In the linear machine, the surge of protons runs from copper electrode to copper electrode. The surge of particles, says Wilson, is "the electrical equivalent of a surf wave. The protons are accelerated as they ride this electrical wave down the tube, and when they emerge, their energy has been increased to two hundred million electron volts." Once out of the linear track, the protons are shot into a "booster ring."

The protons travel always within a sealed steel tube, from linear machine to booster ring to main ring. In the vacuum within the tube, the protons fly easily, guided only by the electrical and magnetic fields of the surrounding machinery. The protons take twenty thousand turns around the circumference of the booster ring. Then they are bumped magnetically out of the booster, guided down a connecting tube, and released into the main ring's vacuum tube.

The thin jet of protons which is the product of this process cannot be seen directly. But even with the beam sealed up inside a tube surrounded by magnets, the likely result of just being in the tunnel while the machine is on is death. The few stray particles from the beam are enough to raise a great amount of radiation by knocking particles off the tube, the magnets, and the walls.

When the Fermilab beam is accidentally bumped off its course and hits the side of the steel vacuum tube, it pops a hole in the steel like a Buck Rogers disintegration ray. If it were not too dangerous to do it, shooting the beam off into the air would cause—apart from the disintegration of whatever it hit—a sharp line in the air. It would be thin, like a line drawn with a newly sharpened pencil. The beam's passage would excite the air about this line and cause it to glow, a translucent fog of pure spectrum blue.

Using remote videotape equipment, films have been made of the beam striking a target. In one such film the target was an aluminum rod about three quarters of an inch around and three feet long. The idea was for the beam to hit one end of the rod, end on, producing a shower of particles out the other end. When setting up for the film, the physicists were not sure what to expect. Usually, only small portions of the proton beam are peeled off and shot at targets. But for the film, they decided to shoot the full beam at the aluminum rod in pulses, one brief burst every ten seconds. Vice clamps were used to hold the rod down to a metal base. When the first thread of beam hit the rod, the target, its clamps, and its base were lifted up and thrown out of range. After a hasty reorganization, the target was clamped down to a series of twelve-pound steel bricks. The next pulse bowled over a target, clamps, and steel bricks. Finally a longer, heavier target was used. It was welded in place. When a beam pulse hit it, the rod's temperature jumped in a quick step 150 degrees Fahrenheit. The rod flashed like a light bulb—on for the second it was being hit, and then off. Another pulse struck it and the rod began a continuous glow. The next pulse caused the metal to smoke, the next caused it to bubble, and finally the metal just drooled out of range of the pulsing beam.

The beam carrying this withering energy is only a tiny spot of protons. There are so few protons in the beam, relatively speaking, that a single bottle of protons no bigger than a sixteen-ounce Coke supplies enough to make a beam pulse every ten seconds, twenty-four hours a day, for more than three months. The bottle used is a bottle of hydrogen gas. About twelve dollars' worth feeds the accelerator for a year.

8

Wilson worked for Ernest O. Lawrence from the time he was eighteen until he was twenty-five. What he did and what he learned in those years formed his style of physics for the rest of his life. The lab was a place of continuous excitement. Wilson says now that he can remember Ernest Lawrence in a number of moods and poses, but the one thing he cannot remember is Lawrence walking—"even if he was going only a few feet, or across the room, he ran. And he sort of expected everyone else to run all the time, too."

Lawrence's style drew impressive quantities of work out of those in the lab. One of the important pieces of work Wilson did was to work out the theory of the cyclotron—the details of the magnetic forces and precisely how the particles circulated within the machine. Later, he studied how closely bunched together the particles were within the particle beam.

He found as he was doing this work that a surprising number of the particles accelerated within the cyclotron were not being effectively brought out of the machine to the target. The results were something of a shock; it was known that *some* protons that started in orbit never came out of the machine. Lawrence and his laboratory had struggled for years to pull out all the particles possible, both for experiments and because the cyclotron at Berkeley was for a time the single most important source of radioactive material. (By using the cyclotron beam to bombard substances like phosphorous, radioactive versions could be produced. These materials were primarily for medical research, and much cyclotron time was spent making them to produce revenue for the radiation lab.) Since nine tenths of the protons accelerated by the cyclotron remained *inside* the machine and were not brought out to hit the target, Wilson proposed putting another target within the machine. He designed a system by which both internal and external targets could work simultaneously.

A crucial requirement of the system was a special vacuum seal. Wilson's private moments at his attic workbench now made their way back into his life; he had made a vacuum pump once like the valve of a bicycle pump, but reversed. For the cyclotron he needed something like it, so he put a ring of rubber around the metal rod which penetrated the cyclotron and held the internal target. Air trying to push its way into the vacuum inside the cyclotron would automatically suck the rubber up tighter and tighter against the rod. It would hold the ring so tightly against the rod that little air could get through. The pressure of air trying to get into the vacuum would itself be the sealer. This ring seal, called the Wilson seal, might have earned Wilson a fortune had it been patented. It later became important in some industries, such as the process of pasteurizing milk, and his seal was forerunner of a common seal used today, called the O-ring. Wilson thought about patenting his seal and asked Lawrence what he should do. Lawrence told him to forget the idea. He pointed out that the patent process can devour time and energy, and if a physicist were going to try to patent everything he invented, he would not be a physicist any longer. He would be merely an inventor.

Both the discovery of the Wilson seal and the use of internal targets to catch the nine tenths of the protons in the cyclotron were published in a single paper in 1938. Chemist Martin Kamen helped Wilson carry out the work, and not long after the internal system was set up, Kamen used it to discover one of the most useful of all radioactive materials—carbon 14. Two years following Kamen's discovery in 1939, physicist Edwin McMillan of Berkeley used the cyclotron to extend the table of elements for the first time in a century; it had been assumed since the nineteenth century that ninety-two was the fixed number of elements. McMillan found number ninety-three, which he named neptunium. He found also the famous counterpart into which neptunium decays after a couple of days —plutonium. McMillan won the Nobel Prize for the work.

There was, in Wilson's 1938 paper, one rather odd line. It was a warning, couched in the obscuring prose of *Physics Review* style, which said soft solder must never be used to attack a target inside the machine.

One day Wilson wanted to change the material on the interior target. In order to shut down the machine as briefly as possible, he quickly soft-soldered the little target onto the rod, closed up the machine, and told his colleagues to go ahead with their work. Things went perfectly; lab workers went on with their work without too much grumbling about the delay. But Wilson had not thought of everything. Author Nuel Davis wrote of the incident: "He had overlooked, what the [high-energy protons] might do to the solder." They melted it. And blew it all over the inside of the cyclotron. Wilson, it turned out, had spray-painted the cyclotron's bowels with a beautiful coat of radioactive phosphorous. It took the whole laboratory staff weeks to scrape it off. Signs were hung on the machine while the laborious scraping was carried on: KILL WILSON!

Wilson managed to get his colleagues angry on a number of other occasions as well. Though he was a withdrawn and somewhat reclusive young man, he had an unusual sense of drama which seemed to burst out of him when he was alone at 4 A.M. In his Fermilab office, Wilson told me of one of his dawn pastimes. Getting up from his chair, he walked toward the window that looks out over the main ring. There was a telescope aimed out the window; Wilson paced for a moment as he talked, swung the telescope absentmindedly on its pivot, then offered with a smile:

"I've looked into more nothing than any living person."

"What?"

"I hold the world's record for looking at nothing. When I was working with the cyclotron, I had developed a vacuum seal— the Wilson seal—that allowed you to put a probe, a long metal rod, into the machine without losing the vacuum. You would put the rod in, and pump down the vacuum, and you could move the rod around, and manipulate targets *inside* the machine without breaking the vacuum seal.

"Well, when you're working late into the night, about four o'clock in the morning you begin to feel a little peculiar. You can do some odd things at that time.

"What I would do is turn off the machine, pull out the rod real fast, and put my eye up to the hole as fast as I could, so I could see—*nothing*. The vacuum. Before the air rushed in. I would look across to where the hole was on the other side . . ." The vacuum was the most pure nothingness then available on earth.

"What did it look like?"

"Nothing." Wilson grinned. "I said before that I have looked at a more intense nothing longer than any *living* person. There *was* one guy who looked at more of nothing longer than I did. He fell out of an airplane at a very high altitude. . . ."

Trying to achieve his record, Wilson said, was not without its hazards. He got more than one black eye by placing his eye to the hole so fast that his eye was sucked up against the machine like a plug to a bathtub drain. Once when he yanked the rod out to get a look, a rubber gasket fell off the rod into the machine. Wilson didn't notice it. Later, when he found it was missing, he poked about inside the machine but didn't find it. He gave up the search. The following day when the machine was turned on, the gasket blew the racing particle beam out of orbit, causing chaos and repairs that took days. As it happened, Ernest Lawrence was to show off the machine on one of those days in a fund-raising demonstration to a group of distinguished visitors. When he found out what had happened, he found Wilson, screamed at him, and threw him out of the lab. He told him not to return.

Wilson fell quickly into a deep depression. He was lost. He continued to work on his physics as best he could; it wasn't until about two weeks later that he saved himself with an idea. Lawrence was a bold man and a far better leader than he was a physicist. From the beginning of the building of one cyclotron, he had always pushed to make another one bigger and more powerful. There had been one of four inches in diameter, one of seven inches in diameter, one of eleven inches, one of twenty-seven inches, one of thirty inches, one of thirty-seven inches, one of sixty inches— And the energy rose; when the machine was producing eighty thousand electron-volt particles, Lawrence was talking about a million volts. When a million volts was reached, Lawrence had for some time been fund raising on the basis of twenty-five-million-volt particles. He soon raised that figure to one hundred million volts. But once he had broadcast the one-hundred-million-volt figure, there was a period of embarrassment. Many of Lawrence's supporters, professionals with experience in cyclotron work, believed it would be impossible to achieve the one hundred million. A powerful figure in physics, and later a Nobel Prize winner, Hans Bethe, published a theoretical paper which stated that there was a limit to how high the energy could be pushed and that limit was fifteen million volts, seven times less than Lawrence was boasting he could reach. A few thought Lawrence had gone too far; he was called a megalomaniac. Others were kinder, but knew he would not achieve anything like one hundred million volts.

As this controversy grew, Wilson remained exiled from the lab. But while he was away, he came up with a theoretical solution to the argument. He passed a message through an intermediary to Lawrence and was cordially invited back to the lab to talk about his idea. The limit of energy, he later wrote in the *Physics Review*, could be raised far higher if better methods of focusing the beam down into a sharp line were used. The power of the particles was eventually pushed far past fifteen million volts. By the end of World War Two, particles were coming out of the other circular accelerators at more than one billion volts.

When a visitor points out to Wilson the similarity between Wilson's and Lawrence's machine building, even down to explosions of temper and tactics for generating excitement in his workers, Wilson pauses to think about it. "I don't think I copied Lawrence's methods," he says finally, "but I must have been very impressed with the sense he had of how to get things done. I guess I learned to think that way . . . despite all the facts and arguments to the contrary."

The Wilson seal, and the internal beam and targets, along with the papers on the theory of the cyclotron, gave Wilson something of an aura. "Bright boy Wilson," he was called in a letter by one senior lab man, as he explained how Wilson had solved yet another problem of the machine. Among the nuclear physicists of those years—Oppenheimer, Bethe, Lawrence, Fermi—he soon became known as a very bright young man who had much ahead of him. When he published his 1938 paper, Wilson was twenty-four years old. He received his doctorate from Berkeley two years later, and was then offered a job at Princeton University. Einstein was working there, and many others gravitated to the place. Robert Wilson arrived in 1940.

9

I T was a December evening in 1941, and it was dark outside when young Robert Wilson left the Princeton physics laboratory. The walk to his apartment was a few blocks, past the eating clubs which were set in a row on the Princeton campus. Wilson had been morose and irritable for days. He had been prowling, throttling bushes and kicking rocks in his mental terrain. He was searching out a problem, and he thought he must be near a solution. He still had nothing when he began his walk home that evening.

In the year leading up to that evening, Wilson had been diverted far from his expected course. The nucleus of the atom had been his puzzle, and in particular the forces within the most simple nucleus, that consisting of a single proton. One force, called the strong nuclear force, emanates from protons and pulls them toward each other to form nuclei. This force seemed to be the single structural element upon which the stability of the universe rested. If this strut were removed, nuclei would fly apart and the universe would collapse into a plasmic soup, a porridge of hot electric charge.

At Princeton, Wilson had begun to shoot protons at protons, measuring deflections, exploring. Wilson's object was to examine the fabric of the strong force. Did the pull emanate from a single-point source in a smooth wave, or did it emanate from more than one point inside the proton, creating several conflicting waves? In other words, did the proton appear to have an intricate structure within, or was it a solid, featureless sphere?

But an urgent telegram from Ernest O. Lawrence interrupted Wilson's brief start on the problem. In the cable, Lawrence asked Wilson to come to an emergency meeting at MIT. The Nazis had invaded Britain by air, and science was being startled out of its political sleep. Even those with the most somnambulent sense of isolation were becoming fitful and troubled. Wilson had considered himself a pacifist. He recalls a moment when he was at Berkeley, sitting in the student union drinking coffee and talking about the war that had just started in Europe. He had attended Leftist discussion groups and antiwar demonstrations at the university gate; then the epithets were passed quietly over hot drinks. Munitions makers were the "merchants of death" who had stirred the trouble and little but evil could come from the fighting in Europe. Wilson and a friend agreed that no matter how justified the cause against Hitler might seem, it would only serve the engorged, blood merchants to join in. The two of them made a coffee pact that they, at least, would not be fooled. They would oppose any action in the war.

But when Wilson got to Princeton, he met scientists from Britain and Europe, and he met some who had lived under Hitler's system and wanted to go back with a rifle. Wilson's opinion was hacked away as one argument followed another. Finally, he was asked to go to that meeting at MIT which was surely a call to involvement in the war. He went, without committing himself. He listened to British scientists give a powerful description of the Battle of Britain. They helped in the battle, they said, by using radio waves to detect approaching enemy airplanes. Some of the same sort of work should be done in America, Lawrence concluded, and a laboratory should be set up for the purpose. Wilson was asked to join it. He did not give his answer immediately, but went to bed. He did not sleep that night. His conscience scratched at him. He could not participate in slaughter, but he did not want to bear the responsibility of Hitler's success either. "That night," Wilson wrote later, "I chose against the purity of my immortal soul and in favor of a liveable world worth living in. I joined the new laboratory in the morning."

But when he came back to Princeton to pack, physicists Harry Smyth and Eugene Wigner cornered him. Not long before, it had been found theoretically possible to shatter the nucleus of the heaviest element, uranium, in such a way that the fragments would then go on to shatter more nuclei, and those fragments in turn would break more. The result would be a bright burst of binding energy. The physicists told Wilson that a team led by the brilliant Italian physicist Enrico Fermi would try to create and to control such a fission. It would be a source of power for use in the war. They convinced Wilson, eventually, that he would be more useful to Fermi's nuclear team than to the MIT radar team. Again, he joined.

His group met with Fermi about once a week, and he worked with physicist E. C. Creutz on the central question in reactor making—how uranium absorbs neutrons before splitting apart in a fission reaction. The neutron is nearly identical to the proton, but is without the proton's electric charge. It can therefore penetrate the electron shell of any atom without being electrically repelled. It glides into the heart of the uranium nucleus carrying enough weight and energy to split open the quivering and unstable nucleus of uranium.

One idea Wilson had was contrary to the beliefs of the time (though it has since proved true): Wilson figured that the fission process exhibits the behavior of a "resonance," that is, that it might occur more strongly when induced by a neutron of certain energies rather than other energies. To test the idea, he made a fast beam of uranium particles and shot it at resting neutrons.

He was thus on the fourth remove from the work he started to do at Princeton. But he was to be taken still another remove from his nuclear puzzle. Just as Wilson was playing with the notion of a beam of uranium particles, a visitor from a British nuclear lab arrived. He had news. New measurements had demonstrated that it would take only a few grams of the rare uranium 235, about the weight of a dime, to make a bomb. A fission bomb had not appeared to be practical up to that time because of the huge amount of the rare isotope of uranium believed to be required. It would have been an impossible amount to obtain. With the new information, a bomb was conceivable, even though the few grams of U-235 would still be extremely difficult to obtain. In fact, obtaining the U-235 would be the most difficult of all the technical problems of making a bomb, but it might be done. Wilson became excited; this news reduced the problem of making a bomb to the straightforward problem of purifying uranium, U-238, to extract the traces of the isotope, U-235. Wilson already had conceived a beam of uranium, and surely the stream could deposit a few grams of uranium at the end of a tube. All he needed now was a means of separating, in flight, the U-235 and U-238, before they were deposited at the end of the tube.

The problem was on his mind when he left the physics laboratory on his way home on that December night. The solution would not be an easy one, but he felt somehow that he could not let go of the problem. The normal form of uranium, 238, is practically identical to the rare form, 235. They are very nearly the same size and weight, and each combines and reacts chemically in an identical manner. Both have precisely the same number of the important electrical particles—the protons and electrons. U-238 however, has three more neutrons, and when uranium is taken out of the ground the raw product has about 150 times as much of this form of uranium.

How could these two nearly identical particles be separated if they always behaved in the same way? Wilson ignored his other work and became absorbed by the question. He gradually sank out of easy communication with the world for some days. There are times, he once told a reporter, that ideas work themselves out over a long period and at other times the solution appears as a sudden apparition. "If you have finished the long business of putting together lots of data, then, as a picture gradually emerges you get a certain sense of pleasure. But the real kicks come when you have the more typical creative experience. You've filled yourself up with as much information as you can. You just sort of feel it all rumbling around inside of you, not particularly at a conscious level. Then—it can happen anytime —you begin to feel a solution, a resolution, bubbling up to your consciousness. At the same time you begin to get very excited . . . pervaded by a fantastic sense of joy."

Wilson felt near a solution to the uranium separation problem when he began the walk home. He was musing over the problem when he left the lab. He remembers that there was a

sharp wind blowing across his face and the air was
"I had the sense suddenly that I knew the answer. I c
coming," Wilson says. His mind raced, his pulse
The world was suspended as his mind took off on its flight. "By
God, it's going to come, I'm going to solve it," his mind muttered to his mind. He felt for an instant like an observer, interested and amused, as the idea began to present itself. It appeared all at once, wholly formed. "I saw it. I saw the particles
speeding along, separating. One set were getting bumped off in
one direction, one bumped off the other way. . . ." The slightly
lighter particles, when in flight, would move faster and get
slightly ahead of the heavier U-238. With a sort of electrical
paddle, the bunching of lighter and heavier particles would be
exaggerated. Then, at the end of the flight path, fast bunches
would be flipped off into one can, while those coming behind
would fly straight ahead into another. In two simple electrical
actions, the uranium beam would become bunches, and the
bunches would become deposits at the bottom of two cans.

"My mind was going a mile a minute. I was thinking of all
kinds of things at once. I thought, my God, I am the man who
knows how to make the bomb! I, a man of about twenty-five
years old, would almost by myself win the war. It could save the
world. I knew within a year we could test the idea, get some U-
235, make the bomb and end the war." Wilson pauses. "We
might have. It *was* actually possible. I had all sorts of other
fantasies as I was walking; I imagined women throwing themselves at my feet, I imagined myself making a fortune, even
imagined myself becoming president."

When Wilson arrived home that night, he immediately began
writing out his idea on paper, several longhand pages of notes.
The idea did not evaporate. The next day it was there, and
after he retold the details to his colleagues, it was still there.
Harry Smyth, Wilson's boss and mentor at Princeton, became
nearly as excited about the idea as Wilson, and he quickly
helped him collect the money and the physicists to carry out the
first tests. The team working on it eventually grew to about
fifty, and the money came to about a million dollars—extraordinary support for the project of a twenty-five-year-old who had
been at the university a single year.

From the moment he took that evening walk, Wilson was

never quite the same. "It was at that moment I matured," he says. "Suddenly I felt very sure of myself. When I was going in to see Rabi to ask for help, I really had no trepidations. I didn't need to be tongue-tied. I had something important to say, I thought I had a bombshell. I don't think I have ever recovered from that experience. It changed my whole personality."

He fell into his work with an enthusiasm which dismayed his new wife, his former late night sweetheart, Jane Scheyer. The two had hardly passed their first anniversary, and Jane says, "There was a period, from about October to April, when Robert was not home one single evening, or one single Sunday. Young ladies nowadays would not put up with that I'm sure. I remember going to New York one day with my mother, who was visiting. We went into the city to visit some young friends. I remember going to their apartment and to my surprise the husband was there. I remember his saying, 'You know, all I live for is my family . . .' or some outrageous statement like that. It struck me as quite comical. I mean, I could not imagine Robert saying all he lived for was his family. All he lived for was his physics."

Within a matter of months, Wilson and his team had built the first model of the uranium isotope separator. The machine was called the Isotron. (Later, the name appeared in Dick Tracy. There was a scientist named Brilliant in the comic strip who was blind, but who otherwise looked unusually like Robert Wilson, especially his porcupine hair. At the end of one day's episode, the blind scientist held out a book to his mother: "Before setting up my lithium dehydrator, Mother, I'd like for you to read me the chapter on the Isotron." Mother: "Certainly, Brilliant, sit down.") The first model of the machine was small, and produced a few dozen milligrams of pure U-235. But the operation was successful enough to project the possibility of building a separation plant which would use many machines and produce one kilogram (2.2 pounds) per day.

By the time the Isotron had gotten this far, there were at least three other projects attempting to obtain pure U-235. One of Wilson's opponents was the powerful Ernest O. Lawrence of Berkeley. Lawrence's project, called the Calutron, had started earlier and had more force of manpower and money behind it than the Isotron, though the Calutron method was far less elegant and direct. Wilson visited Lawrence, and Lawrence worked to persuade Wilson that the competition of both their projects was wasteful. The Calutron was far enough toward the actual production of U-235 that scarce resources should no longer be split up. Wilson found some sense in the argument. Not long afterward J. Robert Oppenheimer came to dinner at the Wilsons and he quickly convinced Wilson to join a new group, a group that would construct a bomb to end the war. Practically the whole Isotron team moved, as a group, to Los Alamos with Wilson.

When Wilson abandoned the Isotron, he felt no great sense of disappointment. His idea had worked, it was pretty, and the new work he had to do was urgent. He was going to Los Alamos in the company of some of the great physicists of the century. Besides, as he once said, "In this business of creativity, it's pretty much all pleasure . . . the intensity of the elation lifts you far out of yourself. The disappointment is a more normal reaction—one that you're quite accustomed to." He was perhaps also aware that the riches and reputation of which he had dreamed in a small moment of delusion had actually come within half an accident of being real. Small circumstantial changes—if he had the idea a little sooner, if the construction had gone more quickly, if anything—might have made his Isotron the chosen machine. Nearness to that success was itself satisfying.

At Los Alamos, Robert Wilson became a government employee. As such, all his inventions, small and large, were patented and the patents were handed over to the government for the usual "one dollar and other considerations." But Wilson noticed that no one ever got the dollar. "I would insist on getting my one dollar," he says. "I would go in and eagerly start arguing and negotiating. The poor patent lawyer would go through it all kind of sadly. I negotiated some of the patents for thirty cents if they really weren't whole-dollar inventions. I sold some for ten cents," Wilson says.

"How much did you get for the Isotron?" I asked. "I got a dollar for the Isotron, which was not bad. It was a fifty-cent idea."

10

J. Robert Oppenheimer had transparent blue eyes and his stare seemed to those who knew him like a mystic's gaze. He could recall passages from theoretical physics papers in four languages, and he could also repeat passages from Proust, from Dante's *Divine Comedy,* and from the *Bhagavad Gita* which he had read in its original text. He was a guru among physicists. In 1942, he convinced a major portion of the world's great scientists to give up science, to retire with him to the desert, and to work out a problem that was technically interesting but scientifically barren.

When the new establishment at Los Alamos had started up, Oppenheimer gathered together a technical board. There were sixteen names on the list, including Enrico Fermi, James Chadwick, Hans Bethe, I. I. Rabi, Edwin McMillan, Edward Teller, Luis Alvarez—with the exception of Teller, all Nobel Prize winners. Two more consultants were celebrated as well, Niels Bohr and John von Neumann.

Robert Wilson was no less susceptible to Oppenheimer's mystical charm. First as the head of the cyclotron group at Los Alamos, and later as head of the research division there, Wilson worked with Oppenheimer from the time before the New Mexico site was settled. "I was soon caught up by the Oppenheimer charisma," he wrote in a recollection of the period. "I became a loyal and devoted lieutenant, a confidant, a friend . . . Oppenheimer stretched me. His style, the poetic vision of what we were doing, of life, of a relationship to people, inflamed me. In his presence, I became more intelligent, more vocal, more intense, more prescient, more poetic myself. Although normally a slow reader, when he handed me a letter I would glance at it and hand it back prepared to discuss the nuances of it minutely. Now it is true, in retrospect, that there was a certain element of self-delusion in all that, and that once out of his presence the bright things that had been said were difficult to reconstruct or remember. Nor, as I left, could I quite decide what it was we had agreed to. No matter, the tone had been established. I would know how to invent what it was that had to be done."

The change in Robert Wilson which began with the moment of the Isotron was apparent at Los Alamos. "Los Alamos was very important to Bobby," says Jane Wilson. "I have told you he was kind of a lone wolf, and didn't have very many friends. He was very introverted. But a very nice thing happened when we went to Los Alamos. Everyone was discovering this magnificent countryside, and this wonderful Western culture, with its layer on layer of Indians and Spanish Americans, of horses and hiking and mountains. Anyhow, Robert was an authority on the West—he wasn't a dude. I think he was the only one at Los Alamos. You know, if Oppy were buying a horse, he liked to have Robert's advice. He had a very respectable position in the lab, and then in a nonphysics way, being clever about pack trips and where you put your bedroll to avoid the rain—you have no idea how popular he became.

"Yes," she said, "I think Robert began to talk at twenty-eight. I don't think he said many words before that."

One of Oppenheimer's first chores for Wilson was to help acquire a cyclotron from Harvard University and to take it to Los Alamos to help in the technical studies there. The fission-bomb project was secret, and so the machine could not be bought outright. Wilson and two other men had to pose as officials of an army medical station in St. Louis, and say they wanted to buy the cyclotron for medical research. One of the men, an army engineer, was disguised as a civilian lawyer. "Unfortunately," Wilson says, "he was given very brief notice to assemble his cover. He had managed to find a business suit all right, but his socks and shirt were of army khaki and his tie was regulation black." Wilson was disguised as a physicist who knew something about cyclotrons.

The three were not a very convincing trio of negotiators but they bargained long and hard with the representatives of Harvard. The price rose, and Wilson began to be embarrassed as the price was pushed up over ten, or twenty times what he knew the machine was worth. His colleagues argued, but still the price went up. Finally, one of the men from Harvard concluded the negotiations with the remark: "Well, if you want it for what you say you want it for, you can't have it. But if you want it for why I think you want it, then you can have it." As the trio left Harvard, and Wilson felt thoroughly fleeced, the disguised lawyer turned to him and chortled: "What a bunch of innocents. I was authorized to go much higher!"

Later, Wilson encountered General Leslie Groves, commander of the Los Alamos project. He had been told about the outcome of the negotiations. Wilson recalls the conversation:

"Wilson," the general said in his preemptive fashion, "we certainly fooled them up there at Harvard yesterday, didn't we?"

"Well," said Wilson, "I'm not too sure that we really fooled them. . . ."

"Wilson," the general barked loudly, "we certainly fooled them up there at Harvard."

"Yessir," Wilson said as the general turned away.

Wilson and his colleagues from the isotron project disassembled, shipped, and reassembled the roomful of machinery that was the cyclotron. With it the team measured the behavior of neutrons when they were fired at uranium 235—how many neutrons were produced in the collision? How did the fast neutrons slow down when they hit the target? The numbers produced filled in the blanks in the calculations which determined what was a critical (explosive) mass of uranium and how the bomb should be designed around that mass.

The proton is the arbiter of atomic behavior. The periodic table is built up from this fact: The first element has one proton, the second element has two protons, the third element has three protons. And so it goes up the scale; hydrogen, helium, lithium, beryllium, boron, carbon, nitrogen, oxygen. Electrically repelling one another in the nucleus, the protons are held in confinement by the attraction called the strong nuclear force. It is the pin which holds all the concentric wheels of nucleus, atom, molecule, and body. Going up the periodic table, atoms with greater and greater crowds of protons have more electrical repulsion, which strains against the strong nuclear binding. With the addition of each new proton, more electrical pressure is added. The heaviest elements are the most unstable, and there is a natural limit to the number of protons that can be confined within a nucleus. The number is ninety-two. There are ninety-two elements which exist in nature and are stable. The elements above ninety-two can be made artificially, but when left alone they spontaneously break into smaller, more stable atoms.

Uranium is element number ninety-two, and it exists on the verge of bursting. Neutrons, with no electric charge, can glide without electrical hindrance into the atomic core, and after they were discovered in 1932, it was soon found that a single, rather slow neutron could snap the unstable uranium atom in half. In the break, the two halves, plus two neutrons and a small amount of binding energy, were released. The meaning of this little event was lost on nearly all the physicists of the time, except émigré Hungarian Leo Szilard, who had read the science fiction of H. G. Wells. In his book *The World Set Free,* published in 1914, Wells wrote about the possibility of releasing nuclear energy. "Those who knew Szilard," wrote Herbert Anderson, Enrico Fermi's collaborator, "would understand instantly why this idea would excite him and why he would keep turning it over and over in his mind until he could figure out what he could do with it . . ." Wells predicted 1933 as the year in which the necessary method would be found. He knew that the disintegration of an element was a process more powerful than any chemical process; it yields a million times more energy in each reacting atom than the energy released in the chemical action of burning fuel.

When, in 1933, Szilard attended a conference in London, where he then lived, he heard the eminent Lord Rutherford declare that, "whoever talks about the liberation of atomic energy on an industrial scale is talking moonshine." Szilard disliked the absolute sound of that, and because he was a man of some humor and crankiness, he immediately set himself the problem of proving Rutherford an ass. As he was walking to work at Bart's Hospital shortly afterward, he was musing over the problem. He stopped at Southampton Row for a red light and the solution came to him as a sudden apparition. By the time the light turned green, he realized that if an atom struck with one neutron releases two neutrons from its nucleus, then those two neutrons could shoot off to hit two other nuclei, and those two nuclei would release four more neutrons. In 1934, Szilard filed a patent which contained the phrase "chain reaction." Szilard was only uncertain about which element it would be that would release two neutrons in collision. It was in the last days of 1938 that it became clear that the natural element which works is uranium; the artificial element which does the same is plutonium.

When he learned of the work of Otto Hahn and Fritz Strassmann, who were the first to split the uranium atom, Szilard knew at once what the information meant physically and politically; he had left Germany just ahead of persecution. Szilard left immediately for the United States to relay his understanding to Enrico Fermi at Columbia University.

As early as 1939, Germany had begun work on a fission bomb, more than a year ahead of the West. For the West, the war was already going badly, and promised to go worse. And so Oppenheimer, who could with his entrancing manner stir feelings of fear, excitement, and seemingly deep understanding, could gather an army of physicists at Los Alamos, and they would be willing to work out the technical details necessary to change the equation $E=mc^2$ into a demonstrable physical fact.

The physicists working on the bomb were aware that its presence in the world would alter war and politics. They knew there was a potential for the bomb's demonic use, but there was so much certainty in the cause against Hitler and so much fear in the chance that that demon would succeed, that the worries and moral doubts were dampened. Only afterward did Wilson have serious doubts about the enterprise, as he also had doubts about the Isotron: "The idea of the isotope separator came to me in a flash of inspiration. But, at the same time, I fully realized the consequences of the idea were it to be successful. At just that moment of creation, I might have said to myself, 'This

is diabolical. To hell with it.' Instead I saw the Isotron as a
factor in reversing the tide of defeat and in stopping the carnage of Europe . . .

"At Los Alamos, we worked frantically so that a weapon
would be ready at the earliest moment," he wrote. "Once
caught up in such a mass effort, one does not debate at every
moment, Hamlet fashion, its moral basis. The speed and interest of the technical developments, the fascinating interplay of
brilliant personalities, the rapidly changing world situation outside our gates—all this worked to involve us more deeply, more
completely in what appeared to be an unquestionably good
cause. Occasionally we did pause in the hot race to wonder
where we were going—and why . . . Niels Bohr, a great humanitarian as well as a great physicist, did most to inspire the
introspective conversations that were held there, and kept them
to a high moral level. Although I do not remember that he ever
questioned whether we should be making a bomb or not, he did
cause to be examined many of the serious consequences for a
world that could continue to be divided . . . Perhaps even I, as a
very young and insignificant member, contributed to that moral
atmosphere. Something like a year after Los Alamos had started
I called a meeting in the cyclotron laboratory (Building X) . . .
I remember placing notices around Los Alamos that announced
a seminar . . . entitled 'The Impact of the Gadget on Civilization.' "

There was much talk at that meeting about the United Nations about to be established. The feeling was that the bomb
should be, must be, built and exploded before that meeting or
else the politicians would be likely to make terrible errors about
what the postwar world would be and how the United Nations
should be organized. After the meeting in the cyclotron lab,
and a short time after the United Nations had been launched,
Germany surrendered. But still, oddly, the work at Los Alamos
went ahead with the same speed and enthusiasm.

"I have often wondered why it was that the defeat of Germany in 1945 did not cause me to re-examine my involvement
with the war and with nuclear bombs in particular. The
thought never occurred to me. Nor, to my knowledge, did any
of my friends raise any such question on that occasion. Surely, it

seems that among those hundreds of scientists at Los Alamos it might have been expected that at least one would have left. I regret now that I did not do so . . .

"Perhaps events were just moving too fast. We were at the climax of the project—just on the verge of exploding the test bomb in the desert. Every faculty, every thought, every effort was directed toward making that a success. I think that to have asked us to pull back at that moment wo¹ld have been as unrealistic and unfair as it would be to ask a pugilist to sense intellectually the exact moment his opponent has weakened to the point where he will eventually lose, and then to have the responsibility of stopping the fight just at that point . . ."

The test site for the fission bomb was in a sand and lava desert, about two hundred miles south of Los Alamos. The tract of land was called Jornada del Muerto, the journey of death, by the first Spanish who had to travel across it. Robert Oppenheimer had to find a code name for it and, after a John Donne poem he had been reading, he decided on Trinity. Donne implored his "three-personed God" to destroy and renew him: "Bend your force to break, blow, burn, and make me new . . ."

In its casing, the bomb itself looked like a great gray egg of metal, with four flight fins attached at one end. The shell, useful in the flights of the other two bombs constructed at the same time, was removed from the test bomb. Only the yolk of the gray egg sat in the test tower. At its center was eleven pounds of plutonium 239. It was an apple-sized ball of material, a fissionable substitute for uranium. The physicists who got on intimate terms with the bomb called it "Fat Man," or even more familiarly, "Fat Boy." The more mechanical term, as Wilson's meeting notice suggests, was "the gadget."

The Fat Man perched on a tower that was one hundred feet high, an open lattice of steel. Short ribs of metal were welded a few feet apart and ran up the outside of the structure as a ladder. Wilson was one of the last men to climb the ladder before it was vaporized in the dark morning hours of July 16, 1945. Wilson had to climb to the bomb to turn on an experiment of his. Two feet from the sphere and arranged around it were sets of tubes called photomultipliers. They detect light and turn it into an amplified signal. In Wilson's experiment, some 250 of the tubes were connected by cable to another device some hundreds of yards away on the sand, which would change the signal into useful information about the atomic fission. The object was to gauge the amount of light thrown off during the first microseconds of the fission and use it to determine how fast the reaction grew. The difficulty, however, is that when such devices are set next to an atomic bomb, all the equipment is reduced instantly to atoms in the explosion. The only way to get information away from the bomb fast enough, Wilson realized, would be to carry it away with the speed of light. The signal would move through the equipment and the wires just ahead of their disintegration.

In the nights before that night, Wilson had a recurring, frightening dream about climbing the Fat Man's tower. Though he would climb up and stand within inches of the deadliest device the hands of man ever dared to make, Wilson's fears were not about the bomb. They were human-sized and mundane. One hundred feet is about nine stories and Wilson would have to go up the distance in the dark, hand over hand, on small footholds. He had nightmares about falling off.

Those in the bunker watched the clock at the announced hour. Those in the base camp a few miles away knelt on the sand, as instructed. Though it was dark as midnight, they put on sunglasses. They put their heads down near the ground, and their backsides faced the gadget. Ignition occurred at 5:29:45 in the silent desert morning.

The first fraction of the first millionth of a second was read by Wilson's phototubes. The equipment then disappeared, the signal shot down a wire, chased by the disappearing cable. It took thirty millionths of a second for the desert to exchange night for noon. To the observers, the world—the desert bushes, the red rocks, the bald hills, and the mountains with their sharp crevices and shadows—appeared suddenly like a slide flashing onto a movie screen. For thirty seconds, there was no sound from the huge white fireball, but those watching were not passive. They felt a visceral excitement and fright. I. I. Rabi, lying on the sand, recalls watching the gooseflesh rise on the backs of his hands. "It was not like watching an ordinary explosion scaled up," he said. "It was awful, ominous, and personally threatening." One physicist was frightened by the sudden heat on the back of his neck; another thought for half a moment that the atmosphere had ignited, that the racing light and heat would soon overtake them, fusing and frying them with the sand. But in a moment the searing white ball dimmed. Fermi got up from the ground, clutching bits of paper. Wilson recalls that the objects of the desert around him seemed tiny. For an instant, the desert was a painted miniature; the physicists did not look across, but *up*, into the monstrous orange flame and translucent purple clouds billowing around it. The events and memories of life which seemed important before that moment now became insignificant motions. For the rest of their lives, this thing would stand as a towering shadow among other puny memories.

After thirty seconds, the sound arrived. The boom slammed their eardrums. The hard surface of an air blast slapped their clothing against their skin and pushed their bodies backward across the ground. Fermi, who had waited for days to do it, released his bits of paper and watched them skitter out into the air away from him. The roar continued to boil in the air, and the percussion beat against the mountains like a drum, sending the tympanic echoes back to the stunned physicists.

When the shock waves subsided, the emotions of those present were a vegetable soup of postadrenaline confusion. There were fear, pleasure, giddiness, and shock in degrees. Physicist Samuel Allison looked at the military men standing around him, and thought that the horror they had just watched was now the property of the military. In a sudden fright, he sought out a civilian colleague. "Oh, Mr. Conant!" he whined. "They're going to take this thing over and fry *hundreds* of Japanese!" For a moment Robert Wilson stood outside his own life, and looked down at it, at the physicist and the man involved in a war. He was disturbed. Perhaps the whole thing had been an awful mistake; perhaps even accepting loss in the war would have been better than allowing the conception and birth of this white abyss of force. Oppenheimer was congratulated in mixed tones. One physicist, with feelings of achievement, necessity, and resignation, complimented Oppenheimer. He then added: "Now we are all sons of bitches."

Some years later, Wilson's eleven-year-old son Jonathan returned home from school angry and distraught. He accosted his father: "How could you do it, Pop? How could you?" Explanation was not easy the moment after the explosion, not easy when his son confronted him, and even today is not easy. When he talks about it, he looks down at the floor. Though there was some good reason for what he did, he feels nonetheless a sense of sin. Not long after the war, Wilson walked through the rubble of the cities hit by the bombs. He was working on a project to assess radiation damage. He made the terrible calculations of the effects of intense radiation on human flesh. Wilson became the first president of the Federation of American Scientists, and he worked actively in the Association of Los Alamos Scientists. Both organizations were formed, as he puts it, "for the expiation of our sin," through full public knowledge and through support of disarmament.

Wilson and the others thought for a time during the Los Alamos project, and just after it, that the scientists would naturally be consulted about how this terrible force would be used. They hoped to confine it. But they were politically naive. Their illusion was soon removed. "In fact," he says, "we were just like the slaves building the pyramids."

11

Robert Wilson spent the middle portion of his life, a little more than twenty years, in the constant company of protons. He looked at them this way and that, considering their riddles in sequence. He spent some years—just after leaving Ernest Lawrence and then again just after the war—attempting to picture the insides of the proton. Does the proton, which is gear and wheel within the atom, have gears and wheels of its own? Or is it a smooth, structureless drop of force?

Wilson shot protons at other protons to find out. He looked to see how they would rebound from one another. One pattern of deflection would suggest wheels within the wheel. Another would mean that the proton was featureless—or that the proton collision was too soft to reveal anything.

Wilson collided protons with energies of eight million electron volts, and the proton seemed featureless. He went on to ten million volts, then fourteen and a half million volts. The results continued the same. But there were practical limits to this proton-on-proton method of measuring, and as more powerful experimental equipment came along, eventually Wilson began to use other means of probing the anatomy of the proton. He fired electrons at the protons, and since electrons are far smaller (and simpler) particles, they would be likely to give cleaner results for the energy expended.

The chief investigator using this electron method at the time was Robert Hofstadter of Stanford University. He had dedicated himself to years of scattering electrons off many things—from each atomic element on down to the single proton. Wilson jumped right in and began bombarding protons with electrons from the powerful machine he built at Cornell, the most powerful machine of its time. Soon, Hofstadter and Wilson were competing avidly. Hofstadter might achieve a result first, then Wilson would achieve one first, and each anticipated the other's next move. Wilson was once so anxious to put across a finding that he raced to write it up and publish it in a journal he had not used before—because its printing schedule was faster. "I knew," Wilson explained only partly in jest, "that if I waited to get it into the *Physical Review,* Hofstadter would hear about it, run to look for the same thing himself and try to publish it first."

Wilson and Hofstadter together learned, with Wilson a little ahead, that the proton *does* have an internal structure. There are overlapping layers of force within it, and from this discovery followed the discovery of a long list of new particles, and a major step toward the current attempt in physics to make a grand synthesis—under which all the particles inside the nucleus are composed of quarks, while all the particles *outside* the nucleus are variations of the electron. In 1961, Hofstadter was awarded the Nobel Prize for his years of electron scattering and his exploration of the proton. By some accounts at least, Robert Wilson earned a small piece of that prize as well.

During those years that Wilson worked on the proton problem, his enthusiasm took him leaping from one idea to another through several other projects. Half a dozen of them were noticeable achievements in the physics of the time. In 1958, Wilson discovered a new state of the proton and predicted two more states. He found that when protons are created in high-energy collisions, at about 750 million electron volts, they form something of a new particle. It is a proton with a different spin than the familiar one, and is called an excited state of the proton.

In earlier experiments, Wilson had determined the range of the proton—the distance it will travel through air and other fluid media before coming to rest. He saw that protons disturb the medium somewhat along their path of flight, but that most of the electrical havoc they create occurs in the last two centimeters before they stop. He realized that this meant protons might fly through the skin and through some depth of tissue with small damage done, but then do far greater destruction to a malignancy lying deep within the body. Wilson's was the first suggestion that protons might be used for radiation therapy.

While at Cornell, Wilson also created a device and coined a word which are still in common use in physics. One crucial measurement in physics is the amount of energy in the particles of light passing through experimental equipment; such measurements of energy are essential to keep track of the conservation of energy. A number of devices had been used to do the work, but the measurements from each were calculated differently and comparisons were chaotic. Wilson created a simple package, twelve plates of copper in a chamber, which gave an accurate and direct measurement of the energy. It measures the total number of energy quanta, and Wilson called it a Quantameter. "I think I like the word even better than the device," he says. "It's a QuanTOMeter, pronounced just that way with the accent in the middle." Quanta, a pretty word, is among the most important of all ideas in physics. Meters of various sorts are, in being both common and critical, like hands and eyes to a physicist. So quanta and meter meet, a neat label, a simple device. It has been twenty years and Wilson still grins about the pleasing combination.

In print, the career of Robert Wilson amounts to only two black binders of articles—there are about two dozen physics papers, a few pages each, and another dozen popular articles. As a literature of nonfiction works, the papers from a physicist's life are shocking in their small number, and in each paper's thinness. Torrents of concentrated human energy are expended to produce a few lines of knowledge. It is like a perverse version of the magician's trick—a gallon jug is emptied into a thimble, which is then inverted to release a single drop onto the table.

Wilson's place as a physicist was once described by a colleague: "On a scale of ten, I'd say he was ahh, about eight plus, maybe 9 minus. He is in the top five percent of all active physicists." A Fermilab physicist put it another way. "Wilson is a superb physicist. You could argue whether he was Nobel quality or not. But the amazing thing about Wilson is that, if he is not the best in one thing, he is extremely good at *several* things." A little like the decathlon athlete or the gymnast who wins the all-around title but is champion in no single event.

When he was fifty years old, Wilson had begun to complain to his wife. He was not doing much physics anymore, and he did not want to just roost as lab director at Cornell. He had a fantasy about what he should do in retirement. When he was at Los Alamos, he noticed that in the town of Santa Fe there was a small group of old Spanish men who sat in the plaza every day. They came in the morning, drank and told stories all day, then went home in the evening. "For my retirement, I wanted to go to Santa Fe to be an alcoholic. These old men would sit and drink, and spin marvelous tales. They were not just stories, but were very philosophical, and they would draw fine meanings out of them. It was quite an art. Santa Fe is now too big a city, and I don't think the old men are there anymore. But probably in one of the villages around there . . ."

More seriously, he thought of taking up sculpture full time. He had observed that sculptors only get better as they get older. Sculpture yields to experience and skill, while physics demands boldness and youth for the grand jeté. He had sold some pieces already, and at the urging of Oppenheimer had completed a large piece which stands at the Institute for Advanced Studies in Princeton. As his thoughts were pushing him this way, Wilson received an invitation to a conference in Rome. Among the things to be discussed were the plans for a new accelerator that would be more than three times bigger than anything then built. First plans called for an energy of two hundred billion volts; these were the first plans for the machine that would become Fermilab. Wilson was not receptive; he felt he had participated in the building of enough machines. If he was not going to do pure physics anymore, he did not want to do doggerel either. When he got the letter, he thought only that it would be very nice to get over to Italy because he had some small female figures made in wax that he wanted to have cast in metal. The craftsmen for the job were in Italy. He sent a letter saying he could not make it to the conference because he was short of money. Soon he had another letter which urged him to come, and offered to pay his way. He hesitated. Then he decided that he could put in the necessary appearances at the conference and still have time to oversee the casting of his works.

He recalls sitting in the conference room with his body a little numb, his mind not fully attending the talks, which were presented by young, professional accelerator designers from Berkeley. They lacked the fire of the old Ernest Lawrence team, Wilson mused.

At lunch occurred one of those important accidental meetings which Wilson believes in. He sat with a former colleague from Berkeley, a Nobel winner. His colleague was now leader of the Berkeley delegation at the conference.

Wilson ate in silence. He was feeling awkward, and wanted to say something to make conversation, but he couldn't think of anything. The silence went on. "Well," he finally tossed out, "I heard the papers presented at the meeting today."

"What did you think?" the Berkeley man asked.

Wilson was not really prepared to say what he thought. He fished for something and pulled out an unfortunate line: "I didn't like the way they were presented," he said. "Remember when you and Lawrence or Oppenheimer presented one of these things? They did it with gusto, with enthusiasm. They didn't seem to have any of that today. . . ."

"That was one of the most shallow things I have ever heard," his colleague said in effect to Wilson. "Who cares *how* it is presented? It's the substance that counts!"

"No, these things count too," Wilson replied. A few more shots passed across the table, and the more Wilson defended his remark, the angrier his friend got. Wilson says now, "Hell, I was only trying to get through lunch. Trying to make conversation. I hadn't intended the conversation to go that way."

The bitter exchange got worse until, as he left the table, Wilson took a final stab: "Well, I didn't like some of the substance of the things that were said, either. . . ."

"Do you think you could do any better?" shouted his friend.

"Any day. Any day!" taunted Wilson. He strode away.

Wilson was now angry, ashamed, and he was hooked. He would not be able to let the subject go without doing some serious thinking about what was actually wrong with the plans. It was the sort of emotional encounter that keeps rising unpleasantly up into one's thoughts, like the stomach's regurgling of an overspiced meal.

Wilson left Rome for Paris, where he hoped to play squash with a friend and join the drawing sessions at the Grande Chaumière. "I told myself that would be the end of that, I would not think about the plans for the accelerator anymore. But when I was sitting at the Grande Chaumière—you pay a franc and can join in—I was drawing this beautiful, curvaceous model and I found my mind wandering. When they would say 'Repose,' I found myself sitting there without much to do, so I began making drawings, circles, and short calculations about the accelerator. I was thinking about my experiences at Cornell, ways to do things cheaper and more cleverly. Wherever I went that week—the bistros or sidewalk cafés, I sat and made designs of accelerators. I was completely engrossed."

It was not the first time he had been in Paris and had his thought swept away with the subject of accelerators, though he says "that subject is not what one should be thinking about in Paris." He had been in Paris earlier, in 1954, when he was a professor D'Exchange at the Sorbonne. "I was professor D'Exchange, but in a sense, though, you're a tourist. It's very hard to be a tourist and not to go into a cathedral, in fact go into *lots* of cathedrals in France. You're bound to go into a couple dozen of them.

"At first when I went in, I was disappointed," Wilson says. "I was not particularly moved. Perhaps I thought that I should have some kind of a religious experience. I didn't. But after a while I noticed I had a different kind of feeling. I began looking at those things very much the way I would look at an accelerator. . . . I wondered how they put them up, how did they know enough physics to assemble those things and not have them *fall down*? . . . I was just amazed at the height. I mean, I was a *rube* with my mouth open, looking at high buildings!"

He had stood looking up. The threads of time and layers of culture began to dissolve, and in the gray stone he recognized something. "I am sure that the builders of the cathedrals would have said that they were making beautiful sculptures in stone, and that these things were an expression of their religious faith. And I would say that I am doing physics research, and there is another kind of faith . . . but somehow these two things short-hand into the same thing. I was trying to make high energies, and in the cathedrals there was a great energy of height. . . ."

He wrote later that, "Thus carried away, I looked into cathedral building a bit further. I found a striking similarity between the tight community of cathedral builders and the community of accelerator builders; both of them were daring innovators, both were fiercely competitive on national lines, but yet both were basically internationalists. I like to compare the great Maître d'Oeuvre, Suger of Saint-Denis, with Cockcroft of Cambridge; or Sully of Notre Dame with Lawrence of Berkeley, and Villard d'Honnecourt with Budker of Novosibirsk. Cathedral builders were considered to be artists, but even they recognized themselves as technically oriented; one of their slogans was *Ars sine scientia nihil est*! (Art without science is nothing.)"

In the papers and sketches of the cathedral builders, the mix of art and technology was complete; in the notebooks of Villard d'Honnecourt, sketches of human figures and technical designs of cathedrals overlap and blend. Wilson's nudes and accelerator calculations together graced his sketch pad at the Grande Chaumière.

Setting the height of Fermilab, Wilson created something of a permanent gesture of kinship between the cathedral and the accelerator. To determine how high the Fermilab high-rise should be, Wilson rented a helicopter. He asked the pilot to ascend slowly, stopping every twenty-five feet, so he could judge how good the view was from each height. "I plotted the aesthetic factor as a function of height," Wilson said, "and I found that it increased rapidly up to about a hundred and seventy-five feet. Above that height the view was equally good." In order to have several floors with the best view of the Fox River Valley, Wilson set the height of the building at 250 feet. The Fermilab high-rise is the same height as the cathedral at Beauvais.

When Wilson returned home after the Rome conference, he wrote a letter to his colleague, the leader of the accelerator group from Berkeley. Wilson formally challenged the plans for the two-hundred-BeV accelerator. He hoped that his criticisms would be useful. Wilson was not a professional machine builder, but he had worked with accelerators for more than thirty years and had designed half a dozen bold machines. He had just finished a ten-billion-volt machine for Cornell; it was ahead of schedule and came in five percent under an already tight budget. Though he was a renegade, Wilson was taken seriously, at least by some.

At a meeting of physicists at the Biltmore Hotel in New York, a debate was arranged so the two sides could openly present their ideas about the plans and how they should be carried out. "Yes, there was a shoot-out arranged, with me on one side and the men from Berkeley on the other," says Wilson. "I lost. It was a debate and they just chewed me up. I don't think I convinced anyone of anything. I was debating with these men who had built big machines before and had studied machines for years. No one had any reason to believe someone who hadn't done it. Besides, I had very little to back up my point. All I could say is, 'Well, I believe it could be done better.' They either had to believe me or not. They didn't. So I left the thing there. I thought I had said my piece. I was only trying to give some helpful advice, after all."

He wanted to drop the thing. But the politics were conspiring oddly. The scientists at Berkeley wanted to design and run the whole show, putting the accelerator in California. They thought it only natural since the East Coast already had a large machine, the thirty-BeV accelerator at Brookhaven on Long Island, New York. East and West fought. In addition, the Midwest Universities Research Association was lobbying strongly and complaining bitterly that all the science money was being poured into the East and West in the United States. Why, they asked reasonably, was the Midwest being slighted? On the side of the Midwest was Senator Everett Dirksen. The solution of the politicians was to appoint a committee to examine all the possible sites around the nation to see which would be best suited for the machine. It was a great prize, desperately sought after. Leon Lederman of Columbia University, and now Fermilab's director, recalls that Southern states were even willing to put on a great show of tolerance to attract the construction. He recalls saying to the Louisiana governor, "Wouldn't it cause some kind of difficulties bringing all those physicists, including the blacks and Jews and others, down there to Dobbs Ferry? We couldn't bring them in, could we?" The governor agreed. "No, you can't. But *we* can. We're the power structure down here."

The site chosen was a spot near Weston, Illinois, called by the locals Coon Hollow. The place was quickly dubbed Dirksen

Junction in honor of that man's influence over the final decision. After the choice of a site, the next question was the choice of a director. Wilson's name had been put on the list, and he had withdrawn it. Another name on the list was Edward Lofgren, of the Berkeley contingent. The job was offered to Lofgren. But Lofgren was having no part of Illinois and the low budget which Wilson said would be enough.

"There was a meeting held after it was clear that the Berkeley proposal had been defeated and Lofgren was not going to be the director," Lederman says. "Myself, and Norman Ramsey [head of the federal panel which had suggested building a large accelerator], and Wilson all went out for a beer. We sat talking after the Berkeley group's defeat. After some conversation and a drink or two, there was a small pause in the conversation. It seemed as if all at once each of us was thinking the same thing: Okay, if it's not Berkeley and Lofgren, who then? Ramsey and I both turned to Bob. He looked, and said, 'Oh, no!' But he was the obvious one, even though, to this day, he looks like a harebrained, wild-eyed outsider to professionals like those at CERN."

Jane Wilson urged him to do it, Lederman and Ramsey urged him. Finally, Lederman delivered the line which moved him to accept: "Bobby, your days as a physicist are over, and you're feeling in a rut. You need a big challenge. This is it. You've shot your mouth off and now you've got to produce!"

12

THE first particle machine Robert Wilson ever made, in his attic in 1929, was a gaseous discharge tube a few inches long for which he blew the glass himself, invented a vacuum pump, and fashioned the other parts by hand. When he visited the radiation laboratory in 1932, three years later, the twenty-eight-inch cyclotron was among the most important news in physics. At Princeton, Los Alamos, and Harvard in the 1940s, Wilson had constructed and used machines that were about four feet in diameter. The first accelerator he had built at Cornell was six and a half feet across. The last he had built there, four machines later, was about a hundred times as large. Six hundred and sixty feet across. The job before him at Coon Hollow was to construct, at one and a quarter miles in diameter, the greatest machine of physics. It would end the questions of one era in physics and begin the interrogations of the next.

Wilson began buoyantly, and the work went deceptively well. A group at the neighboring Argonne National Laboratory in Illinois expected to hear a dry and detailed talk when they went to hear the director of the new accelerator project. But Wilson, with his best cowboy grin, told them about the soil expert hired to tell them about Coon Hollow's soil characteristics. Wilson said the expert had told him that no matter how many different sorts of tests you ran on the soil, the only good way to know what you had in the soil was to pick up a handful, take a bite, and study the taste. Wanting to be the complete director, Wilson had done that; tasted pretty good, he said. Wilson also told the group that the way he figured it, statistically speaking, the laboratory was already on a downhill slide. When the director was the only one on the payroll, the average quality of employee was very high. But from that point on, the hiring of more people could only make the average quality of worker go down. Unhappy but necessary prospect, Wilson supposed.

Wilson had made the outrageous claim that they would come in so far under the $250 million budget that he could afford to add several expensive experimental facilities not in the plans. He made the outrage worse when he said the thing would be finished in five years, several years ahead of any reasonable estimate. (The Berkeley study had called for eight years of construction.) After a year of work, Wilson added another straw to the pile by revising his estimate of when the machine would be completed. Not five, but four years, he announced.

At the end of the first year, there was a meeting in Illinois to which the wounded Berkeley contingent came. The Wilson plans were to be reviewed. "The Berkeley sharpshooters came loaded for bear," says Leon Lederman. "Before we went in there I talked to Wilson, and I made him promise that he would go in and treat these guys with respect, that he would not shout or dismiss them with contempt. He promised."

The Berkeley plan had called for a main ring tunnel to be bored through the earth, and the floor anchored in bedrock to make the machine stable; if the ground shifted by even a few hundredths of an inch over four miles, there could be a disaster in the delicately placed beam tube. Wilson decided he'd take the chance. The fancy, anchored, air-conditioned tunnel would be far too expensive. Wilson had the ring dug as cheaply and simply as a sewer pipe, a cut-and-fill operation.

The beam tube, with its crucial high vacuum, runs through the middle of the 1,014 boxcar-shaped magnets around the ring. If one magnet failed, there had to be a way of taking it out and putting it back in without wrecking the ability of the tube to hold a vacuum. There was such a device, an elaborate clamp seal which could be placed at either end of each magnet. When a magnet failed, the clamps could be popped open, the magnet pulled and fixed, and then put back. The clamps would then be popped on, making a tightly sealed tube again. The problem with this system was that each clamp seal cost something like three hundred dollars. Multiply that times one thousand, and that one precaution became a major budget item. Wilson responded to the situation by declaring that there would be no clamps between magnets. The high vacuum tube would be in one piece. What about when magnets fail and have to be removed? We will build them so they won't fail, he said. We won't have vacuum leaks.

For the faint heart he might have provided a translation of his bravado. It was impossible to believe that magnets would never fail; the edict seemed irrational. But the meaning of the irrationality was this: Wilson hoped to get away with very few failures. If those failures occurred, a method would be worked out to cut away the magnet and weld it back in without vacuum problems. Even if this "can-opener" procedure was crude, time-consuming, and perhaps in failure cases more expensive, more caution was unnecessary. The cost of can opening would be less in the long run. Risks had to be taken. Wilson thought if a machine worked as soon as it was turned on, with no scrambling and reworking, that machine was overdesigned and thus overexpensive. The Berkeley design had five hundred magnets producing a two-hundred-billion-volt beam of particles; Wilson had the magnets mass-produced in a risky manner and could afford to buy a thousand of them which could thus make a four-hundred-billion-volt beam.

In the meeting with the Berkeley sharpshooters, questions were raised about these risks. One after another of the Wilson innovations were poked at. A square tunnel with cranes placed strategically around it to haul magnets in and out was the reasonable approach. But, as in cathedrals, square structures take weight poorly and so have to be expensively reinforced. Arches can be thin and strong. Wilson built the tunnel in an arch form. Cranes could not work with curving walls and ceiling, so Wilson designed a machine that would move around the ring on wheels, to take the magnets out and put them in when a failure occurred. The machine was slow, but effective. Each detail was criticized by the Berkeley group, and Lederman says, "Bob was good. He answered their questions politely. And there were some damn fool questions, too. But they got into asking, 'What happens if . . .' Finally, they were talking about the machine which would go around the ring, cutting out magnets in the event of a failure. 'Suppose,' they asked him, 'that this machine jams and won't go around?' Wilson couldn't take any more. With a perfectly straight face he said, 'Well, yes, in that case we would probably go out to the spot and plant a dynamite charge under the thing, blow it up, and then start rebuilding . . .'" Lederman broke in, lest the Berkeley men either take Wilson seriously or get angry at the leg-pulling: "Bob! Now you promised you would be nice. . . ."

Wilson was riding the crest; the design shaded into construction. He wrote of the design process, recalling his experience with cathedrals: "I am sure that both the designers of cathedrals and the designers of accelerators proceeded almost entirely on educated intuition guided by aesthetics . . . Modern accelerators are exceedingly complex machines characterized by large mechanical and electrical forms which are pierced by vacuum pipes, and immersed in magnetic fields in which atoms are jiggled by electric fields. . . . Informed and informing this complex is a nervous system that consists of a ganglia of microprocessors that are governed by a large computer. Now to understand each complicated component and its relationship to the whole would go well beyond my own technical knowledge. So how do I go about designing? . . . I find out a little here, by a calculation, and a little there . . . then I draw those parts of the design on paper. After that I just freely and intuitively draw in pleasant appearing, smooth connecting lines; lines that cover my ignorance of detail. I keep drawing, correcting here and there by calculations until the accelerator appears that it might work. When the parts and forms have essentially the same relationship that parts of a sculpture should have to the whole, then I am satisfied by the design. . . ."

Wilson pressed on, behaving as a manic artist on the problem he took up, behaving as a drill sergeant in the problems he assigned to others. He deliberately understaffed each project, and liked to see the satisfying flurry of people in motion. One group was headed by Father Timothy Toohig, a physicist and a Jesuit. At a meeting that was required by the AEC to discuss emergency evacuation of each lab in case of radiation or some

other danger, after some serious and irritable argument about
the notion of evacuation plans, Wilson turned to Toohig.
Toohig hadn't said anything yet, so Wilson asked, "What
would you do in the case of that kind of emergency?"

"I guess I would get out my rosary beads and pray," said the
father. The meeting broke up in laughter. But two weeks later,
after Toohig had made a desperate plea to Wilson for more
workers, saying the understaffing was genuinely difficult, Wilson
sent out a package and a little note to Father Toohig. In the
package was a rosary, made of large plastic beads—the beads
were made of scintillator material which glows when struck by
radiation. The note with the beads said, in effect, "I wouldn't
want to insult you and your abilities by sending you more
workers. But since it may not be too safe out there, I had this
scintillator rosary made for you. . . ."

When Fermilab's Meson Laboratory area was under construction, Toohig recalls another encounter with Wilson. "We
wanted a large crane to move things around in the lab. We had
hundreds of tons of equipment, and we couldn't think of any
way to get the stuff around if we didn't have a crane. But
Wilson said, 'We have no money for a crane. But, if you want,
you can have your crane without a building around it.' We
could imagine ourselves out on a concrete slab, in the cold
Illinois prairie wind, freezing and doing our experiments and
moving things around with a nice crane. We chose to have a
building instead. Later, when we were planning the size of the
building, he had planned to put the walls of the building right
up against the edge of the experimental equipment. He saved a
foot or two on the size of the building, so it was cheaper. We
told him that we had to have another foot or so, at least, so that
when one experiment was over, we could move the experiment
out and put the next set of equipment in. 'How often are you
going to move them?' was his answer. We said it wouldn't be
too often. 'Well,' he said, 'when you need to move things, take
out the wall. It'll be cheaper.' "

The Meson lab was put together without the essential crane,
without needed doors, without the necessary foot of space; the
rest of the Fermilab suffered the same stringency. "You find
only later," says Father Toohig, "that you really don't need a
lot of these things. You find out after a time just what *is* sensi-

ble and necessary. What's really essential might get put in later." Extra money was spent at Fermilab, however. It was spent on bright colors of paint. It was spent on the sculpted texture of the central laboratory and on the lofty interior court.

By 1971 the preaccelerators, both linear and circular, were built and running. The main-ring magnets were in the tunnel and were connected to the power supply. The radio-frequency devices, which actually give the protons their accelerating kick, were in place. The computer and its control equipment were ready. Protons had been accelerated in the linear machine, pushed into the small booster accelerator, and fed into the main ring. They had actually raced around the full four miles for a few turns. This was less than four years after Wilson had walked into a vacant rented room, set up some folding chairs before a blank blackboard, and chalked a circle on it.

But the elation ended abruptly. The protons would not circle the machine any more than a few times. The trouble, it was discovered, was in the four-mile stainless-steel vacuum tube in which the protons were to fly. "The donut," Wilson calls it. The donut was filled with debris. Everything from metal shavings to workmen's lunches were found in it. Removing them would not be easy. To take the debris out by hand would mean breaking open the machine in a thousand places, at great cost and long delay. But one Britisher on the staff recalled hearing of the trained ferrets that chased down narrow rabbit holes after their prey. He suggested training a ferret to pull a cleaning device through four miles of rabbit hole. Felicia, a fifteen-inch ferret, was purchased for thirty-five dollars. She was introduced first to short pipes, then longer, up to three hundred feet of tubing. But the ferret would not enter the four-mile tube. So a mechanical ferret was made for the job, and Felicia was relegated to cleaning out sections of a few hundred feet.

After the vacuum tube was cleared, worse difficulties began. The Fermilab tunnel had been built during the winter, when the ground and its moisture were frozen. The tunnel and magnets inside remained cool until the heat and humidity of the following July, when water condensed in the tunnel and created a rainstorm over the magnets. The water should not have caused a failure. But magnets began to burn out electrically— thousands of volts shot through the insulation and crashed to

the ground, burning up the magnetic coil. They blew excruci-
atingly, one magnet at a time. Each one had to be cut from the
thousand-magnet train with the can opener, pulled out of
place, repaired, and laboriously placed back in the main-ring
train. Each blown magnet cost a day of labor and brought more
doubts and bewilderment. It was later found that there were
invisible cracks in the fiber-glass insulation of the magnets. In
a dry tunnel this would have caused no trouble; in a wet tunnel, water worked down through the cracks in the magnets'
insulation to the high-voltage coils. The power jumped from
coil, to water, to ground, and blew the magnet.

It was impossible for the Fermilab technicians to tell how
many of the magnets had these cracks. They simply had to
turn the magnets on each day and wait to see if one would
blow. When one did, the whole system went down. The magnet
had to be cut out of the train, hauled away, and fixed. After
a magnet was replaced, the machine would again be turned on.
The physicists then waited to see if another magnet would
blow. Day by day, magnet by magnet, the physicists watched the
beautiful new machine come apart. The threads of morale
burst, one by one, magnet by magnet. The number of blown
magnets reached twenty, then fifty, and the number still went
up, a day at a time. One hundred magnets blew, one hundred
and fifty. Two hundred magnets burst their bindings.

Over these months, Robert Wilson aged ungracefully. Frantic
suggestions were made to him about how to get the lab out of
this growing disaster. He refused to listen. He said he had to
wait, the whole staff had to wait. The work at each stage was
monstrously time-consuming. At one point, the chief engineer,
Hank Hinterberger, informed Wilson that one problem alone
—checking each of the thousand vacuum pumps for leaks—
would require about two and a half months of labor by Hinterberger's staff. "Okay, you've got two weeks," snapped Wilson.

"Jeeeses! It would take everyone in the whole damn lab
working full time to do that!"

"Okay," said Wilson, "you've got everyone in the lab."

The entire population across the Fermilab site was ordered
from its regular work and into the crisis. But there was no sign
of relief. Two hundred and fifty magnets, three hundred magnets blew, and the number continued to rise. Wilson's decisions

appeared to many to become wild and loose. The whole project seemed to lose its moorings. As physicist Robert March reported a staff member's remark: "We thought Wilson was done for. Either he would quit, or have a heart attack, or one of us would go berserk and shoot him."

Professional accelerator builders at Berkeley and in Europe became a little gleeful, and there were jokes made about cowboys and accelerators. Friends and some colleagues from Cornell became worried. When Wilson accepted the job as director of Fermilab they thought it might be too much for him. He had only worked with a small group of old friends from the Isotron, through Los Alamos, to Cornell. He could handle the small bunch, and his odd behavior had long since been understood. Physicist Al Silverman joined Wilson's group at Cornell in 1950. When he arrived, he said, "I thought Wilson was kind of nuts. He ran around making all sorts of arbitrary statements. He tossed off statements about very important matters with a flip of his hand. The width of the vacuum tube—he'd say, 'The gap will be half. an inch.' Why? 'It's a good number.' At first it seemed to me that he might be a complete crackpot. I was not sure for a while, and I kind of watched how other people reacted to him." He soon realized that Wilson's style and his physics were both good.

But Fermilab's crisis continued for nearly a year. More than 350 of the magnets exploded before the drier winter and the end of the ordeal. Again, physicists tried to produce a beam of protons in the machine.

Physicist Drasgo Jovanovich, who was among those coaxing up the beam in the control room, noted the weary entries in the logbook for the night of January 21, 1972. Diagrams and fragments of writing were mixed, and the book looked like the log from a struck and foundering ship:

8:30   Troubles   Troubles
       Beam doesn't go all the way out. Tune splitter has bumps on it—being worked
9:00   Tune splitter tripped out, in resetting it, Main supplies tripped out correlated?
       Software
       Quad readout doesn't change monotonically with know.

Nav-(word broken)   Wiped out.

Hangup—numbers wrong.

transmission system down. . . .

The fragmentary reports continued that night. At ten o'clock, Jovanovich reports, Robert Wilson walked into the control room. The room was dim, the scopes and digital counters flickered. Wilson produced a small book from his pocket, and read aloud from it a ballad in ancient French:

> *"Paien s'adubent des osbercs sarazineis*
> *Tuit li plusur en sunt dublez en treis;*
> *Lacent lor elmes mult bons, sarranguzeis . . ."*

He read on, stanza after stanza, through hundreds of lines, his arm motioning and his voice echoing down the hall. It was the *Song of Roland,* a ballad sung to French soldiers since ancient times to give them courage as they marched to battle; it recalled wild and fierce deeds of comrades to save one another, to avenge, to protect, to rise suddenly above life and blood into honor. It had been sung by Taillefer, a bard and warrior with the Normans in England. From William the Conqueror he obtained the great honor of striking the first blow in the great Battle of Hastings. He began by singing the *Song of Roland* before the army. He died in the first hour of combat.

"We didn't understand the ancient French," says Drasgo Jovanovich, who listened to the ballad, "but we understood very well the occasion." Work in the control room went on through the night and the next day. Then there was a break in the mood of the scratchings in the logbook. Beam appeared in the main ring; it was sustained and the energy of the shooting stem of protons grew from forty billion volts, to fifty, to a hint of one hundred billion volts. The fever of gloom had been broken; over the next four weeks, the magnets were edged slowly up, juice increased, proton energy going up with it.

Wilson left Fermilab during this period to testify before Congress about what was happening with the project. He spoke about his comrades at the machine. "Last night they were making final adjustments. Their blood was up. I could just feel that those 200 Bev. protons were in our grasp at last—and then

another magnet exploded . . . I have complete confidence in my
colleagues; they are a skillful, an utterly determined, if a small
group, and they will make it; if not today, they will make it
tomorrow; if not tomorrow, the next day . . ."

At this point, the *Congressional Record* is interrupted. There
are brackets, and a note. *NOTE: 200 Billion Electron Volts was
reached at 1:08 P.M., central standard time, March 1, 1972.* It
was accomplished three days before Wilson's fifty-ninth birthday; in March of the following year, Fermilab achieved four
hundred billion volts. In May of 1976, Fermilab achieved five
hundred billion volts. During years when the slopover alone in
a defense contract could amount to more than a billion dollars,
the Fermilab was built on a $250 million budget. Actually,
$243 million was spent.

There was one moment before a congressional committee,
when Wilson was being questioned by Senator John Pastore,
which has since become something like the summary punctua-
tion to the career, the art, and the physics of Robert Wilson.
Leon Lederman quoted it in the keynote speech at the Fermilab's dedication, as he stood in a ripping prairie wind on a
platform before the central laboratory building.

Senator Pastore pressed Wilson, asking him for evidence of
the practical applications of particle physics. Wilson answered
that physics is not merely a path to more technology, not a step
toward the gadgets of the future. It is a much more fundamental human act.

What then is the purpose of Fermilab? Pastore asked.

"To get answers to questions that men have been asking for a
very long time," Wilson said. "One of those questions has to do
with simplicity. Is there a simple understanding of nature . . .?"
Can the workings of nature be held within the grasp of the
human mind?

Pastore was unsatisfied with this thought. He pressed Wilson
for a more practical answer.

Senator Pastore: Is there anything connected with the hopes of this
                    accelerator that in any way involves the security
                    of the country?
Dr. Wilson: No sir, I do not believe so.
Senator Pastore: Nothing at all?

Dr. Wilson: Nothing at all.

Senator Pastore: It has *no* value in that respect?

Dr. Wilson: It has only to do with the respect with which we regard one another, the dignity of men, our love of culture. It has to do with those things. It has to do with, are we good painters, good sculptors, great poets? I mean all the things we really venerate and honor in our country and are patriotic about. It has nothing to do directly with defending our country except to make it worth defending.

Two

On Divinity Avenue
Mark Ptashne and the
Revolution in Biology

1

I N recent years biologists have found a number of the fundamental principles that govern life. This extraordinary knowledge produced a double reaction in society. Businessmen went politely potty, buying the stock of biology companies for ten times its worth, venturing capital in companies that have nothing yet to sell. At the same time, protesters raised their voices and were rewarded with laws that are unique in the history of science. In two states and five cities the practice of biology is now restricted by those laws.

One place unique as the center of the new research, the protest, and the biotechnology business as well is the Harvard Biological Laboratories. The temple that houses the whirlwind is on Divinity Avenue. There I went to find the offices of Professor Mark Ptashne. He is chairman of the department of molecular biology. He is also an important figure in the new advances of biology, and has been involved in fighting the protests and joining the business boom, each in a way that was interesting enough to draw national publicity.

The old laboratory building where I first visited him is literally crawling with specimens of the science. Grasshoppers, horses, wasps, and other things in sculptured menagerie extend around the circumference of the building. Inside there have at times been complaints of rivers of ants, Pharaoh ants, leaking into the building and trickling upward to all five floors of the lab. The lack of air conditioning, and thus open windows, invites a number of winged subjects for study. But the biologists seem uninterested. Their concern is with biological matters that are several orders of magnitude smaller. Genes, chiefly. DNA.

The first time I entered the labs I went in through the wrong door. I found myself walking down a basement corridor. The names on the doors fascinated me. DROSOPHILA KITCHEN, said one. (It's a fruit fly.) CONSTANT TEMPERATURE, said another, and UNIQUE INVISIBLES. There was COLD ROOM, and AUSUBARIUM. (Apparently after an assistant professor there, Ausubel.) On another corridor, I saw NO LIGHTS, 8 AM to 8 PM. THE ALGAE INVASION. Under it was a headline taken from a newspaper: AT END OF DAY, SIMPLE RHYTHM CONTINUES.

I climbed the stairs to the fourth floor. In the year I first met Ptashne, he had just turned forty. Still, he dressed like a student. His summer uniform comprised a pair of frayed blue-jean shorts, a dark tee shirt, and sandals. He wore long sideburns and glasses with black aviator frames.

He is one of the prominent researchers in applying the techniques of gene splicing, and has made significant original contributions to the understanding of how genes are self-controlled. I had learned from another biologist that Ptashne has been a political activist, that he is a good amateur violinist, that he owns a Stradivarius. Ptashne had also been described to me as a character with "a Picasso view of life—two eyes on one side of the head . . . adventurous . . . always getting himself into ludicrous situations."

It appears to me now that some of his unusual personal habits and ways of thought have been essential to his work in science. One example is Ptashne's habit of contrariness. His home is quite tidy, with fine Japanese art on the walls and handsome oriental rugs. But to break the sense of elegance he has planted unexpected surprises. One guest pleaded with him to buy a sugar bowl because he got tired of spooning sugar from a bag to sweeten his coffee. Yo-Yo Ma, the noted cellist, is a close friend, and says he delights to see the studied contradiction in Ptashne's life. "He wears khaki army shirts and then puts on Calvin Klein jeans." He recalls being in Paris with Ptashne once and spending the evening in a fine French restaurant. Afterward Ptashne insisted on going to McDonald's for chocolate shakes. The professional musicians left their instruments behind, but Ptashne carried his violin into McDonald's.

At the same time that he can wear cutoff jeans and a tee shirt, he is very careful about his hair. He owns a single suit, one that his friends say he has worn perhaps twice in fifteen years.

"He wants to be anti-the-norm at all costs," Yo-Yo said. "He loves these little contradictory things."

Though for many scientists the habit is not carried out so elaborately in their personal lives, it seems that contrariness is crucial to critical, creative thinking. What is accepted as true might be wrong; what is impossible might be tried. It is almost a rule of science; it is the norm of Ptashne's personality. It is what led him to his chief work in science and continued through the sixteen years he spent on it.

He and Walter Gilbert, whose labs are one floor below, did a classical series of experiments which solved one of the more important biological questions of the era, perhaps the single most important question after the discovery of the role of DNA in life. The question, roughly, was this: Every cell in the body contains the same million genes. So why does the heart cell make proteins for muscle contraction, but fail to make insulin, adrenaline, brain peptides, and other things made specially elsewhere? The heart cell has the genes to do all these things; so what turns off the inappropriate genes?

When I met Ptashne to ask if I might use his life as a starting point to write about biology, I found he was in midleap. He had just admitted to himself that fifteen years of work on a single trait of a single minute virus was finally near an end. (Later he would find a new level of understanding to study and retract this hasty conclusion.) He was just taking up the chairmanship at Harvard, just helping to begin a new gene-engineering company called Genetics Institute, and leading a team which was seeking to produce the sought-after antiviral substance called interferon.

Ptashne was not only on the cusp between parts of his own career, but also stood where all of biology does now—between the time when a number of stunning penetrations in the study of life had been made, and the time when that knowledge might find its useful and proper place in the society at large.

The change in biology over the previous two decades had

been startling. When Mark Ptashne was in high school and already beginning serious work in biology, he was advised to avoid the field of genetics. It was a stagnant discipline, he was told, which had advanced only a little since the middle of the nineteenth century, when Gregor Mendel had crossed tall and short pea plants. In the *Encyclopædia Britannica* current in the 1940s, only three paragraphs were devoted to the subject.

Little enough was understood about the nature of life that a form of vitalism was still a common way of thinking, even among biologists. Vitalism held that the perfection of beings and their generation endlessly through time must occur because of some unknown principle. This principle was given a variety of names through time: first the soul, then intelligence, and for a time "plastic nature." Eventually it was called the "vital force" and it attempted to pinpoint that peculiar quality that makes the difference between living and nonliving matter. These beliefs were possible even after World War Two because the chief mechanisms of life and heredity were largely unknown. Up until the 1950s, it appeared that no answers would be gained soon.

But between Ptashne's graduation from high school and his graduation from college an eruption had taken place. It was on the scale of the Newtonian or Einsteinian revolutions in physics. Its beginning could be marked with the 1953 announcement by James Watson and Francis Crick that they had found the structure of DNA, the material of genes. Within a few years, biologists approached for the first time within sight of a complete scientific description of a living creature, the bacterial resident of the human intestines called *Escherichia coli*. James Watson, codiscoverer of the key facts which created the revolution in biology, wrote that we have already learned about a third of all the chemical processes which comprise life for the *E. coli.* "This conclusion is most satisfying, for it strongly suggests that within the next 20 to 25 years, we may approach a state in which it will be possible to describe essentially all the metabolic reactions involved in the life of the *E. coli* cell . . . [The modern biochemist] unlike his nineteenth century equivalent, at last possesses the tools to describe completely the essential features of life."

The late Jacques Monod, one of the honored figures of the

new biology, put it more simply when he replied casually to a question not long ago, "The secret of life? But in principle we already know the secret of life."

The knowledge has come suddenly, and it carries the odor of sacrilege. We have found out how bare, insensate molecules compose life and carry it on moment to moment without the intervention of gods or men. This new knowledge ended the possibility of belief in any form of vitalism, and it is not a coincidence that it also sparked a protest.

For the first time since Darwin, biology got open, active opposition. The new biology appeared to abuse the sacred. Opponents saw the tabernacle opened and its contents spilled and searched by irreligious robbers. These were the biologists who claimed to have captured a secret that was imagined to be God's alone.

The biologists themselves have said only that the mechanisms of life are now open to inspection. If there is something else to life beyond these mechanics, it has always been something permanently beyond the prodding fingers of science. But, yes, genes can now be read, removed, and even exchanged between distant species—frog to monkey, man to microbe. And it has now become clear that this knowledge of life gradually will become the manipulation of the substance of life. Ptashne and others have already begun that work.

My first lengthy talk with Ptashne occurred at his Cambridge home. As I sat at the table, he moved from phone to sink to refrigerator, and back around again. Opening a bottle of wine, taking the fourth call in ten minutes, cleaning a plate, he is quick, impatient, restless.

Like many scientists, Ptashne distrusts journalists. As would become his habit in eight or ten conversations over a year, he began by worrying out loud. He has refused many requests for interviews, he said, and many people have told him he is foolish for allowing himself to be a subject in this book. First, it is thought immodest among scientists to speak publicly of personal matters. Publicity is counted as an evil, sometimes necessary or even useful, but always dishonorable. Ptashne said that "any personalized account must necessarily minimize the role played by others in the science, which spreads ill will." Second, journalists distort the rightful proportions of things. All that journalists want to talk about, he says, are the hot political topics—the furor over recombinant DNA, or biology as big business, without dealing with the science in a serious way.

When the technique of recombinant DNA was being debated, and scientists managed to alarm the press and the public about what dangers might be connected with the work, Ptashne was at first concerned about the hazards. But gradually as the work proceeded, and as the scientists voluntarily restrained themselves from working with disease organisms, Ptashne began to argue that enough precautions had been taken. More would be an irrational barrier to science. But by then reporters had only begun to warm up to the issue. Mayor Alfred Velucci of Cambridge had only begun to speak of the Frankensteins who worked in the Harvard labs.

Velucci held public hearings before a packed council chamber and television cameras to decide whether Harvard was to be allowed not only a building permit to make a new biology lab, but official permission to carry on biology within the city limits. Before the loud, fearsome Velucci and the silently running cameras, came Mark Ptashne as the chief witness for Harvard. He was prodded, poked, and lectured by the mayor and council for three hours.

Later, when genetic-engineering businesses had found their prospective products in such demand that stock in the companies sold for spectacular prices, Ptashne, as mentioned earlier, was involved in the formation of one such company, Genetics Institute. Harvard, which was planning to help finance, and profit from, the venture counted on Ptashne's participation. He did not agree when he was first approached, but finally said yes. Eventually the origins of the arrangement seemed forgotten and it was "Ptashne's company" to some Harvard faculty. An argument began about whether Harvard ought to make such an investment and become a partner with one of its faculty. The press again was there to repeat the points at the loudest possible volume. Ptashne felt himself portrayed as a broker about to sell Harvard's academic purity. Finally, after what Derek Bok, president of Harvard, found to be intolerable public debates, Genetics Institute was disinvited from linking itself with Harvard.

Picking up a pipe from the scarred, round wooden table in

the center of the kitchen, Ptashne says, "The reason I worry is I'm afraid you'll emphasize all the wrong things. You'll emphasize the recombinant DNA debate, or the Harvard business thing, when really these are just side issues, not even that, a millionth of a percent of what I'm doing or what I care about." Actually he cares a good deal more than that, but the reverse emphasis irritates him greatly.

What Mark Ptashne cares about is a small organism that exists on the border between life and the lifeless. It is called lambda, it is a virus, and like all others of its kind, it can do nothing on its own. It is no more than a string of genes, a length of DNA, wrapped in a layer of protective molecules. It has no cell walls, no activity within, no organized cellular machinery. It cannot even reproduce itself without using the reproductive machinery of others, of real cells.

Lambda and other viruses are organisms so simple they appear to be nothing more than a string of molecules bent on making endless copies of themselves. Viruses are like parts from the machinery of life, moving about within living creatures like bodiless spirits. They come so near to the least behavior possible from an organism that its chemistry almost seems intended merely to demonstrate the principle: chemistry can look and act alive.

But because it is the simplest chemical mechanism made of DNA does not mean that it is actually simple or that its behavior lacks drama. Even at this crude level, life is surprising.

By the early part of this century, it had already been established that bacteria were agents of disease. One after another bacterium was discovered to be the cause of disease; these small creatures—some as tiny as one twenty-five thousandth of an inch—were identified and studied. But in the last decade of the nineteenth century, the Russian bacteriologist Dmitri Ivanovski found a disease of the tobacco plant, called tobacco mosaic disease, which was caused by something far smaller than any known disease bacterium.

The juice of a diseased plant would infect a healthy one; Ivanovski filtered the juice through extremely fine filters and still the juice produced disease. A Dutch researcher independently discovered the same phenomenon a few years later and called the agent of disease a "filterable virus." In Latin, the word *virus* means simply "a poisonous slime," and this one could pass through the finest filters. Eventually, it was found that these poisons which passed through filters cause a large number of diseases on their own. In man they are responsible for polio, malaria, measles, yellow fever, typhus, and the common cold.

Viruses are far smaller than bacteria and cannot be seen through any light microscope, though all the bacterial organisms can. They were studied with some intensity for at least fifty years before researchers really had any sense of what they were like. One of the first to see viruses, using an electron microscope capable of magnification hundreds of times as great as light microscopes, was Thomas Anderson. In 1942 he sent some of the first pictures of the things to another dedicated researcher in viruses, J. J. Bronfenbrenner. Anderson reports that when the old professor, who had worked for decades on viruses without the slightest sense of what they actually looked like, first saw the pictures he was astonished. He clapped the palm of his hand to his forehead and said, "*Mein Gott!* They've got tails!"

The most interesting kinds of viruses are those that were found to enter and destroy bacteria. When they were first discovered they were called bacteria eaters or bacteriophages, since in Greek *phagos* is "to eat." For a brief time scientists became very excited at the implications of this, as they have gotten excited in advance over the medical value of interferon. It was believed at first that the "phages," as they are now called, might be used simply to destroy the bacteria of disease and thus be something of a miracle cure for most any disease caused by bacteria. Unfortunately, the bacteria were able over a short time to transmute themselves and to become resistant to the phage viruses.

This single piece of behavior which phages are capable of may not be useful medically, but it is rather macabre. Ptashne's lambda phage, to take an example, attaches itself by its tail to the outer surface of a bacterium. The phage has a squarish head, and when attached by its stiff tail to the bacterial skin, it appears like a lamppost on a tiny planet. DNA is packed in the square head of the phage virus. The tail is a hollow tube, and through it the DNA is quickly shot into the bacterium.

The empty viral shell hangs like an empty cicada husk on tree bark, while its DNA enters and commandeers the machinery of the bacterial cell. The new DNA orders copies made of itself, complete with its lost hull and tail. The copying goes on within the helpless bacterium until finally a hundred to a thousand of the viruses are produced. The bacterium finally is burst by the phage, and a new crop of potent viruses begin to float out toward other bacterial skins, where they may attach themselves and begin again.

But life, being perversely complex, has given some viruses an additional property. Lambda is the chief example of the phage with this unusual property: it can attach to the bacterium and enter it as usual, but instead of taking over and immediately duplicating itself, the lambda DNA can instead become a "sleeper" set of genes. It becomes part of the bacterium's normal DNA. Its potentially lethal genes are dutifully reproduced and passed on to all the progeny of the bacterium. Then, a hundred or a thousand generations later, the lambda gene may burst out again, coming to life to make a hundred copies of itself, bursting the body of its host to get free.

It is this stunning ability to turn off its normal life cycle, remain inactive, then later spring to life that Mark Ptashne has studied since about 1965. And, in a sense, he solved it. He and several colleagues have, through hundreds of experiments, now been able to produce detailed drawings and descriptions of exactly what occurs with the sleeper lambda and why. This is interesting in itself, but the principles worked out along the way are far broader and more important than the tiny lambda and its unusual bit of behavior.

Soon after the discovery of the "secret of life"—the elegance and importance of DNA in the life of all living things—it seemed that all of biology turned to the next question. If each cell in our body contains all the DNA, and thus all the genes, then the genes for muscle proteins exist in nerve cells, and the special chemical character of blood cells exists as well in toenails.

Within a year or two of the famous DNA paper of James Watson and Francis Crick, a pair of French biologists (the great Jacques Monod and François Jacob) began to set out a theory to explain this odd state of affairs. Most of the DNA messages must be turned off most of the time. Only those signals useful to each specialized cell are allowed to be turned on in that cell. So, Monod and Jacob said, there must be some substance within the cell that shuts off, or represses, many genes.

This repressor substance could be many different kinds of chemical beast, from RNA or DNA itself to some protein. It might act directly or indirectly. It might act on the DNA itself or at any number of other sites in the cell machinery between the gene and the products made from its instructions. But whatever it was and however it worked, the repressor was a completely new and extremely important actor in the functioning of living things. It was suddenly a new principle of life. When Jacob and Monod published their repressor theory, it was at once a challenge to molecular biologists to find out if the repressor was real, to attempt to isolate it, and to find out how it worked.

Among those drawn into the chase for the repressor, along with Nobel Prize winners and many eminent men of biological science, was Mark Ptashne. Many prominent men had already made attempts to discover the repressor—it was said that Jacob and Monod would not only create the theory of the repressor, but find it themselves. There were others. The influential Sydney Brenner of the British Medical Research Council worked on the problem. Numerous failures were either recorded or rumored; the problem had become one of notorious difficulty.

2

IN the first laboratory where Mark Ptashne worked, in the first summer weeks he worked there, he was both so intent and so clumsy that people began to move glassware when he came near.

There was in the laboratory a recorder used to measure brain waves; its thin wire pens were balanced finely so that they might glide very rapidly across the paper. Once, when the teenaged Ptashne, the youngest of the students in the lab, was forcibly defending an assertion, he began to gesticulate excitedly. He backed up, lost his balance, and sat down heavily upon sixteen delicately fibrillating pens.

The laboratory was that of Dr. Frank Morrell at the University of Minnesota. The work there was on epilepsy—the electrical storms which seize control of the brain for a few moments. Dr. Morrell was a friend of the Ptashne family, and when Mark asked to see what was going on in Morrell's lab, Morrell accepted. Ptashne knew nothing of laboratories, nothing about medical research, though he said he wanted to be a doctor. Or, perhaps less seriously, a violinist.

Ptashne looked like an awkward child: his ears were a little too big, he was quite short, and he wore the black frame glasses and carried the briefcase that denoted an intellectual boy.

He did have perfect grades throughout high school. He did

win the state debating championship. He studied the violin. He raised bees and played in the school theater. Beyond the requirements of being an intellectual, little Mark Ptashne also played baseball well, and became captain of the golf team in high school. All these things he did in three years of high school, because instead of taking a fourth year, he went off to Reed College in Oregon.

Ptashne's father was a businessman who started a number of businesses and tried to make them go until finding something that suited him. But probably more importantly, his parents were Socialists who helped found the Progressive party in Chicago in 1948. They went to endless political meetings. They raised funds for the Lincoln Brigade to fight in Spain, and for civil rights. Paul Robeson came to their house on one evening to raise funds. By age nine, Mark insisted that he should attend meetings alongside his parents. So for the Robeson visit he sat beneath the piano in his pajamas. Robeson noticed and sang "Water Boy" to him.

But whatever else may or may not have distinguished Ptashne as a child, his chief feature was his unrelenting energy. He slept a little and ran much.

Dr. Morrell took Ptashne into his lab for a summer's work in 1956, and was surprised at both his attitude and his energy. "He was brash, rambunctious, argumentative, critical, unrelenting in his disparagement of sloppy thinking—qualities which rubbed people the wrong way. But I found him exciting, didn't mind his brashness." Though Ptashne enjoyed the game of dipping the ideas of others in a bath of acid, he made many mistakes of his own. He thought fast; self-analysis and self-criticism dragged behind at some distance. "But once his thinking has been analyzed and criticized I never found him to be pigheaded," Morrell said.

"On the other hand," Morrell continued, smiling, "he would neglect certain elementary realities. Such as the fact that wet paper tends to rip."

Morrell's experiments were done on rabbits, which daily had to be sacrificed and their skulls opened. Ptashne once carried a wet paper bag filled with rabbit parts on the hospital elevator. The elevator filled with patients, relatives, and hospital staff, who were stunned when suddenly a bagful of bloody parts were unloaded all over their shoes.

In the laboratory, rabbit surgery rotated among the students and doctors, but work that could be done by one meticulous medical student, or two inexperienced ones, took a laboratory full of people to stand ready to close off inadvertently cut blood vessels when Ptashne took his turn with the scalpel.

"He was very clumsy," said Morrell. "But the great thing was when the data began to come out of the experiment." Among the squiggles and scratches on the long, long sheets of brain-wave results, Ptashne could quickly see relations between a shadow of a bump from one part of the brain and the same from another area of the brain. Said Morrell, "Without question, Mark, who had no background at all in this area, always asked the most perceptive questions and made the most challenging remarks."

The first scientific papers with Mark Ptashne's name on them came out of Morrell's laboratory. And, sometime during that first summer in a laboratory, Ptashne gave up the idea of becoming a doctor. He was surprised at the arrogance of staff doctors, disgusted by the gore in the work. His plan had been to go to medical school, "until finally I had to face the fact that I just couldn't make it through. I just couldn't put up with it. I can't memorize."

When he left for college, at Reed in Oregon, he declared his major to be philosophy, but soon he began instead to think of biological research; it had the intellectual challenge of medicine without the annoying physical impediments.

Reed College was an unusual place to get a college education because the students were, on the whole, more distinguished than the teachers. It was a place that supposedly did not grade students (it did, but the students were not told of it), and its life for male and female students was among the most open and liberal of the time. It was so much what intellectual children from public schools desired that the place must have seemed a dream. "Because the academic standards were taken so seriously, about half of every class dropped out before graduating," Ptashne says. "When I came to Harvard, I was amazed at how much less intense was the intellectual atmosphere here . . . and how much easier it was to get a B.A. at Harvard than at Reed."

Ptashne flourished. By the time he graduated, he had already published a scientific paper of his own, with no senior co-authors, on the subject of fruit-fly genetics.

Then and now, the predominant mode of communication used by Ptashne is argument. In 1960 when Ted Kennedy, younger brother of the presidential candidate, came to speak to Reed students, Ptashne ended his visit with a series of sharp questions about the third Kennedy: Was Bobby not a red-baiter when he worked for Roy Cohn? Did Ted condone that? After a brief argument, Kennedy left quickly.

In the regular assemblies of the Reed student body he became something of a hero for this sort of thing. Perhaps the most famous case among students was the debate over the college's policy on what was called "intervisitation" between male and female students. The debate was sparked when a male student was caught in a female dorm, very early in the morning, shaving. Which in itself would have produced little reaction, except that the captor was the mother of one of the girls. This brought down threats of the end of "open door" from the college president, and counterthreats of a strike from Ptashne.

Roughly speaking, the policy was that intervisitation was allowed, provided nothing went on which could not go on with the door open. This did not mean that the door had actually to be open, but merely theoretically open. A Talmudic debate ensued before the assembled body of some 250 students, in which two philosophy professors tried to unfold the logic of the principle and elucidate just what it was that might be done in front of an open door. They arrived finally at an explanatory principle: What one could do before an open door is no more than one would do in public in a bus station.

Ptashne rose. "Does this mean we can't masturbate in our rooms anymore?" The debate ended in pandemonium.

It was during the summers away from Reed that Ptashne acquired the obsession which he has not yet left behind. Through a Pakistani teacher at Reed, Ptashne went during his sophomore summer to the Rocky Mountain Biological Labs to work under a biologist there named Edward Novitski, then during his junior summer to work at the University of Oregon with Franklin Stahl and Aaron Novick, two biologists in the circle of experimenters—along with James Watson, Francis Crick, François Jacob, Jacques Monod, Sydney Brenner, Max Delbrück, and others—whose work began the biological revolution. In these laboratories he first read of what seemed to be the most romantic and exciting problem of modern biology—the search for the molecule that controls DNA. It existed in theory, chiefly in the work of the Frenchmen Jacob and Monod. But none of the great laboratories had yet been able to find it.

Ptashne did not think of himself then, or now, as a natural scientist, or even as one who logically should have spent his years in science. Rather, it was these summers—he also spent one at a music camp—and this problem that sent Ptashne into molecular biology. Quite deliberately, before finishing at Reed, he went to visit the professor whose work brought him closest to the work he desired to do. Matthew Meselson, a biochemist at Harvard, as Ptashne remembers it, treated him coolly. But Ptashne did make his way to Harvard, and into Meselson's laboratory, where he began to tell people who asked him that he intended to find the repressor.

His boldness was his mark. After earning his Ph.D. under Meselson, Ptashne was elected to the most distinguished club at Harvard, the Society of Fellows. Very few graduates are selected from each season of students, and the chief formality for those who have joined is that they must attend the dinners at which fellows from the arts and the sciences exchange views. The dinners are typically old-worldish, quietly formal affairs. One of the fellows recalls his first sight of Ptashne after Ptashne's election as a junior fellow. Ptashne throttled up to the front of the somber Elliot Hall and stepped from his motorcycle. With his helmet under his arm, he strode into the dining hall. His short stature and assertive manner created an instant impression of how Napoleon must have appeared, as Ptashne entered the assembly to dine with a few of the more eminent American scholars. Not long thereafter, Ptashne, arguing the Vietnam War, irritably instructed W. B. Quine, the aged and famous American logician, that his thinking was abominably illogical.

3

EVOLUTIONARY biologists point out that we are the instruments of our genes, the tools they have shaped to assure their survival. We are used and discarded in each generation. "We, and all other animals, are machines created by our genes," writes Oxford zoologist Richard Dawkins. "We are survival machines . . . An octopus is nothing like a mouse and both are quite different from an oak tree. Yet in their fundamental chemistry they are rather uniform, and, in particular, the replicators which they bear, the genes, are basically the same kind of molecule in all of us—from bacteria to elephants. We are all survival machines for the same kind of replicator—molecules called DNA—but there are many different ways of making a living in the world, and the replicators have built a vast range of machines to exploit them. A monkey is a machine which preserves genes up trees; a fish is a machine which preserves genes in the water; there is even a small worm which preserves genes in German beer vats."

The objects of study in physics, atoms and particles, are permanent structures. But the objects of study in biology change and perish even as they are being watched. Hundreds of generations of bacteria—in human scale, what would be all of historical time—pass in a few days. For example, one of Ptashne's experiments involved irradiating bacteria at a certain stage in their growth, at one moment in life of a bacterial civilization. He started growing them before going home in the evening, and just before lunch the next day, the bacterial population had grown and reached its zenith, ready to be bombarded with radiation. Nothing else on earth survives very long either. Eventually all living boundaries are burst, all bodies taken to bits and hauled off piecemeal to be of use elsewhere, in service of that which is most permanent in biology—the genes.

Because the shapes of things grow and decay so quickly, like a wave forming, breaking, and receding back to water, it has even been a little difficult at times to distinguish in the abstract between living and nonliving things. Crystals grow, replace lost limbs, reproduce themselves, but are not alive. And Shakespeare's brief candle: *Encyclopaedia Britannica* defined a living thing as a discrete mass of matter, with a definite boundary, undergoing continual interchange with its surroundings without itself changing over the short run. The steady flame has a definite boundary. It draws into itself one kind of substance and releases another without appearing to change itself. And it seemingly can both grow and be divided.

The whirlpool is another case. Thomas Henry Huxley, grandfather of author Aldous and biologist Julian, said that "the parallel between a whirlpool in a stream and a living being, which has often been drawn, is as just as it is striking. The whirlpool is permanent, but the particles of water which constitute it are incessantly changing. Those which enter it, on one side are whirled around and temporarily constitute a part of its individuality; as they leave it on the other side, their places are made good by newcomers . . ." The living body is itself a vortex of chemical and molecular change.

Ptashne's lambda virus is far more complex than these things and does actually contain the information needed to multiply itself. Yet it is not alive. Unlike the fire, it has no metabolism. It demonstrates that the distinction between the living and the nonliving is merely verbal.

But though living things are ceaselessly changing, and soon perishing, their genes persist through time. They maintain their own form by copying it, not roughly, but in precise detail, tens, hundreds, and thousands of times over generations.

To lay out the matter simply, the genes are the particles of life. There are on average a few thousand molecules to make up one gene. These genes are then linked together, with some intervening strands, to make up the long strand of DNA. DNA itself is actually two long chains stuck together. The two strands, linked by small molecule pairs at closely spaced steps all along the chain length, are twisted around each other into a tight helix. The result is a strong but flexible structure very like a rope ladder, with the molecule pairs as the rungs and two sugar-phosphate chains as the outside supports.

What is structurally fascinating about this molecule of DNA, apart from its curious and pleasing shape, is its dimensions. It is about ten atoms wide and billions of atoms long. If the coiled and folded DNA within one of our cells was unknotted and stretched to its full length, it would not only be longer than the cell which contained it, but would reach completely out of atomic scale. It would be a filament six feet long and far too thin to see.

The proper question about genes was put clearly four hundred years ago. Montaigne, ignoring the mystical prejudice of his time, wondered how inheritance was possible, mechanically. "What a wonderful thing it is that the drop of seed from which we are produced bears in itself the impressions, not only of the bodily shape, but of the thoughts and inclinations of our fathers! Where can that drop of fluid harbor such an infinite number of forms? And how does it convey those resemblances . . . ?" The answer is simple enough that Montaigne might have guessed it, and simple enough that for twenty years in this century biologists had the answer and did not believe it. In building a human, each detail of structure is assigned a bit of code. The code is in solid form, in a sequence of linked molecules. The Irish freckle, the Roman nose, the Hapsburg lip, are preserved in molecules as if in a jar of formaldehyde.

Embedded in the ropelike form of DNA, in the center between the twisting strands, are small, flat molecules. They are the carriers of the coded information and describe the mechanics of all life. In our alphabet, twenty-six symbols can make a virtually endless number of meaningful words; in DNA, four symbols suffice to make an alphabet. The letters are A,T,C, and G. They are the first letters of the four sorts of molecules stacked within the length of the DNA helix.

The four letters combine into words. As it happens, nature

uses only words of three letters: TGT, TGA, CAC, TAC, and so on. These are combined into sentences containing from six to several hundred words. Each sentence is a command, to be carried out by chemical machinery of the cell: Make insulin. Break down milk sugar. Make this or that enzyme. Each sentence, for the most part, is a command to make a specific enzyme.

Biologists were both stunned and amused when they first learned that DNA actually operated by a code, a code exactly like the Morse code in principle. Playfully mimicking this new-found code, Max Delbrück, the great physicist-turned-biologist, sent a telegram to his friend George Beadle when it was announced Beadle had won the Nobel Prize for work in genetics related to DNA. The text of the telegram read: ADB ACB BDB ADA CDC BBA BCB CDA CDB BCA BBA ADC ACA BDA BDB BBA ACA ACB BBA BDC CDB CCB BDB BBA ADE ADA ADC CDC BBA DDC ACA ADB BDB DDA BBA CCA ACB CDB ADC BDB BBA.

Beadle could not solve it immediately, but when someone suggested that the BBA was a repeating sequence that must have special significance, he soon read the message: BREAK THIS CODE OR GIVE BACK NOBEL PRIZE. Beadle sent a reply in a code of his own. Delbrück finished the exchange when he sent a DNA model to be presented to Beadle at the lecture following the Nobel awards ceremony. The model had each of the stacked center molecules, or bases, stained in one of four colors. When decoded, the model read: I AM THE RIDDLE OF LIFE. KNOW ME AND YOU WILL KNOW YOURSELF.

Only four years before this exchange, until as late as 1953, it was believed that this molecule was a "stupid substance," a "stupid molecule," whose extremely monotonous structure could not be useful for much of anything. Over the molecule's enormous length, it was believed, four subunits repeated themselves millions of times without variation: adenine, thymine, cytosine, guanine; adenine, thymine, cytosine, guanine.

Nobody, Delbrück reportedly said, ". . . absolutely nobody . . . had thought that the specificity might be carried in this exceedingly simple way, by a sequence, by a code. This denouement that came then—that the whole business was like a child's toy that you could buy at the dime store—all built in this

wonderful way that you could explain in *Life* magazine . . .
That there was so simple a trick behind it. That was the greatest surprise for everyone."

It has turned out that the four molecules stacked in the helical center of the DNA are not in a repeating sequence. Rather, the order varies, and each gene is denoted by a unique sequence varying in length from about fifteen to several thousand molecules long. The sequence CTATTAC is the signal for the beginning of one message that instructs the cell to make an important protein molecule, hemoglobin. The molecule which colors our blood red and which captures and transports oxygen throughout our bodies, hemoglobin is encoded by about 440 "letters" in the DNA chain. A change of a single letter, from a thymine to a guanine in the seventeenth position among 440, changes normal red blood cells into the sickle-shaped cells that afflict blacks with sickle-cell anemia.

The genes are the particles of life. They are passed through the sex cells to progeny. They direct the construction of living bodies, determining which will be milkweed and which human.

But even more than conveying traits from generation to generation, genes run the machinery of living cells. There is no action or thought without the genes first having created a little chemical cascade in the cell. In bone marrow cells, a gene's code orders the production of hemoglobin. In the immune system, where defense of the body against foreign substances begins, genes direct the manufacture of antibodies, the proteins which attach themselves to foreign molecules thereby disabling them. In muscle cells, the key element that genes direct to be made is myosin, a protein that has the ability to change its length and thus make muscles contract. In the brain, genes direct the making of chemicals that transmit electrical impulses across the gap between nerve cells. From this chemistry arises thought as well as action.

DNA molecules have been recognized as components of the nucleus of living cells since 1869, but they sat in laboratory jars—a white, gummy substance in the dry form—for some eighty years before biologists began to realize what DNA was. Now it is the center of attention in thousands of the best biological laboratories in the world.

The gene's housing is the cell. Looking from the cell wall

inward toward the tangle of genetic filaments, we see that the cell's skeleton is on the outside. The stiff outer wall gives the cell integrity. Just inside the wall is a filter, the membrane. This prevents the organic chemicals that the cell produces from seeping out. But it is permeable to some molecules. In fact, the membrane actually contains a number of "metabolic pumps" which draw through the membrane certain useful molecules to create greater concentrations of them where they are needed inside the cell.

Besides the DNA contained within the cell, there are a large number of other molecules, perhaps two thousand large ones and as many different kinds of small ones. It may seem odd, but there are extremely few medium-sized molecules within the cell. This lack of middle-sized molecules occurs chiefly because the cell likes to work in small units; it takes less energy. So the cell creates a good variety of small molecules, and then, to make the larger ones, simply links a number of the smaller units together in long, simple chains.

In carrying on its daily traffic, the chief chemical problem to be overcome in the cell is that the thousands of chemical reactions necessary to life do not occur very readily. In ordinary solution at room temperatures they would occur very slowly, if at all. To overcome this reluctant pace, the cell employs catalysts. (While inside the cell, these chemical agents are called enzymes.) For every chemical reaction, there is a specific catalyst, a particular enzyme, to force the reaction through its cycle quickly. These catalytic enzymes are proteins. Protein molecules are built by chaining smaller units, though they are themselves far smaller than the great DNA chains. Protein is the dominant material used in construction of the cell, as well as the agent used to catalyze all chemical action.

With its recumbent DNA and swarm of active proteins, the cell is a tiny chemical factory. When raw materials flow into it, protein molecules may catalyze their transformation into other small organic molecules. Proteins then join these together, forming the large molecules that make up the important parts of the cell. This constant production can go on until the cell is nearly bursting with useful manufactured products. It then must divide, creating progeny nearly identical to itself. Such division and procreation is the way single-celled organisms reproduce, and, with little modification, is also the way a human is built from a single egg cell.

In that event, the DNA of a single cell must be able accurately to build a creature sixty trillion times in its own size and millions of times more complex. If such a construction job were given to humans, say to build a city a few thousand times the size of New York, humans could not do the job without networks of planning boards, phalanxes of computers, platoons of engineers, and armies of tradesmen. Probably we could not do it. Cold chemicals, on the other hand, accomplish the thing casually and without the benefit of intelligence.

Any understanding of such things in biology is very recent. Unlike physics, which flourished and used rather modern terms quite early, biology could not be carried on openly virtually from the time of Plato to this past century. Physical forces could be observed more dispassionately; life, on the other hand, was both an immediately personal matter and sacred ground within the province of the Church.

Doctors were forbidden, on pain of losing their immortal souls, from opening a dead body to determine its structure and contents, no matter how useful such information might prove to be. And on the matter nearest the heart of life—the begetting of new men, animals, and plants—the subject was not a matter of physical events. It was no simple physical junction at which two meet and three depart. It was a piece of unfathomable spiritual mystery. Things did not get born without the breath of God to liven them, and men were not men until the spark of the soul was infused by God.

Creatures did not necessarily breed offspring like themselves, and in fact life could sometimes spring up from nonliving things. "Every humid body which dries up breeds life," Aristotle said. Said Helmont: "The emanations arising from the bottom of marshes bring forth frogs, snails, leeches, herbs, and a good many other things." He believed that a dirty shirt and some grains of corn, if placed in a pot for twenty-one days, would produce mice.

If living things might be engendered this way, they also might be jumbled: "Nature always tries to create its own likeness," wrote Ambroise Paré in 1573, in a book called *Monsters and Prodigies*. In an odd example of nature straining to have like produce like, he said, "A lamb with a pig's head was once seen because the ewe have been covered by a boar." The creatures which appear in the literature of many centuries including such delightful monsters as a child with a frog's face, a lion covered with fish scales, a fish with a bishop's head.

The most fearful aspect of these things is not that such monsters were believed to exist, and rather commonly, but that any animal or person might give birth to such a thing. Gestation and birth were not so much physical events as mystical ones; a pregnant woman's sinful thoughts might transform her baby into a monstrous shape, physical evidence of her unclean soul.

It was not until 1860 that someone thought to actually keep track of how like seemed to beget like, and to keep careful track of specific traits through generation after generation. The monk Gregor Mendel, an Augustinian friar not much suited for the life of prayer in his Austrian monastery, began the modern work in his garden, with the cultivation of peas. Friar Mendel found that each of seven physical features of the peas was inherited accurately every generation. As one writer put it, Mendel showed that traits (or their genes) were inherited as though they were real things; that is to say, they couldn't be diluted, subdivided, or mixed during inheritance. Genes, then, seemed to be little inheritable packets of information, each governing a particular trait of an organism.

It was in the 1920s that the actual physical location of the genes within animal and plant cells was found, by zoologist Thomas Hunt Morgan, a Southerner who found his way to Columbia University in New York. A rare, white-eyed fruit fly once alighted on a bench in Morgan's lab, the fly was noticed by Morgan's wife, and after a hectic hunt by Morgan, his wife, and a posse of students, the fly was finally captured. It was soon forced to mate in captivity with a male of the usual red-eyed variety. But the result, over generations, was odd. It apparently did not follow Mendel's rules. And through the hunt to discover why not, Morgan found that the location of the genes must be in the center sphere, the nucleus, of the cell. He also saw there tiny, threadlike structures. The threads seemed doubled themselves and split into an identical pair every time reproduction occurred.

In these threads which mysteriously made copies of themselves must be carried the genes and the information to direct the body's cells. The threads, which had been seen by other biologists, were named chromosomes by Morgan, from the Greek for colored or stained bodies, which they were under the microscope. Morgan eventually showed that the chromosomes had multicolored bands, or beads, which were the sites of the genes themselves. An abnormality in a bit of chromosome was the reason for his little fruit fly's peculiar progeny.

One odd note in the events leading up to the discovery of genes, how they are made and how they work, is that the magical substance itself—nucleic acid—was discovered at about the same time Abbot Gregor Mendel was finishing his garden experiments. The substance was discovered by a Swiss chemistry student, Friedrich Miescher, more or less by accident. He was assigned by his teacher to analyze the contents of some cells, and he tried stomach acid to break down the cell walls so he might then gather up the chemicals in the interior of the cells and analyze them.

To his surprise, Miescher found that the cell nuclei survived the treatment. Curious, he made a chemical analysis of the nuclei and found the material totally different from the proteins and other substances that fill the remainder of the cell. The chemical substance within the nucleus Miescher called nuclein, or later, nucleic acid.

From the time the nuclear chemicals were discovered, until 1944, their importance was not recognized. The reason was that throughout this time it was becoming more and more apparent that proteins, those extraordinary molecules composed of very long chains of little chemical clumps (called amino acids), were the fundamental materials used by the body to carry out virtually all its activities. It was long assumed that proteins were not only the building materials and messengers among the cells, but would also turn out to contain the instructions—the genes—to govern the whole elaborate production.

In fact, when American physician and biologist Oswald Theodore Avery finally proved the contrary, that proteins were not the genetic material, his extraordinary and carefully composed work was simply set aside by others for lack of understanding. The Nobel Prize, given only to the living, thus was

handed to geneticists before and after Avery, but not t
man who finally showed what genes were made of. One of the
chairmen of the Nobel Committee now concedes that this failure was probably the greatest blunder in the history of the
Nobel science prizes.

Avery was a small, meticulous man who worked at the Rockefeller Institute in New York. The event which set him off on a
quarter of a century of labor was the discovery of an odd fact.
In the 1920s it was found that there were two bacteria which
were nearly identical except that one caused pneumonia and
the other did not; it also was found that the innocent version of
the bacteria could be transformed, as Jekyll into Hyde, by the
addition into its culture dish of a small amount of the virulent
bacteria.

The single fact about this whole business which spoke most
loudly to Oswald Avery was the fact that the transformation
could be effected by dropping in among the innocent live bacteria bits of the virulent bacteria that were dead—physically and
sexually inert. It seemed plain that some chemical substance
from the dead bacteria was being taken up into the live creatures and that this substance could then permanently take over
the life of the mild organism, transmuting it and all its progeny
into a malevolent one. This onetime transmission of lasting information had to be an exchange of genes. So Avery labored for
years to answer the single question, as he put it, "What is the
substance responsible?" The substance would have to be the
substance of the genes.

In 1944, DNA, the chief molecule of "nuclein," was still a
rather obscure chemical. It was known to be present in the cell
nucleus, but its size, shape, and function were all unknown. By
then Avery had gone through one kind of chemical after another derived from the dead bacteria, and now DNA had to be
tested as well. So Avery added to a mass of dead cells a chemical
that breaks up DNA into nonfunctioning molecular bits. He
reasoned that if DNA was the sought-after substance, destroying
it would also destroy its power to transmit virulence.

Crumbling the long DNA molecules into pieces did, in fact,
stop the virulence from being transmitted. DNA was thus
shown to be the actual material basis of heredity. Avery's work
showed that, as one writer put it, inheriting something meant

getting a piece of DNA. Genes are DNA. Information is DNA and DNA is information.

What came about ten years after Avery's crucial work is better known. Gradually, Avery's work was confirmed by others and the question gradually became one of how DNA worked. How might the physical shape of the chemical both hold and transmit information so effectively?

The discovery of the shape was made by James Watson and Francis Crick at Cambridge University in England. The shape turned out not only to be functionally important, but to strike the imagination as a formulation both charming and powerful. The basis of life turned out to be a magical shape—as alchemy was always supposed to turn out.

Within about five years of the discovery of the double helix and the code by which it functioned, during the time that Mark Ptashne was in high school and his first years of college, the great men of biology were pulled into the work at hand. First the helical code had to be examined and proved to be what it seemed. The next question was how the commands in this code were carried out, physically and chemically. Most genes in the cell are turned off most of the time. They are switched on only when there is a demand for their chemical products. This became the great question of molecular biology: How are the genes controlled?

During the middle 1950s, Monod and Jacob informally gave the idea of DNA control a name and a theory. Some "repressor" material blocked action of the DNA at places, preventing untimely access by the materials within the cell, they said. Among those drawn into the question, along with Nobel winners and other eminent men of biological science, was a young researcher, Mark Ptashne, beginning his first postgraduate work at the Harvard Biological Laboratories under James Watson.

4

WHEN Mark Ptashne stood taking his doctoral exam before Nobelist Salvador Luria and other professors of biology, Luria asked him, now that he had finished his experimental work for the doctorate, what would he do next? He was not interested in what he had been doing, Ptashne said. It had only been something to do until he could solve the repressor.

His answer "created much mirth and merriment," and with some justification, Ptashne says now. It was 1965 and the problem of the repressor had stood for twelve years, a principal question since the structure of DNA had been worked out in 1953. Leading biologists of the world had worked more or less seriously on the problem more or less constantly for the entire period. They had failed.

Biologist Nancy Hopkins was in 1965 an undergraduate student taking courses from Matthew Meselson, James Watson, and teaching assistant Mark Ptashne. "I remember that even within the first two lectures it was clear to me, with no experience, that the repressor was THE problem. I asked Mark, if he was such a smart guy, why wasn't he working on the repressor? He laughed and said it was hard." She also asked the eminent Dr. Watson. He said that there was no chemical test, no assay, for it and so he couldn't do it. From another lab, she heard that Nobelist Arthur Kornberg—who had proved that DNA as a chemical completely apart from living systems, purely mechanically, works just as Watson and Crick predicted it should in live organisms—said that if he were twenty years younger he might try the repressor. But as it was, the problem was too hard. And there were Jacob and Monod, who had created the theory of the repressor. Their failure to find the repressor was a source of great disappointment and tension. They worked together less and less, then finally not at all.

Ptashne, though, had more ambition than even the usual ferocious twenty-five-year-old, and more physical energy. He also had a streak of boldness that made the situation provoke him almost beyond his own control. He could not resist it. He had come into the fraternity of biology by working directly with the two eminent scientists, Franklin Stahl and Aaron Novick, who had done, just before he met them, some of the classical papers in modern molecular biology. Ptashne also met H. J. Muller during his Reed summers, and later Matthew Meselson as well.

The revolution in modern biology was made by these men and others, a band as fascinating as the great circle of physicists that included Einstein, Bohr, and Szilard. Meselson was a student of the eminent Linus Pauling, and Stahl worked with Meselson on an experiment that has been called the most beautiful in biology. Muller had worked at Indiana University and had taught James Watson and Salvador Luria. Novick collaborated with Leo Szilard (who had magically moved from the great circle of physics to that of biology). Novick had been a student of Max Delbrück. Into this group stepped Mark Ptashne, a recruit from the next generation.

He was enthralled with their work. And what he heard from the time he came into those laboratories was talk of the repressor. Even after the completion of his Ph.D., after his pursuit of a place in the Harvard labs of Watson and Meselson, the problem still stood.

"This problem had certain earmarks, certain aspects, which don't normally exist in biology," Ptashne says. "It affected me deeply and aesthetically. It was a beautiful formal problem: either the theory was correct, or it was not. If not, there were certain clear alternatives. Biology rarely presents you with a problem that neatly."

The problem was hard, chiefly because there were too many guesses that had to be made even to start. But Ptashne realized that this uncertainty had apparently prevented all the older biologists from taking on the problem squarely. "The fact that so many people were working on it, fancy people," said Ptashne, "was grounds for asking on what basis an amateur like me has to attack the problem. But as I looked into it more . . . it became clear that the others were willing to take risks only to a certain point. The question was, how hard are you willing to work with the possibility that you'll have nothing at all to show for it? You may work for two or three years, simply fail and look like a fool. If not a fool, at least empty-handed."

It involved risking a year, or two, or three, on a problem that was filled with hazards and might produce no result at all. And a negative result in this case would be completely meaningless.

Ptashne would risk it. He wondered from time to time what a huge crater it would make in his life if the enterprise failed. But the thing about boldness is that it ignores consequences. The first time physicist Sidney Coleman met Ptashne, he recalls, "He impressed me, impressed everyone, as being a very hard-driving individual. Ambitious. Extremely energetic. Anyone who stood between Mark and what he wanted would soon have a Mark-sized hole in him."

The first time he went skiing, a friend recalls, Ptashne spent a little while on the learner slopes. But soon he slid over to the top of the Alpine run, a run that has dangers for experienced skiers, and he announced to his friends that he was going down. No, they said. "Yes, I am," he said, "and furthermore if I kill myself when I go down it will be your fault for not helping." His friends dragged along and tried to keep him from the worst injuries by placing themselves at the most difficult spots in the run. But soon Ptashne came flying down toward them. "His feet were three feet apart and his poles were tucked under his arms —he was in a racer's schluss! We screamed, 'Fall, Mark, fall!'" But Ptashne shot past with a look of mixed elation and terror. Out of control, he finally drove straight into a curve and a great snowbank. His injuries, luckily, were not permanent.

Ptashne began work on the repressor in 1965, after he joined the Society of Fellows and earned himself his own laboratory on

the fourth floor of the Harvard labs. On the third floor was
Walter Gilbert, a physicist who had recently switched to biology and who also had decided to find the repressor.

The two figures contrasted: Gilbert, soft-spoken, taller, a
decade older, and an experienced scientist with a sharpness of
mind and toughness of manner that engender tales. Gilbert was
a natural scientist whose interests did not extend greatly beyond the laboratory. Repressor or no, success or failure, Gilbert
would continue on in science, said Ptashne. "He would be a
scientist no matter what. Put Wally in a room and give him a
pencil and a pipe cleaner and he will do an experiment. I
admire that," Ptashne said.

Ptashne was the louder, shorter, younger man. He had come
into science chiefly because of the repressor. He felt he might
have entertained other careers. "My relation to science has been
much more tenuous. In those days I never regarded myself as a
scientist. I was a person who got caught up by this great enterprise," by the search for the "holy grail" as Gilbert called the
repressor.

He admired Gilbert and thought of working with him. "I
had a chance of working directly with or under him, or in
opposition to him. But I felt right from the beginning that
Wally was much too strong a personality to survive under. My
personality was sufficiently egotistical that it would have to survive independently."

So they began to compete in the search, but by different
methods and on different genetic systems. Both worked with the
common and best-understood of bacteria, *Escherichia coli*. It is
a creature that inhabits the human gut, largely harmlessly, and
looks like nothing so much as a piece of gray Good-n-Plenty—a
tube with rounded ends. Its great advantage, like other beasts
of the genetics lab, is that it reproduces quickly. A generation
passes every twenty minutes. It is grown simply in tubes or
dishes filled with a nutritious broth of fundamental chemicals.

Gilbert chose to work with a gene of *E. coli* called the lac
gene, short for lactose. *E. coli* has the ability to live off many
varieties of food, and one of them is lactose, milk sugar. But to
do this it must begin making an enzyme (beta-galactosidase)
that will find, bind to, and cleave into two pieces the incoming

molecules of milk sugar. The pieces are directly usable by *E. coli*'s system. When lactose is absent from its environs, however, *E. coli* does not need the cleaving enzyme, and so shuts down the gene that makes it. Gilbert sought the repressor that could do this.

Ptashne worked with the bacteriophage lambda, and its ability in some cases to be harmlessly stored away in the *E. coli* genes for a thousand generations at a time, rather than its more common behavior of entering the bacterium and within minutes filling it to bursting with its progeny.

The chief difficulty of the experiments was that there are no more than about ten or twenty molecules of repressor in each cell—amid hundreds of thousands of other molecules. The repressor might also be composed of any one of a number of different substances: Some evidence hinted that it was a protein, and François Jacob, who should know as much as anyone about it, said it should most logically be RNA, the DNA-like substance that carries the genetic code to the place in the cell where DNA instructions are carried out. How it acted was also unknown: it could block DNA directly or block the next step, the RNA's attempt to make proteins.

Or, the whole idea of a simple repressor could be wrong. To do any experiment at all required making a series of unjustified assumptions, just in order to know what sort of test to use for the unknown substance.

Ptashne did have the advantage, as he puts it, "of being an amateur, that is, neither a geneticist nor a biochemist. Most geneticists would not do the messy biochemistry that was required, and on the other hand, most biochemists would not consider doing these outlandish experiments while being guided" by the rules of heredity.

Ptashne had one idea to begin with. He knew that there was another phage (434) besides lambda that was nearly identical to it, except that it had a different repressor gene and apparently a completely different repressor. "So whatever magical operation you did you always had a twofold system to look for differential effects," Ptashne says. "That was the charm of the idea. Drop them into an extract containing the presumed lambda repressor, and lambda will be repressed while four

thirty-four infects the bacteria and pops out. On the other hand
you can drop them into an extract containing the four thirty-
four repressor, and only lambda will come out."

The first scheme began with a procedure in which he took an
extract of ground-up bacteria with repressed lambda, and thus
by implication, repressor in it. Into this extract he dropped
some cells with the cell walls removed. "I hoped the proteins
(and the repressor) would get into them once the cell's walls
were removed. They certainly did not, though. It was a completely crackpot scheme," Ptashne says.

Some weeks were lost on it. He turned to a second and a third
variation of the idea. And a fourth. Months were lost, with
nothing but dead cells and dirty glassware as a result. He had
long talks with Gilbert, whose experiments also were sinking
without releasing even a bubble of hope. Gilbert knew he himself could go on, but suggested, in a friendly way, that Ptashne
should go do something more useful to himself and science.

Ptashne tried new methods. By his own count over the first
year of work, he tried some thirteen ways of making the repressor separate itself from the chemical confusion in the cells. They
failed completely. Gilbert's experiments were not going well
either; at one point he realized that a single wrong assumption
had kept him working impotently for nearly a year. Lab workers who recalled that period said the competition between the
two became rather sharp, as when Gilbert's colleague Benno
Muller-Hill would come up to Ptashne's lab to brag about a
successful day and taunt Ptashne.

"The competition may have been sharp," says Ptashne, reflecting on the matter, "but I think it's important to point out
that the relationship between me and Gilbert was one of
mutual support and openness." Ptashne was working nights and
weekends. Dinners with friends were cut off early so he could
return to the lab. If he scheduled even an hour or two off, he
worried about it for days beforehand. The thought of two or
three lost hours became unbearable. The tension appeared in a
variety of physical symptoms as well. He once went to a doctor
who said he was simply exhausted and he could either see a
psychiatrist and start taking pills or take a couple of weeks in
bed. "I think I asked for the pills," Ptashne says.

Ptashne now does not remember what sort of pills they were,

perhaps only aspirin, but he recalls reviving himself quickly and getting back into the lab. Sidney Coleman, who was a good friend of both Gilbert and Ptashne, said of the period, "They were all going crazy. There was an intense competitiveness—though very little hostility. Each of them was saying things like the other's system would never work. They were driving themselves into the ground in a fever of industry and excitement."

It was nearly eighteen months after he started that Ptashne began work on "hysterical scheme number 14." This time the idea was to get *E. coli* to stop making everything except the repressor. To do this he first had to irradiate the lambda-infected bacteria with ultraviolet light. This fouls the DNA, but does not debilitate the machinery where the proteins are actually fabricated. Nor does it damage the proteins already made and contained within the cell—among them some repressor.

So into this radiated, devastated cell, Ptashne thought, he might introduce a fresh lambda virus. When it entered the cell it would encounter the repressors already there, shut off forty-nine of its fifty genes, and settle into the dormant state in which it makes nothing but repressor. In fact, he could introduce ten or twenty fresh lambdas, and together they would produce more and more repressor until the repressor molecule existed in large quantities within the cell.

In theory.

Ptashne soon found that the amount of radiation needed to shut down *E. coli*'s DNA was also enough to completely disintegrate the bacterium. It took a number of failures before he noticed, or his assistant Nancy Hopkins noticed, that there was a moment in the life of his bacterial populations that they seemed more vigorous. At the moment the cells were crowded, but just before they became overcrowded, they were most able to absorb the radiation and continue functioning. The cells had to be watched closely for hours to catch the few minutes in which the little civilization reached its peak of growth. Only then could Ptashne irradiate them and infect them with lambda viruses.

He also found that, even under heavy radiation, some DNA continued to work. Even severely damaged, it produced other protein molecules at twenty times the rate it made repressor proteins. Still, this was an improvement over what he started with—a rate of ten thousand to one.

Another failure which dogged the work was that, unknown to Ptashne, the usual amount of magnesium added to one stage in the experiment turned out to foul the works. Other failures came and went without explanation.

Quite a few physicists who have left their neater discipline to enter biology have found themselves mumbling about the uncertainty of it all. Max Delbrück once wrote that "A mature physicist, acquainting himself for the first time with the problems of biology, is puzzled by the circumstance that there are no 'absolute phenomena' in biology. Everything is time bound and space bound. The animal or plant or microorganism he is working with is but a link in an evolutionary chain of changing forms, none of which has any permanent validity. . . . The physicist has been reared in a different atmosphere. The materials and the phenomena he works with are the same here and now as they were at all times, and as they are on the most distant stars."

The uncertainty in biology is apparent in the daily lab work: a biologist, working alone at a bench full of flasks, filters, pipettes, and other simple implements of hand labor, may do the same experiment a dozen or two dozen times before it works. He will likely never know precisely why it did not work so many times before it finally did. Failure may come because of dirty glassware, an improper temperature, a bit too much of one chemical ingredient, or no discernible reason at all.

Ptashne says that he has tried to forget most of this unpleasant period and has succeeded. "I remember the strain of working fifteen hours a day, under pressure, and having nothing at all to show for it. Day after day after day desperately trying everything, and going over and over the same thing. And there was the competition with Wally . . ."

Thinking back over it, he says that his memory is bad and it may be slighting the experience simply to say it was unpleasant. There were exhilarations and a sense that he was impelled forward under the weight of the problem itself. "Kierkegaard said or according to some people, he did not say, that a scientist does not chase truth, but truth chases the scientist," Ptashne says.

He had misgivings about what he was doing. "I thought I was extending myself in this crazy way. I was driven to it. I can't explain it rationally," he says.

It was in this period that Ptashne devised the theory that the chief experience of science is failure. "I think the most important experience you have as an experimental scientist is realizing the extent to which you can be fooled, the extent to which your impulses and aspirations lead you to believe things which have nothing to do with the way things actually work. . . . I have notebooks full of crackpot experiments, theory upon theory, wonderful constructs. . . . I had done everything right, and now from x, y must follow. Y didn't follow at all. I'd find it enormously amusing that the world could conspire to make something fit so beautifully with your constructs, which just happen to be wrong. . . . You find out that no matter how much you want something to be true, no matter how much you're just sure it must be true—the scientist learns that what he thinks could well be completely false." In this experience is the difference between science and religion, between poems and scientific papers.

Ptashne's schemes grew more elaborate to accommodate obstacles. Because the amount of repressor, compared to the other proteins still being made in the damaged cells, was still very small, his extracts were not pure enough simply to filter out the repressor.

So he irradiated *E. coli* as before, but this time divided the colonies into two parts before infecting them with the fresh lambda virus. To one batch he added the fresh phage and a radioactive amino acid. When the phage began to manufacture its repressor protein, it would take up this radioactive molecule. So would other proteins still being made in the damaged cells. The result was that he could count radioactive clicks from repressor proteins and background proteins. For comparison, his second batch got radioactive amino acids as well, but a fresh phage that was damaged so that it could not make repressor. Thus, its radioactive clicks would count only background proteins, no repressors.

When he compared the two batches all the proteins were spread out, by weight, along a line. In both cases, the line was jagged but nearly flat. The background proteins gave radiation counts very nearly the same as the background proteins plus the repressor. But, borrowing a striking thought from an experiment he read, he simply let the two batches sit in the radiation counters for many hours. Whereas he could count only a few clicks difference in the beginning, as the hours went by he could see the tiny difference become visible as the clicks went up into the thousands. With the proteins spread out in two jagged lines of counted clicks, eventually one line grew a bump, then a sharp spike above the haze of background counts. It was the repressor.

Sitting at the kitchen table after dinner on one August afternoon, Ptashne said, "I think this could only be embarrassing if you make it sound as though it was some great heroic event." Quietly he placed a fork on his plate. "But when you are doing something like that the only way to keep yourself going and take all nature's blows is to build for yourself a Faustian conflict. Every day you get up in the morning and you are shaking with rage, and you must go and fling down the doors of science. There is an enormously inflated sense of self-importance and historical moment. It may be false, but for me it's necessary."

By the time he had isolated the repressor, there was some disappointment waiting. Partly it was because the achievement had dribbled out over months at the end. Partly it was because Gilbert finished a few weeks ahead of him and was ready to send his paper into a journal when Ptashne finally had consistent, repeatable results.

"I had no sense of elation, just of relief," Ptashne says. "It is like having a headache for ten years and suddenly it goes away. It comes back, unfortunately, the next week, if you're crazy enough to be doing experimental science."

He was and it did. Though the repressor was found and proved to be a protein, the work was not done. In fact, though all the time and emotion were concentrated on this first question, the second was actually more important. The repressor may exist, but how did it work? It was still possible that the repressor might be only one chemical in a chain of agents and reactions that accounted for its action. It was possible that the simple, elegant model in the Jacob and Monod theory was wrong.

Because Ptashne's experiments ended with purified, radioactively labeled repressor, he could begin immediately to test the second question. Gilbert could not.

With Nancy Hopkins, who had assisted in the final months of the repressor isolation, he mixed repressor with a batch of DNA that contained the dormant lambda. There were two possibilities. If the theory was right, the repressor would act simply by binding tightly to the DNA to block the dormant lambda genes from being expressed, from making new lambdas. If the theory was wrong, the repressor would not stick to the DNA.

He put his mixture of repressor and DNA into a centrifuge. The repressor protein was smaller and lighter, and so it should stay floating near the top of the tube. But if it bound to the long, coiled strands of DNA, the two should drop together to the bottom of the tube.

The results came one morning as Nancy Hopkins was running the experiment. She took the numbers, scratched out on a sheet of graph paper, to the seminar Ptashne was attending. This time the answers came without pain or labor, the result fell out quickly. This time there was more than relief. The two began hurrying down the hallways and talking excitedly to anyone who would listen.

Unfortunately, Walter Gilbert was in the hallway and walked by as the revelers were telling their news to James Watson. Taken by surprise, he was upset and failed to conceal his disappointment. According to the researcher, he went back to his laboratory and said he now had to beat Ptashne into print.

Ptashne soon turned his paper in to James Watson, head of the lab, to be sent on to the journal *Nature*. Though Ptashne now claims he does not remember the incident well, Watson held onto Ptashne's paper—perhaps at Gilbert's request and perhaps on his own—waiting for Gilbert to race through his work to catch up. It was perhaps the only truly bitter moment in the long, productive competition.

From the work came several notable scientific prizes, such as the Charles Léopold Mayer Prize of the French Academy of Sciences for the two researchers, as well as election to the National Academy of Sciences in America.

5

I T is hard to recall now, but during the late 1960s and early 1970s, pure research in science was regarded with suspicion, was criticized, was argued over. The urgency in the public mind of poverty, war, and racial trouble made it common to hear that work in the service of no one was selfish. The phrase used was "copping out." It meant evading social responsibility. There was, in addition, a growing sense that science itself, so often in service to illegitimate ends, robbed people of their humanity.

Ptashne's political sensibilities put him at pains to do something, to spend time on something besides science. He was one of the student-bohemians who wore their shirttails out and listened to folk songs, who had pride in their sensitivity to social issues, and in their rebellious mode of life.

Ptashne, earlier than most, crafted his life carefully to contravene respectability. His hair was long enough that one friend claims to recall watching the Ed Sullivan show in curiosity about the new singing group called the Beatles: "My God," he reports saying when they came on the screen, "they're four young Englishmen with Mark Ptashne haircuts!" Ptashne had a motorcycle. He lived with his girlfriend in a scruffy apartment whose toilet did not work and whose furniture was covered with hair from his three cats.

Over the years of the 1960s, he gradually became more certain of the need to do something about the war. He began to circulate petitions, raise money, help arrange protests. In 1968, he traveled to Cuba with two other scientists and on the way met playwright and cartoonist Jules Feiffer in a Mexican airport. "He was part of a traveling trio of mad scientists," said Feiffer. "They were traveling without passports in order to circumvent the State Department's rule against visiting Cuba: if they didn't have passports they couldn't have them taken away. . . . Mark was then twenty-eight years old and talked incessantly about how young he was and how old everybody else was, especially me.

"The first thing that came to mind is that I was watching this guy who claimed to be a scientist but who I knew was Groucho Marx. He was zipping back and forth very, very fast. Terribly funny. Very competitive. Challenging everybody around him. But the challenges are free of hostility. I usually rise very badly to challenges or resent them. But somehow with Mark that threat didn't occur. Underneath it all there is an amiableness, a good-naturedness. But the surface is naked aggression." Ptashne visited Cuba twice to lecture in 1968 and 1969. In 1970, linguist Noam Chomsky, a friend of Ptashne's, traveled to Hanoi as a gesture of sympathy to the government of North Vietnam, not to mention as a gesture of defiance toward the Nixon government. While he was there, the North Vietnamese asked him to lecture on linguistics and told him they wanted to receive more Americans, especially doctors and biologists.

So, on short notice, Ptashne flew to Hanoi. He found the mood toward science there quite different than in the United States at the time. Though without current knowledge of molecular biology, the biochemists were quite interested in the work of Jacob and Monod, and asked Ptashne if his work was in any way related to theirs. It was, he said, and spent eleven hours at a blackboard before a packed classroom delivering the news about lambda and the repressor. He was asked again and again to go over the work in detail, the logic of each step.

He asked about Socialism and the course of its development in Vietnam. He was told frankly that there would be no time for such talk; there were too many questions about science to be asked and answered. Ptashne says he thought then of the slackening numbers of American students interested in science and the guilt acquired by many of those who do work in it. At the end of his day of lecturing, he asked about academic science amid war. The implication in his question, and in the ones he would be asked repeatedly when he returned, was that research was impractical, perhaps even callous, when so much other urgent business needed doing.

One professor offered to explain: He said they were building a society and that requires knowing about such things. He smiled and added something which brought a laugh from the group. Perhaps, he said, the Vietnamese have a gene which makes them want to learn.

As Ptashne continued his work on lambda, he also had a part in the Harvard student strikes and their aftermath, chiefly as a member of the faculty's liberal caucus and as one of those who negotiated with Harvard's administration. He was the architect of a parliamentary maneuver which put the Harvard faculty firmly on record as opposing the Vietnam War, an act which gained him some notoriety.

Beginning about 1970, his work on lambda began producing interesting new results. The problem was essentially the same one he started with, but in the meantime he had acquired a lab full of students and colleagues to help him sort out the details of how the repressor works to hold lambda harmlessly inside the bacterial cell that it would normally devastate within an hour.

It had been just about fifty years before that H. J. Muller made a startling conjecture in an address. He thought it remarkable that the new substances then just coming into experimental vogue, the phage viruses, should actually behave as if they had genes like larger organisms. Of course, said Muller, they were too small to have genes. On the other hand there was the possibility that these things were genes themselves. He predicted the opening of an entirely new way to study genetics, essentially the one which has followed and produced the great revolution in biology during the past few decades: "If . . . these bodies were really genes, like our chromosome genes, they would give us an utterly new angle from which to attack the gene problem. They are filterable, to some extent isolable, can be handled in test-tubes, and their properties, as shown by their [destructive] effects on bacteria, can then be studied after treatment. It would be very rash to call these bodies genes, and yet at present we must confess that there is no distinction known between the genes and them. Hence we cannot categorically deny that perhaps we may be able to grind genes in a mortar and cook them in a beaker after all. Must we geneticists become bacteriologists . . . chemists, and physicists . . .? Let us hope so."

At the time, few believed genes could or ever would be reduced to chemical substances, or all the processes of life reduced to interactions between molecules. But fifty years after Muller suggested the possibility, a young man who had once met Muller and been inspired by him was standing knee-deep in molecules, showing for the first time those intricate and lovely mechanisms and how they behaved. Ptashne's work began to lay out the workings of a curious molecular machine. It is essentially a switch that can change the entire chemical state of the cell. It is the elaboration of this sort of mechanism which has abolished the last possibility of believing rationally in the élan vital, the mysterious principle underlying life.

After Ptashne isolated the repressor and found that it bound directly to DNA, much about the way it worked needed to be elaborated. So far, he knew that when the lambda parasite injected itself into a bacterial cell, its DNA was inserted by some enzymatic mechanism among the DNA of the bacteria itself. Then, it could either reproduce itself immediately or remain dormant, to be passed silently from generation to generation of bacteria. In the dormant state, virtually the only working gene is the one which directs the making of repressor molecules. The repressors, once made, bind themselves to the bacterial DNA just upstream of the chain of lambda genes. They settle adjacent to the "start" signal, where "reading" of the lambda genes would normally begin. The presence of the repressor blocks the gene reading and thus keeps the lambda genes unexpressed.

This picture raised for Ptashne a number of questions about the action between the repressor and the binding site. Working now with a long list of collaborators, including Nancy Hopkins, Thomas Maniatis, Vincent Pirotta, Paul Chadwick, Russell Maurer, Keith Backman, and others, Ptashne found that his image of the repressor action was too simple. There was not one site where the repressor bound itself, but three adjacent sites, and the repressor bound to each with a different affinity.

It was later found that the system contained not one repressor, but two, to regulate each other. The repressor not only held dormant other lambda genes, but also the gene that would make the second repressor. When lambda genes were freed, so was the second repressor. It then bound to the DNA to block manufacture of the first repressor so lambda genes could be made without interruption. The lambda system contained a two-way switch.

But to study the molecular details of the lambda switch, Ptashne needed relatively large quantities of the repressor molecules. In his early repressor experiments one of the greatest troubles was the small number of molecules he had to work with. The experiments operated near the limit at which results dissolve into noise. Now he used the repressors in experiment after experiment to test and compare their action in differing situations. So Ptashne and his colleagues now created a number of tactics to get the gene machinery to overproduce by a thousandfold or more the number of repressor molecules produced in *E.coli.*

The discovery of the new recombinant-DNA techniques of biology began with the realization that DNA is not perfectly stable. It can be broken by such environmental agents as radiation and cancer-causing chemicals. Thus cells have a series of molecules which have, among other abilities, the ability to repair DNA. These enzymes first cut and then rejoin the DNA strands. (In formal biological language, they are called restriction enzymes.)

These splicing enzymes are at the center of the whole recombinant-DNA technology, for biologists have no tools of their own to work at the submicroscopic level of molecules. They can mix vast hordes of molecules in test tubes and cleverly play off their effects against one another. But they cannot see or manipulate DNA directly, let alone cut it precisely between chosen base pairs. But this is what the splicing enzymes do, they break DNA neatly and predictably, cutting between the same base pairs every time. Since there are more than a hundred different cutting enzymes, each of which cuts in its own characteristic place, mixing the different cuts can give biologists strips of DNA of different lengths. Many of the enzymes cut in a way that also makes it easy for the DNA to join together again.

Thus it is possible for biologists to separate bits of DNA and recombine them with others specially chosen.

From this power extends many others. Biologists now speak of the technology, without trying to exaggerate, as the single most important tool of biology to be created since the microscope. Until now, genes were only something inferred from recurring appearances of traits. But the new techniques allowed genes to be cut out and read, letter by letter. They allow the cloning or multiplication of exact copies of genes for study. Letter sequences can be altered to determine which strings within a gene make the gene do what it does. Finally, DNA can be mixed even across the widest biological distances. Rabbit genes have been put in mice and operated. Human genes have been placed in bacterial cells and operated.

The technique for cloning a gene, once the gene has been identified and extracted from a living cell, is relatively simple. Plasmids, or rings of DNA from within a cell, are cut open with splicing enzymes. The stretch of DNA containing the gene to be cloned is prepared so that at either end it is "sticky." That is, it has single, unpaired nucleotides that will readily join with their usual partners (A to T, C to G). The gene with sticky ends will now attach itself to the loose ends of the opened plasmid. The plasmid becomes a closed circle again, this time including in its DNA the new gene.

The recombinant plasmid now can be placed in its natural place in the bacterial cell. When the bacteria multiply, so will the plasmid be multiplied. And the new gene will be read and its gene product made alongside the usual bacterial gene products.

Ptashne and his students created a system which would not only get gene products made in *E. coli,* but get them made at an enormous rate, virtually making the cell produce that gene product and little else. He modified the natural system in several ways. The "start" sequence at the beginning of a gene is not equally strong in all genes. Some attract the enzymes that read genes more efficiently than others. Ptashne took a particularly strong one and inserted it into a plasmid. He also inserted a sequence of DNA (called the Shine-Dalgarno sequence) which assures that once the gene is read, the cell machinery will efficiently translate the genetic message into a protein molecule. And he found that up to a hundred plasmids containing the new gene might be inserted into one *E. coli* cell before the cell begins to fail.

In this way, he got *E. coli* to produce 190,000 molecules of the second repressor in each cell. That is about two thousand times the normal amount. Now his laboratory has reached even higher multiples.

Such a result helped produce repressor and solve the purely scientific problem. But like a beacon it also drew the attention of commercial interests. In 1973, a number of scientists, including Paul Berg, Stanley Cohen, and Annie Chang at Stanford, and Herbert Boyer at the University of California at San Francisco, discovered, in rough terms, how to splice genes. Ptashne had taken another step when he and his colleagues at Harvard worked out how to use gene-splicing techniques to make super-producers—genes that could be put in harness to make virtually commercial quantities of specified chemicals.

Ptashne said in a rather offhand manner in his papers that virtually any gene might be put in his superproducer plasmids. The implication was clear that even such useful substances as interferon, insulin, human-growth hormone, and so on might be made in relatively large quantities by the method Ptashne reported. At the time, he himself expressed no interest in the commercial applications. But companies began to approach Ptashne and all the members of his group, even down to graduate students in the lab. Before these matters fully developed however, another historical anomaly intruded.

6

I N the midst of success, the first indication to biologists of political trouble came in the summer of 1973.

It came in New Hampton, New Hampshire, at a Gordon Conference on nucleic acids, one of those regular events where scientists have the opportunity to exchange their latest results. At this one, chairwoman Maxine Singer, biologist at the National Institutes of Health, wanted to bring up the issue of risk. Many resisted, but finally discussion of the risk of the new experiments was put on the agenda as a final item—a few remarks, less than thirty minutes allotted.

There was some concern that Paul Berg and his colleagues at Stanford had been carrying out dangerous experiments. He had been mixing the genes of *E. coli* with the genes of a cancer-causing virus. The virus, called SV40, is lethal to small animals but apparently not harmful to humans. Nonetheless it seemed too risky to insert any kind of cancer genes into a bacterium that can inhabit the human gut.

Two proposals came up for a vote at that meeting. First, whether the group should send a letter to the National Academy of Sciences asking for a study of the risks of the new gene experiments. The second vote asked whether that letter should also be made public by printing it in *Science,* the country's chief science weekly.

Mark Ptashne's instincts, and those of a large number of the scientists, were toward social concern and openness. The era of the sixties had produced that impulse in some and strengthened it in others. And it was this impulse rather than any sense of a real hazard that decided him to vote yes to both questions.

"Did I really believe there was any hazard? Well, God knows what I really believed," Ptashne says. What he did know was that he had strong feelings. He wanted to be responsible. He did not think about the details of infectious-disease containment or about the political consequences of saying publicly that his line of work had unknown and perhaps very serious hazards for society.

But it was done. The letter was published, the National Academy formed a committee to consider the issue. Chairing the committee was Paul Berg. He had already decided that his own SV40 work, and work like it, should stop at least until an investigation of the question could be done.

Berg organized a meeting in April 1974. He set as the agenda just the question "whether or not there is a serious problem growing out of . . . experiments involving the construction of hybrid DNA. . . ."

The ability to extract DNA from any organism and insert it effectively into any other was, although new, already widespread. For example, a bacterium could accept a gene from a mammal and make some protein useful only to the mammal. One of the early experiments included taking a gene for resistance to antibiotics and inserting it into *E. coli*. Conferring resistance to antibiotics on any set of genes is clearly a business that may have some hazards.

The basis of this work was a principle found and first used by Berg, Cohen, Chang, and Boyer in 1972 and 1973. Together with an amplification of the technique like Ptashne's superproducer plasmids, these new technologies became the basis for trumpeting the possible uses of the new biology and sounding the alarm about possible dangers.

Biologists realized that they might artificially use both the cutting and splicing enzymes. Since the genes of all living things are chemically identical, it thus became possible to circumvent all the rules that keep genes and species apart. A biologist might clip out sections of frog DNA and transfer the cuttings to a test tube holding *E. coli* DNA. Given the right cutting and splicing enzymes, applied in the right order, the two sets of DNA splice themselves together. Mixing up many genes of widely differing animals early enough in their development makes any number of strange, chimerical creatures possible in theory, even though the things cannot survive in practice. As Cambridge's Sydney Brenner was fond of saying, one might even mix the DNA of a duck with the DNA of an orange.

Stanley Cohen and Annie Chang of Stanford Medical School were the first to perform the simplest version of the technique. They transplanted genes of *Staphylococcus aureus* into *E. coli*. Whether the transplant was successful could easily be told: This staph is resistant to penicillin. So, if the experiment worked, the *E. coli* would become resistant to penicillin and survive a dose of it. If the experiment failed, a dose of penicillin would kill the *E. coli*.

Quickly the Stanford team also proved that great distance between species was no barrier to this technique. They soon had the genes of an African toad functioning within *E. coli*.

Besides this technique, biologists soon began using another, more indiscriminate kind of experiment, called the shotgun experiment. In it, not one or two, but all the genes of some organism are chopped into bits. Each of these bits then is separated and inserted into *E. coli*. The result is tens or hundreds of tubes with bacteria carrying separate sections of the organism's DNA. Thus, each piece of DNA can be tested separately to isolate genes and their powers. But this technique also means that if there are some dangerous genes in the lot, they too will be put into *E. coli* and reproduced unknowingly in literally hundreds of millions of copies.

In April of 1974 Berg and a handful of other researchers in the new biology met at MIT to discuss the problem of risk. They quickly decided that an international meeting should be called to discuss, as Berg wrote later, "Were there any experiments which should not be done? How could such a moratorium be proposed or enforced? . . . we expected a frank and searching review of what people were doing or wanted to do, particularly from the point of view of whether they should be done. But as we talked we realized that the pace of events might not wait for February [1975] and that some of the experiments many people would agree could be hazardous would be done by then."

He gave as an example attempts he had heard of to insert into *E. coli* genes of the herpes virus. Herpes causes ulcers of the skin and of the membranes in the mouth and genitals.

The sense of worry was increased by an event little known in the United States, the most serious incident in this century of dangerous organisms escaping from the laboratory. Not long before, a lab technician who had worked on smallpox at a laboratory in England became ill and was admitted to the hospital. Before it was discovered that he had a mild case of smallpox, he received two visitors. Both caught the disease and died. Though the incident had nothing to do with mixing DNA, and represented a hazard of medical work as old as knowledge itself, nevertheless the incident had an important effect on thinking about biological hazard.

Clearly, to understand and defeat dangerous organisms, scientists must work with them. What had presented itself, a simple way to cut and mix DNA, was one of the most powerful tools ever found in medical biology. But the Berg group determined that while waiting for an international conference, precautions ought to be taken. A letter was sent to *Nature* and *Science,* the two chief journals of science in English. They asked biologists to halt and defer experiments which might obviously be dangerous, at least until the conference could consider the matter.

Just before the letter was published, Ptashne sent a letter to Berg about an experiment he was considering that involved the use of SV40, the monkey tumor virus. The experiment was odd, because he did not want to put the tumor virus into a microorganism. He wanted to do the reverse, put lambda genes into SV40. It was not easy to imagine a hazard resulting from the mixing of lambda with SV40 that wasn't already present in SV40 alone, but the climate of worry moved Ptashne to write a letter he later wouldn't think of composing. He asked if the experiment might be dangerous. Berg replied: Ask God.

A few days later, the Berg group's call for a moratorium was published. The letter was unusual, and its publication in the United States was accompanied by a press conference. An accompanying letter from British biologist Michael Stoker, published with the letter in *Nature,* said that over the aeons, nature had mixed its own dangerous and clever concoctions of DNA (such as the tricks of the parasite lambda). "No doubt a good many dirty tricks have been attempted and discarded by nature in the course of evolution, but the disquiet arises from the utterly novel associations of genetic material which are now possible . . . it is encouraging that the very leaders in the field have taken the initiative."

Up to the point of the press conference, all the activity had been more or less private among the scientists themselves. When Berg was asked to attend the press conference he recalled that he was surprised. "We hadn't thought the public would be in on it," Berg said, "and I must admit I didn't give much thought at all to the press." He found the press conference boring, the reporters uninformed. But the next day, "When I saw the headlines—SCIENTISTS URGE BAN ON GENETIC RESEARCH—I realized that what we had done was being misconstrued."

The call for a moratorium was followed seven months later by the international conference, held at the Asilomar conference center near Pacific Grove, California. The meeting was a confused affair in which it soon became clear that the fears of the scientists were quite vague and their knowledge of what might happen mere guesswork. Although *E. coli* is perhaps the best understood organism on earth, scientists simply could not tell the results of splicing into *E. coli* genes that it had never had before. There was discussion of the K-12 strain of *E. coli*. It was a specially weakened strain that, it was believed, could not easily survive outside the specially warm and nutritious environment provided in laboratories. But one scientist pointed out that, if it was accidentally swallowed, even if it lived only twenty-four hours, that would be enough time for it to pass through fifty generations. *E. coli* was also known to exchange some bits of its DNA with other *E. coli*—so the weakened strain might pass on a harmful bit of DNA to healthy *E. coli*. And what if it got into the rich environs of a sewer where billions of its relatives live in every square foot of water? It was all speculation, but no less unnerving for that.

That there are public health hazards hidden in our ignorance of biology and medicine has been proved more than once. Examples mentioned at the Asilomar meeting were the accidents which occurred with the polio vaccine and with hybrid corn. Though it was not known at the time, between ten and thirty million Americans, and even more Russians, received contaminated doses of polio vaccine in the 1950s. They were contaminated with the same agent—the SV40 monkey virus— that started the trouble for mixed-DNA experiments. It is not yet known what the health effect, if any, of that accident may be. The other example of an accident was the crop disaster of 1970. A large proportion of the nation's corn crop at the time was hybrid, the product of crossbreeding different strains. Most of these hybrids carried a similar genetic failing. A variety of fungus quickly adapted itself to the new varieties in the field and took advantage of their vulnerability. Twenty percent of the country's corn crop was wiped out.

Some at Asilomar objected to making any sort of rule about future experiments because too little was known. "We have to make some decisions," said Berg, "if you concede there is a graded set of risks [depending on the danger of the organism being worked with], that is what you have to respond to." James Watson replied: "But you can't measure the risks. So they want to put me out of business for something you can't measure."

At the end, when it was clear that nothing was clear, the lawyers spoke up. Alex Capron, then a professor of international law at the University of Pennsylvania, said, "This group is not competent to assign overall risk. . . . It is the right of the public to act through the legislature and to make erroneous decisions." It was exactly what the scientists feared. Legislators and erroneous decisions.

Roger Dworkin, a lawyer from the University of Indiana, put the matter even more squarely before the naive group. His talk, as he described it to one reporter, was about "conventional aspects of the law, and how they may sneak up on you—in the form, say, of a multimillion dollar lawsuit." Professional negligence is not something that juries and judges are sympathetic to, Dworkin said. He named an Oregon case in which an ophthalmologist was sued for malpractice. The charge was that he failed to give a glaucoma test to a young patient who had no symptoms and who had about a one-in-twenty-five-thousand chance of having the disease. The jury decided he was guilty of negligence. Dworkin went on: "The law has a tradition of listening to and respecting expert groups that regulate themselves. On the other hand there is precedent for ruining groups that don't." Doctors, for example. Dworkin said that malpractice has always been hard to prove, and made much harder because doctors have refused to testify against each other. As a result, they are now massacred in court.

The next action of the meeting at Asilomar was to write and vote on a set of voluntary rules for those who wanted to recombine DNA molecules. The vote was not close, and for the first time in the history of science, so far as anyone knows, scientists barred themselves from some research. Even during World War Two, when pleas went out to nuclear scientists not to stop some research, but merely to stop publishing openly for fear that Germany would learn too much, the scientists flatly refused.

The effect of what the scientists believed were responsible measures was immediately unpleasant. Journalists had attended Asilomar, and their stories, as all newspaper stories tend to be, were blunt and faintly alarmist. The public, expecting each profession to minimize its own difficulties, was shocked. If the scientists were themselves so worried, then the trouble must be truly great. As one magazine said on its cover, the work is no less than SCIENCE THAT FRIGHTENS SCIENTISTS.

7

A SILOMAR was the alert, but the battle began in Cambridge City Hall in the summer of 1976.

It was sixteen months after Asilomar, time enough for biologists to gain experience from hundreds of experiments with recombined genes. There had also been time enough for scientists to get used to the rough guidelines set down at Asilomar: First, the most dangerous experiments, such as putting the genes for making botulism toxin into *E. coli*, were to be avoided altogether. Three other categories of experiment were set up—low, medium, and high risk—and for each of these, biologists were urged to use the appropriate level of special protection. In the high-risk category, experiments involving organisms that might possibly harm humans, the scientists were to use special sealed laboratories with negative air pressure, so that when a door is opened, air is drawn only into the room. Special protective clothing should be worn and experiments done inside containment boxes. Further, the *E. coli* used should be a specially disabled variety that could not live long outside the test tube. The scale went down from these precautions to the low-risk category, which might be carried out with the simple precautions such as thorough washing of glassware and cautious handling of biological materials.

The precautions, which apparently were honored by biologists, did not prevent protest. What the biologists began to realize for the first time was that they had started an argument in public, and that such street debates invite brawlers. The Asilomar conference had considered only the narrow question of how the new experiments may proceed safely. The technical issues of safety were most important to the scientists. But in a street brawl, technicalities are lost.

A number of older scientists who had given up their biology for philosophy gave the protests a large measure of credibility. Erwin Chargaff of Columbia University and Nobelist George Wald of Harvard spoke up sharply. So did Robert Sinsheimer of Cal Tech.

George Wald's office is one floor below Ptashne's in the Harvard Biological Labs. From 1976 onward, Wald has been willing not only to speak up, but to actively seek the podium. He is now in his middle seventies, with a shoulder-length mane of white hair and a medallion dangling perpetually from his neck. His hands shake with age, but his voice is clear. He has been an activist since 1969 when he startled himself by making a thoughtful and impassioned speech against the war in Vietnam. The experience, he says, transformed him. He has since spoken out against the continuing nuclear arms race, for the Ayatollah Khomeini and the Iranian revolution, and against recombining DNA molecules.

In the summer of 1976, he and his wife, biologist Ruth Hubbard, went to visit the mayor of Cambridge, Alfred Velucci. As it happened, the mayor was then contemplating holding public hearings on the issue of recombinant DNA. Harvard wanted to build a medium-level containment laboratory and had applied for a building permit. It was an opportunity Velucci could not pass up. Wald and Hubbard walked into Velucci's office at just the proper moment, delivering to the mayor the weight of a distinguished biologist, ready for the action Velucci hoped he could take—a total ban on mixed DNA experiments within the city limits of Cambridge.

It was the first such public battle over recombinant DNA in an American city, and it sparked similar conflicts from the U. S. Congress and the New York State Assembly to the city halls in such places as San Diego, California, and Bloomington, Indiana.

It began on the hot night of June 23, 1976, in the old, balconied, and wood-paneled City Council chambers. The City

Hall is in the center of town, about halfway between MIT and Harvard, and as an institution, traditionally hostile to both of them. Cambridge is a working-class, industrial town that also has powerful enclaves of academia within its limits. The feuding over taxes and real estate and other issues is traditional; Mayor Velucci made it somewhat more vociferous when he threatened, repeatedly, to turn Harvard Yard into a parking lot and the *Harvard Lampoon* building into a public urinal.

For the university, Ptashne was the chief witness and came up first. Ptashne wore jeans, a long-sleeved sport shirt, and sandals; practically formal attire. The mayor, in his business suit, stared down from the dais at him.

From his early concern and willingness to take some cautionary action, Ptashne had begun to listen to those in biology who had experience with the most virulent of organisms. These organisms were shaped by evolution over millions of generations specifically to infect animals. But despite a total lack of care by workers experimenting with these organisms, and no complete facilities to speak of before World War Two, biologists said that through half a century of monitoring, only a relatively small number of accidental infections had occurred. Virtually all those infections were limited to people infected in the laboratory. In a few cases, the infections had spread from a lab worker to a second person; but in no case had it gone further than that. Even extremely infectious microbes, handled carelessly, seemed little or no direct threat to the public.

Ptashne began to realize that the issue was not one of science or of health. It was one of politics. He also began to experience in a brief space what most of us experience over decades—the sense of the world changing color, changing all political terms and leaving him alone among strangers who used to be friends. Without changing, he had changed, from radical to establishmentarian.

"Let me begin by giving you a blanket statement of fact," Ptashne said as he looked up at the mayor and the television lights. "No known dangerous organism has ever been produced by recombinant DNA experiment. For what it's worth, during the past two years, millions of bacterial cells carrying pieces of foreign DNA from other bacteria, from yeast and fruit flies . . .

have been constructed in many laboratories in this country. So far as we know, none of these cells containing foreign DNA has proved itself hazardous . . . We must realize that unlike other real risks," and here Ptashne referred to all the virulent, infectious bugs that are used daily in labs around the world, ". . . the risks in this case are purely hypothetical."

He said he could not construct any plausible scenario among the experiments intended for the low- and moderate-risk containment that would result in any real danger. There is a greater risk in keeping a household pet, he said.

He was thinking of cats. One microbe commonly carried by cats can infect pregnant women and kill the growing fetus. The event is rare, but not hypothetical. In fact, he said, standard biological labs having nothing to do with mixed DNA are more dangerous because they keep roomfuls of animals that carry organisms that can cause disease in man.

Velucci waited for half an hour or so, listening. Then he began a litany. He said they were questions he wanted answered, but he did not pause for reply:

"Did any one of this group bother at any time to write to the mayor and City Council to inform us you intended to carry out these experiments . . .?

"Can you make an absolute, one hundred percent guarantee that there is no possible risk which might arise from this experimentation? Is there zero risk of danger? . . ."

His voice was rising in volume and expression. "Is it true that in the history of science, mistakes have been made . . .?

"Do scientists ever exercise poor judgment?

"Do they ever have accidents?"

By now the audience was cheering. "I have made references to Frankenstein over the past week, and some people think this is all a big joke . . . this is not a laughing matter. If worse comes to worst we could have a major disaster on our hands."

Other City Council members began to prod. Why, if the matter was so simple, did scientists themselves—George Wald, Ruth Hubbard, Jonathan King—want the dispute put before the City Council? If the scientists have a vested interest, how could they regulate themselves?

Councilman David Clem said, ". . . Now, you made a statement, 'There's no known dangerous organism which has ever been produced by a recombinant DNA experiment.' "

"Yes," Ptashne said. The TV lights were making him sweat. He sat forward in his chair, his legs tensed, he tugged nervously at his sideburns.

"Now just what the hell do you think you're going to do if you DO produce one," Clem said with irritation. Velucci warned: "Don't put it in the sewer."

Ptashne tried to answer the shot in the typical academic way. ". . . near as we can tell, the probability that that event will occur is extraordinarily low. Now I know that you don't like to hear scientists telling you that . . ."

Ptashne had tried to explain the different levels of risk and containment, from P (for physical containment) 1 to P4, in which P1 and P2 are essentially standard laboratory practice. P3 and P4 containment include some special equipment and precautions, like those used in the labs where the deadliest organisms—for use in biological weapons—are made. Ptashne tried to explain that all experiments have some risk, even those to be done at P1 and P2. One could simply not say there was zero risk for experiments of any kind. Or for any other activity in life.

Clem passed all this by, and said of the new containment lab, "I do not think that it is worth the risk of the City of Cambridge to allow that to go forward without establishing a moratorium . . ."

"Does that include P2, sir?" Ptashne asked.

"If you want my personal opinion," Clem shot back, "I don't think you have any business doing it any way. . . ."

Velucci jumped in, reading the proposed action for the City Council, "That the Cambridge City Council insists that no experimentation involving recombinant DNA should be done within the City of Cambridge . . ."

Above the applause and boos, Ptashne said, "If you pass that resolution virtually every experiment done by members of the biochemistry department of Harvard will have to stop, and virtually every experiment done by about half the members of the biology department would have to stop—including experiments that no one, sir, NO ONE, has ever claimed had the slightest danger . . ."

The next week, the City Council passed an altered version of Velucci's proposal. It banned DNA experiments at the P3 and P4 levels for three months, and established a citizens' committee to make recommendations about the next step. The council later adopted a law that was somewhat stricter than the federal rules administered by the National Institutes of Health.

Similar though less stringent laws were passed by New York State and Maryland, and by at least five cities around the nation. The laws were the first of their kind to be applied against the practice of science.

At the Cambridge hearings, Ptashne finally realized how naive scientists had been from the beginning. The initiative began with himself and other scientists at the Gordon Conference three years earlier. Then there was the letter asking for a voluntary moratorium, the press conferences. Then Asilomar, again organized by scientists and guidelines written by scientists.

Standing at the beginning of a technology that awed them, scientists simply got frightened of all that was uncertain ahead of them. In their hands, they realized, was a power which stretched out beyond their vision. At the 1973 Gordon Conference in New Hampshire, the scientists decided to do the responsible thing, to openly voice their concern about what dangers lay beyond their sight. And later they moved to a voluntary ban on some experiments.

But the effect of the voluntary ban was something they had not expected. Their voluntary ban became involuntary when the ban hardened into federal regulations and finally into laws.

Expensive P3 laboratories had to be built. For a period of two or three years a number of experiments became impossible. Virtually every laboratory of advanced molecular biology in the nation was affected, with work delayed months or halted altogether. Of course, the most sensitive experiments were those with human genes. They were also the experiments which seemed the most important, for they were experiments to find the genetic base of human diseases.

In the first years after Asilomar, scientists as a group had changed their opinions rapidly, even though the public machinery they started ran on far beyond that time. It was two things, chiefly, which changed the minds of the biologists. One was a series of experiments conducted to determine the likelihood of an accident with *E. coli.* The particular strain of *E. coli* used in experiments, the K-12 strain, was tested to see how long it could survive in the human intestine alongside the wild and well-adapted *E. coli* that naturally lives there. The answer, roughly, was that the laboratory strain reproduced poorly and could not last more than a day under most circumstances. So the chance of such a bug causing disease and being spread from lab workers to the public began to appear near nil.

In addition to such experiments, molecular biologists soon learned a great deal from their colleagues in the branch of biology that dealt with infectious disease. They learned that it is no simple matter for a bacterium to become a disease-causing bacterium. Very few bacteria are capable of it, and any random combination of new traits added to bacteria are likely to make them less capable of it, not more so. For a bacterium in the intestine to become pathogenic it must acquire the ability to make a toxin. That toxin must be able to act specifically on a group of human cells. The bacterium producing it must be able to bind itself to the cell wall. It also must be able to defeat the human immune response.

But the reasoning that affected scientists in this matter did not spread to the public, as the alarm had. And in this, a political fact, the scientists were quite naive. It was not until the Cambridge hearings that Ptashne and others began to be awakened to the nature of the game.

"I was astounded by that meeting. Absolutely astounded. . . . I really thought that if one wrote this out and was very precise, and so on, it would just be like arguing in front of the [Harvard] Research Policy Committee. But it was just an unbelievable joke. Maxine Singer was introduced, and Velucci asked for her phone number."

"I guess . . . you just have to be very inexperienced to think that what you say matters . . . it doesn't," Ptashne says. "Only as I got to know them [the City Council members], and saw how they were lining up, and on what basis they were making their decisions, did I realize how foolish we were to think that an intelligent presentation in front of the council would make any difference. . . . We were being so anally precise. . . ."

Scientists had named the danger in very clear terms, and now it would not go away. Ptashne found, for example, that the argument that other things are more dangerous than recombinant DNA and yet are not tightly restricted, simply leads to the reply that those things ought to be stopped as well.

Behind it all is really no scientific argument, but a religious one. One opponent of mixed DNA research, Jonathan King of MIT, was asked in the Cambridge hearings whether he was even worried about the experiments classified safe enough to need no containment. King said yes. "I am personally, privately, organically afraid . . . It's tampering, as far as I'm concerned, at the most profound biological level. I hate to say it here publicly because my scientific colleagues, you know, are going to give me a lot of abuse. I think it's sacrilegious."

Says Ptashne, "My general belief is that if somebody wants to make the argument and attempts to make it on principle—that knowledge is dangerous—I'm sympathetic to that argument. . . . It's not a nonsensical argument." But, he says, "frankly I think some of these guys are just disingenuous about it. . . . What [they] say is 'These experiments are dangerous and therefore they should be stopped,' when what [they] really mean is the other argument [that knowledge itself is dangerous]. Then you're using a salient issue to play on people's general fears. . . . The tack you're using in doing that is dishonest."

In retrospect the Cambridge struggle was just another example of something that the scientists appeared to bring on themselves. The whole series of events was built on what appears now a foolish decision, politically, at least.

The containment lab being built at Harvard, which gave Velucci his opening to hold public hearings and pass a law, was intended originally to house the experiments of Thomas Maniatis. Maniatis wanted to work with SV40 monkey tumor virus. There was no rule or restriction at the time which said he could not simply sit down at the bench and go to work, with no precautions at all. Many labs were doing just that. "You have to be so dumb to get yourself into this position," Ptashne said later. "We were acting like a bunch of stupid children. The argument is this: Well, if we spend an extra half a million to be careful, people are going to love us, and they're going to think that the work's okay. And we can say to everyone: Look, those other guys grow SV40 on the bench top. We do it in a half-million-dollar lab.

"We made the mistake of assuming that people would appreciate our expensive efforts to be supercautious, to go beyond any reasonable safety requirement," Ptashne says. Joshua Lederberg of Stanford warned his colleagues against this approach. People do not react as scientists expect. "It's completely crazy," Ptashne says, "because what they do is—" And here Ptashne mimics arguments carried out over months:

They ask, "What if an ant walks in?"

Ptashne replies: "What if an ant walks in? It doesn't make any difference. The stuff's not dangerous."

"If it's not dangerous, why are you spending half a million dollars building the containment lab?"

"Well, okay," says Ptashne, "we'll try to get rid of the ants."

"But how can you get rid of every ant? There are little tiny ants in this building."

Reflecting on this argument, which actually took place in an expanded form, Ptashne says, "It got to be Looney Tunes. . . ."

Ptashne says there was one particular point that struck him rather hard, not precisely like Saul's conversion, but still a rather sudden strike at the heart. The meeting included some chemists, who as a group are more industry-oriented and conservative than most scientists. It included Ptashne and Jonathan King, an MIT biologist and probably the single most active and effective opponent of recombinant DNA work. At one moment King was saying, "All over the country, there are people who are arguing that we soon will have the technology to genetically engineer humans. It will change the people. It will change their genes . . ." He was holding up before the audience of scientists, to illustrate his point, a copy of MS. magazine with a screaming gene-engineering cover.

The scene "affected me personally somewhat," says Ptashne, "because I've always been, as I say, rather strongly tied to the Left and very skeptical of institutions and experts, and I generally regard the chemists as, on the whole, a reactionary lot. And yet, here I could see a case where what one desperately needed in this sea of absolute bullshit that we were being flooded with was some group of guys who would just ask what the facts were. I remember the chemists pressing King for numbers at some point and they were not getting them."

When he reflects on the recombinant DNA debate as it

stretched over nearly ten years, he begins to talk again about the war in Vietnam. The scientists' impulse at the beginning of the whole affair, to disclose in public their concern about safety, was an impulse born in that era.

But also in that era, the American Left was taught how to disbelieve "experts" and despise technology which the experts were hawking.

Definitions had shifted. "In my experience, the most striking misuse of rationality was manifested by people like McGeorge Bundy, Robert McNamara, Dean Rusk, and so on, who perpetrated and defended the war in Vietnam," Ptashne says. "It was they who misused rationality with disastrous consequences." But in the DNA wars, it was the Left which had become irrational, Ptashne says. And because of the confusion of responsibility, the serious questions raised by the Left are not being addressed. How well is technology used? What should the relationship between science and society be?

He says that he has always thought of basic science as a form of culture to be placed alongside art and music. Such serious questions as "Should people have the right to say what kind of basic science is practiced?" should be asked, and should be asked of all forms of culture. "Should people have the right to say what kind of music is composed? I happen to believe—and so did Plato—that what kind of music is composed is very important for what effect it has on people's lives . . . there are no simple answers to these things." He does not advocate regulation of culture, but the application of cultural work to social ends presents a serious problem.

It was not until 1982 that the federal regulations were, for the most part, lifted from biology. But the public attitude of suspicion remained, and so did the laws in some communities.

8

SOMETIME after the repressor work, Ptashne intensified his work at the violin, as if he were beginning a new career in it. He has played steadily since grade school, and so was no beginner. But he began an impassioned search for the right violin technique, and he acquired successively a large number of teachers in the effort.

His method of learning a subject, any subject, is well known to his friends. As Michael Fried, professor of art history at Johns Hopkins, says, it can be embarrassing if Mark chooses your own discipline as the subject he next intends to ravage. "Within two weeks he will know more important people than you have met in ten years. He will end up introducing you around in your own field."

The method is simple: a perpetual student, he picks up the telephone and calls this or that eminent scholar. This is how he sought a really good doctor for his aching back, a coach to teach him tennis, and several teachers to instruct him in the subtle techniques of the violin.

He began to rise in the morning and pick up his violin for two or three hours before going to the lab. A professional musician staying at Ptashne's house was surprised one morning by the sound of Ptashne playing; he told a friend that he was touched by the sound, and by the thought of a man Ptashne's age rising early every day to struggle with the instrument, to attempt to perfect his playing.

In this, music is unlike science. One's power may increase steadily with practice in music. The pleasures of discovery and the mastery of small matters are more frequent. The instrument and the muscles to be controlled are not capricious and evasive, as the truth about nature is. "Also," Ptashne says, "I perform occasionally at various scientific things, mostly because scientists don't expect too much. When I can control my muscles to the extent that I can play in tune, and can do it in front of other people, it's a tremendous kick, something you can't get out of science."

He elaborated in some detail on his experience of science and how it differs from his experience of music. "The experience of continuity, or of time itself, in experimental science is highly discontinuous. That is, viewed from within, things seem to be happening very, very slowly. The results lag behind the mind, I think, so that day in and day out, nothing seems to be happening. Viewed from a broader perspective, however, things, especially in a field like molecular biology, happen with astonishing swiftness and brutality. As Chargaff says, every few years, the mirror of science is shattered. . . .

"The point is," says Ptashne, "that the problems formulated at any given time with their associated flavors and aromas periodically disappear. Thus the problems you grow up with . . . are periodically destroyed in a rapidly moving field, and one must start over again. This means that continuity in science is not something that is easily experienced.

"Music is different. If one works at it seriously, then one's powers of expressiveness will gradually increase, and that is a most wonderful feeling. Spinoza's phrase is, I believe, that pleasure is the feeling that one's power is increasing. Here, we are talking about the power of expressiveness," Ptashne said.

He now takes lessons once a week at the New England Conservatory of Music. Every summer "religiously, I go to Italy to study chamber music. . . ."

But, in the 1970s, Ptashne had just achieved enough new skill that he decided to take a step up in the quality of violin he could own. "I have always been conscious of looking for a violin, and in fact, I think you could trace my economic status by what kind of violin I had at any given period of my life. So, for example, as an undergraduate I had one kind, and as a graduate student when I was slightly richer, I had another. As a junior fellow I could afford a slightly better one yet. I was always going into debt to buy the best violin I possibly could. I always had a rule, of course, as everybody should; namely, never to try with any seriousness a violin that was out of my price range," Ptashne says.

Ptashne had no intention of going the whole distance and buying a Stradivarius. He would have advised himself strongly against it. But he found himself once taking lessons from Joseph Silverstein, the concertmaster of the Boston Symphony Orchestra, and Silverstein was trying out a Stradivarius that a New York dealer had given him. Silverstein asked Ptashne to return the instrument to New York for him, as Ptashne was going down to the city in a few days.

"I took it home, played it for a week, and by the end of the third day, I could not sleep; I had visions about it. I was bewitched and seduced by the thing," Ptashne said.

Ptashne had by now risen to a reasonably large academic salary and a professorship, and had acquired some prize money. So he was looking for a violin of quality, one that might cost tens of thousands of dollars. He had tried a number of the Italian instruments fashioned in the seventeenth century—the Amati, the Guarnieri. But finally, against his own and others' advice, and with no hope of actually putting together the sum that the thing cost, Ptashne decided nonetheless he must have the instrument.

In typical Ptashne manner, he approached Harvard's president Derek Bok and attempted to convince him that Harvard should make him a loan. He reasoned that Harvard made special loans to faculty members so that their children might attend college; he is a bachelor and this would be the closest thing in his life to a child; therefore, Harvard should consider the two situations equivalent and lend him the money. Harvard considered, and declined, though it did help him get a rather large loan at a local bank. Still, he needed more money, and he decided that because the violin's value could do nothing but increase, the natural way of financing it would be to sell shares in the violin which he could later buy out. Eventually, he managed to do it.

After purchase of the violin, within a year he had also bought a fine house in Cambridge. He learned to care for the violin daily, and filled out the house with art, carpets, and furniture. His relations with women gradually began to change into a single long-standing commitment. He was tidying up the world as he grew older.

The change also extended to the laboratory, chiefly in how he treated those who worked under him. In the years just after he isolated the repressor, when he was about thirty years old, said James Watson who was his mentor at the time, "Mark was hopelessly irresponsible for other people; he is getting a sense of responsibility now. Mark is self-centered and really didn't care about other people. He was interested in other people—I was probably the same way—only when they were interesting."

Ptashne's method of teaching is to demand much and praise little. He is a sharp and intelligent critic. As one friend assessed it, "There is a brusque, businesslike exterior . . . but he is a very generous person and a tremendous educator. I think he has the capacity to change people when they come in contact with him. He's very abrasive, sometimes because he can't stand a person, but often because he cares and really wants to get under your skin. He really wants to tell you that you ought to be buying a different kind of comforter because it ought to have down feathers in it. Or you really ought not to be eating so much cholesterol. Or you shouldn't have such and such a record player, or shouldn't like Stern's intonation or whatever. He's always taking on causes and making people think their way through things."

The method, said Ptashne's friend, is "not for the weak, or for the gentle, or for the modest. But I think there's a great deal of caring there . . ."

The chief, recurring theme in conversation among the students and laboratory workers was, at least in the first years he ran a laboratory, Ptashne's harshness. Though he was fair, and concerned, he was unable to take an amiable attitude toward students and their work. The ambition he applied so ferociously to himself he began to apply to those under him. His common mode of communication was to make critical remarks or to press for progress on a project. For some it was a powerful stimulus; others left the lab.

Says Ptashne, defending his aggressive style: "I think my methods can be misinterpreted. I do needle and goad students, at least those for whom I have the greatest respect. The reason is that most people do not understand just how difficult science is, how difficult it is to do something truly first-rate or original. Many of the people who have the ability to do it, do not, because they don't realize the extent to which they must extend themselves.

"A potentially creative young scientist can sink into cynicism if his early efforts are all failures; one taste of success can inspire a career," Ptashne says. So he pushes the best students rather hard.

He goes on: "Students tend to be too conservative, not appreciating that ideas can come from anywhere, and that there are many different styles, influenced by personality, that contribute to science. . . . Being lackadaisical with people is not always the way to succeed in this endeavor."

As evidence of his success, he gives a list of some of the students he trained who have succeeded: Nancy Hopkins, the lab assistant who became a full professor at MIT; Bob Sauer, a graduate student who moved directly into an assistant professorship at MIT; Thomas Maniatis, the postdoctoral fellow who became a full professor at Cal Tech and then at Harvard with his own lab. The list goes on—Barbara Meyer of MIT, Lenny Guarente of MIT, Carl Pabo of Harvard, Tom Roberts of the Harvard Medical School.

Ptashne is one of those chiefly responsible for building the current strong department of molecular biology at Harvard. It cannot be said that the Ptashne style has no results to show for it.

The characteristic mood of the Ptashne style is impatience. "He is constantly in a hurry," said Tom Maniatis, once a worker under Ptashne and now a notable molecular biologist. Maniatis recalled visiting England with Ptashne. Ptashne drove too fast, once nearly mowing down a queue waiting for a bus when he forgot which side of the road he should be driving on.

Another time when he was in a rush, he left a broken hood latch partly open so he wouldn't have to pry it open later. The hood blew open at sixty miles per hour and sent him off the road into a ditch.

"This is characteristic," said Maniatis. "He sometimes ends up doing things in a haphazard way, and it ends in disaster." In the lab he would try to rush experiments and sometimes end with no result because he forgot a step. "The great concern in the lab," said Maniatis with a grin, "was when he would not be teaching and so he'd come in and say, 'I finally have all these things finished. I'm going to get into the lab.' We all threw up our hands. The classic image of Ptashne is a picture of him rushing around, dropping a tube, and frantically trying to recover an experiment by pipetting it off the floor."

In one often-recounted experiment, a large number of tiny circular filters were used to identify genetic material. Each should have been carefully labeled and held in place with a pin. Ptashne did not trouble with detailed labeling; he dropped the tiny bits of filter on the floor and was found by lab workers on his hands and knees studying the disaster, trying to reconstruct the array and determine which was which.

In the laboratory during the 1970s, the question Ptashne and his team were working on was how, at the level of molecules, does the gene direct the production of important substances. There is, as Ptashne and others found, a series of purely mechanical signals which are quite important in the process.

The substance which binds to the DNA and begins to read it, as a recording head picks up sound from a tape, must first be attracted to a "start" sequence, or set of signals, on the DNA at the beginning of the gene. A second set of signals, important in going from gene to gene product, is one that is used to facilitate reading later in the process, when the DNA has been transcribed into RNA, which must then be used as a template to make the desired molecular product.

The strength of these signals at the start of a gene determines how efficiently the cell will make what is coded in the gene. This efficiency is measured by the number of molecules of the desired substance actually produced in the cell.

Ptashne found that it is possible to make an artificially strong sequence of commands that would get a cell to produce far more than usual. He linked together more than one of the start sequences to achieve a hundred to a thousand times the ordinary rate of production in the cell.

It is at this point that a glimmer appears in the eye of the businessman. It is possible to view the cell as a miniature machine which naturally manufactures a large variety of interesting substances. A large number of the things made by cells cannot yet be made by man, and so the most important ones must be collected from dead bodies. In other cases, getting cells to make a substance in relatively large quantities may be cheaper than some manufacturing processes.

Many things made by cells have immediate application to medicine, for example, the hormones. Shortages of one or another hormone cause disease or gross defects. Human-growth hormone is lacking in dwarfs; some of the stuff is now collected bit by bit from cadavers, and the result is an extremely expensive drug that is not widely available. A twist on the same idea might be to enhance the bulk of cattle with bovine-growth hormone mixed in the animals' feed.

Insulin is now fairly cheap and effective, but what is being used by humans is pig insulin. Human insulin is chemically just a little different. It may not matter, but the pharmaceutical companies realize what a selling point they would have if they could offer human rather than pig insulin to their customers. Advantage or no, it could be sold.

Male hormones and female hormones also have their uses. The endorphins, a related group of substances which appear to be the body's natural pain-killing chemicals and which flood the system during childbirth and other desperate moments, might be a candidate for mass manufacture by cells. Vasopressin, a drug which appears to restore or enhance memory, is another candidate.

Another class of useful and profitable substances are the vaccines. Genetic technology may be able to produce vaccines for hepatitis, malaria, venereal disease, and a variety of agriculturally important diseases such as foot-and-mouth. Enzymes, proteins that act to trigger some chemical reactions, are also among the materials now being eyed by gene-technology companies. They can help transform sugars into alcohol, they can be used to separate ores from rock.

Even more interesting are the chemicals made by the human immune system. This is not merely one cell making one useful chemical product. Rather, it is a system that produces tens of millions or hundreds of millions of different kinds of molecules. The problem faced by the immune system is that it leads the body's defenses against invading foreign substances. There are viruses, bacteria, poisons, and other damaging chemicals in the environment which can enter the body in significant amounts. These must be recognized and disabled by the immune system. But of course the system cannot know ahead of time which of the millions of hazards in the world will suddenly enter and endanger the body.

Still, the immune system succeeds not only against common hazards, but also against substances that did not exist on earth before man created them. The immune system also has in it already the ability to disable substances not yet conceived by man or nature.

The system manages this with antibodies. Each antibody is a molecule of a slightly different form. Because of the differing forms of the molecules, each type of antibody made is specific; it chemically recognizes and binds itself to one hazardous substance. Of course, there is some overlap. A few different antibodies may find and attach themselves to different parts of the surface of the incoming, dangerous molecules. But primarily, one antibody is responsible for disabling one foreign substance.

If the genetic system made these antibodies by the simplest method, however, the effort would overwhelm the system. There are only a million or so different genes in the entire human complement of DNA. But the immune system would need a hundred million all to itself to make the necessary antibodies.

So the immune system instead makes each antibody in four basic parts. There are a different set of genes for each of the four parts, so that the possible combinations become very large. Of half a dozen genes, any one may make part one, while from another group of genes one is chosen to make part two, while from a group of a few hundred genes one is picked to make part three, and so on. The process is like making billions of poker hands with only fifty-two cards. Hundreds of millions of antibodies are made with only a few hundred genes.

In the body, each cell in the immune system picks one variety of antibody, one poker hand, and permanently produces only that one kind of antibody. Thus when a foreign substance enters the body, it faces different antibodies from tens or hundreds of millions of cells. One of the cells makes the antibody that fits this particular foreign substance. Then, the action of an antibody locking itself onto an incoming substance becomes a trigger, setting off a rapid increase in the growth of the one cell line that makes the antibody which successfully found its target.

For businesses, the important part of all this is the active, binding parts of the antibodies. The genes for just these active parts can be cloned. This will produce a reagent, a chemical with the specific property of binding to another particular chemical.

Such one-on-one binding could be a useful and profitable tool. (There is even one new gene-engineering company, called DNAX, devoting itself entirely to making these bits of antibodies.) In the treatment of high blood pressure, there is a substance called renin which doctors would like to draw out of the system to reduce blood pressure. A chemical that might bind to renin, rendering it harmless, could offer a new approach to the treatment of hypertension.

Some poisons people swallow cannot be removed from the body fast enough to prevent death or severe damage to the system. Digitalis, barbiturates, tranquilizers, and even aspirin present some difficulties for emergency room doctors. None of the present methods of counteracting these poisons acts directly on the dangerous molecules, but only indirectly. Some of the filtering processes are long and expensive. Some produce serious side effects of their own. So a chemical that might enter the body, bind itself to the poison, and allow the two to be harmlessly flushed out of the system would be important and possibly profitable.

Other possibilities for the immune system's molecules are new industrial filtration techniques and drug purification.

If an antibody's active site can be linked up to a large chain molecule to give it weight, the two together can capture most any chemical and hold it in a filter while other things wash through. The many costly industrial processes, such as filtering pollutants and purifying chemical products, are now carried out by laborious methods of many steps. An antibody filter could be an inexpensive, one-step method of doing the same thing.

One of the chief concerns about proteins such as insulin and interferon is the difficulty of removing impurities from them. It is often the impurities in drugs which give them their worst side effects. Another use for a sensitive filter might be in intravenous feeding. Any time a patient must be fed through tubes, there is a danger that bacteria can get into the system and introduce their toxins into the liquid. The reactions can be severe.

Because Ptashne had coaxed *E. coli* into making large numbers of the repressor molecule, up to a thousand times what *E. coli* on its own would make, Ptashne was very early doing things of interest to the growing gene-engineering trade. The whole basis of commercial gene-engineering is the ability of biologists to manipulate genes in a way that will get microbes to overproduce some chemical. They commonly insert a hundred copies of the gene for the desired substance. They also insert extra "start" signals to get the manufacture under way more effectively.

By 1980, Ptashne got a chance to try producing a medically interesting chemical when Japanese researcher Tadatsugu Taniguchi spent some months in Ptashne's lab. At the Foundation for Cancer Research in Japan, Taniguchi had successfully purified from human cells a variety of interferon called fibroblast interferon.

Interferon is a protein whose function in the body appears to be defense against invading viruses, and possibly against the growth of cancers as well. Little is known of the mechanism of interferon, but cells challenged by viruses begin producing it. Unlike antibodies of the immune system, interferon does not attack the viruses directly. Rather, it appears to be a messenger. It leaves the challenged cells and migrates to neighboring, healthy cells, where somehow it starts production of substances that prevent the virus from using the cell's machinery to reproduce and continue their invasion.

Interferon is the most general and promising agent yet tested against viral infections. Vaccines, the primary treatment, are limited to defense against a single viral type. They also carry the danger of accidental infection with the very disease they are trying to prevent. Toxic antiviral chemicals are now being tested but have not yet reached general use, and apparently carry some strong side effects. Interferon has so far been tested with some success against a range of viral infections, including rabies, herpes, chicken pox, German measles, and hepatitis.

Some years after interferon began to be tested as an antiviral agent, Ion Gresser, an American researcher working in France, tried interferon against tumors in mice because a number of animal tumors are known to be caused by viruses. It stopped early tumors and shrank others; within a few years interferon began to be thought of as one of the chief hopes for cancer treatment. But the substance was extremely rare, since the cells manufacture it in quantities countable in molecules rather than milligrams.

By 1980, when I first visited Ptashne's lab, a fierce competition had developed among the new gene-engineering companies to make interferon. Ptashne's lab was in the contest, for better or worse.

9

THE first night I met Mark Ptashne, at his fortieth birthday party in the summer of 1980, I also encountered the new wave in commercial biology. At the party were a number of people from Ptashne's lab, and Keith Backman, the former Ptashne lab member now at MIT.

Backman had worked under Ptashne for a number of years. When Backman got his Ph.D. and left for MIT, the relations between the two were tense and difficult. Backman later became a consultant to Genentech, teaching its staff the tricks which had been worked out in some detail in Ptashne's lab. Gradually the ill feeling between the two faded, and on that warm June night, Backman came to the crowded party at Ptashne's.

Genentech was one of several companies working on the problem of interferon and how microbes might be coaxed to make this famous protein. Ptashne at the time led no company but appeared on the verge of joining one, and his lab was also deep into the problem of interferon. Another company on the same trail was Biogen, with Walter Gilbert competing for them against Ptashne, Genentech, and one or two others.

By the summer of 1980, Biogen had announced that it had made interferon by gene-engineering methods. Actually, it had produced only a precursor molecule of interferon, but a press conference was held nonetheless and the stock of Biogen's parent, Schering Plough, jumped in value and the paper worth of

Biogen rose from fifty million dollars to a hundred million dollars. (The Securities and Exchange Commission later investigated the timing of that press conference to see if anyone may have profited illegally from it, but eventually the investigation was dropped.)

At the time of Ptashne's party, Genentech was preparing its own announcement. Rumor had put Genentech's production of interferon at ten thousand molecules per cell—a substantial quantity, large enough for commercial production. Backman had helped in Genentech's jump forward, and at the party he was pressed several times to talk about the work. Was ten thousand units right? Ptashne's lab had that much too, but no sooner were the molecules produced than they seemed to be degraded. The final result was a count of no more than one thousand per cell. How did Genentech overcome this degrading?

In watching Backman I saw something I had never seen before in several years of traveling among academic scientists. Backman refused to talk about the Genentech results. "I can't," Backman said. "You know I can't."

Not long afterward I was speaking to one of the researchers in Ptashne's lab, Tom Roberts, and asked about the methods used to produce interferon. He refused to talk about it. I asked about what the obstacles were in general terms. Again he refused, saying he didn't know me and so couldn't speak. It took me some days before I realized what he was saying—that I might not be trusted with the information. I was not sure, finally, whether I was accused of being a gene spy.

Ptashne found the incident "rather shocking. I cannot understand why Roberts would not talk to you. It is silly. . . . There is a lot of spoken concern about secrecy, and so on, but I think it is mostly misplaced." The actual number of times such secrecy occurs, he feels, is small and at variance with the usual openness of his lab.

But the reports continue to circulate nevertheless. Later I heard of bitter battles over who owned genes and the methods of gene splicing. Lawsuits were begun in California. In one laboratory locks had been installed on refrigerators and lab doors.

For biology, fear and secrecy were largely new. Until the

middle of the 1970s, the scientists in molecular biology seemed little different than monks toiling in scholarly poverty and obscurity. Openness was one of the chief virtues practiced. They discussed results openly. They sent one another not only ideas, but also samples of their work in tissue cultures and extracted genes.

Graduate students who wanted to work in the field were expected to live on salaries at the poverty line. Those with new doctorates were expected to take laboratory jobs paying in the ten-thousand-dollar range, while graduates in law, business, and medicine from comparable schools received two or three times as much.

As a compensation, the biologists had their intellectual purity. There was a special honor in the poverty of the dedicated researcher, and a suggestion that money could not tempt a talented biologist from the rigors of his work. Industrial laboratories were full of secrets and unimagination.

But suddenly in the mid-1970s biologists emerged from their cells, blinking. They found themselves in demand. Their science had not only begun to master the principal mechanism of life, but the mechanism turned out to be exploitable. It might clone dollars as easily as genes.

The standard tale of biotechnology is the story of Genentech. Though it was not the first gene-engineering company, it was probably second or third. In 1976, an employee of a venture capital firm, Robert Swanson, who has a degree in biology, became interested in exploiting the promise of gene-engineering. He sought out Herbert Boyer of the University of California at San Francisco, one of the three or four scientists credited with inventing gene splicing. Boyer and Swanson each put up five hundred dollars. Within the next four years, Genentech had announced bench successes in making, by gene-engineering, human insulin, interferon, human-growth hormone, and a brain hormone.

On October 14, 1980, the company went public, asking buyers to pay thirty-five dollars a share even though the company had no products. Within twenty minutes of the time trading began, the stock price rose to eighty-nine dollars per share, one of the better performances by a new stock in market history. Between breakfast and lunch, Swanson and Boyer each made, on paper, about eighty-two million dollars. Though that paper money has since deflated considerably, the two are still millionaires many times over.

"This whole business thing is really fascinating," says Tom Maniatis. "It is fascinating to see the effect on the minds of all these scientists." The arguments over what is happening to biology and biologists include "the worry about whether you should dive into the money pile, or whether the pile is corrupting everybody."

At first, he says, those who began to consult for a fee with gene companies were criticized. Over the years, academic "purity is something which developed out of necessity. Since there was no money, a sense of saintlihood was required in the situation. Now it's not required."

The best academic researchers could now name their price. Ptashne was pursued by several companies. One offer stunned him a little. "They actually told me I could name any amount. Literally write my own check," he says. A postdoctoral researcher in his lab was making about eleven thousand; to join their company full time, Genentech offered him more than thirty thousand. Plus stock, and a chance to increase his salary rapidly.

Though commercial consulting arrangements are common among faculty members in law and business, as well as sciences such as chemistry and computing, somehow the entry of commerce into biology still did not seem natural. Because of this setting apart, once again a national debate began about the new biology, and once again Ptashne was a chief player. This time the fight was not with the city of Cambridge, but among academics themselves.

Ptashne had resisted offers from companies for several years. Partly, he felt that it was the universities who should stand to gain from the biology they had created. But when Harvard approached him with the idea that his work was quickly applicable to industry, Ptashne doubted it. He also defended pure, academic science and tried to set himself apart from Wally Gilbert, who had made the transition to corporate gene work easily.

The university did finally get Ptashne to file for a patent on his methods for expressing large amounts of gene product in a cell. A venture capital company in the General Electric family of companies, Business Services Development, Inc., made an offer to Harvard of about half a million dollars to make use in some way of Ptashne's work.

It was then that serious negotiating began between Steven Atkinson of Harvard's Committee on Patents and Copyrights and industry. From early in the negotiations it was clear that both sides wanted to create a separate company to exploit Ptashne's methods, and that company should be owned partly by Harvard.

The negotiations continued at length, and Ptashne was introduced to an entirely new world of people in the fast lane of speculative business. In a conversation with writer Michael VerMeulen, Steven Atkinson said of the time, "So many people were chasing Mark Ptashne that I could get a dozen executive vice presidents to fly into Boston just by calling their corporations' main switchboards and saying we would like to discuss Ptashne technologies." Among the supplicants at the professor's door were Cetus, Genentech, Eli Lilly, Abbott, Hoffmann-La Roche, and Pfizer.

The negotiations went on and gradually the role for Harvard and faculty members like Ptashne was altered substantially from an early position in which Harvard might have fifty percent of the stock and university professors might participate in managing the company, have equity in it, and maintain their positions at Harvard. Eventually, when the matter was presented before the faculty, the proposal was far simpler. The company would have no Harvard management, no Harvard name or facilities, and Harvard would no longer even put up some of the capital. Harvard would merely have owned some 10 percent or so of the shares. In exchange for that, the company would have the right to use Ptashne's work and whatever patents came out of it.

But before the wrangling was over, the original GE company offer was out, and other companies were in and bidding. The Harvard patent committee which started the whole thing was out, and the Harvard Management Corporation was in. But matters became more entangled, until finally Ptashne decided he himself would jump into the action. He got a call from William Paley, chairman of CBS, who was interested in investing in biotechnology, and told Ptashne that all the scrapping among the lawyers and businessmen was not making the deal any better and that Ptashne himself could do better. And he did.

As might be expected, once Ptashne was drawn into the arrangement, he began to shape it himself. Paley was brought into the negotiations, and where the Harvard management failed to put together a deal with subordinates in the interested firms, Ptashne went directly to the company leaders and succeeded. Besides Paley, Benno Schmidt of the prestigious J. H. Whitney and Company venture capital firm was brought in. Venrock, the venture capital firm of the Rockefeller family came in, and also a venture company called Greylock.

Ptashne found himself enjoying the role of business entrepreneur. Not long after his fortieth birthday, Ptashne explained his entry into business. "If all this had happened a year or two ago, when I was still in the midst of despair understanding how the lambda works, I probably wouldn't have done it." Winding up work on lambda, as it seemed to him then, after fifteen years' work, left him open. "That, plus becoming forty, God knows. And the desire to see my whole extended family [from the laboratory] reassembled again" under the aegis of a new business.

Tom Maniatis, who eventually joined Ptashne in consulting for the company, gave an added reason. There was, beyond the pure interest in business and getting a good bunch of people together, also the sense of making some kind of hard practical contribution to the world. This was not often directly possible in academic science.

Then, too, there was the money. "I think Mark wants to make money. He wants to be rich—there's no ifs, ands, or buts about that. And Mark, of course, wants to do that in the same style that he does science. He wants to do it big and he wants it to be interesting while he's doing it."

Ptashne says that it would have taken an enormous effort of will to stay out of the business entirely. "Having been one of the few molecular biologists who worked in this area [of getting overproduction from bacteria], having one of the leading labs in this area—to have no commercial relations whatsoever is almost . . . it's mind-boggling. I'm courted every single day.

Yesterday, some guy offered me literally millions of dollars to go direct a research outfit on the West Coast. . . . He said any price. Any price!"

But more fascinating to him is the entry into a new field. Putting the company together "is like a puzzle with five thousand loose pieces. It's night and day, up and down, this guy's out, that guy's in. The money's in, the money's out. The building's here, then . . . It's all quite extraordinary."

In the fall of 1980, rumors of the "Harvard company" spread through the campus, and though the Harvard faculty had no official power in the matter, enough negative comments were heard that Bok felt he had better openly bring the matter before the faculty. Harvard already had a financial interest in T. A. Associates, a venture capital firm which owned part of Biogen, the company Walter Gilbert helped to found.

But a company in which Harvard has direct ownership at the same time Harvard professors are key consultants and board members seemed a different matter. Some members of the faculty thought the situation might change the way research is chosen at Harvard. The possibility of profit for Harvard might draw scientists and their superiors toward practical, profitable research instead of research that is only intellectually exciting.

The idea of a "Harvard company" infuriated Walter Gilbert. It would put him in the position of competing against Harvard with his own company. He did not mind competing against other companies, even with Harvard professors as their consultants. But he said he did not want to fight against a company that would, in some sense, be Harvard's own.

After a bitter debate among the faculty, a debate that was reported nationally, Derek Bok announced on November 17 that Harvard "has decided not to become a minority shareholder in a new corporation in which one or two of its professors will play a prominent role. The preservation of academic values is a matter of paramount importance to the university," Bok said, "and owning shares in such a company would create a number of potential conflicts with these values."

Finally, although Derek Bok had at one time tentatively committed Harvard to the deal, it was he who halted it and gave the clearest summary of reasons why a company linked with Harvard might conceivably be dangerous to the academy:

"First, the prospect of reaping financial rewards may subtly influence professors in choosing which problems they wish to investigate. Academic scientists have always feared what Vannevar Bush once termed 'the perverse law governing research,' that 'applied research invariably drives out pure.'

". . . [Another] danger is the risk of introducing secrecy into the process of scientific research. Secrecy, of course, is anathema to scientific progress, since new discoveries must build upon what is already known. . . .

"The final danger is a threat to the quality of leadership and ultimately to the state of morale within the scientific enterprise . . . The traditional ideal of science was based on a disinterested search for knowledge without ulterior motives of any kind . . ."

It was not clear why the current interests of professors and the university had not already caused these kinds of academic erosion. Or perhaps they already had. But this debate was an emotional one. The outcome was finally decided not by which arguments were the stronger, but simply by the fact that enough faculty members had created enough sparks and noise that the university, politically speaking, could not afford to put itself in the awkward position of appearing to go commercial.

The Harvard decision began a debate that was heard at all the major universities and in several hearings on Capitol Hill. Stanford declared itself against such arrangements. MIT soon made a deal with the wealthy Whitehead family which went several steps further than the Harvard arrangement. It even provided for twenty faculty members to have joint appointments at a Whitehead Institute and at MIT. Control of these faculty members and their graduate students was to be shared between the nonprofit institute and MIT. The financial arrangements between companies and universities continued to increase. The effects of these new ties are still being debated.

Though Harvard stepped out of the deal, the company went ahead, with Ptashne and others at Harvard in tow. Called Genetics Institute it was one of the last well-respected and well-financed groups to join the overcrowded pack of new gene-engineering companies.

In fact, by the end of 1981 the gold rush in biotechnology

had virtually ended, at least its first phase, though not before an official count had put the number of new gene-engineering companies at 150. Gabriel Schmergel, the new president of Genetics Institute said, "I know of seventy-five or more companies in the field, out of which one third or one half exist only on paper." It was estimated that more than four hundred million dollars in venture capital had been put into the new companies by the fall of 1981. Most of it was generated on the basis of expectations that were intentionally generated by such things as Biogen's press conference and Genentech's press releases. Eventually the claims came to be seen as dangerous exaggerations.

Genentech, one of the most successful companies in the field, began to complain openly about exaggerated hopes and claims. Genetics Institute's Schmergel said, "What I am concerned about is the hype. What has been exaggerated is the short-term profits. Highly exaggerated. It's exaggerated by people who have a self-interest because they want to issue stock." In that sort of situation, "many people will get hurt," he said, especially the average investor who cannot easily distinguish good investment risks and bad ones.

The deflation which naturally follows exaggeration began in 1981. By the end of that year, virtually all biotechnology stocks had dropped. An index of the stocks, put together by the investment firm of Dean Witter Reynolds in April of 1981, dropped steadily from the beginning. It fell thirty-five percent between spring and fall, while the Dow Jones stock average fell only 14 percent. From Genentech's peak of eighty-nine dollars a share in 1980, the company's stock slipped gradually until it dropped past its opening price of thirty-five dollars and hit bottom near twenty-six dollars.

At the end of the year, Scott King, a biotechnology stock analyst for the brokerage firm of F. Eberstadt in New York, said, "A year ago, any deal that was proposed got made. Now it's much harder. I know of several private stock sales that fell through." One such failure was the $50 million deal between E. F. Hutton and DNA Sciences. It collapsed because not enough money could be raised.

Of more than a hundred companies competing in the market,

Scott King believes that no more than two dozen will survive. Though he is still enthusiastic about the prospects for gene engineering, he is not enthusiastic about the gene companies as an investment. Progress in such things as the study of the immune system, he said, "in a few years is going to be the most important thing in all of medicine. I am tremendously excited by it. . . . But there is too much competition among these companies already. The way to make money is—don't compete. If there are too many in the field, it becomes a price war. You don't make money in a price war."

What many investors did not realize about the biotechnology boom is that the companies will take five to ten years to show the certain signs of success or failure. In other industries, the first profit is expected in less than three years. The difference, chiefly, is in the whims of bacteria.

One-celled animals that are easy to handle in the test tubes, and can be readily coaxed into producing valuable chemicals by methods such as those Ptashne worked out, behave differently when asked to grow in great metal tanks. The trouble is not with the gene-engineering end of the work. It is the same trouble faced by other industries which depend on growing microorganisms. Because the animals must devote most of their energy to making a useless, foreign substance, they cannot defend themselves against natural hazards. Small temperature changes can become fatal. Contamination may be the most serious problem: If only a few organisms of the wild type are present among the billions of domesticated ones, or can enter the tanks through leaks, a researcher may come in one morning to find his tank of engineered bacteria dead at the hands of a horde of wild bacteria which have quickly taken over the tank. One British company, ICI, spent twelve years trying to get its big fermentation vat working properly, and wrote in its report of the struggle: "The number of individual manual operations of valves, instruments, and pumps can, even for the pilot plant, run to many hundreds. Failure to observe the precise sequence can lead to . . . failure by contamination in a few days."

However long it takes gene companies to produce their first marketable product, one problem that will remain is the effect commercial ventures will have on universities and the way biology is conducted in them. Ptashne believes that much of the worry is needless, though secrecy is something to be avoided. He tried to help establish Genetics Institute with special ties to Harvard in order to keep lines of communication open.

Now, though, he believes the separation of the two is best. "I keep the two entirely separate. Applied research, goal-oriented research of a very high level goes on at the Genetics Institute. . . . In my lab at Harvard, more basic matters continue to be investigated concerning genes and the mechanisms by which they are controlled," Ptashne says. "I also find, in a curious way, that my connection with Genetics Institute makes my research path at Harvard clearer; that is, far from corrupting that work at Harvard, it frees it to be pure and directed along lines that could be of no direct interest to the company. Any more direct commercial interests that I might have are then satisfied by the company itself."

One of the more subtle effects of commercialization may in the long run be the final, residual effect of the whole matter. University biology departments have been one place people might turn for the opinion of dispassionate scholars. But if there are no molecular biologists without company connections, this may no longer be true. Conflicts of interest, though they may not matter most of the time, will be the rule. It is already apparently true that there is no notable biologist in this field anywhere in America who is not working in some way for a business. I interviewed some two dozen of the best molecular biologists in the country and found none.

The best hope, biologists say, is that eventually the interests of the academics and the companies will diverge again. In a few years most of the companies will have failed. The academics will again set off down avenues of no immediate interest to the companies. Then, if no permanent damage has been done, the monks and merchants once again will go their separate ways.

10

THE last time Ptashne and I talked, it was again in his kitchen, again over a chicken and wine, in the summer of 1981. I had been visiting with him every so often for nearly a year, but he was no less nervous about having agreed to put himself in the hands of a journalist. He continued to tell me stories about journalists he had encountered. One writer from the *Boston Globe*, he said, listened while Ptashne explained at length the details of recombinant DNA and why it was not the danger it had been portrayed. After listening for some time, according to Ptashne, the writer said, "I have never seen anyone explain it all so patiently, and completely reasonably. But still I just know in my heart of hearts that this science is potentially evil, that it is dangerous, and is all the more dangerous when a person explaining it appears so rational."

Ptashne reiterated: "People tell me I'm crazy for doing this." He paused. "You know, the standard objection to these things is that what gets lost in the story is the science and the real reason one is doing the science. Instead there appear all these peripheral things. . . .

"For me, and maybe it's just an indication that I'm an old fart, things like the recombinant DNA and all that other stuff were done in order to solve the lambda problem. What you will find is that other people may jump from thing to thing; sometimes that's very effective. But it's a different thing to be intellectually and emotionally and physically committed to one problem. This can be worse or better, but it is what I have done."

Despite his reservations, Ptashne was excited to be able to talk about his work. He had just come back from Cold Spring Harbor laboratory on Long Island where he had given a talk on his work as it stood then. At the time, he thought his fifteen-year bout of work was essentially over; he had described the whole picture of the lambda sleeper system for the first time. Those who listened, including James Watson and Francis Crick, found in Ptashne's description a little epiphany. It was the first complete, pictorial description of a tiny molecular co-operation—no more than two molecules leaning against one another—that controlled the balance of an entire biological system.

"As I told you, I have gone through periods of real depression with this thing," Ptashne said as he took a bottle of white wine from the refrigerator. He was told more than once that he had finished with lambda and he could go do something else. He stayed with lambda and sometimes regretted it. Though he might again regret it tomorrow, on this night he was pleased. "I have stayed with this lambda thing for—I don't know how many years now, practically speaking all of my scientific career." He popped the cork on the wine bottle. "Through all that time we have developed these techniques for recombinant DNA, and done this and that other thing, all of which were done for one intellectual point. And now, just now, in the last few months, have we been able to formulate in simple and elegant terms how the system works and why it works the way it does."

He said that biologists did not recognize it before, but that organisms have a serious problem that must be overcome. Having worked out the biochemistry of it, now it's clear that the difficulty does indeed exist: how can genes be kept steadily in one state, and then, when challenged by some change in the environment, switch rapidly and efficiently to another way of operating?

First there was the idea of the repressor. Genes could simply be turned off by such a chemical. That would explain the possible existence of two states, on and off.

But how it might actually switch back and forth was not clear. Ptashne moved from the simple repressor idea to the realization that there was a double-repressor system. The lambda system has only two states: one in which the lambda genes are dormant and the repressor holds them in as well as helping to make plenty of repressor to keep the state stable. The other state is one that can be triggered by, for example, a dose of ultraviolet light or the entry of a carcinogen into the cell— many things that might endanger the cell. In this state, the second repressor, called cro, operates. Its job is to shut down the first repressor, thereby allowing the lambda genes free to produce new lambdas, which can then escape the endangered cell.

Working with Tom Maniatis, Barbara Meyer, and others, he found that the repressor mechanism operates in a complete loop, like those which form the basis of computer programs. It regulates itself. The details, in rough terms, are these:

We can picture the *E. coli,* grazing and gently spinning its motorized flagella. The small lambda settles on the outside of *E. coli,* like a mosquito, and inserts a protein syringe into the *coli.* Through the syringe it injects DNA into the bacterium. The parasite now can either use the *E. coli*'s gene machinery to manufacture more of its kind. Or, it may become dormant. There is some speculation about why it might like to wait for a thousand generations before reproducing. Perhaps it is a mechanism to avoid bursting out into some environment not suited for it.

When the lambda has become dormant, virtually the only one of its fifty genes that is working is the repressor gene. It must make repressor to keep the lambda in its sleeping state, and it does this simply by sitting on the "start" signal just ahead of all the lambda genes. Because of the presence of the repressor, the enzymes which normally would begin reading the lambda DNA and carrying out their instructions do not recognize the genes as sequences to be read. There must be a free, recognizable "start" signal to attract the enzymes of transcription.

This much was shown, roughly, by Ptashne's early repressor experiments. But the intricacy of the system only became clear later: There is another repressor in the system. This one represses the repressor. The system is a closed circle, like the M. C.

cher work entitled *Drawing Hands,* which depicts two hands
on a piece of paper each using a pencil to draw the other.

Under normal circumstance, the repressor remains in place
and keeps this second repressor silent. But there are substances
that can change this balance and allow the second repressor to
come out and repress the first. It is during what biologists call
the SOS response, when *E. coli* begins to be damaged by any of
a number of materials, the cell releases an enzyme that cleaves
all sorts of repressors up and down the DNA, allowing a number of silent genes to be expressed. They are genes that make
enzymes to repair damaged structures in the cell that must be
quickly put to use.

As it happens, one of these repair enzymes, called Rec A,
cleaves the lambda repressor. It cuts it exactly in half and
renders it unable to hold back the lambda virus any longer.
The repressor can no longer block the "start" signal. The first
of the lambda genes freed, it turns out, is the one that orders
manufacture of a second repressor which returns to block the
first repressor's gene.

Repressing the repressor is important in switching the system
from one stable state—producing repressor and holding back
lambda—to the next state—producing lambda and holding
back the repressor. In fact, the double-repressor mechanics of
the system work so that the change of state occurs quite suddenly.

It appears, says Ptashne, almost as if the lambda virus could
detect an insult to the cell, and so breaks out to evade the
danger. To a novice, the whole elaborate scheme also has the
appearance of a Rube Goldberg sort of machine. But it provides an important biological model for fast-switching systems.

The molecular details of the act are important, and the
switch works like this: The place that repressors act to shut
down a gene is called a binding site, or in the confusing biological jargon, an operator. In lambda this binding area, or operator, is split into three separate sites where the repressor can
land. Each site has a small electrical force arrayed in a way that
attracts the special configuration of atoms that is the repressor
molecule. Site one is closest to the gene to be shut down. It has
a moderately strong attraction for the repressor. It fills up first
when there is repressor available in the cell to bind to it. Site

two has one fifteenth the power to attract repressor molecules.

This is the trick that runs the system: The molecule that binds to site one then bends itself over to site two, where it adds attractive power to this otherwise weak site. Site two has about ten kilocalories of binding power on its own. With the help of repressor bound at site one, it gains two more kilocalories of binding power. "The important point is that the small differences, of just a few kilocalories that you get from this interaction between molecules, turn out to completely dominate the biology of the system," Ptashne says, or at least, "is a special feature that enables the whole system to work efficiently."

The two sites are not just an effective repressor system. It turns out that their configuration also aids the system to boost the rate at which even more repressor molecules are made. It is a kind of self-sustaining repressor pump.

The system thus has both negative and positive controls—a repressor action that is negative and a boosting action that makes more of the needed molecules. This keeps the whole system stable in its dormancy. It also makes the system capable of halting suddenly. The repressors sitting on the DNA not only block a "start" signal, they are partly responsible for making their own kind and keeping the binding sites filled. When one function is disturbed, both collapse. The system flips suddenly to its second state: free manufacture of lambda.

The third of the three binding sites operates in this new state. Though it usually remains empty, the third site is the place that the second repressor, cro, can attach itself. It can be filled when the SOS response begins, or in a few other situations in which the repressor molecules are destroyed, leaving open the binding sites.

When cro fills site three, it halts completely the making of the first repressor (it blocks the "start" signal of the repressor gene). With no repressor being made, binding site three is filled by the new cro repressor. Site one is open. Lambda's genes are then open to be read and obeyed by the cell. Soon hundreds of new lambda parasites have been made within *E. coli.*

The whole switch is actually a little more complex and subtle than I have described. Repressors and cro repressors each can occupy all three of the binding sites at times—repressors filling the sites from right to left, and cros filling the sites from left to right. In a crude sense the system is like one of those modern V-shaped light switches. Pressing one end turns the lights on; pressing the other turns them off.

Such a molecular switch, elaborated in detail first in lambda, has apparently been found in some detail in half a dozen other systems, from monkey virus genes to frog genes. It is one sort of molecular mechanism by which life operates and which looks to the eye like thoughtful "behavior," or a considered reaction. It is what might be described as a "smart system," one having a crude ability to take information and react efficiently to it.

There is another interesting point about this switching system. Many different substances can trigger the SOS response and cause lambda to rise from its dormancy. As it happens, all these substances cause cancer. A test called the induct test has been devised to exploit this curious fact.

To test whether a substance causes cancer, it is put into a batch of E. coli containing dormant lambda. Within twenty minutes, the bacteria have burst and the lambda, much multiplied, are free. The substances which cause the lambda to awake and lyse the bacteria are probable carcinogens. The test is about ninety-nine percent accurate.

This result has led Ptashne and his colleagues to think it possible that there is some fundamental biological similarity between cancer and lambda release. A portion of the Ptashne lab is now devoted to exploring the question.

But it occurred to me that the molecular details of the lambda dormancy seem surprisingly complex for so rudimentary a creature, a system that is not even, officially speaking, alive at all. It is a nonliving bit of chemistry.

I asked Ptashne if that meant that the chemistry of higher organisms, the cells of plants or animals, for example, would be still more elaborate and thus more difficult to figure out.

He said it was not at all certain that higher cells have more complicated schemes for control. They might very well be cruder and simpler. It is not often appreciated outside biology, he said, that it is the small, short-lived creatures that are favored by evolution. Modern man has existed only for about ten thousand generations. But E. coli generates that much history within days. These organisms, by definition, are more highly evolved. Their numbers in nature reflect it. The great British biologist J. B. S. Haldane, when once in the company of theologians, was asked what he could conclude about the nature of the Creator from a study of His Creation. "An inordinate fondness for beetles," Haldane is said to have answered. Since zoological classification began in 1758, more than a million species have been identified. Seventy-five percent are insects. Sixty percent of these are beetles. But if you count by population rather than by type, the microorganisms are vastly the greatest number.

As one of Ptashne's colleagues put it, "The systems in *E. coli* may not do as much as the larger human systems, but they certainly do it better. Higher systems haven't had the time to strip down their [biochemical] systems of unwanted features or time to develop such elaborate controls."

For sixteen years Ptashne has been closeted intellectually with a single problem, one passage in the life of one of these elemental bits of genetic information, the lambda. But finally, he told me, he had laid down his last major doubts, admitting that this work was "probably" complete and he would have to move on to something else.

Unlike the achievements in the arts, which can be voluminous and accessible to the world, this intellectual achievement was more typical of science. The greatest mental effort of Ptashne, and perhaps ten other people under him, had been laid out over years upon a single fine detail. The total work came down at last to six pages of narrative in the journal *Nature*, published at the end of 1981.

"To whatever extent I justify my scientific life, it is in that I stuck with a simple biological system, realizing that one doesn't understand it . . . driving it to the point where one really has a clear picture of how it works and why," says Ptashne. Coming back on his thought, he added, "To a certain extent, this is a rationalization. You are never sure why you do what you do, but . . ."

The phone interrupted. When he hung up, he moved between the sink and the table, the table and the refrigerator, talking softly about the cruelty of science.

"I mean cruelty in the deepest sense. In the sense that your problem disappears." He went into science, he says, "to exert my will on the world. To actually have a measurable effect." He had thrown his whole mental and emotional life into it. The problem, then, was over. He was too old to begin with a great new problem like the repressor, or at least he felt he hadn't the energy to face one. At middle age, too, choices are more difficult. Fears are larger, mistakes hurt more and heal less.

He scraped the chicken bones into the garbage. He rinsed the plates and turned to lean against the sink. He said, "But in no field is the end of a problem so sudden or so final." He said he has several smaller problems which may lead somewhere. He has a new business he can use to lead him off into other fields. And finally, he has his violin. As I took my leave that night, he was talking about the way that music presents an endless challenge, but always allows you some small, pleasing progress.

Later, in February of 1982, I picked up the phone to find Ptashne at the other end, in a different state of mind. The rumors of the death of the lambda problem were premature. Ptashne was excited about a new detail. Carl Pabo, then a postdoctoral researcher in Ptashne's lab, had just begun to elucidate in detail, through crystallographic work, the detailed shape of the repressor and the cro proteins. Ptashne had carried the detail of the lambda system down to the level of molecules. As we spoke on the phone, he said, "Now, for the first time, we are able to carry the studies down to the ATOMIC level! And this means . . ."

And this means the work goes on.

Three

Doll Inside a Doll

John McCarthy
and the Evolution
of Artificial Intelligence

1

THE fellowship of man and machine, I have always thought, is a provocative subject. The idea led me to poke about on the science shelves at bookstores and to thumb through magazines. My glance, while moving through the reclining bodies of the technical words in one of these articles, was halted by a phrase standing upright: . . ."the artificial intelligence laboratory." The tone was matter-of-fact, as if it were referring to something more common, like a saw factory. I did not know what artificial intelligence was or what one of its laboratories might do. But all the images which lined up behind the phrase seemed to be pictures of the world in some other time—brains of bright metal, spindled humanity, and arrays of clean, well-lighted hardware.

Eventually I got the chance to go to California and to visit the Stanford Artificial Intelligence Laboratory. On a hot June afternoon I met the lab's director, John McCarthy. I had driven up from the main campus of Stanford University to his outpost in the hills. He was late, so I waited in his office. It was the head of a long snake of a building which sat coiled on the hot hilltop. Two walls of the office were glass, and through them I could see the hills outside which were the color of straw. The short, yellow bristles of grass made the hills look like the scalp of a marine recruit. With the wiry dark hair of bushes and trees shaved off, the bumps and scars of contour were visible. The few trees out the window were eucalyptus, and they looked dusty and dry as fence posts.

John McCarthy's appearance, when he finally strode into the office, struck me as extraordinary. He is about average height, five feet nine inches. His build is average, with a little age trying to collect itself around his middle. But his hair encircles his head and his face with a great cloud of silver needles. Amid this prickly gray mist his eyes are two dark rocks.

Our first meeting actually consisted of several conversations, between his bouts of work. I remember most clearly one moment, a pause between talks. There is a long wooden table in his office, and I recall the form of Professor McCarthy seated before it. His body was hunched slightly in the shoulders, held motionless, and his eyes were rapt. A small screen and keyboard were in front of him. The machine was in a little clearing amidst a jungle of papers and ragged envelopes. I had come in and sat down, but for a moment my presence was immaterial, a shade at the rim of his consciousness. He continued staring into the screen. I recognized this sort of catatonia. Scientists (as do writers and artists) wander into the paths in the background of their work and cannot find their way back immediately. I didn't interrupt him.

I watched as McCarthy leaned toward the keyboard. His hands were suspended over it for a moment, curled as a wave, but in suspension. Then a rapid tapping of his fingers broke sheets of pale green words across, then upward, on the dark screen. His computer terminal lay at the end of a wire which could be traced to a room down the hall containing a constellation of computers. The computers hold in a file all of McCarthy's professional work, and dozens of other files and services which he can use. He was pondering, via his terminal, a paper he was composing on the philosophy of artificial intelligence.

He stood up without breaking his gaze. His hands hung loosely at his sides. He looked into the screen as if he were standing at a cliff and looking down into a distant valley laid out before him. I could not see over that cliff, and as he looked down, I wondered—what would I see if I could look with his knowledge, through his eyes? A passage I had read not long before came to mind: "The computer is, of course, a physically embodied machine and as such it cannot violate natural law," wrote Joseph Weizenbaum in *Computer Power and Human Reason.* "Electrons flow through it, its tapes move, and its lights blink, all in strict obedience to physical law to be sure, and the courses of its internal rivers of electrons are determined by openings and closings of gates, that is, by physical events. But the game the computer plays out is regulated by systems of ideas whose range is bounded only by the limitations of the human imagination. A computer running under the control of a stored program is thus detached from the real world in the same way that every game is. The chess board, the 32 chessmen, and the rules of chess constitute a world entirely separate from every other world. So does a computer system together with its operating manual. . . . The computer, then, is a playing field on which one may play out any game one can imagine. One may create worlds in which there is no gravity, or in which two bodies attract each other, not by Newton's inverse-square law, but by an inverse-cube law, or in which time dances forward and backward in obedience to a choreography as simple or as complex as one wills. One can create societies in whose economies prices rise as goods become plentiful and fall as they become scarce, and in which homosexual unions alone produce offspring. In short, one can single-handedly write and produce plays in a theater that admits of no limitations." My mental picture fixes John McCarthy that way in that pose: working at his terminal, playing out the moves and countermoves in an idea he created, on a field he imagined, all obeying rules he made up.

There are about three million computers in use in the world now. But not millions or thousands, or even hundreds of them, are dedicated to the sophisticated work of artificial intelligence. Though there has been much celebration of the coming of the computer revolution, it can hardly be said to apply to our current use of these machines: They do little beyond arithmetic and alphabetical sorting. In practice they are no more than automated filing systems with central controls, and still the chief task they are assigned around the world is to keep track of company payrolls. The promise of computing—"the steam engine applied to the mind" as one professor of computing put it—still remains largely unrealized.

The one tiny academic discipline in which the limits of computers are being tested is the field of artificial or machine intel-

ligence. Of the hundreds of thousands of computer programmers in the nation, only a few hundred have devoted themselves to the question of what computers are finally capable of,
asking whether the old science fiction saw about brains and
computers being equivalent is, in fact, actually true. It has been
said for fifty years that computers are "giant brains" and that
the human mind is merely a "meat computer." In a slightly
different form, the same idea has been expressed for more than
two thousand years in the construction of automatons that imitate human and animal behavior. It is only in the past twenty-
five years, however, that the questions—what is intelligence and
how can it be made mechanical?—have actually been raised to
the level of serious academic questions.

Even within universities where a good deal of work goes on
about computers, the field of artificial intelligence is a sub-
subdiscipline. In universities the research and teaching about
computers is generally housed within schools of electrical engineering. Within this designation are the schools of "computer
science," where the physical details of computer operation are
studied alongside the mathematical disciplines of computer
languages. Within this discipline is the still smaller one of artificial intelligence. There are only three or four universities in
the country which have more than two professors in the field.

Where most computer researchers work to make machines
faster, smaller, and better organized internally, those who devote themselves to artificial intelligence do not take for their
subject the operation of computers. Rather, it is in some ways
more closely related to philosophy or psychology than to electrical engineering.

Within this small, exotic field, John McCarthy is one of the
three or four people who have contributed most. As I sat waiting for McCarthy to finish, I could see him blink a few times
and retrieve his thought from the screen before him. I could
see he was beginning to recover. He rubbed his eyes beneath
black frame glasses.

He began by saying that in artificial intelligence the object is
to find out what intellectual activities computers can be made
to carry out. He is rather certain that an intelligence smarter
than a human being can be built. From time to time, journalists who discover the existence of his laboratory call up Mc-

Carthy to ask him about such robots: "Can they be as smart as people?" McCarthy smiles. "No. That is one of the science fiction fantasies, that robots will be *just as smart* as humans, but no smarter. Robots will be smarter, because all you have to do is get the next-generation computer, build it twice as big, run it a hundred times as fast, and then it won't be *just as smart* anymore. . . ." The field of artificial intelligence is a collective attempt to create such machines. There are now about three hundred souls in the United States and perhaps another two hundred in the rest of the world working to make them.

To the journalists, who take their ignorances quite democratically from romantics who fear technology and from science fiction fans who adore it, McCarthy routinely explains that the popular images of both the intelligent computer and the "computer revolution" are mistaken. First, the computer revolution, which is supposed to have occurred in the past twenty years, has not begun. It will not begin until the home computer terminal is a commonplace. Second, he says, in the future there are likely to be machines of many sizes, shapes, and degrees of mobility, not a single race of manlike beings. Third, these machines will not be seeking control over humans, or as more modern science fiction writers would have it, seeking to be liberated from their status as an oppressed minority. In fact, these machines are unlikely to have any sort of motivation.

"My idea is that there is a fundamental difference between intellect and emotion," McCarthy told me. "I think that all intelligent beings will have similar *intellects*. When we program a computer to solve a certain class of problem, what it does is fundamentally similar to the way a human being solves those problems. Intellect takes the shape of the problem it has to solve. But motivation is a different matter. I regard human motivation as very eccentric and peculiar," McCarthy said. "If you were designing a machine to be intelligent and optimize the performance on some job or other, you wouldn't make the machine much like a human." There are too many hazards in human behavior. Rather, the machine would be given its goal, and working toward that goal it would set out subgoals and work on them.

"But these subgoals would remain subordinate. It seems to me that one of the odd characteristics of human motivation is that subgoals become independent of the main goal, and then come up to dominate it. Let's say your interest in writing was somehow related to a desire to please your mother. You could argue, as a Freudian would, about the origins of it. But you would have to say that you are writing now even if it would *displease* your mother. So there is this characteristic of human intelligence, that subgoals take off by themselves." As examples of human peculiarities, McCarthy mentions that humans don't like to be bored, that they don't want to die, and that they get angry. "Machines couldn't care less about these things unless you specifically build it into them. The kind of motivations that might be built into a machine are simpler ones, like accepting a problem, working through it, and stopping. Or, doing a problem, but instead of stopping, listening for another problem. But in any case, we wouldn't be inclined to imitate human motivational characteristics. There is no reason to make something that gets angry, if angry means to do damage to the enemy even at a cost to itself. . . . There is a science fiction writer, David Gerrold, who was much interested in the subject of machine intelligence. He wrote a book and asked me to criticize it because he was going to write a sequel. The thing that I found most wrong was that he had a big machine with *all* of these human motivations. But I wasn't able to suggest any way you could change that and still have a story. . . ."

McCarthy, who is now fifty-five, is one of the three acknowledged fathers of the field of artificial intelligence—he in fact coined the phrase artificial intelligence to name the field in 1956. Of the three most important centers of artificial intelligence in the world, McCarthy founded two—the one at MIT in 1957 and the one he now directs at Stanford in 1963. He conceived and crafted the computer language in which most of the field's intelligent computers work. He founded and solved the first problems in a subbranch of mathematics called the semantics of computation. He has created a continuing succession of ideas which have over the past twenty-five years become successful computer hardware or programs. And he now, more or less by himself, upholds the philosophical wing of the study of artificial intelligence.

His life seems almost to be a machine for making ideas. He

not only has a computer terminal in his office, he has one at home, and there is no time of the day or night which is reserved for the disengagement of the mind. It seemed to me that he was not living in the world the rest of us inhabit, but rather in a mental model of what the world could be like. In it, all the concrete objects of the world are replaced by descriptions of their function. One result of this is that he has great trouble with social exchange.

When he entered the office the first time I met him, his greeting consisted of an expectant stare. No words at all. Discourse by his visitor brought from McCarthy a series of mumbles, which slowly increased in volume and clarity, like the sound of a man emerging from a cave. Only when his mind reached the surface was something similar to normal conversation possible. His colleagues confirmed this: that John McCarthy's mind is a vehicle streamlined for rapid passage through the fluid of thought, capable of maneuvering with little outside friction. But in the open social terrain, his streamlined concentration becomes awkward and unwieldy.

"A large part of his creativity," says Les Earnest, associate director of the lab, "comes from his ability to focus on one thing. The *hazard* of that is . . . everything else gets screwed up." While most people can be said to socialize by talking to one another, McCarthy's manner of socializing around the laboratory consists mainly of walking around in the halls, stepping into an office here or there, picking up something from the desk, and reading it. "Sometimes he'll walk in when you're there, not say anything to you, just pick up something and read it, then walk out," Earnest says. "When I really want him to read something, I don't go in and put it on his desk. It would get lost. I put it on *my* desk. He'll come in and pick it up."

One of McCarthy's chief accomplishments in the field of artificial intelligence is to have created the language in which most intelligent computer programs are written. It is called Lisp, a shortening of List Processing Language. One fundamental unit of the language is the ordinary pair of parentheses used in natural languages. But in McCarthy's Lisp, the parentheses are used forcibly and often. Expressions hide within expressions, hiding within expressions. One nests within another for as many as eight or ten levels deep. And each level may be a complex program by itself, with all its own set of Russian folderol—the doll inside a doll inside a doll inside a doll.

In a sense, McCarthy thinks the way his programming language is built. During a day he may nest one activity inside another, with one conversation broken by another, then return to the first as if each unit were marked with parentheses. If he had a clock on the wall of his office, it might well have parentheses on its face, for he seems to measure time in problems and subproblems rather than in hours and minutes.

One researcher at Stanford recalls standing in the laboratory's snack room chatting with McCarthy about some complexity. The researcher ended a reply and turned to hear McCarthy's response. But McCarthy had disappeared. Two days later the researcher was standing near the same spot, McCarthy walked up without greeting, and resumed the conversation in midthought. Edward Fredkin, one of the pioneers of machine intelligence who joined McCarthy at the MIT lab very early and became his friend, recalled that on another occasion he and another friend were walking near the MIT labs. He wanted to introduce his friend to McCarthy because the two had some mutual interest. McCarthy at that moment approached them on the sidewalk, and Fredkin stopped him to make the introduction. Fredkin's companion said hello and asked McCarthy a technical question about his work. McCarthy looked at him, turned his back, and paced away. Fredkin was surprised, his friend quite angry. The friend turned and walked away. A moment later McCarthy, having walked about twenty paces down the street, returned. He looked blankly around. He was ready to answer the question, and wondered where Fredkin's friend had gone. "You see," Fredkin explained, "John has a habit of pacing when he starts thinking. He didn't mean to walk away, but he was thinking and couldn't help it. . . ."

It is characteristic: McCarthy is a man whose life is arranged around ideas. Not only in mathematics and computing, but also in politics, music, literature, or plumbing. He once had to struggle with moving a piano up a flight of stairs. Soon afterward he was deep into the problem, which was to move heavy objects over difficult and uneven terrain. There have been invented all manner of vehicles, carts, and robots designed to transport things over smoother terrain—why not over the really difficult spots? His answer was a cleverly designed six-legged mechanism which could walk up and down stairs carrying pianos.

He builds ideas, he breaks them down. There is nothing which delights him so much as this endless game of Chinese tangrams, arranging and rearranging scraps of thought to make chimerical creatures. Some of his mental beasts, the few best ones, may stand by themselves.

2

THE central question in artificial intelligence is actually a very old question. The idea of making artificial beings that move and speak could not have come much after the invention of static sculpture. From before the time of Homer, mechanics in their shops and writers at their tables have imagined mechanisms that would mimic people. Probably, the craftsmen and scholars of three thousand years ago found artificial beings easier to believe in than we do, even though we are closer to actually making them. We are coming around to complete the circle now, as scholars and craftsmen again see the possibility of artificial creatures in real terms. This time, however, the creations are more than clockworks and are without the need for the old "life-forces" of the vitalists.

It is an old tradition that the building of a humanlike machine calls for dark magic and the use of forbidden knowledge. Still, the generations have never failed to conjure images of such beings. Each century has built its mechanical mimics. The first clockwork automatons we know of were built in Egypt, about 1550 years B.C. Palace artisans crafted water clocks with human figures that announced the hours by striking bells and blowing trumpets. A thousand years later, Homer wrote of the clockwork creatures used by one of the gods. These clockworks were built by the only lame god, the ugly and gentle blacksmith Hephaestus. The Romans later called him Vulcan. For the executive sessions of the gods, Hephaestus made carts which wheeled themselves into the conclave, delivered their burden, and wheeled themselves out again. He built, according to Homer, armor for Achilles that was imbued with strength and virtue, so that "light from that fair, elaborate shield shot into the high air . . ." and for others he made gold and silver guard dogs. For himself he made women of gold; they could speak and carry out the tasks of apprentices. But Hephaestus' most powerful creature was the bronze giant Talos. He was a gift to King Minos of Crete, who used the giant to guard his island. Talos walked the circumference of the island three times daily; he sank unwelcome ships with great boulders thrown like pebbles. Medea finally destroyed this creature when she found that a vital fluid in his body, which charged him with energy, was held in by a plug in his foot. She pulled the plug.

Craftsmen were inspired to do the work seriously, and make their fortunes by the invention of mechanical amusements. Archytas, who lived in Tarentum, Italy, in about 400 B.C., constructed a wooden bird that fluttered up on a wire, "and actually flew, so delicately balanced was it with weights, and propelled by a current of air enclosed and concealed within it," said one writer of the time. A mechanical engineer named Hero made a model of Hercules and the dragon, and he also created the first vending machine—it acted out little scenes after one denarius was dropped in its coin slot.

There was from the beginning a fear about these things. The forbidden knowledge which lay behind the animation of life seemed in danger of being exposed, unleashed. In the thirteenth century Albertus Magnus spent thirty years building a machine he called an android, which in Greek means "man-form." Albertus' android was a butler which stood by the door at his monastery in Cologne. When someone knocked, the android rolled to the door, opened it, greeted the visitor, and asked his business. There are some accounts which describe the visit of Thomas Aquinas to the house of his teacher, Albertus. When Thomas was greeted at the threshold by the mechanical man, he became enraged at the sacrilegious boldness of the creature. He leaped on the butler and violently disanimated it.

Regular as struck hours, the automates appeared over the

centuries, and through the nineteenth century they were put on tours around Europe. There was a "writer" doll which scratched out little poems on paper, and the "artists" which drew rather complex pictures (Marie Antoinette, Louis XVI, a ship at sea). The device named most lifelike of all the automatons by its viewers was a duck. The advertisements for the duck's tour (which included the La Scala Opera House in Milan) said it was "an artificial duck made of gilded copper who drinks, eats, quacks, splashes about on the water, and digests his food like a living duck." The part about digesting his food was a polite phrase to convey the fact that the duck shat an odorous substance after a performance. The clockwork constructions got more and more elaborate—clockwork theaters with stage and players, whole clockwork towns in miniature. Finally there was a clockwork fraud. An Hungarian inventor, Baron von Kempelen, built a chess-playing machine. It was a wooden man dressed in Turkish costume mounted on a large cabinet which contained the convincing embellishment of hundreds of gears. The wooden man was a fine chess player, a great success, and he toured Europe and the United States until the dwarf inside the box finally became too ill to go on with the exhibition.

There was no clear connection, though, between man's artificial works and the real mechanisms of nature. The craftsmen could not really imitate nature because they understood it mystically, not mechanically. They thought in terms of things like "vitalities" and "essences" which seemed to have no physical structure.

The first to grasp the fundamentals of the machine and how to imitate nature's machinery was Leonardo da Vinci. He understood it partly through his art. Art during his time had just abandoned the flat, myth-centered icons. Realistic, convincing three-dimensional pictures were painted for the first time. The world was seen without its vestments. Painted leaves must look just as leaves look, the painters said; leaves have *this* number of veins and lobes, and must be just *that* color of green.

In addition to seeing things plainly, Leonardo made the next step of deduction and was the first man to do so. From his meticulous drawings of plants, of human anatomy, of skeletal birds and flying machines, he learned that the details of nature are not accidental. The things of the world have certain appearances because of the way they *work*. The surface oddities of nature are not mere facades, they are clues. Leonardo could look through the transparent hide of nature and see how the actions of things flow from their structure; he understood that the objects of the world are harmonious *mechanisms* with simple purposes and few needless parts. From this insight grew Leonardo's passion to make machines and automata of all sorts.

Just as Leonardo studied each motion in the hinges, levers, and pulleys of the human hand to learn how it spun wool, or the motions of the bird's wing to discover how it took off, so intelligence researchers now try to use machinery to mimic gestures of the mind. If the mind can produce, for each word you may mention, a string of associated words and descriptions within the mind, then the brain must have a mechanical method doing this storing, recalling, and associating. And that mechanism ought to be imitable. Artificial intelligence researchers quote Leonardo as a proof for their own work: "The bird is an instrument working according to natural law, which instrument is within the capacity of man to reproduce in all its movements," wrote Leonardo five hundred years ago. So it should be with the mind, according to the researchers in artificial intelligence. (They add the thought that the difference between the metallic force of the airplane and the feathered darting of the bird can also give some idea of how different artificial and human intelligences will eventually be.)

Up to the nineteenth century, all the mechanisms built were merely clockworks. For each doll or demon, a single prescribed pattern would be enacted from the beginning to the end of its routine. Then the identical sequence would begin again. But to make convincingly intelligent automata, we ought to find out how intelligent creatures perform such varied behavior in response to the world.

One thing common to all the intelligent beasts is that they have brains, arranged behind a screen of perceptual organs. The eyes, ears, skin, organs of balance, all send signals, symbols of their stimulation, to the central processing organ. The information is sifted, then forced into useful interpretations. Intelligent creatures thus do not have only one automatic pattern of behavior. Instead they behave on the basis of a constant stream of new information—information about both itself and the world. Choice is created. The continuous newness of behavior arises from this—a reasonably small number of mental processes being fed a large and constantly changing number of new configurations of time, place, and condition in the world. Intelligent behavior is contingent. So, a mechanism without perception, without mental interpretation, and without a way of acting flexibly on these, will never be a convincingly intelligent machine. Machines of intelligence must perceive and interpret the environment in at least a crude form. Nothing like this could be achieved until the creation of modern computers.

The first thing which might have been called a modern computer was created in Britain in the early part of the nineteenth century, more than a hundred years ahead of its time and even before the discovery of the electric currents which we now associate so closely with computers. This machine was called the Analytical Engine by its maker, Charles Babbage. It was a computer rather than a calculator because in theory it could manipulate any symbols, not just numbers, by any operation that can be specified, not just the four usual operations of arithmetic. Calculators which could perform simple arithmetic operations had existed for several hundred years before Babbage's Analytical Engine.

Babbage's feat in creating the modern computer in a mechanical, embryonic form was not well recognized until recent years, partly because he failed to actually build the one he had put down in blueprints. Babbage himself was an irascible and rather sad figure who succeeded throughout his life at works completely unimportant to him. He created the postal service when he made calculations which proved that it would be cheaper to deliver mail than to maintain large post offices where people could pick it up. He is also given credit for creating the field of operations research.

At the time Babbage created his Analytical Engine, there was no clear distinction between mathematical calculation and intelligent thought. Though we now see arithmetic as mere rote manipulation of numbers, it was then seen to be far more fundamental to intelligence, probably because only the most highly educated, and not even all college graduates, could do arithmetic.

So, when Babbage made a calculating machine that could operate by itself after certain numbers and operational information were put into it, it was seen by some as a threat to the integrity of human intelligence. In Babbage's blueprints, the engine was to have been more than ten feet long, five feet wide, and comprise hundreds of polished brass gears and rods stacked in tall, handsome columns. Babbage and his superiors apparently spent some time protecting the machine from attack by arguing that the machine was not intelligent, but merely able to do complicated, preset tasks.

From childhood, Babbage had been fascinated with automata. He often recalled the times he would be taken as a child to see the exhibitions of automata, one of which he described as a silver figure twelve inches high, "an admirable danseuse, with a bird on the forefinger of her right hand which wagged its tail, flapped its wings, and opened its beak. The lady attitudinized in a most fascinating manner. . . ."

Babbage kept in his parlor the unfinished brass towers of one of his machines, in the hope that he might persuade his guests to help in his projects. This forlorn machinery sat beside a small, graceful automaton—one he had bought after years of fondly remembering the exhibitions of his childhood. The machine from his childhood and the one from his adult life made him bitter; he was hurt that all his guests, except for a few foreigners, ignored his own works while they gathered eagerly around the frivolous figure, the silver dancing lady. Babbage died in 1871. He had worked fifty years on his calculating engines. He finished none of them.

Another figure whose life ended tragically, Alan Mathison Turing, took the next important step in the progress from clockwork gadgets to machines of intelligence. Turing, another British mathematician, was a rather odd and shy man. He had pale eyes, and such a childlike gaze that for fifteen years after achieving his degree, he was still accosted by school proctors when he walked at night—they took him for an undergraduate violating curfew.

Some of his pastimes seemed rather childlike as well, such as the thing he called the "desert island game." The object was to build useful objects out of the common materials around him. He made cleaning fluids and weed killers by extracting nonpoisonous chemicals from things in the house and then recombining them into the substances he needed. In a biography his mother wrote, she said that Turing "would have preferred if possible to make his own electric light bulbs and batteries. He went so far as to contemplate making bricks to pave his garden path, but he thought it came near to 'cheating' to buy clay from a builder instead of digging it up himself . . . pottery in his laboratory suggests he had made a start on work with clay."

This was a way of thinking with Turing, and when he became interested in problems of the ultimate forms of computing, he approached them in similar fundamental terms. He broke the problems into parts and then put them in terms of vivid mechanical models. The original question was abstract— what problems have solutions that, in principle, are not computable? To start, he had to make a definition of "computable." He decided that it meant whatever could be expressed as numbers and calculated by a machine. That is, it must be able to be done in a definite series of steps without any abstract or indefinable moments along the way. Arithmetic qualifies as computable, but can good poetry be created by a machine's computations?

The kind of machines he was talking about were machines that manipulate information. He was not concerned with the other sort of everyday machinery, the brutes like the internal-combustion engine that change fuel into force. In the past century or two, much has been learned about that kind of engine. But information machines—and that phrase is often meant to include all living creatures in addition to a few made of inert metal—are more engrossing and less well known. In a famous paper written in 1936, Alan Turing claimed that there was a machine that could be built that would be a sort of "universal machine." He said it could do every possible computation. By extension, it could carry out any operation that any other information machine could do, whether it was an abacus or an animal's brain. This was possible, he said, because this ultimate machine could simply take for its instructions a complete description of the machine to be imitated.

It was actually not practical to build a universal machine at the time Turing suggested it. It was the idea that was important. Had anyone attempted to build one, it would have operated by laboriously punching holes in a paper tape to record and manipulate information, and this would make it far slower than a person using a pencil and paper. But his description of the machine proved mathematically that one information machine could encompass all others, and do any computation, provided only that all the steps it needs to follow were explicit. This means that if the brain operates by a series of discrete actions of the neurons (or some approximation of that), then it is *certain* that machines can be made as intelligent as people.

In 1946, ten years after he created the idea of the universal machine, Alan Turing went to work for the National Physical Laboratory in Britain, with the object of making his machine real. At the time, no distinction had yet been made between ordinary computing and really intelligent computing.

The director of the laboratory, Sir Charles Darwin, told a British radio audience: ". . . Turing set himself out to find out the ultimate limitations that [computing machines] must have. The answer cannot be given simply, of course, but it is roughly that you could make a machine do anything which can be . . . [done according to rules]. It was an idealized machine he was considering, and at that time it looked as if it would be so fantastically elaborate that it could never possibly be made. But the great developments in wireless and electronic valves during the war have altered the picture, because through complicated electric circuits you can do many things at enormously greater speed than you could do before mechanically. Consequently, Turing, who is now on our staff, is showing us how to make his idea come true."

Several teams in America were already building computers when Turing started making one in Britain. But all the machines built did embody Turing's ideas, and all the modern computers that have followed from those made in the 1940s have been "universal machines." From the beginning, silhouetted behind all the mathematics and mechanics, was the great question of whether these machines would be real thinkers; might they sometime surpass their stumbling makers?

This question made all the first computer builders consider natural thinking machines. How are they organized, and what are the rules by which they operate? Human and animal brains, they reasoned, must have some method of doing what they do.

Turing became fascinated with biology. The great mathematician John von Neumann, who followed up Turing's early work on computing, studied physiology. "The computer injected something into modern scientific thinking beyond mere technology," wrote physicist Jeremy Bernstein, the author of a book on computing called *The Analytical Engine.* "For the first time, I believe, it has presented us with a machine-tooled model —still primitive—of ourselves. In his early papers on the logical design of computers, von Neumann took his notation from two physiologists, Warren S. McCulloch and Walter Pitts, who were trying to make a mathematical model of the human nervous system. Von Neumann was trying to create what might be described as an electronic nervous system." McCulloch and Pitts concluded that the neurons in the brain were equivalent to the basic components of the computer—to the vacuum tubes of 1948, to the transistors of today. They wrote: "Anything that can be exhaustively and unambiguously described, anything that can be completely and unambiguously put into words is, *ipso facto,* realizable by a suitable finite neural network." In other words, the network of neurons in the brain might carry out the same calculations, in the same way, as Turing's universal machine.

Computer scientists began to see in their metallic creatures the potential stirring of life. Von Neumann began thinking about Turing's universal machine as a sort of elemental model of life. Could it, in theory at least, reproduce itself? He decided to make a list of what things were necessary for a machine to reproduce. First there must be raw materials to make an offspring. Then, there must be a set of instructions for turning the raw materials into the new creature. Then there must be some tools or mechanisms that can carry out the making of the offspring. He added that there also must be a method of copying this whole process, a blueprint, so that future generations will also be able to reproduce. Von Neumann actually made a mathematical sketch of such a self-producing Turing machine.

As one writer pointed out, we are by now so used to the idea of computer analogies to biological systems that they may appear obvious. But they are not obvious. Actually they are only a few decades old. Von Neumann's analysis was five years ahead of the discovery of the double-helix structure of DNA, and preceded by several more years the full unfolding of what is called the central dogma of genetic replication.

In casual conversation, those who worked on the early computers let their thoughts go further. The wife of one eminent mathematician recalled to Alan Turing's mother how she had listened to her husband and Turing talking. They were talking about the computer Turing was building. "I couldn't take part in the discussion and it was one of many that had passed over my head, but suddenly my ear picked up a remark which sent a shiver down my back. Alan said, reflectively, 'I suppose when it gets to that stage we shan't know how it does it.' "

That attitude toward the possibility of intelligent machines was infectious. John McCarthy was a gangling graduate student in 1949; he knew nothing about the nervous systems of computers. But that year at his school, Cal Tech, he went to an event called the Hixon Symposium on brain mechanisms and behavior. Von Neumann, who was then composing his ideas about self-reproducing machines, went to the symposium and so did an array of other notable computists. Almost all the papers and talks at the meeting were strictly about the brain, and the computists wanted to absorb all they could on the subject. But in one paper, McCarthy recalls, he first heard the arguments about machines and intelligence. He started turning the ideas over in his mind. He decided that the next logical step in thinking about machines and biology ought naturally to be evolution. He thought that, in theory at least, the best way to make a smart machine would be to put one through the same process which made the human brain smart. "My idea was to experiment with automata," McCarthy said. "One automaton interacting with another which would be its environment. You would experiment to see if you could get a smart one." One automaton, in other words, would play the part of a primordial bit of life, and the other automaton would play the part of the world in which it lived. Assuming each played its part effectively, the result would be a rapid, miniature version of evolution, a speeded-up movie of life blooming. After the Hixon Symposium, McCarthy wrote to von Neumann about this idea, von Neumann liked it, and when McCarthy went to Princeton to take his doctorate the next year, the two talked about it. "Write it up, write it up!" von Neumann told him. McCarthy thought the idea was premature, and though he did some preliminary experiments, he never put the idea to paper. But he had begun to think about machines and intelligence, and the fascination never left him.

When the first universal machines had been built, at the beginning of the 1950s, the era of the first computing machines ended. It was now clear what the limits of computation were, at least in an abstract sense, and it was certain that very powerful computing machines would be possible. The first computers were fast, and had tens of thousands of "neural" bits. They didn't approach the complexity of the brain, with its ten billion neurons and trillions of connections between the neurons, but there was enough computing power in the first machines to attempt intelligent tasks with them. The computer, said Dartmouth computer researcher John Kemeny, began to look "remarkably human. It starts with limited abilities and it learns more and more by imitation and by absorbing information from the outside."

The field of artificial intelligence begins at just this point. Digital computers were made and were waiting—empty matrixes of computing power. They were ready to be given eyes, ears, memory, reasoning, intuition. It was left to the generation of John McCarthy to begin building programs into these computers that might resemble, however remotely, the fundamental parts of human intelligence. Though he was a relatively young man at the time, Alan Turing did not live to see the field of artificial intelligence firmly established as a new scientific discipline. He was poisoned on the night of June 7, 1954. The verdict of the inquest was suicide. Many of his friends did not believe it; they felt his death must have been a freak accident. He had swallowed a fatal dose of potassium cyanide. Turing had synthesized the same chemical, in the few days before he had died, for use in one of his "desert island" experiments. It is unclear whether he could have accidentally swallowed enough of the substance to cause his death. In any case, he had worked late that night, eaten an apple, and gone to bed. The housekeeper found him dead in his bed on the morning of June 8. He was forty-two.

3

U<small>P</small> to the time John McCarthy became creator to little machines which might evolve on their own, he had no experience in computing. In school he studied mathematics unrelated to computers, and he was no good at gadgets, which in those days computers still were. They were metal racks packed with raw relays, wires, and switches. The machines sat in the shops of electrical engineers and, according to Jeremy Bernstein, "one could go in and listen to the gentle clicking of the relays, which sounded like a roomful of ladies knitting." Without any special qualifications, McCarthy wandered into the field of computers and the specialty of artificial intelligence. It was the habit of mental tinkering, established in his childhood, which drew him into the field.

John McCarthy and his younger brother Patrick were born in Boston. Their father, John Patrick McCarthy, laborer, had landed in Boston in the early part of this century. He was something of a refugee from the politics and bloodshed then going on in Ireland. He worked the docks, he carpentered, he fished, he organized union men. His sympathies were with the Irish Republican Army and he worked for their causes here. A newspaper clipping from August 1920 describes "John P. McCarthy, the well-known Irish leader" as he led three hundred Irish dock workers in a strike against British shipping. At a noontime rally, McCarthy exhorted the longshoremen to stop unloading goods from the British ship anchored there. He said the workers must help stop the British massacre in Ireland by halting the flow of British goods. He criticized President Woodrow Wilson, who claimed to be a supporter of democracy around the world, but who in a recent trip to Britain had failed the Irish cause. "For a night's lodging in Buckingham Palace, he sold democracy," McCarthy said. McCarthy, an Irish Catholic, later married Ida Glatt, a Lithuanian Jew. Her newspaper clips say that she once led a squad of Goucher College students in a march on the White House. They demanded suffrage for women. John McCarthy, senior, went to school only to the fourth grade, but he enjoyed reading and he built a fairly large library in his home. He memorized poetry. He led conversations at the family dinner table every evening that covered politics and literature and most any other subject; and, what may have been most important for the children, he took their contributions to the conversation seriously. The family politics was Marxist, the family religion, atheism.

Marxism, in the 1930s, was imagined to be the "scientific" approach to politics and government. It's now obvious that it is as irrational as any other form of government, but at the time it was natural for John McCarthy's two sons to develop intellectual views of life early, as Marxism recommended. The boys read widely and did well in school. The way some boys followed every pitch and swing of their baseball team in the newspapers, the McCarthy boys followed the adventures of the Red Army in China and the innings of the Spanish Civil War. Young John also watched as his father created and put together various gadgets. John's father eventually got patents on two of his devices—an orange juice maker that used water pressure to squeeze the orange and a small machine for caulking ships. John began reading about science early, titles such as *The Boys' Book of Electricity* and later the philosophical *New Background of Science*. "It was obvious to me," McCarthy said, "that from the age of eight or ten, I was going to be a scientist."

He admits to fitting, in all the particulars, the image of the bright, clumsy, and obnoxious child ahead of his years. He was small and unhealthy. He skipped three grades in school. By the time he got to college at Cal Tech, he could not face the physical education course. He never went to the class and was thrown

out of school for it. "The physical education courses at Cal
Tech were terribly oppressive," he says. "It was tough enough
that I found basic training in the army a relief. They had a
much worse obstacle course at Cal Tech." But he admitted that
he was bad at athletics. "I was bad at it, partly from lack of
interest and partly from an accumulated lack of success."

When McCarthy went to public school, in Boston, New York,
and finally Los Angeles, where the family moved because of
John's health problems, the teachers were not so suspicious of
academic success as they are now. "The teachers really appreciated, and pushed, smart kids," he says. "Oh, there would be a
little bit of talk about their social development being hampered
by skipping grades (the rot that eventually came to dominate
the system had started), but mostly the teachers hadn't become
anti-intellectual yet. . . ." As might be expected of him, he tried
to quantify the question of intellectual versus social development. He did a survey. At one point in his complex student
career, he entered MIT and found he was several years younger
than others in his class. "I did a study of the people who had
entered MIT at an early age. I interviewed about fifty people;
everyone who was still around," McCarthy says. "They had
somewhat differing views about whether they thought skipping
was a good idea in general. All but one thought it was a good
idea in his particular case."

By the end of high school, John McCarthy had chosen mathematics as his field. It was some time later that he realized he was
following a historical pattern in this choice. "The curious fact is
that in the United States, and even in Russia, the fraction of
leading Communists who become mathematicians is very high."
He thinks that "the original promise of Marxism—science applied to society—leads to an interest in science. Then after some
experience of the real world they retreat. They head in the
direction of the purest possible science." This might be the
equivalent of a religion among the Communists. If there is
anything outside religion which requires faith and which pulls
whole self-consistent worlds out of immaterial hats, it is
mathematics.

McCarthy entered Cal Tech in 1944, intending to study
math. After he was thrown out and was unsure what to do next,
the army drafted him out of his predicament in 1945. He put in

his time as a supply clerk in a collapsing postwar army. "Though I was a fairly obnoxious character, I was treated rather tolerantly," he says. "I only remember one guy who really tried to bother me when I was in the army. There were four guys in my hut with me, Midwestern farm kids, and they offered to beat him up for me." When McCarthy returned to Cal Tech, he was admitted. Then, after graduating in 1948, he went on to Princeton, where he earned his Ph.D. in mathematics in 1951.

All of this put John McCarthy squarely in the middle of what C. P. Snow called the scientific culture. When McCarthy joined it, an argument with the literary culture about man and machines had already been going on for a few hundred years. In fact, in a little broader terms, the argument had been going on since Plato. Even in 400 B.C., the literary culture scorned engineers and their machines. Plato wrote of the engineer, "You despise him and his art, and sneeringly call him an engine-maker, and you will not allow your daughter to marry his son. . . ."

Leonardo, in his time, was spurned by literary society. He was the bastard son of a laborer, fit for manual labor and work with machinery, but not fit according to the lights of the time for "pure" intellectual work. On either side of the gulf between the literati and the scientists, separate literatures grew up.

It was between 1810 and 1820 that Charles Babbage in England contrived the first automatic calculating engine. At the same moment, the Luddites were rioting and destroying machinery in mills all over Britain. Mary Shelley was publishing the first story in which science was used to make an artificial, and evil, man. Her nameless creature gave a body to many fears about science, and it has by now become the single strongest image of man's works gone wrong. Throughout Babbage's sad life, literature was producing, with mechanical regularity, stories and opinions that opposed the progress of machines. In a burst of spleen, a year after Babbage died Samuel Butler wrote in *Erewhon:*

> If all the machines were to be annihilated at one moment, and if all the knowledge of mechanical laws were taken from him so that he could make no more machines, and all machine-made food

destroyed so that the race of man should be left as it were naked upon a desert island, we should become extinct in six weeks. . . . This fact precludes us from proposing the complete annihilation of machinery, but surely it indicates that we should destroy as many of them as we can possibly dispense with, lest they should tyrannize over us even more completely.

Alan Turing, in his time, saw no less of the literature that derided mechanist progress. In the 1920s, Karel Čapek published *R.U.R.* It was a play in which he coined the word robot, from the Czech word used to describe enforced labor, and had these creations destroy the human race for efficiency's sake. Fritz Lang created *Metropolis,* a film considered by literati to be among the best films ever made, but also a film which is, to the technical mind at least, an example of extreme intellectual sloppiness in the way it treats issues of science, technology, and government.

The split between technical and literary culture is something which worries John McCarthy. It is something which has affected his thinking and to a degree governs society's acceptance of new ideas, including his.

"You know," McCarthy says, "there are not really two cultures at all. It would be better in some ways if there were two cultures. But really there are only one and a half." From the time he began reading in childhood, McCarthy has enjoyed stories, folk songs, and poetry. But he has found no scientific faction within the arts. "My students are all in the sciences," he said, "but they don't have a separate set of novels, films, and plays that they can go to. They see the same antitechnological stuff as the students in literature and are influenced by it." From childhood, McCarthy has been conscious of being different, separated in some way from the culture at large. He has always written squibs, notes, poems, stories, almost any sort of passing thought which he can tap out and file in the computer's memory. Along the way, he has written a little story-puzzle which expresses the difference he feels between the literary and the technological approach to human affairs.

When he told me the story, we sat in the den of his large, modern home in Palo Alto. It was past midnight and he was showing me a few of the scraps he had filed away in his computer, the way a writer might pull out yellowed clippings and spidery notes from an old cardboard box. On his home terminal (which is connected to the computer at his laboratory a few miles away) he typed out DOCDIL.ESS. On the screen, a short article appeared in green type. It was titled *The Doctor's Dilemma*. "Suspend your natural skepticism and imagine the following miracle to have occurred," the story begins. "A young doctor working in a hospital discovers that he has the power to cure anyone under the age of seventy of any sickness or injury simply by touching the patient. Any contact, however brief, between any part of his skin and the skin of the patient will cure the disease. He has always been devoted to his work, and wants to use his gift to benefit humanity as much as possible. However, he knows that his gift is absolutely nontransferable (this was explained by the angel who gave the gift to him), will last for his lifetime only, and will not persist in tissue separated from his body.

"What will happen if he uses his gift? What should he try to do, and how should he go about it? What is the most favorable result that can be expected? I consider myself a member of the scientific rather than the literary culture, and my idea of the correct answer to the question reflects this. However, in order to mislead the reader, I shall give a number of pessimistic scenarios, together with some related literary exercises."

With some delight McCarthy goes on to predict the sort of answers which everyone gives to the problem. The dilemma seems to offer a terrible moral choice. After McCarthy told me the problem, but before I had a chance to read as far as the solution, I spent more than an hour sorting through the possibilities. An army of the maimed, legions of the infirm, would besiege the doctor's door. How would he choose among them? The children would be first, probably. What about his own friends? What about people of importance? Perhaps he should reserve his touch for those without money and without hope of even conventional medical treatment. My thoughts ran that way for some time. When I got a copy of McCarthy's story the next day (obligingly printed by the computer), I read on. Before offering his solution, McCarthy lists some of the common "literary" answers. He has a list of eighteen plausible tragic and comic consequences in the life of the gifted doctor. "The doctor uses his gift," reads one exercise, ". . . other doctors are jealous and disbelieving and drive him from the hospital. He cures patients on the outside, but they get him for quackery and put him in jail where he can't practice. . . . He cures a guard of cancer, and then the little daughter of the warden of the prison. This arouses the fears of the insecure, narrow-minded, brutalized, and bureaucratized prison doctors to the extent that they have him sent to a hospital for the criminally insane to be cured of his delusion. There, they lobotomize him. Write scenes in which the doctors disbelieve cures taking place before their eyes . . . and the report justifying his commitment to the mental hospital." Another of his scenarios begins, "His gift is judged sacrilegious by the church of your choice. Fanatics are aroused by preachers and our hero is burned at the stake . . ." Another puts the government in charge of deciding how the healing gift should be used. The government mishandles the job of administering the gift. "Write a description of the computer bungle that requires him to cure the same person 103 times, and 102 people zero times each. Describe the questionnaire that has to be filled out even by the dying in order to be cured. Describe humorously how a dying man completes the form in the nick of time, but is prevented from being cured at the last minute because he has written 'same as the above' in a space where he should have written his address for the third time."

Pessimism is a powerful element in literature. The number of great works of literature of an optimistic tone or happy end is extremely small. In science, the tendency goes the other way. Literature examines the sorry state of the present and extrapolates it. Science ignores the sorry state of the present, asks instead what else is possible and attempts to produce it. The pessimism that seems to be a part of the doctor's dilemma really resides in the literary culture's view of things; McCarthy's solution replaces it with optimism.

There is no moral dilemma in the problem, McCarthy says. Everyone in the world under seventy whose illness can be identified in time to bring him to the doctor can be cured. He calculates: "Approximately sixty million people under seventy die each second. We build a machine that can move twelve people per second past the doctor on each of ten moving belts.

A mechanism should be provided to stop the motion of the finger of the patient momentarily, so that it touches the doctor rather than brushing his skin. On the basis of the arithmetic, the doctor need only spend one sixtieth of his time curing people, that is, twenty-four minutes per day. In order to reduce transportation costs it might be desirable to build a number of machines in different regions of the world and for the doctor to make trips to these machines, say once a month, to get the slow diseases, and to fly emergency cases to wherever he happens to be. . . ." McCarthy's technical analysis goes on, pointing out that the solution would contribute to the population problem in the world, but not very much. To make a stable population, he says, "the elimination of death under seventy would require that couples limit themselves to an average of say 2.1 children rather than the 2.2 children that might be allowable otherwise."

From his childhood on, John McCarthy has tinkered, in this sort of mechanical manner, with the way the world seems to us. When he does it seriously, and applies it to current difficulties in computer science, it becomes his work. When he does it in less serious moods, he concocts ideas like a privately vinted beverage, which he then serves to friends or guests on social occasions.

"Did I tell you my bicentennial idea?" he asked me. He had this notion about five years before the U.S. bicentennial year, he says, at a time when thoughts about America quickly sank into grim visions of riots and radicals, of carnage in Vietnam, of racial holocausts and crime. As a sort of tonic, McCarthy started thinking about the bicentennial celebration.

"I calculated that it would be possible for the United States . . . to have a birthday party and invite everyone," he says. He means the entire population of the world. "I calculated that if we devoted our entire aluminum production between 1971 and 1976 to the thing, we could build enough double-decker 747s to move the entire population of the world in thirty days and out again in another thirty days. . . ."

"Where were you going to have this party?" I asked with perhaps a little skepticism.

"Well, you'd wanna have a place that had a reliable, good climate, and since it's in July, then New Mexico or Arizona, the higher altitude areas. . . . You figure that if you built a double-deck structure there, so all the services were underneath, then a twenty-mile-square array of people would be about right for the whole world. Then you'd put the show up on a cube about a mile high . . . with two shows, which you see is determined by which way you flip your glasses. One of them would be the ceremonial parts and the other one would be nominally for the kids. . . ."

"I see; the fun parts?"

McCarthy laughed. "Right!"

The night he called up *The Doctor's Dilemma* on his home screen for me and told me about the United States birthday party, McCarthy also called up on his home terminal a number of other scraps of thought. Among the items in his file are notes on J. R. R. Tolkien's ring trilogy. McCarthy read it and liked it. He can recall parts of it in the smallest detail. But his liking it, of course, does not mean that he wouldn't want to change it. So there is a McCarthy Sequel to *The Lord of the Rings*. "Of course, it can't be published," McCarthy said. "It was intended as a genuine piece of *samizdat* [a work for the drawer, one that is unpublishable]." In the McCarthy Sequel, the Orcs, who were Tolkien's rude and ribald infantry of evil, are given a dignity which Tolkien had refused them. "He invented a race to be prejudiced against," McCarthy said. "They even smell bad!" As a historian of that period of Middle Earth, McCarthy has uncovered a good explanation for the Orcs' hostility to Hobbits and other northern folk. Tolkien mentions that in an earlier time there was a campaign which "cleaned" the Orcs out of the mountains by such means as murder and well poisoning. The Orcs remembered it. McCarthy's revisionist history of Middle Earth also included a new view of the lordly elves and a correction of Tolkien's mistaken perception of the Hobbits as a lowly and somewhat backward group. The Hobbits were in fact the only group in Middle Earth with currency, private ownership, densely packed farms, and other signs of a society advanced far past the tribal and feudal societies described for the "higher" groups. In later years of Middle Earth, recounted by McCarthy, the Hobbits discovered and learned to use a whole new technology of magic.

A click banished the Tolkien *samizdat*. Typing SHORT.ESS into the terminal brought up thoughts on many subjects. They were numbered. Fifteen said: "The steam shovel was not invented by the world's best ditch digger. This is my excuse for proposing innovations in fields that 'belong' to other people." Item 17 said, "The best way to solve a moral problem is to make it a technical problem. The moral problem of chastity has been relieved by birth control. . . ." Number 10 began: "The most important price is the current price of a human life. Many activities are undertaken to save life, and many activities are undertaken in the knowledge that they will cost life. Many of the activities intended to save life are suboptimal in that the same money would save more lives spent some other way. Suppose there were a publicly known 'value of a human life.' Anyone who could show that his proposed lifesaving activity would save lives cheaper than the standard would have a prima facie case for his proposal. Someone proposing an activity that cost lives would have them charged to his project at the standard rate.

"What about the humanitarian argument that it is wrong to put a price on human life? Well, he who *refuses* to put a price on life will kill more people than he who *knows* the price. . . ."

4

AFTER a cramped and intent childhood, John McCarthy emerged into the world at a good time and a favorable latitude. He emerged into a field of work that was brand new. Artificial intelligence was ready to split off from computing of the kind that prints paychecks. It could have advertised itself in help wanted columns. Pioneers Wanted. Low Pay. Good Benefits. The basic ideas of machine intelligence, such as Alan Turing's, were already down on paper and the basic hardware was already assembled in the shops, but the social agglutination which makes a domain of study—papers, journals, seminars, and conferences—had not yet begun.

From some time in the middle of the 1950s, the study of artificial intelligence and the life of John McCarthy bloomed together. The social awkwardness which McCarthy had carried with him like a second skin was overcome enough for him to find and marry a young woman in 1955. The physical gracelessness that hobbled him was overcome enough for him to take up some sports such as sailing and mountain climbing. Beginning in about 1955, McCarthy had an extraordinary string of good ideas in artificial intelligence. It was also during the middle 1950s, and the early 1960s, that artificial intelligence itself grew from virtually nothing to a discipline producing a thousand books and papers a year. A current of excitement, started by the success of the first programs, increased steadily for a decade. It caused an unnaturally fervent glow about the field—for a time at least.

After his first summer of working directly with computers rather than with the theories of them, McCarthy thought it would be a good idea to get together in one place all the people most interested in mechanical intelligence. They could come to a summer-long research conference, work hard, and at the end produce the first major report on the subject. This extended brainstorming session took place at Dartmouth College in the summer of 1956. It was the first conference on artificial intelligence (it was in creating a name for the conference that McCarthy coined the term "artificial intelligence," which eventually became the name of the whole field), and the two dozen or so participants came bristling with ideas.

A group from Carnegie Tech, where a center to study machine intelligence was just starting, came to the conference talking about a computer program they made called the Logic Theory Machine. In trying to understand the methods people use to solve problems, they reasoned that there must be only a few clever methods behind all human mental abilities. So they gave their logic machine three simple methods to use in trying to prove equations of logic. The program could substitute one expression for an equal one, it could break up a problem into a series of subproblems, and it could decide which subproblems to solve by a method called chaining. Their program found proofs for thirty-eight of fifty-two theorems it tried in the *Principia Mathematica,* the epic work of mathematical logic by Alfred North Whitehead and Bertrand Russell. It would take a college student to do as well. But the program also found at least one proof more elegant than even the version offered by Whitehead and Russell, a feat still talked about twenty-five years after it was accomplished.

Arthur Samuel, a pioneer of artificial intelligence, was also at Dartmouth for the summer and was talking about his program that could play checkers, a game which he discovered was far more difficult to play expertly than most people are willing to believe. Samuel was helping to build the first commercial computers for IBM, and was working on his checkers program in his off-hours. "We were building several of IBM's 701 model, and the machines were out on the factory floor. I would go down at night to play on them. I had as many as three machines playing checkers through the night," he said. His checker-playing program was the first program to change its behavior to profit from its own errors and successes; in essence, it was the first program that could learn. It soon was beating its maker. It once beat the state champion from Connecticut, who was also one of the best players in the nation. "It is very interesting to me," commented the checker champion after his loss to the machine, "that the computer had to make several star moves in order to get the win .... In the matter of the end game, I have not had such competition from any human being since 1954, when I lost my last game."

At Dartmouth, McCarthy contributed an idea on computer chess. The problem in chess is that there are about 120 different sequences of moves that are possible. The fastest conceivable computer, one of immense capacity operating at the speed of light, could not look at all the possibilities, not even if it spent more years at it than there are atoms in the universe. So computers, like humans, must apply some sort of cleverness in deciding what moves to consider. Chess grand masters look ahead at only about thirty-five possible sequences, and most of those only as far ahead as three moves and countermoves. But chess programs that were discussed by the machine intelligence researchers would be looking at far more, hundreds more, possibilities than a grand master, at the same time playing a game so poor that a talented child could beat them. There was something wrong, and McCarthy realized that the programs were looking at far too many moves. All but a few of the paths examined by the computer were false trails chasing hopeless moves.

So McCarthy created a mathematical method which, in a later streamlined form, was called the alpha-beta heuristic. Once stated, it was obvious that this is one way people avoid useless searching: look for your most promising move and look for the most damaging thing your opponent can respond with. Then, stop searching all the lines that give your opponent a powerful answer. (If I make *this* move, my opponent can make *that* move to trap my queen. Forget that move. He may not see the trap, but I had better not take the chance. . . .) "It turns out that the alpha-beta heuristic is absolutely compulsory for playing chess," McCarthy says. "It doesn't matter whether you're a human, a Martian, or a machine. You must use it if you're going to play a good game. The solution takes the shape of the problem to be solved.

"Much of our intelligent behavior is like this—it is not determined by heredity, or by culture, but is shaped by the difficulties of the problem to be solved. Many linguists and psychologists have not grasped this idea yet. But it's what artificial intelligence *is*—studying the relationship between problems and the methods for their solution."

These ideas are contrary to popular ideas in some other fields, most notably the field of linguistics. Its current light, Noam Chomsky, argues that the ability to produce sensible, grammatical language is inherited genetically. Even though thousands of languages have arisen in many different cultures, he argues, there are likenesses in all the languages. So if language is not based on culture, it must be genetic, according to Chomsky.

"This ignores another possibility," McCarthy says. It ignores the possibility that language structure is similar in every culture not because it is genetic, but because language could not work if it did not have those traits. Every culture creates languages along similar lines, because it is impossible to make a working language without doing so.

"Do you know the story of the monkeys and the typewriters?" McCarthy asks. "A statistician one day remarked to his friend, a rich and eccentric gentleman, that numerically speaking if one sat a troop of monkeys at typewriters and got them to hit the keys randomly, eventually the beasts would write all the books now in the Library of Congress. The eccentric gentleman decided on the spot to try it out, despite the astonished pleadings of his friend that the probability that they would write any book at all within the next million years is impossibly small. The monkeys would write nothing but gibberish for billions of years, he pleaded. The eccentric carried on anyway, and as the story goes, the troop immediately began producing sensible copies of famous books. This result so enrages the statistician that he grabs a pistol and begins shooting the monkeys. The last monkey puts a sheet of paper into its typewriter and as it is dying, types out *Uncle Tom's Cabin* by Harriet Beecher Stowe, and then it slumps over and dies. It is sort of a meaningless story, but it's becoming funnier now because the Chomskyites are beginning to be seriously embarrassed by the monkeys. You've heard of the apes that have been taught to speak in sign language? I expect to hear of monkeys being shot any day now," McCarthy laughed.

It was about the time of the Dartmouth Conference in 1956 that McCarthy began to articulate his ideas about intelligence in man and machines. He realized that the knowledge missing to make intelligent machines is not technical or mechanical, but is fundamental knowledge about knowledge. "I think it's a lack of understanding of the relationship between problems and the methods for solving them. It is a question of understanding what is known about the world, what people know about the world, and how one can express it in terms which machines can use. If this is close to any field of science, then philosophy is the traditional field which has the closest connection," McCarthy says.

At MIT, John McCarthy reached his season. He had just married a woman who had been a student with him, and they had two daughters, one in the first year of their marriage, and the second four years later. McCarthy's young family soon began to look, from the proper angle, like the family of his father and mother. Politics were a family observance, and the ideas that came through the family circle acquired a familiar deflection to the left. The outlook was intellectual, the mode active. Brother Patrick recalls visiting the household once and noting that the family had no television set. He visited a few years later when there was a television, but found it sitting broken and unnoticed in a corner. No one in the family had the time or the interest to care for it. He also recalled going down to breakfast in John's home. As a matter of habit, he brought something to the table to read. As he sat there, each member of the household wandered in, one by one, each absorbed in his own reading.

When McCarthy took up athletics, he did so in a particularly McCarthian manner. Edward Fredkin recalled a number of outings with his friend. "I went rock climbing with McCarthy. It is kind of funny, the way he approaches it. He is not strong. He doesn't have endurance. When he is out there he gets what is called sewing-machine leg as fast as anyone—the typical thing that happens is that he would be hanging on a ledge by his fingernails, with one foot up here and it has all his weight on it. He can't move from there for a while until he feels around and calculates where next to climb. It's an awkward position, hard on the leg that's carrying all the weight, then all of a sudden his leg would start jerking of its own accord, as if it were pumping the foot pedal on a sewing machine. It happens to you when you are out of shape. . . . Despite all this, John does it and does it well at times. The reason is this: What you are doing out there when you're hanging on by your fingernails is that you are solving an intellectual problem. Now where will I go? Will I reach for a handhold here? Where will my foot go if I do? And so on. So, even though John is bad at these physical things, once they are reduced to mental gymnastics instead of physical ones, he is good! He learns fast. He remembers everything. He can develop skills. So without any natural ability he's still sort of conquered . . ."

"Mind over matter?" I suggested.

"Exactly. Very much that."

The trouble, of course, arrives when circumstances become unruly and the body is forced to act before the mind can discover an exit, compose a plan, and command the body to obey. Both Fredkin and McCarthy have flying licenses. Fredkin has flown with him a number of times, and remembers quite vividly the flight in which John McCarthy decided to promote himself from the clunking little machines with wheels fixed in place and airspeeds of about eighty miles per hour. The two flew in a "Moony," a single engine craft with retractable gear that can manage just under two hundred miles per hour. When McCarthy flies, he does not do it by feel or by physical instinct which is the common way for pilots of some experience. He keeps lists and sublists of things to do in his mind and clicks off items one by one as they need to be done. Fredkin recalls him doing just this as he was trying to land the racing aircraft. "Prop feathered . . . Mixture full rich . . . Airspeed check. . . ." McCarthy was talking to himself softly. "Coming in now. Okay, now we'll do this. Okay. Now that. . . ."

The airplane landed on the runway and was racing along the ground for several seconds before McCarthy got to the landing part. He looked up, a little surprised. Fredkin looked at him.

When they parked, McCarthy had a little grin. "Yes," he said to Fredkin, "I've decided that the Moony is about the highest performance aircraft that I should fly. . . ."

On another outing, Fredkin was teaching him how to bring a spinning airplane back to level. "You have to be careful how you do that," said Fredkin. "There are certain rules to follow, like not trying it unless you are up high enough to pull out before you hit the ground. Well, we had flown out over the ocean and done a number of them, stalling the left wing and spinning down, stalling the right wing. Then just after pulling out of one, John said, "Let's do another one. Right now!" For a second I didn't say anything, but my instincts were telling me that we shouldn't do this," Fredkin said. Finally he turned to McCarthy: "John, do you realize that at our altitude, there is no possibility whatsoever of our recovering before we hit the water?"

John McCarthy's sense of adventure, for some reason, is not hampered by his physical shortcomings. He has flown from Boston to San Francisco in a light plane, he has flown up to the Arctic Circle, and down into the mouth of canyons at Lake Mead and Yosemite. He has made twelve parachute jumps from up to ten thousand feet. In such things, McCarthy's mind wanders out ahead of his body. He imagines possibilities and then drags his carcass after.

5

I T was at MIT in 1958 and 1959 that McCarthy created the
Lisp programming language. In 1959, he started single-handedly a new branch of computer science called the semantics of
computation, in which hundreds of papers a year are now written. "He laid the foundations of the whole field," said Joseph
Goguen, a computer semanticist of UCLA. "He defined the
questions. He produced the methods. He is extremely important to the field, the most important person of anyone, I think
almost anyone would agree." The object of McCarthy's work
was to find a way to prove that a computer language and the
machinery connected to it do exactly what they are supposed to
do, to demonstrate that they are not full of errors. Without this,
no one using a computer can be sure the error is his own and
not the fault of the computer system. "In the long run,"
Goguen said, "in the field of computer science, advances like
the development of the first language, Fortran, are insignificant compared to what John McCarthy did. The first thing you
invent is the computing machine and the idea of a program,
then you try to create a mathematical theory of it so you can
show that things do what they are believed to. The first thing
was done by Turing and von Neumann, and the second thing
was done largely by John McCarthy and also a man named
Peter Landon."

In 1958, McCarthy conceived a new form of time-sharing on

computers called interactive computing. In 1959, he created the idea of the practical home computer linked to a public "information utility." Over the same period he outlined his method for making a computer with general intelligence, using what he called programs with common sense. Any one of these ideas would have been enough to make a successful career in computer science; they were only the start of McCarthy's.

The achievement McCarthy is most famous for is his creation of Lisp. Of the hundreds of programming languages now in use, it was the second to be written. Fortran, a language strictly for mathematical formula translation, was created in 1956. Lisp followed about a year and a half later and was a wholly different sort of language. Though computers are imagined by nonspecialists to be great number-crunching appliances, they are not. They are really machines capable of shifting and combining *any* kind of symbol—words, signs, pictographs, any sort of symbol at all. Lisp was the first language built to use the whole range of symbols rather than just numbers.

As one mathematician put it, "The new expansion of man's view of the nature of mathematical objects, made possible by Lisp, is exciting. There appears to be no limit to the diversity of problems to which Lisp will be applied. It seems to be a truly general language, with commensurate computing power."

Programming languages, to the minds of most of us, seem arcane and artificial. They might make ideal symbols of the ingrown, superspecialized, and sterile world of the computers. But these computer languages are not so alien to those familiar with the history of natural human languages. In fact, the invention of computer languages fits neatly into a historical cycle of growth. Human language was created as a collection of markers, of placeholders so to speak, by which man could keep straight the objects and events in his increasingly confused world. But eventually this oral language found its limits. Cities had been created, and people were having difficulty keeping track of the buying, selling, and trading of animals, food, and other goods. Oral language had become overloaded. So a new system was developed—*written* language.

At first, this new system used small clay pebbles or counters shaped into things they were to stand for—a round one with a cross for a sheep, an oval for a jar of oil. The tokens were kept in a jar. The number, or the kind, were changed as animals were bought, cloth was sold, oil was stocked. Eventually, these computational symbols were cut into the outside of the jar, or onto a tablet, instead of being shaped into tokens. Gradually these symbols evolved into alphabets—writing had been created out of calculation.

When the computer was created, a new level of symbol manipulation was reached. The computer was quickly adopted for use in everyday business transactions, just as spoken language and then written language were each adopted first for practical purposes. Only later were they raised to the level of arts.

It is a little surprising to us now, but just as computing raises fears and objections, the adoption of writing had its opponents as well. In Plato, we find the plea of an inventor to his king in Egypt: "This invention O King will make Egyptians wiser and will improve their memories; for it is an elixir of memory and wisdom that I have discovered, but the king was not convinced and feared that the invention of writing would impair the memory instead of improving it, and that the people would read without understanding."

The essence of a computer programming language is, like ordinary language, abbreviation. It lets a word or phrase stand for a complex of operations in the way that English nouns stand for accumulated experience or a welter of meaning. The differences between English and a programming language are chiefly that programming languages are exact and explicit where English is uncertain; they have total access to small memories, where users of English have haphazard access to an extremely large memory; and programming is well understood though so far rather limited, while the action of English in the brain is not understood but is quite general and powerful.

Programming, partly from prejudice and partly from deliberate obfuscation by programmers, is usually thought to be extremely complex and difficult, a subject fit only for mathematical adepts. But writers trying to unmask the mystery of computer programming have often pointed out that it is not much different from knitting. The simplest actions inside the computer might be compared to the simplest hand motions in knitting. Inside the machine, every click or switch that occurs must be named and called into action by a specific instruction, as if in knitting a pattern were described by naming each individual jerk or motion of the fingers. The operations inside the machine are simple and easy to understand, as are the finger movements in knitting. "The operations are few in number and simple in type," writes author Margaret Boden, "for instance, copying an item of information in a specified position in the storage register, shifting an item to another specified position, and counting the instructions executed so far (the comparable operations in knitting include passing the wool *over* the needle, passing it *around* the needle, pushing the point of the needle into the front of the first stitch . . . and so on)." The whole sequence of instructions is called the program. Written in this level of detail, where every action is specified, it takes dozens of written steps to accomplish the addition of two numbers, or the simple matching of a word with a list to see if it appears there. To avoid these tedious steps, programmers take the often-used sequences (such as "add" or "match"), and then use these as if they were units. They are called subroutines and can themselves be collected into bunches and used as units. When subroutines and collections of subroutines are given names so that they can be called on, then you have a programming language. Knitting, too, has its own language and it is no less perplexing than Lisp. In a beginner's book of knitting we find:

```
K4, P1, yo, sl 1, K2 tog, psso, yo
P1, K6, P1, yo, sl 1, k2 tog, psso, yo, P1, K4
. . . Row 1:   P3 * K1 back loop (k1B) , P3, repeat . . .
```

From a beginner's book of Lisp we read:

```
(label match (lambda (x y)
(Cond (( or (null x) null y)  (quote no))
       (( eq  (car x))  (car y))(car x))
       (t      (match   (cdr x) (cdr y))
```

The likenesses between knitting and programming seem a little whimsical, but they aren't. The reason for the similarity is that writing programs and writing knitting patterns are similar mental processes. Both the programmer and the pattern writer *think* in the abbreviated terms they use. The habit is innate.

All complex thinking abbreviates concepts and then manipu-
lates the short forms. A dramatic example of this occurs in chess.
A chess grand master, glancing for only five seconds at a chess
game in progress, can later recall where every piece on the
board was. A novice at chess given the same test can recall only
a third or less of the placements. The ability to "see" the board
in abbreviated units—"Lopez position," "Four knights
opening"—makes the difference. This was proved when the
same grand masters and novices were given a similar "five-
second glance" test. This time, the grand masters and novices
did equally badly. Neither could remember the place of more
than four pieces at the most! The test that reduced grand master to the level of novice was the same as the previous test which
showed they were so different—except that the pieces were not
in positions where they might be found in some chess game, but
were instead in randomly scattered positions around the board.

When Shakespeare said that brevity is the soul of wit, the
word meant "knowledge," and so Polonius was giving a formula
for intelligence: The whole method of intelligence is to ab-
breviate and manipulate knowledge. A computer programming
language provides the way of abbreviating knowledge, just as
the chess master's experience provides him with a profoundly
effective method of doing the same. So in the late 1950s, when
John McCarthy wrote the programming language that could be
the crucible for intelligent programs, it was a significant marker
in the progress of the field.

Parts of the Lisp language were revolutionary events within
the world of programming languages. One example of this is
McCarthy's creation of the "if, then" expression; it is now used
in all computer languages and it allows long, branching chains
of speculation by a computer. It gives the machine, in a rude
way, the ability to ruminate over many trials and errors before
setting off on a line of thought.

In addition, there is one other feature often mentioned by
those who write about Lisp. Technical writers will often segre-
gate their mention of this attribute by commas, or cloak their
praise with brackets, but they say it nevertheless—the language
has a purity and mechanical grace unlike any other. It is not an
accident. John McCarthy sacrificed efficiency more than once to

achieve a certain abstract beauty in the forms of Lisp. There is also a cumbrous grace in the way a program moves forward in Lisp. The parentheses coil and uncoil, shell to shell to shell descending through the dolls of a problem, and step to step to step coming back up again.

By the 1960s the flush of hope which accompanied the 1956 assembly at Dartmouth had become a public excitement. Not only were computers playing championship checkers and passable games of chess, not only were they solving problems of geometry and logic, but a score of other interesting programs were running. One program behaved like the investment officer of a bank: For two quarters in 1960, the program chose a portfolio of twenty-nine stocks for the bank to invest in. The bank's human trust officers also chose twenty-nine. Twenty-four of their choices were identical; three more were nearly identical. There was a program to answer questions about baseball scores and baseball players' performances. There was a program that translated Russian into English, a program to solve integrals in freshman calculus, and a program to solve those arithmetic word-problems that drive sixth graders into frenzies of spitballing.

The researchers became bold. "It is not my aim to surprise or shock you," wrote Herbert Simon, one of the creators of the Logic Theory Machine. "But the simplest way I can summarize is to say that there are now in the world machines that think, that learn, and that create. Moreover, their ability to do these things is going to increase rapidly until—in a visible future—the range of problems they can handle will be coextensive with the range to which the human mind has been applied." He wrote that in 1957, and then predicted that within ten years from that time "a digital computer will be the world's chess champion," that within ten years "a digital computer will discover and prove an important new mathematical theorem," and, also within ten years, "theories in psychology will take the form of computer programs."

Another researcher said that in "three to eight years we will have a machine with the general intelligence of an average human being. I mean a machine that will be able to read Shakespeare . . . play office politics, tell a joke, have a fight. At that point the machine will begin to educate itself with fantastic speed. In a few months it will be at genius level and a few months after that its powers will be incalculable." Man's limited mind, he added, may not be able to control such immense mentalities.

The optimism drew a cloud of reporters and critics. The ancient debate about man and machine started up again. "The coining of the term 'artificial intelligence' in the 1950s," wrote computist Donald Fink, "was the signal for a particularly acrimonious expression of conflicting ideas. The defenders of intelligent machinery predicted rapid progress in the intellectual attainments of computer programs. The detractors were equally vigorous in denying that the word 'intelligent' was then, or ever could be, properly applied to any machine." Journalists began to appear in the laboratories of artificial intelligence. They came with the usual baggage that journalists haul about with them—bright, curious intellects completely unmarred by knowledge, and dark, skeptical frowns that hide gullets large enough to swallow anything. The result of putting these journalists in the same tank with schools of excited and fiercely technical-minded scientists was predictably farcical.

A tide of articles of reaction appeared over the next few years, in publications ranging from *Life* magazine to *My Weekly Reader*. Books appeared with titles like "What Computers Can't Do." Not unusual was the article which appeared in the magazine *Oui*, a Playboy publication. Researcher Kenneth Colby was quoted in it. Colby, who is best known for his program which simulates the behavior of a paranoid, was refusing to be interviewed: "I'm not being paranoid," he said, "I just don't feel I have anything to gain by talking to the press. Journalists want easy answers, and there simply aren't any in this business. People keep asking me if robots are going to take over the world, and I say, 'Yes, as soon as we can get them to work. . . .'" The article, naturally, turned out to be a feature on the ways that robots are going to take over the world. The headline was: THE ROBOTS ARE COMING. The subheadline advised: FROM NOW ON, WALK SOFTLY AND CARRY A BIG CAN OPENER. The article opined: "Scientists have created a whole new generation of robots that will one day manage your household, mow your lawn, chauffeur you to dinner, tutor you in French,

join you in Monopoly, diagnose your ailments, or psycho-
analyze you. And this is only the beginning. . . ."

Later the article gets down to its nub. It uses some comments
that had been attributed to Marvin Minsky, the director of
MIT's artificial intelligence lab for more than a decade. The
author noted that Minsky denied having said these things, but
still couldn't resist quoting them:

"Minsky sees no reason why robots shouldn't win out over
mere mortals. Two years ago he told writer Brad Darrach: 'The
human brain is just a computer that happens to be made out of
meat.' And he warned, 'Once the computers get control, we
might never get it back. We would survive at their sufferance. If
we're lucky, they might decide to keep us as pets.' Publication
of those comments in *Life* outraged Dr. Minsky and the robot
community. This is a view artificial intelligence experts prefer
to confine to private sessions. They fear that a public backlash
to the robot population explosion might undermine their research funding. Factory workers might rise up; government officials might be frightened about being replaced by robot
bureaucrats; intellectuals would fret about alien machines coming to dominate our culture. Of course, Minsky and his colleagues don't want their robots to undermine the world. It's
just that they can't offer any guarantees. . . ."

Poor Minsky. Through endless articles his quote will be repeated, like muddy footprints tracked across the popular record
of the subject. And following the quotation marks there will
always be the little comment that he claims not to have said it
at all. Minsky will forever be leading a secret gang of "alien
machines coming to dominate our culture."

But the predictions of the researchers and of the journalists
came to nothing. Expected advances failed to occur; the performance of programs that *were* written began to look less and
less impressive. One good example is the program by Joseph
Weizenbaum that was called DOCTOR. It was mentioned by
the writer in *Oui* as a program that will "one day . . . psycho-
analyze you." The program conducts a psychiatric interview,
imitating a Rogerian therapist. This is an example chosen because it shows the program answering at its best; and it sounds
convincingly like it knows what is going on. (The program
speaks in capital letters):

Men are all alike.
IN WHAT WAY
They're always bugging us about something or other.
CAN YOU THINK OF A SPECIFIC EXAMPLE
Well, my boyfriend made me come here.
YOUR BOYFRIEND MADE YOU COME HERE
He says I'm depressed much of the time.
I'M SORRY TO HEAR YOU ARE DEPRESSED
It's true. I am unhappy.
DO YOU THINK COMING HERE WILL HELP YOU NOT TO
BE UNHAPPY
I need some help, that much seems certain.
WHAT WOULD IT MEAN TO YOU IF YOU GOT SOME
HELP
Perhaps I could learn to get along with my mother.
TELL ME MORE ABOUT YOUR FAMILY
My mother takes care of me.
WHO ELSE IN YOUR FAMILY TAKES CARE OF YOU
My father.
YOUR FATHER
You are like my father in some ways.
WHAT RESEMBLANCE DO YOU SEE
You are not very aggressive but I think you don't want me to
notice that.
WHAT MAKES YOU THINK I AM NOT VERY AGGRESSIVE
You don't argue with me.
WHY DO YOU THINK I DON'T ARGUE WITH YOU
You are afraid of me.
DOES IT PLEASE YOU TO BELIEVE I AM AFRAID OF YOU
My father is afraid of everybody.
WHAT ELSE COMES TO MIND WHEN YOU THINK OF
YOUR FATHER
Bullies.
DOES THAT HAVE ANYTHING TO DO WITH THE FACT
THAT YOUR BOYFRIEND MADE YOU COME HERE

If one didn't look any deeper, to see how the program works, this would be an impressive demonstration. But the method that the program uses is transparently mechanical and silly when it is discovered and seen in a more typical interview. The program's method is to watch for key words in the patient's sentences—such as mother, family, anxiety, and so forth. Then,

twisting around the sentence that the patient spoke, it turns the
patient's own responses into questions. Another example:

I've come to discuss a very serious problem I have.
PLEASE CONTINUE, THIS MAY BE INTERESTING
I suffer from what you could only describe as menu anxiety.
PERHAPS IN YOUR FANTASY WE SUFFER FROM WHAT
EACH OTHER
Excuse me?
DO YOU FEEL STRONGLY ABOUT SUCH THINGS
You mean my menu anxiety?
YOUR MENU ANXIETY
You see, when I'm trying to order dinner at a restaurant, I become
very confused.
I SEE
Sometimes I'll be eating at an Italian restaurant and I cannot
decide whether to order fettucini or clams casino and I become
very agitated and disoriented.
HAVE YOU TRIED
Tried what?
TELL ME ABOUT WHAT
What the hell are you talking about?
WHAT THE HELL ARE I TALKING ABOUT
Can you help me overcome my anxiety concerning menus?
WHY DO YOU SAY YOUR ANXIETY CONCERNING MENUS
Because I cannot cope with them.
IS THAT THE REAL REASON
That is not a reason, but a description of my feelings.
DOES THAT SUGGEST ANYTHING ELSE WHICH BELONGS
TO YOU
Yes, my money, which I appear to be wasting at the moment on
psychotherapy with you.
IS IT IMPORTANT TO YOU THAT YOUR MONEY WHICH
I APPEAR TO BE WASTING AT THE MOMENT ON PSYCHO-
THERAPY WITH I
Yes.
PERHAPS YOU WOULD RATHER TALK ABOUT SOME-
THING ELSE
No. I would like to go on with the same subject.
ARE YOU SAYING NO JUST TO BE NEGATIVE
No, I am being affirmative.
YOU ARE BEING NEGATIVE
No. Affirmative.

ARE YOU USING MONOSYLLABLES FOR SOME REASON
Polysyllabic words seem to escape your comprehension.
WHY ARE YOU CONCERNED OVER MY COMPREHENSION

This program was written by Joseph Weizenbaum of MIT, and he soon found that people, including psychiatrists, were willing to believe in the powers of his DOCTOR. "I was startled to see how quickly and how very deeply people conversing with DOCTOR became emotionally involved with the computer," Weizenbaum wrote, "and how unequivocally they anthropomorphized it. Once my secretary, who had watched me work on the program for many months and therefore, surely knew it to be merely a computer program, started conversing with it. After only a few interchanges with it, she asked me to leave the room. Another time, I suggested I might rig the system so that I could examine all conversations anyone had had with it, say, overnight. I was promptly bombarded with accusations that what I proposed amounted to spying on people's most intimate thoughts: clear evidence that people were conversing with the computer as if it were a person who could be appropriately and usefully addressed in intimate terms. . . ."

Another failure was in programs that were built to translate one language to another. It was assumed that if rules of grammar and a dictionary were stuffed into a computer in the right way, intelligible if not brilliant translations would result. They didn't. What came out was sometimes ridiculous. One often-told story is that a program was given biblical quotations to translate. One of them was, "The spirit is willing but the flesh is weak. . . ." Using only grammar and the meanings of individual words, the computer cheerfully offered in translation: "The wine is agreeable, but the meat has spoiled." One elaborate computer program, which based its translations on syntax, discovered that there were a variety of possible meanings for almost every sentence presented to it. This was a surprise; people looking at the same sentences found them clear and unambiguous. How people instantly and automatically interpreted the lines was something of a puzzle. The simple sentence "Time flies like an arrow" was given four different, entirely plausible meanings by the computer:

1. Time moves in the same manner an arrow moves.
2. A particular variety of flies called "time flies" (not unlike varieties we know of, such as "bottle flies" or "horse flies") are fond of arrows.
3. Measure the speed of flies that resemble arrows.
4. Measure the speed of flies in the same way that you would measure the speed of an arrow.

How is a computer to decide which meaning is the correct one? In a sentence like, "He gave the boy plants to water," how is the computer to decide that the words boy and plant do not belong together in a single phrase—after all, "boy plants" may be something like "boy scouts" or like "house plants." Humans banish these ambiguities without any conscious thought. But by what rules?

Problems similar to this in every area of knowledge confronted the artificial intelligence researchers. The situation was absurd. The researchers had tried the hardest problems first, and they seemed to succeed, but the simple problems confounded them. As Minsky put it, "The results of the first few experiments in artificial intelligence surprised everyone because it turned out that relatively small programs were able to do things that everybody thought would require a lot more intelligence . . . they were able to play a fairly good game of chess, to solve pretty hard problems in college calculus. Well, everybody knows that those things require advanced intelligence. . . ." Or do they? It was on the basis of that "advanced" work that the researchers had made their lighthearted predictions.

The realization came gradually. Bit by bit it was discovered that the things we think of as complex and difficult, the things we expect only geniuses to be able to do, are really the simple things intellectually. What is *hard*, what is quite beyond the ability of today's knowledge and computing power, are things that four-year-olds can do with ease—seeing, hearing, understanding words.

6

ONE of the first computists to speak up on the question of how to get machines behaving as people do, McCarthy said, was Alan Turing. A friend of Turing's, Sir Geoffrey Jefferson, had chided Turing about his interest in trying to squeeze some drop of intelligence from buzzing metal beasts. In 1949, in the Lister Oration for that year, Jefferson proclaimed to his friend Turing and everyone else the reason why he could not believe in such a machine. "Not until a machine can write a sonnet, or compose a concerto because of thoughts and emotions felt, and not by the chance fall of symbols, could we agree that machine equals brains—that is, not only write it, but know that it had written it. No mechanism could feel (and not merely signal, an easy contrivance) pleasure at its successes, grief when its valves fuse, be warmed by flattery, be made miserable by its mistakes, be charmed by sex, be angry or depressed when it cannot get what it wants."

Turing responded to his friend's lecture, the following year, with an article in a philosophical magazine. He did not accept that writing a sonnet would be a good test of a machine's intelligence. What would prove to everyone that a machine was intelligent? Surely there would always be someone arguing that each new ability of the machine was a mere artifact and not really the *essence* of intelligence. So Turing devised a test that could be taken by future machines, a test that would satisfy all.

It went like this: We put in one room a human, in another room a computer, and in a third ourselves, the judges. Teletypes connect us with both the room of the human and the room of the computer. We do not know which room has the machine and which the man. We must try to guess, by putting questions to each hidden participant. If after some minutes of interrogation we cannot be sure, then the machine has won and proved itself a thinker of human level. This test has, since the article appeared in the 1950s, been called the Turing Test. Turing himself offered a sample dialogue of how the test might go, but did not say whether the answerer in the sample was man or machine. He started with a question which slyly needled his friend Jefferson:

Q: Please write me a sonnet on the subject of the Forth Bridge.
A: Count me out on this one. I never could write poetry.
Q: Add 34957 to 70764.
A: (Pause about 30 seconds and then give an answer) 105621.
Q: Do you play chess?
A: Yes.
Q: I have my K at K1, and no other pieces. You have only K at K6 and R at R1. It is your move. What do you play?
A: (After a pause of 15 seconds) R-R8 mate.

Turing wrote that the test "may perhaps be criticized on the grounds that the odds are weighted too heavily against the machine. If a man were to try and pretend to be the machine he would clearly make a very poor showing. He would be given away at once by his slowness and inaccuracy. . . ." Turing went on to talk about Professor Jefferson's objection to machine intelligence. In its starkest form, the argument is the solipsist point of view, Turing said. That is, it is the view that nothing exists except oneself, because that is all that can be verified by "feelings." The rest of the world is an unverified dream. In this view it is impossible to know whether a machine is thinking or "merely signalling," just as it is impossible to know if another human is thinking.

Turing believed that "in about fifty years time it will be possible to program computers, with a storage capacity of about 10^9 to make them play the imitation game so well that an

average interrogator will not have more than a 70 percent
chance of making the right identification after five minutes of
questioning . . . I believe that at the end of the century the use
of words, and general educated opinion, will have altered so
much that one will be able to speak of machines thinking without expecting to be contradicted. . . ." By inventing the imitation game, Turing has set the goal for all those interested in
studying machine intelligence. He also gave a date to aim for—
the end of the century. And, in the end of his article he suggested the best problems to begin with: "We may hope that
machines will eventually compete with men in all purely intellectual fields. But which are the best ones to start with? Even
this is a difficult decision. Many think that a very abstract
activity, like the playing of chess, would be best. It can also be
maintained that it is best to provide the machine with the best
sense organs that money can buy, and then teach it to understand and speak English. . . . I think both approaches should
be tried."

John McCarthy very early added his own reading of the compass. He said that there were essentially two approaches to
machine intelligence: the heuristic, which involves clever programming to mimic human intelligence; and the epistemo-
logical, which involves settling fundamental questions about
knowledge, what it is and how it works, through the use of
mathematical logic. McCarthy took the left fork, the epistemo-
logical, and sent others padding down the opposite path. His
approach was the theoretical one, while the other was practical,
involving as it did the building of one program after another,
trying to imitate fragments of our intelligence.

McCarthy, since the middle 1950s, has been working slowly
on a single computer program called the Advice Taker. His
object is to settle some questions about knowledge first, and
then to actually make the program work. The heart of the
problem, as he sees it, is the commonsense, general knowledge
which people display in everyday situations. Suppose a man was
asked to get to Duluth in a hurry because tomorrow afternoon a
miracle would occur. A person would immediately realize several things without consciously working them out: First, that
there are some things he does not know, but needs to, such as
whether any airlines fly to Duluth, if there are any flights that

might get him there in time, whether he has the money to pay for the trip, and where in Duluth he might look for a miracle. Second, he immediately generates a number of questions that he already knows the answer to: What is a Duluth? What does "get to" mean? What is a miracle, and why would one want to be present for it? What is his time limit, and can he beat it? How does one transport oneself from place to place? For people all these things are trivial matters; for a machine they are not. How is it to realize that it doesn't know enough to work out the problem? And, if it does realize that, how is it to know what things it needs to know?

The problem, really, is one of organization. The brain has billions of bits of information in it; a machine might easily be stuffed with the same information. But the brain is not organized like a garbage can with all the bits in a heap. Recalling from memory any one bit, which the brain can manage in a few seconds or less, cannot simply be done by sifting through a billion-bit heap. If the job were done by sifting, it would take hours or days to get from kitchen to bathroom because each bit of information—What is a bathroom? Is there one near? Where? How transport my anxious self there?—would require a full search of the brain. So, the problem is to organize huge amounts of knowledge in a way that permits us to retrieve it at will, to mix and match pieces of knowledge, and to establish permanent links between pieces of knowledge.

One of the recent bits of progress McCarthy has made in his effort to work out these problems is his invention of a method in mathematical logic called circumscription. He illustrates the problem he is trying to solve with an old puzzle: Three missionaries and three cannibals, standing together beside a river, want to cross to the other side. They have one boat which cannot hold more than two people. The catch is that at no time may cannibals ever outnumber missionaries, otherwise the cannibals will lunch early. McCarthy is not concerned with the trick of the puzzle, but with trying to teach a machine how to understand the idea of crossing a river. Like every action of life, the notion contains many unstated assumptions. He can teach the machine the simple rule: If a boat is on a shore, and a set of things enter the boat, and the boat is propelled across to a point on the opposite shore, and all the things in the boat exit, then the crossing is completed. This statement is easily made in the terms of mathematical logic. But the real world is not so simple. Suppose the boat has a leak, or suppose the boat is a rowboat and has no oars? In logic these things might be fixed by simply tacking them onto the first rule: that there must be no leak, and there must be oars. But there are bound to be more, unthought-of disasters awaiting the boaters. So, McCarthy's solution is to say that "the boat may be used as a vehicle for crossing a body of water unless something prevents it." In ordinary mathematical logic this would not suffice, because everything must be laid out, item by item, and McCarthy has not laid out a list of all the things which might prevent the boat from crossing. But his method, circumscription, offers a formal mathematical way of going ahead with only incomplete information.

McCarthy has been working on such methods of handling knowledge in general. But others have worked instead on how to structure vast quantities of specialized facts within the mind of the machine. At MIT, neurophysiologist David Marr has crossed the barrier from studying the brain biologically to studying it as a computational machine. His work, among the most successful in all of artificial intelligence, has been on vision. The problem is that vision is an extremely complex ability. Seeing is not what it seems. Most people assume that our vision works like a camera, with the tiny inverted image focused at the back of the eyeball being transmitted whole to the brain, creating pictures which are stored in a file and which can then be rummaged like an old trunk in an attic.

Actually, we do not see "images" at all, nor do we store pictures. An image does fall on the retina, but behind this screen of tissues there are unseeing receptors. They merely jerk in little spasms according to the lightness or darkness of the retinal spot they touch. At a bright spot, the receptor fires rapidly, at a dark spot, it fires slowly. Along boundaries, where dark and light meet in the image, an abrupt difference in firing rate occurs between adjacent receptors. This abrupt difference is crucial, because we "recognize" it as an edge. All along one area of a picture, we detect this "cliff" where firing falls off. We recognize such a broad pattern of firing as a unit. Other patterns we recognize in a similar way—lines, surface textures. When the data from such discoveries over the whole image are put together, we begin to identify the particular combination of edges, colors, and surfaces as familiar objects. Since the brain cannot store pictures as such, the "images" we have in our minds are really only a set of such number patterns. The dog of your childhood is stored as a sequence which reads 314—15—9265. Objects of the real world, of course, have a far greater wealth of detail than we pick up on our retina, and the image on our retina in turn has a greater wealth of detail than we translate into firing sequences. From such rough clues, we decide what pattern we are seeing; in fact, it is often necessary to falsify some of the incoming information in order to make a clean interpretation. We guess, and if the clues are too ambiguous we force our interpretation on an unwieldy world.

As it happens, other creatures may take the same visual information about the world and build quite different "images" with it. The world the frog sees is a colorless world; the dominating objects, the ones toward which all its attention strains and focuses, are little blots of moving contrast. They are bugs. A frog can spot and follow moving contrasts with an awesome accuracy. In an instant, its sticky tongue reaches the object and pulls it back. But the bug, if it is not *moving*, will not be noticed by the frog. A frog sitting in a heap of freshly killed flies will starve to death.

We, like frogs, manage. Our vision moves with a fluid grace through a bombardment of information. We cannot hope to deal with all the bits of data, so we ward off most, and select a few million for our use. Out of these we form an idea of the objects in the world, in thousandths of a second. It all passes beneath our notice, like some miniature war, with waves of soldiers moving against each other: We only know the final outcome, who won—what color, what shape, is it flesh or wood? This process and all other sensual processes are the basis of intelligence.

David Marr began his career successfully in neurophysiology and brain studies at Cambridge. He chose to come to America to work on artificial intelligence because neuroscientists had reached a cul-de-sac. In trying to understand the way the brain works, they confronted problems that could be dealt with only by computation on a scale that can only be handled by computer scientists.

"The situation in modern neurophysiology," Marr wrote, "is that people are trying to understand how a particular mechanism performs a computation that they cannot even formulate, let alone provide a crisp summary of . . . To rectify this situation, we need to invest considerable effort in studying the computational background to questions that can be approached in neurophysiological experiments. . . ." Marr's work stands between neurophysiology and computation, using both, since neither is adequate alone to decipher vision. His work, he said, "amounts to findings in visual neurophysiology. The need for these [computational experiments] arises because, until one tries to process an image or to make an artificial arm thread a needle, one has little idea of the problems that really arise in trying to do these things."

So Marr's work has been to make computer programs that can accept signals from a video camera as the eye and brain take light signals from the world, process them, and produce "recognition" of objects. The computer program should mimic the workings of the vision system closely enough to produce the same kind of computational mistakes—which we call optical illusions—as the eye makes. If programs can be made that will on their own produce mistakes similar to those the eye makes, then there must be little doubt that the eye and brain are doing the same computation as the program mimicking them.

Marr's theory of vision is built upon a thorough understanding of neurophysiology and what is already known about the processes of vision. In a similar way, linguist Terry Winograd of Stanford has built natural language programs on a firm base of linguistic theory.

"When a person sees or hears a sentence," Winograd wrote in 1972, "he makes full use of his knowledge and intelligence to understand it. This includes not only grammar, but also his knowledge of words, the context of the sentence, and most important, his understanding of the subject matter. . . . We feel the best way to experiment with complex models of language is to write a computer program which can actually understand language within some domain.

"For our experiment, we pretend we are talking to a simple robot, with a hand and an eye and the ability to manipulate blocks on a table. The robot responds by carrying out commands (in a simulated scene on a display screen attached to the computer), typing out answers to questions, and accepting information to use in reasoning later on."

The result of the experiment was a program with which one could converse rather naturally, as long as the dialogue stuck to the little world of blocks in which the simulated robot lived. Winograd's language program was general enough so that it could easily be adapted to other domains besides the block world. But to cover almost any domain presented, as people can, would require a way of putting more knowledge about the world into the program and a more sophisticated way of using knowledge.

A sample dialogue with Winograd's program, and with Winograd's comments in parentheses, gives a clearer idea of the generality and power of his small program. The imaginary scene in which the robot is manipulating things has two green blocks and a green pyramid, two red blocks and a red pyramid, a blue block and a blue pyramid, and a large box. Beginning partway through a long dialogue, Winograd asks a question:

Had you touched any pyramid before you put the green one on the little cube?
YES, THE GREEN ONE.
When did you pick it up?
WHILE I WAS STACKING UP THE RED CUBE, A LARGE RED BLOCK AND A LARGE GREEN CUBE.
Why?
TO GET RID OF IT. (By keeping track of the original subgoal . . . the system has some understanding of its own motives.)
Why did you do that?
TO CLEAN OFF THE RED CUBE.
Why did you clean off that cube?
TO PUT IT ON A LARGE GREEN CUBE.
Why did you do that?
TO STACK UP THE RED CUBE, A LARGE RED BLOCK AND A LARGE GREEN CUBE.
Why did you do that?
BECAUSE YOU ASKED ME TO.
What did the red cube support before you started to clean it off?
THE GREEN PYRAMID.
There were five blocks to the left of the box then.

NO, ONLY FOUR OF THEM: THE RED CUBE, TWO LARGE
GREEN CUBES AND A LARGE RED BLOCK.
Does a steeple . . .
SORRY, I DON'T KNOW THE WORD "STEEPLE." (The system
interrupts immediately when it sees a word it can't figure out.)
A steeple is a stack which contains two green cubes and a pyramid.
I UNDERSTAND.
Are there any steeples now?
NO.
Build one.
OK.
Call the biggest block "superblock."
OK.
Have you picked up superblock since we began?
YES.
Why did you drop it?
BY "IT" I ASSUME YOU MEAN SUPERBLOCK. I CAN'T
EXPLAIN A NONEXISTENT EVENT. (There is no record in
memory of any block being dropped.)

The work of Marr, Winograd, and others is important beyond the boundaries of artificial intelligence. Winograd's program has already had some effect on traditional linguistic theory.
Winograd learned, as he worked out his program, that the only
way to build a system to understand language is to build it so
that it can use both meaning and grammar to support each
other. This is contrary to the Chomskian view. Chomsky's ideas
are built upon the notion that, as Winograd puts it, "Language
is a way of organizing abstract symbols, and competence is explained in terms of symbol-manipulating rules. . . . Rules have
been formulated which describe in great detail how sentences
are put together. But . . . such theories have been unable to
provide any but the most rudimentary and unsatisfactory accounts of semantics." In other words, Chomsky's grammar is not
enough to allow a machine to understand or to speak. Winograd in recent years has gone beyond block worlds. He is now
building a computer language, called the Knowledge Represen-
tation Language, which he hopes will provide a system into
which huge quantities of knowledge can be placed and from
which bits of information can instantly be retrieved. Its core is
an unlimited array of semantic units—groups of words and

phrases related in meaning and stored together in memory. Gradually, the abilities of man are being better mimicked. Gradually, Turing's Test is becoming more winnable by machines. Fragmentary comparisons between man and machine have already begun, of course, such as occurred inadvertently when Joseph Weizenbaum wrote his DOCTOR program and found that computer programs free of any knowledge at all about human behavior are only a little less convincing than psychiatrists themselves. In a test of the believability of DOCTOR, patients, after talking with the program, were asked about the interview: sixty percent refused to believe, even when told, that the interview was with a machine, not a psychiatrist.

A similar test put the situation in reverse: A program that gives answers like those of a psychotic, a paranoid, was created by Kenneth Colby. In his test, he first had psychiatrists interview patients by Teletype to arrive at their diagnoses. A second group of psychiatrists was asked to rate the transcripts of these same interviews according to the presence or absence of paranoia in the patient being interviewed over the teletype. A third group of psychiatrists was sent the same transcripts, but was let in on part of the secret: some of the "patients" interviewed by psychiatrists were not patients, but the paranoid computer program. These psychiatrists were asked to tell, from the transcript alone, which of the interviews were with patients and which with the computer.

Among the first set of psychiatrists, none realized that they were interviewing computers as well as patients. Among the second group of psychiatrists the same was true: They could not tell the difference between man and machine patients. Among the third group of psychiatrists, who *knew* that some of the interviews were with a machine, they also could not tell the difference between man and machine. They did no better than chance when asked to choose which was which. Of course, this test was unfair. It probably tells more about the state of knowledge in psychiatry than that in computer science.

Turing suggested comparing the new, unprogrammed computer with a baby that needs to be nurtured and taught, and he felt that the computer's growth in knowledge and competence might parallel that of a developing person. But the abilities computers have acquired in the past thirty years have been oddly uneven, very unlike any orderly growth of powers. Rather, the growth of computer ability has been in bursts, forward and sideward, like the ramshackle movement of evolution rather than maturation. It grows broadly, from variety to variety, only occasionally squirting upward to a new species. We can see more similarity between computers and other species such as insects than we can between computer and man.

Insects were once thought to have intelligence, to have the ability to learn and to reason. The behavior of some insects, on first look, would seem to justify this opinion. For example, the sphex wasp. The creature stings its prey, the spider, paralyzing but not killing it. The wasp drags the spider to the burrow where the wasp eggs lie. Before bringing the spider in, however, it leaves the spider outside and enters the burrow to see that everything inside is in order. Then, it goes out to retrieve the spider and place it next to the eggs so they may have food when they hatch. This sequence of behavior is invariable for the wasp. In fact, if an intruder were to move the spider when it lay outside the burrow, move it only an inch or two, the wasp could not accommodate the situation. When it goes to fetch the spider, it drags it back to the burrow entrance and leaves it to inspect the den again. If the wasp is interrupted at any point in the plan, it must halt and repeat the cycle from the point of interruption. If the spider is moved forty times in a row, then forty times the wasp will emerge from the inspected nest, find the spider, drag it close, and leave it again to inspect the nest.

Another insect, the dung beetle, similarly executes a plan to make a ball of dung and roll it to its nest; if the rolled ball is removed from its jaws early on, the beetle will not stop, but will continue to carry out its program as if the ball were still there. In some species of arthropods, there is a tiny ganglion which indicates to the insect whether the hairs on its legs are clean; if this ganglion is removed, the poor creature will clean itself until it dies of exhaustion.

Our computer programs are better than the behavorial systems in the insects. It is common for programs to have what these insects lack—mechanisms that check on the progress of an action and compare it to the final goal, in other words, feedback. But we have only recently developed programs that can see as well as insects, and there may be some abilities of insects we cannot or have not yet programmed. Perhaps, while we wait to try Turing's Test at the end of the century, we might make provisional tests—Can the machine imitate the essential abilities of the insect? Of the reptile or bird?—and so on up the evolutionary scale.

7

JOHN McCarthy left MIT in 1963. He moved to California, where an era of political and social experiment was beginning. Within his own small bounds, McCarthy already had some experience of these things. The dedicated restlessness which had defined McCarthy's intellectual life fit well into the new California surroundings. He left MIT because his work there seemed unappreciated; he was still languishing near the bottom of the hierarchy of professorships. When he moved to Stanford he was made a full professor and was permitted to found and direct his own laboratory there.

Pictures of the new Stanford professor, taken a few seasons after his arrival, show well how he adjusted to the climate of California: His hair, still black but bleeding gray, hung in long locks upon his neck. A varicolored headband, like those worn by hippies, gave him a renegade look. His beard was long and full. (The beard was acquired, not grown as part of the new look, at MIT. A friend recalls that McCarthy entered a bout of the mumps with a bare chin and came out of it hirsute, bearded more or less by accident.) Though McCarthy was approaching the age of forty during the bloom of the flower children, he was entranced by the efflorescent celebrations. "I think a discovery was made between 1960 and 1967 in rock music," he said. "It was a discovery of a new technique perhaps; I don't know exactly what, but it produced an emotional effect in a way that

had not been done before. . . . I think they lost it though. . . ."
He listened to the Jefferson Airplane, The Doors, Big Brother
and the Holding Company. He went to the first rock concerts,
which mixed light with the blasts of sound. He met the John-
nies Appleseed of lysergic acid diethylamide, Timothy Leary
and Richard Alpert, long before they scattered their fantastic
seeds and became cult heroes. When McCarthy moved to California, he sold his house in Massachusetts to the pair. "That is
where they had their first hippie commune," McCarthy said. He
knew Leary and Alpert only casually, but he said, "I had to
worry about their fate, because, shortly after I sold them the
house they were fired by Harvard. I had a second mortgage on
the house. . . ." I asked McCarthy if he went back to visit Leary
and Alpert after he moved to Stanford.

"Yes."

"How were they?"

"Oh, they were high," McCarthy said and smiled. He recalled
that the two had some rather bizarre political ambitions when
he went to see them. "They had just visited an island called
Dominica, and they were going to take over the island, they
thought. They had been treated very nicely by everybody there.
But they had some rather tactless ideas about it. They were
going to import their own food rather than pay the high local
prices. . . . But they went ahead planning. What happened in
the end, of course, was that the next time they visited Dominica
the British colonial office found out about them and the drugs.
They promptly threw them out. . . ."

The evening that Leary and Alpert described their paradise,
McCarthy was also offered a dose of the chemical which had put
such ideas in their heads. McCarthy says he couldn't take it,
because he had to get up at 5:00 A.M. the next day and drive
250 miles. "So I went to bed. I slept in their meditation room—
what they had done was taken my old library, which had an
alcove in it, and they walled off the alcove so that it could not
be reached from that floor. They made a hole in the floor of the
alcove, put a trapdoor in, and had a ladder going down to the
basement. It was a cocoon, layered with pillows, colored light,
and psychedelic art. The house altogether was the prototype of
the hippie pad several years ahead of its fame." McCarthy's
venturesome attitude did lead him eventually to try LSD. A

young woman offered to guide him on the excursion, so he took a dose of the drug and the two went off to a concert of Big Brother and the Holding Company. "The girl had just had a squabble with her boyfriend," McCarthy recalls, "and she also had a phobia—she hated rock concerts. She couldn't stand the enormous crowds. The result was, I took the LSD, and *she* freaked out. . . ."

McCarthy joined the Mid-Peninsula Free University when it started. Mid-Peninsula was one of the largest of the dozens of free universities started during that era. He became involved in the governance of the hodgepodge of courses. Strangely, the free university, which had been created as a Leftist answer to the conservatism of the established universities, became a force that drove McCarthy away from the political Left. His drift away from the Left actually started many years earlier; even while he was in the Communist party in the 1940s and early fifties, he felt himself being repelled gradually from the cause. "What was a scientific theory about society, a wrong one perhaps, but a scientific attitude in the 1920s," McCarthy said, "became in the 1930s just an apologetics for whatever policies the Soviet government wanted to carry out." His interest in the theory relaxed, and he found himself faced with succeeding strains on his belief. He learned about the massacres of the "red terror" which took place after the revolution; he was left to wonder about the occupation of Eastern European countries. There was Beria, who was executed after a farcical trial, and then Khrushchev's admission in a speech to Soviet leaders that there was a Gulag Archipelago and that Stalin had murdered thousands.

By the late 1960s, his sympathy with Leftist causes was still enough alive that he volunteered to help the free university. He once managed to finagle a grant of five thousand dollars to help fund its projects—a bit of fundraising that cost him some effort. But as soon as the money was in hand and a meeting called to decide how to spend it, a group of "ultraradicals" packed the meeting. They voted out everyone else, voted themselves in charge. They used the money to print one large issue of a newspaper whose banner headline read: TEN WAYS TO OFF-ICATE. Translated, the headline and following article suggested ten ways to murder policemen and get away with it. Following that experience, McCarthy visited the Soviet Union for a time. Then he happened to visit Czechoslovakia in October of 1968, just before the Soviets made their argument against free expression there with tanks. ("He came back plotting to build martial robots," one friend remembers.)

The conjunction of experiences chilled him. "The campus radicals and the bureaucrats of Pravda are really the same sort of people," he says. "Granted that Soviet bureaucrats are in their sixties and seventies, and some of these radicals are in their twenties; otherwise I found the parallel remarkable. Both are oppressive in their psychology. Both have the same tendency to abuse what power they can get, and both severely enforce adherence to their beliefs of the moment." McCarthy smoldered as Stanford's ROTC building burned down and radicals laid siege to even the most disinterested parts of academic life.

At the beginning of the 1970s, there was an abrupt change in the weather about John McCarthy. The headband was dropped and he had his long hair sheared. He wore suits. The indicators of his political opinions turned round to face another direction. Some found the change irritating and barely explicable. Arguments with friends occurred over Vietnam and other issues. Others felt the change was more consistent with McCarthy's previous beliefs than an alteration of them. "The main driving force in John McCarthy's political view of the world is individual freedom," Terry Winograd said. "Back in those early days he saw the New Left and the student movement as the chief expression of individual freedom, and therefore was very sympathetic to it. He dressed in a way that was in style with it. As time went on, he began to see that the political situation had changed. The student movement as a spontaneous outburst of individual freedom died away; what was left was the more harsh political element. . . ."

As McCarthy describes it: "I quit the left in 1953, but still remained sympathetic for a long time. I didn't become an actual reactionary until about 1972." After a moment's thought he added, "I suppose I was moving in the opposite direction from most people. I even acquired something of an affection for Richard Nixon!"

During this turbulent period, McCarthy's first marriage ended in divorce. He sank into a period of bachelorhood. Friends noted the changes: a shagginess overtook his habits of grooming and dress, domestic chores went undone, entropy increased across the breadth of his scheduled life. But coincident with the time his political compass shifted, McCarthy had met and begun to keep company with a woman six years younger than himself. She was a programmer for IBM named Vera Watson. After her appearance, much of his life began to be retrieved from neglect. His hair was trimmed, his clothes better kept and chosen, his house neatly reordered. Vera was born in China and lived in Canada and South America before settling herself in California. Among a list of her abilities, probably the most outstanding was her mountain climbing. She is the only woman to climb the Andes peak Aconcagua alone. It was not her intention to climb alone to the top of the 22,800-foot mountain, the highest in the Western Hemisphere. But the rest of the group climbing with her turned back. She refused to. She climbed other great peaks of the Americas before meeting John McCarthy. Together the two climbed lesser rocks in Yosemite and then ascended a 17,000-foot Mexican volcano. But McCarthy's climbing was eventually discontinued. "I got too fat," he says. Vera and John were a middle-life couple, well suited to one another. She was a quiet woman. She was well organized. Both were attracted to technical subjects. Her politics, in addition, were a good fit for his mellowed outlook.

8

I n the 1960s, a fundamental change took place in the relations between men and machines, and among the authors of that change was John McCarthy. In a sense, he is the father of all intimate relations between humans and computers. He is one of the inventors of computer time-sharing. Specifically, he created the form of time-sharing that allows one person to use a huge computer connected simultaneously to hundreds of other users, and to converse with it personally, as if he were the only person connected to it and the sole master of its powers. The significance of his idea, just beginning to be felt as ordinary people learn to use computers, extends outside science and mathematics to politics, merchandising, and other areas of society. It is even possible that it can alter democracy as we have known it.

McCarthy's discovery, as well as his own intimacy with computers, began when he worked on an early IBM machine. The experience was useful to him, but parts of it he found frustrating and even absurd. All computers then, and it is still true with the clumsy machines used by business, were operated in a way that did not allow anyone but a specialized operator to work the machine. The man who submitted his problem to a computer did not actually go near the machine. "For the first two decades of the existence of the high-speed computer," wrote John Kemeny, "machines were so scarce and so expensive that man approached the computer the way an ancient Greek approached an oracle. A man submitted his request . . . and then waited patiently until it was convenient for the machine to work out the problem. Only specially selected acolytes were allowed to have direct communication with the computer. In this original mode of using computers, known as batch processing, hundreds of computer requests were collected by the staff of a computation center and then fed to the machine in a batch."

What was worse, those acolytes who stood guard over the computer were often obsessive mechanists. Entering the domain of computers early, they had a special love of the orderly behavior of the new machines, and so made their systems mimic the same relentless logic. The behavior of ordinary people who must use the machines, however, was plodding, haphazard, and entirely unlikely to be able to follow accurately the thought chains of those specialists.

McCarthy's colleague, Edward Fredkin, described his and McCarthy's first years of coping with this situation. "Those early programmers made systems that were extremely aggravating for ordinary people to use who were not so compulsive as the programmers were. I had to submit my cards in the morning. The following morning they would tell me what the computer did. I would get a message which would say that on line number seven, I had a comma where I should have had a period. Since the machine *knew* I needed a period, it could have just acted as though I had made a period. It *also knew* about mistakes on later lines—fifty-six, seventy-two, ninety-three, and one thirty-four. But it didn't mention these. When I corrected line forty-seven, and spent another day doing it, it then informed me about a missing left parenthesis on line fifty-six. And even at that, it did not tell me in a nice way. It said: YOU HAVE ERROR NUMBER 7313. When I looked that up in the manual, the book would say, 'Either a left parenthesis or a semicolon omitted from such and such a location, or possibly another location.' Of course, the machine *knew* which of these things it was. But the programmers didn't allow their system simply to tell me, even though the machine was quite capable of doing it."

I told Fredkin that I always assumed those irritating features were simply the way computers acted.

"No. Absolutely not. I wondered about this too, because when I first started writing programs they didn't act that way. In fact, there is no good reason for them to behave that way. It is *harder* to write them that way. The world has now begun to force programmers to write better programs. McCarthy was one of the pioneers; he helped force programmers to do it. That is what time-sharing and interactive computing are about. . . ."

McCarthy realized that there was no good reason for the estrangement between a man and his machine. So, in 1958 and 1959, he worked out a computer system in which the batch method was abandoned. Humans are slow to think and act, where computers are fast, and this slowness was used to advantage. While a human takes ten seconds, twenty seconds, or even several minutes to write out a question and respond to its answer, a computer can act in millionths and billionths of a second. A servant capable of working at the speed of light in his rounds can serve many people without any one of them finding a delay in his own service. Just so, if each user has his own terminal connected to the computer, the computer can rapidly turn from user to user. The machine's attention thus shuttles round the circle of users, answering a request at each step, apportioning some milliseconds of its time for each computation. A medium-sized computer can handle fifty to a hundred private terminals working simultaneously. This was McCarthy's inspiration: to allow each member of the laboratory to use the computer as if it were his own: to use it at any hour of the day or night and to have his own file of papers, notes, and programs in its memory. From this, McCarthy extended the idea. He was the first to think of the computer terminal for the home in concrete terms.

In his own home, John McCarthy's terminal is in his study, adjoining the living room. The first time I visited McCarthy at his home, he showed me some of the machine's abilities. We had sat in the living room of his hilltop house for most of the evening, sketching for the tape recorder the outlines of his career. Vera came in from work after we began, served coffee, patched a few memory blanks with names and dates, then softly excused herself and went about her own work. It was after one in the morning that McCarthy and I finished worrying other topics and he led me to the study to show me the machine.

The powers of the terminal are limited, he said, as I was looking around at what hung upon the walls (a futuristic city in Day-Glo colors, a Civil War document he found in a barn, two walls of books: science, fiction, science fiction). There is no public information utility to connect his terminal to. There is no phone system connecting all other home terminals to his. But the machine is part of a network of a few hundred terminals, and it does have many useful programs.

At the center of the screen is an invitation from the computer: "TAKE ME, I'M YOURS." When I asked McCarthy about that line, he said that it was half of an old laboratory joke. Though it was eventually removed from the system, the computer also used to say, when it was overloaded, "NOT TONIGHT, DEAR, I'VE GOT A HEADACHE." Now, when it is idle, the terminal screen displays a list of useful information—the date and time, the temperature, the number of people using the computer, the amount of computer capacity being used.

McCarthy typed his initials on the keyboard. "As soon as I log into the system, it tells me if there are any messages." A message from someone at the lab appeared, and after a couple of stanzas of clicked dialogue, McCarthy returned his attention home. He was conversing with a colleague about two miles away, but the exchange could just as well have been with someone in Europe. Some of the other computer centers in the network are MIT, Harvard, Rand Corporation, Xerox, University of Illinois, half a dozen army and air force bases, and the Advanced Research Projects Agency of the Defense Department, which pays for and oversees the network. There are approximately six dozen "nodes in the net." At each node, there are any number of terminals, up to seventy-five or so.

The number of programs of convenience that McCarthy can use is very large, and if you count his ability to write little programs to fit his needs, the number is practically limitless. When he sits down at the terminal in his lab, McCarthy may choose to call up one of sixteen radio channels piped in or one of three television channels if he cares to. He may check in daily with the news service programs—the computer gets The Associated Press and *The New York Times* wire services. By typing HOT, he can see what is currently running on the wires. But a better way to check the news is to leave standing requests with the computer. The machine can save any stories of interest, provided you can give it a key word to search for. McCarthy asks the machine to save every story in which the word "nuclear" appears, so he may follow the progress of the debate over nuclear power. Another researcher at the lab follows the exploits of those who protest whale hunts: the program saves for him all stories containing the words Greenpeace, whale, dolphin, porpoise, and cetacean. At first, he found Miami Dolphins football stories mixed in with his desired catch. He instructed the program to take all the stories with "dolphin" and subtract from those all stories with the word "football." The same researcher at the lab receives stories touching on his hometown in North Carolina, on airplane crashes, and on space missions. On an average day, he gets half a dozen stories altogether. McCarthy had the news service program designed as a service specifically for use in home computers.

Among the secretarial conveniences of the system is an editor program. While he is writing, McCarthy may delete or insert words, lines, paragraphs, or whole pages at any spot. The effort involved is the pressing of two keys. Another program can correct spelling errors—it has a ten-thousand-word dictionary in it. Once his paper is typed, McCarthy can have it printed by the computer. For the printing, which looks nearly as good as a professional printing job, McCarthy may choose from more than a hundred typefaces, including three in Elvish (from Tolkien's *Lord of the Rings*). He may use the machine to make complex graphic displays in a variety of colors. He may instruct it to print in the staffs and notes of musical notation. The machine can also be McCarthy's adversary in many games, including chess, checkers, go, kalah, and a number of curious games known only to programmers (life, wumpus, bloop, adventure, space wars). The file called YUMYUM is a list of restaurants recommended by local programmers in cities from San Francisco to London.

What a listing of programs does not convey about the network of terminals is the sense of play connected with John

McCarthy's interactive computing. This appears, to begin with, in their jargon. Programmers or researchers are "hackers." The word is an antonym for theorist. A "glitch" in the jargon means a sudden, maddening failure—such as an electrical failure at the worst moment. As one hacker put it, "It is a small discontinuity, something unexpected, especially something that screws you. It is the sound of someone stepping in dog shit." Among hackers, subtlety is respected, and the hacker who uses the grinding power of a large calculation in place of a smaller, more cleverly designed program is said to be guilty of using "brute force," and one who uses brute force as a regular method is a "jock." To "snarf" is to take, or borrow, especially said of a large document snarfed without the author's permission. "Vanilla" is an adjective attached to anything that is standard or ordinary; to "flame" is to speak incessantly and insistently on a boring matter. To return from a digression is to "pop." One word borrowed with appreciation from World War Two is FUBAR (an acronym for Fucked Up Beyond All Recognition). FUBAR has been shortened by hackers to "foo," and is used as a noun to lightly deprecate anything or any situation. A great green sign over the door to Stanford's computer room reads FOOSLAND.

Though each terminal user can see the screen of any other user at any time, there is an etiquette at the lab which discourages users from interrupting each other. But from time to time they do make jokes appear on one another's screens. At MIT a little program called COOKIE BEAR institutionalizes the joke: When a researcher is the victim of cookie bear, his screen will flash and the message appears: BEAR WANTS A COOKIE. The victim must type out COOKIE to feed the bear. He may ignore the message and go on with his work, but the bear will return after an interval. If again it is not fed, it will go away, but return sooner. The cycle repeats, the bear returning after shorter and shorter intervals until it achieves its cookie.

Making the computer behave as people do is also a constant source of amusement to the hackers. It is like the fun zoo keepers might have with the chimps in their charge. They teach them tricks of mimicry. Once, while a Chinese delegation was visiting Stanford during Mao's last years, the programmers taught a mechanical arm to write out a Maoist slogan on command. On another occasion, the mechanical arm in coordination with a camera eye was trained to serve punch. It would swing over, dip a cup, then swing back to fill a waiting glass. The Cyclopean bartender delighted those at the party, but after some time appeared to be consuming some of the punch itself. It started to swing erratically. Soon the arm began scooping up punch and flinging it about in gleeful abandon. The crowd roared. Only later did the programmers understand their error: over a certain threshold of work, tolerance in the mechanical parts was not great enough, and began to cause faulty feedback, which in turn caused erroneous instructions to be sent back to the arm.

Perhaps zoo keepers make sexual jokes about the animals in their care; computists certainly do so with their charges. In Foosland, large printouts are hung on the walls—computer renditions of nude women. In order to make one of these pinups, a woman must pose for the computer to make the drawing.

"For some reason, the women cannot resist it," said a worker at the lab. Some time ago, a young man explored a similar thesis for a project in psychology class. He made a filmic study in abnormality—that is, a porn movie depicting a woman coupling with a computer. The film was shot late one night when, usually, few people are in the lab using the computer. On this night, however, there were so many diligent programmers catching up on their work that they had to be shooed away from the computer room. Instead, the lab's TV camera was pointed in the direction of events, and everyone watched on his own terminal screen.

Those who have used computer terminals linked to a larger system have also developed a dependency on their machines. They work now sans pencil, paper, or typewriter. They enjoy the constant connection to each other through the machine and depend on services the machine offers. The terminal has become an appendage as familiar as the telephone. It has become second nature to the degree that when one poor, discomposed researcher committed suicide some time ago, he filed a suicide note on his terminal, signing only with his meaningless system-name.

9

I T was nearly two in the morning when McCarthy and I finished talking about the terminal and the system connected to it. Vera wandered into the study, yawning. The two, though they had been together for some time, had just been married and had returned only two days before from a short honeymoon. They were planning a longer vacation together, and they eventually took it—to climb a volcano rimmed with ice. McCarthy roused himself from his seat by the terminal; Vera circled his waist with her arm, and rested her head on his shoulder as I left.

I next saw John McCarthy more than a year later. He had just returned from Nepal and China. He had gone with Vera to Nepal, where she would stay to join a major mountain climbing expedition to Annapurna, the tenth highest peak in the world, and one of the most hazardous. This expedition comprised all women climbers, and if it succeeded would be the first group of women to reach a major Himalayan peak, the first Americans on Annapurna. Vera had not done very much ice climbing, nor had she climbed much in conditions of forcible winds and hard cold, but the opportunity to climb with a major expedition was a prize. So she went, with courage to stand in for experience.

When I walked into his office, McCarthy had in front of him a letter from Vera, and he was talking on the phone: "Appar-

ently the Sherpa humor is rather broad . . . they had made
obscene pictures in the snow . . . Yes. The most recent information I have is that they were at camp two, deciding where to put
in the route to camp three. They were just about to tackle the
hard part . . . across the glacier to the ice face, near the bottom
of the steep wall . . . Everyone is having trouble breathing but
no one is thinking mutinous thoughts yet. . . ." After he hung
up, he turned to his terminal, rapped for a moment before
greeting me. We talked about Annapurna. He seemed nervous
until we moved the subject to artificial intelligence and some
questions left unanswered in previous talks.

I asked about the dates of some of his important papers: His
first paper on the correctness of computer programs was written
in 1961. His first paper proposing a time-sharing system with
multiple terminals running together was in January 1959. I said
I was curious to hear him talk a little more in personal terms
about living with computers. Do they really become personalized and continue to give the illusion of animate, if limited, beings? And about the future of artificial intelligence work
—what can we expect?

We somehow began, *en passant,* to talk about chess. Only a
week or so before, McCarthy had lost one of the most famous
bets in chess history, a bet that had been the subject of speculation for ten years since it was made in 1968. During a conference at Edinburgh University in that year, John McCarthy
found himself across the board from David Levy—then reigning
chess champion of Scotland, an international master, as well as
a former researcher in machine intelligence. McCarthy gave a
hard game, but was finally unkinged, and as a careless shot after
the match he said that he would never be able to beat Levy but
soon, in ten years say, a computer program would. Computer
programs at the time were winning only half their games
against much weaker players, and Levy at once offered to bet
500 pounds on his skill against a decade's progress in machine
players. McCarthy and another researcher who had heard the
bet accepted it, 250 pounds each. By the year of the match,
things looked bad for the computists; machines were bigger and
faster but no smarter. But in the event, during September 1978
in Toronto, Levy was surprised at least in the beginning of the
match. In the first game, Levy offered a relaxed, playful game

and was mated. In the next four games, Levy played more soberly and directly against the weakness of all computer chess programs—the slowly developing game of high strategy. He won three and drew one, and took his prize. After the match, several people offered to renew the bet—that ten years from this match he would not be able to hold up. Levy refused the bet. He had not thought that a computer would ever be world chess champion, but he said that his opinion had changed. A computer will be world champion, perhaps within two decades. Within a decade, however, it would be good enough to beat Levy.

McCarthy said he was not much upset at losing the bet. The value of the pound, after all, had dropped greatly during ten years. "I would have been much more upset if I had *won* the bet. When I made it, I assumed that a lot of work would be done on chess programs and some new ideas would be put into them before the match with Levy. But nobody worked on chess seriously, and there were practically no new ideas in the program." It would have caused trouble with McCarthy's ideas about what is necessary for machine intelligence if a program could win by brute force alone.

In the course of conversation, I asked McCarthy if he would play against one of the powerful computer programs. I said I would like to see such a match. It would be, in a way, master against pupil as well as man against machine, because McCarthy contributed ideas to some of the first successful computer chess programs. Working with student Allen Kotok, he wrote a program that played the first major match of computer against computer. McCarthy's program played against a program written in the Soviet Union with the help of a chess grand master.

McCarthy said it would be fairly easy to set up a game against a good program at MIT by simply playing on the terminal at the lab or at his home. We decided to play on a Sunday night, and finish with my other questions afterward.

We started at about ten-thirty on a chilly, foggy night at the hilltop laboratory. McCarthy arrived with the family dog, Caspian, drooling and jingling behind him. McCarthy placed a pocket chess set down on the desk next to his terminal, and researcher Bill Gosper, who made the arrangements with MIT to have the chess program ready to play, typed the moves into the computer and read its responses. The program McCarthy was playing against was one that some years earlier was entered in a human chess tournament in Boston and won the Class D crown—the best of the casual players. With some concentration, McCarthy could beat it. He decided to give the machine the slight advantage of the attack by letting it play first.

The first moves went quickly, but McCarthy, unable to tether his mind to the board, made a slip, and then another one. "I've blundered already," he said. "There's been too much talking." Looking at the computer's evaluation of the position after only seven moves, Gosper added, "The machine thinks it's up a pawn." McCarthy resigned the game. The predictably constant behavior of the machine often allows it an advantage over erratic human behavior, dislocated as it often is by emotion. Worry is as much a part of the human chess game as it is absent from the computer's game. McCarthy was inclined to quit for the evening and go home. But Gosper coaxed him to retract his blundered moves and start over. McCarthy decided finally to take back one of his poor moves, and not the other, to see if he might regain position by the end of the match. He didn't. The machine played evenly, McCarthy slipped another pawn behind. What made the game grimmer was that, with each move, the machine printed out its evaluation of the position and what it expected its opponent would do at each move. The predictions were practically always correct; when they weren't, it was because of a poorer choice by McCarthy. He would have resigned after about thirty moves if he were playing a human. He had a situation in which he might advance a pawn, make a queen some moves later. This kind of thinking—more than five or six moves ahead—is often beyond a computer's ability. McCarthy said, "There is always the chance of running into a bug in the program in which the machine makes a completely crazy move. That is one rule when playing a machine—never give up, not even in the most obviously lost situations." But the MIT program caught his advancing pawn, and neatly made a mate as well.

When he got home, McCarthy settled himself into the swiveling chair before his terminal. I had noticed that he refers to the computer not as he or she but as "it." Then, having picked a neuter pronoun, he uses verbs that reanimate the neutered machine. It wants, it thinks, it asks. I heard one computist describe what happens when the system encounters a confusing situation: "When it hits a bug, it drops over and plays dead. Then it just waits for someone to come and revive it." I asked McCarthy about whether the machine is personified for him or not.

"No. I would love to call it 'he' and think about it as if it had a personality. But it's not yet warranted." Still, he said that one could talk about a machine wanting or knowing; these terms are as legitimate for machines as for people. They may be the only way of describing simply the complex action of machinery. This does not mean that he is attributing these desires and attributes to the machine's "mind." The attributes can appear without the mind.

"As much as possible," he once wrote, "we ascribe mental qualities separately from each other instead of bundling them in a concept of mind. This is necessary because present machines have rather varied little minds; the mental qualities that can be legitimately ascribed to them are few and differ from machine to machine. . . ."

As McCarthy points out, when we refer to the behavior of people—"He wants to eat" or "He knows the answer"—we really do not know what we mean. What *does* it mean to want? Ultimately, to say what "want" is, one would have to describe the physical system at work in detail, telling why each part operates in concert with others, and how this produces the behavior that indicates to us "wanting." In place of this laborious process we use the shorthand, which works rather well. With humans we do not fully understand all the internal rules and mechanisms which account for wanting and knowing, while with machines we do know all the internal rules and could trace fully the reason it wants this or believes that. But still, just as with a human, it is quicker just to talk about the states of mind.

An accident with McCarthy's home heating system during one January was the event which caused him to think about the use of these terms. "Ascribing beliefs to simple thermostats is not really necessary. . . . ," he wrote, "however, their simplicity makes clearer what is involved. . . . First let us consider a simple thermostat that turns *off* the heat when the temperature is a degree above the temperature set on the thermostat, turns *on* the heat when the temperature is a degree below the desired temperature, and leaves the heat as is when the temperature is in the two degree range around the desired temperature.

"The simplest belief predicate B (s,p) ascribes belief to only two sentences: 'The room is too cold' and 'The room is too hot,' and these beliefs are assigned to states of the thermostat so that in the two degree range, neither is believed. When the thermostat believes the room is too cold or too hot it sends a message to that effect to the furnace. . . . We do not ascribe it to any other beliefs; it has no opinion even about whether the heat is on or off or about the weather or about who won the battle of Waterloo. Moreover, it has no introspective beliefs, that is, it doesn't believe that it believes the room is too hot.

"The temperature control system in my house may be described as follows: thermostats upstairs and downstairs tell the central system to turn on or shut off hot water flow to these areas. A central water temperature thermostat tells the furnace to turn on or off, thus keeping the central hot water reservoir at the right temperature.

"Recently it was too hot upstairs, and the question arose as to whether the upstairs thermostat mistakenly *believed* it was too cold upstairs or whether the furnace thermostat mistakenly *believed* the [heating] water was too cold. It turned out that neither mistake was made; the downstairs controller *tried* to turn off the flow of water, but *couldn't*, because the valve was stuck. . . .

"Since the services of plumbers are increasingly expensive, and microcomputers are increasingly cheap, one is led to design a temperature control system that would *know* a lot more about the thermal state of the house, and its own state of health. . . .

"A more advanced system would know whether the actions it *attempted* succeeded, and it would communicate failures and adapt to them. (We adapted to the failure by turning off the whole system until the whole house cooled off, and then letting the two parts warm up together.) The present system has the *physical capability* of doing this even if it hasn't the *knowledge* or the *will*. . . ."

The use of gender when describing machines, in fact, has declined generally. Perhaps that is because of our greater mechanical sophistication, and that computers have superseded simpler machines as the most personified collections of parts. But there is a curious property of computers that is absent from other personified machines of the past. As Edward Fredkin commented, "If you ask me what a home terminal is most like to deal with, I would say it is most like the relations between a writer and his typewriter. I have read some very funny stories about the love and hate relations of people and their type-writers. But there is a great difference, not just in what the terminal can do, but in the quality of the relationship. The computer has the power to punish you. Learning to ride a bi-cycle, if you make big mistakes, you fall down. But you won't fall down if you make little mistakes, and eventually you learn to ride it so that you never fall down. It is not that way with a computer. It sits there with a baseball bat in its hands just waiting to hit you on the head anytime you do anything wrong. You leave out one comma, and it gets you. Most people never learn very much discipline, so they constantly make this kind of small error. . . ." It is for this reason that many of those who take up programming for a living seem to be obsessive creatures —or that obsessive are the ones who become programmers— because they must deal with a superrational machine, one which disallows any error and punishes vagueness.

Part of the problem of making computers accessible to every-one is eliminating the machine's obsessiveness with perfect clar-ity. But still, I said to McCarthy, assuming that can be worked out so that we can use machines for more duties, don't you think people will object? Wouldn't people rather deal with people than with machines?

"The ideology on that point," he says, "is often wrong. Take the phone system as an example. When the phone company was first introducing dialing in places where there had been a man-ual operator, they found an immediate jump of thirty percent in the number of calls that were made. The reason is that going through an operator is a psychological hazard. You prefer to be thinking about what you are going to say to the person you want to reach, rather than what you are going to say to the operator. In fact, you sometimes find yourself inadvertently say-ing to the operator something you intended to say to the person you were trying to reach. . . ." The hazard may occur in other situations—at the supermarket, at the bank, and with other routine transactions in which people are used to carrying out unthinking, repetitive processing of customers.

What about humanizing machines, making them behave in a friendlier, more personal manner? Do you think that might be a good idea?

"I would say that if a machine became too human, people wouldn't like it." McCarthy laughed a little. "If you had to start to worry about the impression you were making on it— *that* would be bad. . . ."

Is that a general rule, people like machines to be like machines?

"I think so. You know there is this remark you hear about people being treated like machines—you could define the issue if you wanted to. There are two ways of looking at the people in those ordinary transactions. One is to think: If I do this, he will do that. (The way you treat a store clerk you don't know— you expect rote responses.) I regard that as treating a person like a machine. The other way to look at people is to think: He has certain goals, and he will act to advance them; he has these desires and perhaps I want to help him realize some of his desires. You can say that you are treating him fully as a human when you want to understand his goals.

"But you may not prefer to be treated as a human. That depends on the character of the interaction. If you are a store clerk, you probably prefer to be regarded as someone who will say, 'Give me the money, I'll give you the goods.' You are not interested in this customer psychoanalyzing your inmost desires. Or—in the form it most often takes—you are not interested in his criticizing you. So to speak, judging you. The clerk wants to keep his privacy."

10

THE Leftish ideology of the 1960s that once attracted Mc-
Carthy nevertheless always contained elements of antitechnological feeling. McCarthy knew that those streaks of thought
were irrational, and he smelled the irony of the situation. The
Left, champions of the people, were opposing the very machines
that could return some political power to the hands of the
people. The computer, McCarthy felt, was the quintessentially
democratic machine. He mentioned these ideas in his writing,
the most public of which was in *Scientific American* in 1966.
"The computer is an information machine. Information is a
commodity no less tangible than energy; if anything, it is more
pervasive in human affairs. The command of information made
possible by the computer should also make it possible to reverse
the trends toward mass-produced uniformity started by the industrial revolution. Taking advantage of this opportunity may
present the most urgent engineering, social, and political questions of the next generation. . . ."

But the slogans of the 1960s became, in the 1970s, pretexts for
political violence. Computers were among the objects of physical attacks. A computer facility not far from McCarthy's constellation of machinery was bombed. A Molotov cocktail was
exploded in the computer rooms of Fresno State College. It
caused a million dollars' worth of damage.

Thomas Whiteside, writing in *The New Yorker*, once cataloged similar attacks made on computers around the world. The computer had become a target, he said, "for the reason that someone had come to regard it either as a kind of electronic destroyer of personal identity or as an abhorrent symbol of corporate capitalism. Sometimes these attacks are committed by programmers or other computer processors in irrational outbursts, and sometimes they are planned, for political or other reasons. Several incidents have involved guns being fired at computers . . . at the Charlotte Liberty Mutual Life Insurance Company, in Charlotte, North Carolina, a computer operator, apparently in a fit of frustration, was reported to have fired a handgun several times at the company computer. In Olympia, Washington, in 1968, an unknown person fired two shots from a pistol at an IBM 1401 computer in a state employment office. And in a municipal office in Johannesburg, South Africa, in 1972, an unidentified person, who city officials suspected may have been the recipient of an exorbitant bill of some kind, fired four shots through a window at a computer."

In addition to sporadic gunfire made in anger, a number of computers have been disabled through premeditated violence. The National Farmers Union spent half a million dollars trying to repair a Burroughs computer—it had broken down thirty-six times in two years—before the true cause of the trouble was discovered and a computer operator arrested. The suspect had been inserting a key in the machine's memory-disc file, thus short-circuiting the memory. The man told police that he had an "overpowering urge" to shut the machine down. Similar assaults have been made on computers using screwdrivers and other sharp tools. During the Vietnam War, several attacks by radical groups were reported. A computer center at the University of Wisconsin was bombed, resulting in the death of one student and damage amounting to one and a half million dollars. Whiteside also records an attack on a university computer facility in Rome. "According to a Reuters dispatch, three masked women armed with rifles and a silencer-equipped pistol, held two professors and an assistant on duty powerless in a computer center at the university while a male accomplice poured gasoline on the center's computer and then set it on fire. The computer-terrorist women gave no motive for their behavior. . . ."

Most people believe as Thomas Whiteside does that such attacks, and the hostility in general toward computing machines, are caused by the nature of the machines. One criminal, after stealing $720 through a company's computers, pleaded in his defense that he had undertaken to outwit the computer because it was "a horrible impersonal machine." The phrase "impersonal machine" has become worn from overuse, and the phrase "computer error" is now accepted uncritically, though it is an obvious misnomer. The mistakes attributed to computers are actually of a more commonplace kind—they are caused by the carelessness of programmers. The assumption that computers are inhuman, impersonal machines is merely prejudice which has been generated to fill those empty places where real knowledge is missing. In fact, the same prejudices expressed in the same language were applied to the other objects before computers existed. Those formerly feared objects are now familiar and cause no emotional charge. The comments of a century past still sound fresh, though the objects of their criticism are not computers but looms, boilers, and carriages:

"The civilized man had built a coach, but has lost the use of his feet," wrote Ralph Waldo Emerson in 1841. "He is supported on crutches, but lacks so much support of muscles. He has a fine Geneva watch, but he fails of the skill to tell the hour by the sun." Samuel Butler thirty years later mimicked the attitude of his time: "This is the art of the machines—they serve that they may rule. . . . They have preyed upon man's groveling preference for his material over his spiritual interests, and have betrayed him into supplying that element of struggle and warfare without which no race can advance. The machines being of themselves unable to struggle, have got man to do their struggling for them. So that even now the machines will only serve on condition of being served, and that too upon their own terms."

In 1888, George Moore wrote: "The world is dying of machinery; that's the great disease, that is the plague that will sweep away and destroy civilization; man will have to rise against it sooner or later." And Henry David Thoreau as well: "Men have become the tools of their tools." It is worth adding that none of these writers, not even Thoreau, though he is famous for attempting it, lived without the support of the technology of their age. Modern writers who use the same slogans do not consider giving up the freedom created by their heated homes, typewriters, autos, and inexpensive books.

The climate of prejudice toward machines worsened sufficiently that protests began to appear, like the one from Isaac Asimov: *"If robots are so advanced that they can mimic the thought processes of human beings, then surely the nature of those thought processes* will be designed by human engineers and built-in safeguards will be added. . . . Never, never was one of my robots to turn stupidly on his creator for no purpose but to demonstrate, for one more wearying time, *the crime and punishment of Faust. Nonsense! My robots were machines designed by engineers, not pseudo-men created by blasphemers. . . ."*

Fear of machinery is a sort of xenophobia, and the slogans— human versus inhuman, feeling versus unfeeling—are found to be empty on close inspection. After all, emotions are precisely the characteristics we know are *not* uniquely human. All the feelings are found, in their full dress, down to a rather low level of animal. It is machinery that is uniquely human. We know of no humans who have been without their own variety of technology, from even before the time of the Neanderthal.

John McCarthy's whole childhood and education prepared him for two things: mathematical science and visionary politics. When home computers are linked in a national network, the two will be melded. One aspect of the new information technology has a particularly acute and personal aspect for him. McCarthy had watched as his brother, a Communist, was thrown out of the army years ago and recently dismissed from a post office job for his beliefs. McCarthy himself has experienced the feeling of being suspected and cataloged by the FBI. "It is easy," he says, "to have fantasies about the government establishing a dictatorship through their access to everyone's personal data, and to imagine people doing each other in with information gained from computerized spying. But the source of the dictatorship isn't the information. It is a monopoly on force and the will to use it. . . ." Actually, linked home computer terminals could be a guard against the surreptitious gathering and misuse of personal information, since users can store their files in code at virtually no cost. The code used could be one of the new computer-generated codes. They are, speaking practically, unbreakable even by code experts using their own computers.

By nature, McCarthy said, computers are democratic machines. Though we call many forms of government "democracies" now, that word truly applies only as it did originally—to a people that governs itself by voting *directly* on all issues of major concern, without the corrupting intercession of elected representatives. If there is any machine which might retrieve that lost relation between a citizen and his vote, it is the computer. It can handle information cheaply, in great volume, and can easily be addressed from distances. The two technical reasons why simple democracy has not been possible are that the people's wishes could not be recorded in a cheap, efficient way, and that it was impractical to deliver, day to day, all the necessary information for people to hear arguments, decide, and vote sensibly on issues. The technology now exists, and is simple enough, for people to recall at least some of the power that was surrendered to representatives over the past twenty-four centuries.

"Inventions that increase the speed and immediacy of information," wrote Ben Bagdikian in his books on news organizations, "have always changed the nature of their world. The introduction in Europe of printing by moveable type in the fifteenth century helped to produce the Renaissance and the Reformation. Telegraph, railroads, and high-speed presses in the nineteenth century led to the overthrow of oligarchies and launched mass politics. Television in the 1950s crystallized the civil rights revolution, rebellion on the campuses. . . ." What has been lacking in each of these innovations is the reverse flow of information. People have received information without having effective means of giving back their judgments on it. Opinion polls, made frequent and reliable by the use of computers, has indirectly begun the movement of information in reverse. But without home terminals, or at least local library terminals, the circle will not be drawn all the way around. The newspaper, Emerson said a century ago, does its best to make every square acre of land and sea give an account of itself at the breakfast table. A terminal beside the breakfast table, Mc-

Carthy believes, will turn the simple accounting into an exchange.

McCarthy thought early and deeply enough about these things that he has written a set of rules which he says are essential to maintaining liberty in the future. Decades ago he wrote in an article in the *Scientific American:*

> Reflection on the power of computer systems inevitably excites fear for the safety and integrity of the individual. In many minds, the computer is the ultimate threat. It makes possible, for instance, a single national information file containing all tax, legal, security, credit, educational, medical, and employment information about each and every citizen. Certainly such a file would be the source of great abuses.

On the other hand, McCarthy says, the political confrontation over the establishment of such a system could provide an opportunity not only to ensure some protection from future information gathering, but also to cure existing abuses.

He suggests a bill of rights:

No organization, governmental or private, shall be allowed to maintain files of its own on large numbers of people apart from a national data system.

The rules governing access to the files shall be definite and well publicized, and the programs that enforce these rules are open to any interested party, including, for example, the American Civil Liberties Union.

An individual shall have the right to read his own file, to challenge entries in his file and to impose certain restrictions on access to his file.

Every time someone consults an individual's file this event is recorded, together with the authorization for access.

If an organization or person obtains access to a file by deceit, this is a crime and a civil wrong. The injured person may sue and be awarded damages.

Credit information shall not be available without authorization from the person concerned.

"To establish such rights," McCarthy said, "people must revise their ideas about the source and nature of their freedom. Most individual rights now recognized are based on the claim that the individual always had them. . . . Technology is advancing too fast, however, to allow such benevolent frauds to work in the future. The right to keep people from keeping files on us must first be invented, then legislated and actively enforced."

Such a set of rules to govern the use of a new technology is as important as the technology itself. But somehow we adopt the one too soon, the other too late. McCarthy for many years has advocated such rules to govern the use of information without much effect. But he keeps on with that as well as his academic work.

The last time I saw John McCarthy, he was tacking down a new layer on his long-building project to give machines commonsense knowledge. He had begun it in 1958; when I saw him, the previous day he had held a conference entitled The First International Conference on Non-monotomic Logic. The title was a joke, since the conference was not international, but consisted of only fifty students and teachers from Stanford and a few others from various parts of the United States. But the conference was the first one on non-monotomic logic, and the first conference in machine intelligence that did not take for its subject computer programs recently written. The conference was on purely abstract aspects of intelligence. It dealt with questions of logic which underlie ordinary human knowledge. The conference was a nice addition to the progress of McCarthy's idea. McCarthy himself, however, was a little wobbly during that week. Not many days before, a ragged hole had opened in his life.

The mountaineering team that Vera was a part of had reached the last camp before the Annapurna peak. The air was thin and brittle, as cold as thirty degrees below zero at times. Avalanches had boomed past them repeatedly in twenty-foot walls of flying ice and snow; one had buried several members of the team briefly and destroyed much equipment. But they reached the last camp, and from it two women and a Sherpa climber had made it to the top. A second team of two women then tried.

John McCarthy received a telephone call one afternoon: Vera had fallen while attempting the summit; her body was still on the mountain and could not be reached. She and a companion, roped together, had been crawling upward on a face of ice. Probably one slipped and then the other; they pulled each other down two thousand feet. The other climbers tried to reach them but twice failed because of exhaustion, cold, and an intervening crevasse. Finally, after three days, they were forced to leave the bodies where they lay. Vera's red jacket could be seen from a distance, lying beside the chasm. The rope that bound the two together dangled over the edge, but no one could see into the fissure, to Vera's end of the rope.

McCarthy told interviewers that those who climb and who know climbers always prepare themselves for the worst. He had been prepared, but found that the shock of grief was different and much worse than any preparation could confine.

I went to McCarthy's home for eggs on a Sunday morning three weeks after the news. I sat at a round wooden table while across a low counter he was scrambling eggs and frying bacon. I noticed that the spare room nearby had a cot in it, with the bedclothes disarranged, and I wondered if he were sleeping there rather than in the bedroom. He had accepted many sympathetic invitations in the previous weeks, had kept himself in constant motion, had avoided fingering the hole in his life where Vera had been.

Breaking eggs, McCarthy commented acidly upon the swings from credulity to incredulity that constitute reaction to his field. One critic finds in John McCarthy an analogy to the man who declared he was on his way to the moon. Climbing up a tree, he announced new progress as he reached each higher limb. Another says that the computer, after all, is only a tool. There can be no "theory of artificial intelligence," but merely clever solutions and clever programs to solve specific problems. It is like civil engineering; is there a theory of civil engineering? No, only a collection of methods for building taller and better bridges. We don't know the limits of clever computing, but they are likely to be short of human abilities. McCarthy's view is that clever engineering, combined with a few good ideas in mathematical logic, need not be confined by the boundaries of human intelligence. At least, there is no reason to erect such a boundary before we get to it. Computing, after all, was once mere arithmetic before it jumped its boundaries.

I once read a quotation from a time when even among well-educated men, arithmetic was a rare skill. Samuel Johnson, who had learned his times tables late in life, wrote, "Nothing amuses more harmlessly than computation, and nothing is oftener applicable to real business or speculative inquiries. A thousand stories which the ignorant tell, and believe, die away at once when the computist takes them in his grip. . . ."

Puncturing yolks, McCarthy was talking about the home terminal and whether offices away from home would still be necessary or desirable if home terminals were generally in use and could communicate freely with one another. Wouldn't that keep people from enjoying the social life within an office? It might, McCarthy said, and offered a few thoughts in compromise. Though McCarthy has ideas that reach far and some which are on a large scale—he once told me of a few galactic engineering projects which might be considered, and another time related his idea for a nation composed entirely of ships floating as an island in international waters—still, he is no utopian thinker. He thinks in details, speculates in particulars. Freedom is something that individuals possess, technology merely a succession of individual machines. He mocks great political and social schemes, and takes some delight in bursting these gaudy bubbles. He once pointed out to me, as we talked quietly one evening in his den while a party was occurring in the rest of his house, the one defect of all utopian schemes. They provide no means for their own demise; they offer no alternatives for those who detest their premises. He said that if he were talking to the authors of one of these schemes, he would put his objection in the form of a single question. "In your world, is it permissible to leave?"

Even if it is successful, artificial intelligence will be no utopian technology, or the foundation of grand social schemes. It is a technology that could pull both ways, but the largest advantage would go to the ordinary citizen. There is also, in so new a discipline as artificial intelligence, the possibility of failure. The foundations are still wet, nothing is firm. There is a personal risk in believing in it; more in expending one's life on it. Ideas brooded for years may end discarded, so many empty eggshells.

I spoke with him about this once. When he began to talk, his eyes sought the center of the room, as if he was slowly reading a script which appeared there in the air. It was not that his mind was not on the question. He was thinking about it, but in a way that was abstracted, objectified, removed from the room and the social situation in which it occurred. He said he did not worry too much about the question, but thought artificial intelligence would be possible. There is, he added, an outside chance that some mathematician will prove that it is impossible. There are impossibility proofs done on such matters. "Yes," he said in a whisper, "that would be discouraging." That is unlikely, however. It is also unlikely that the enterprise will fail on its own within his lifetime, and unlikely that it will succeed in his lifetime. All those things amount to the same thing for him, he said. "I won't ever know for sure."

Scraping eggs into the garbage, McCarthy suggested we take a walk through one of his newer projects. It is a computer system that allows every Stanford student to use a powerful computer, at a very small cost to the university, because the hundred-terminal system operates without staff and virtually without supervision. We took Caspian the dog. We went down to a building with a single large room containing fifty terminals. Though it was Sunday morning, and there was a light drizzle, the room was filled with students. Every terminal was occupied, and each student stared raptly into his screen. We walked through, two men and a dog, unnoticed, mere shades passing at the rim of consciousness.

Notes

Pages

23. Kenneth Evett, *The New Republic*, June 12, 1976.

30. R. R. Wilson, in *Perspectives in Modern Physics*, ed. R. E. Marshak (New York: Interscience Publishers, John Wiley and Sons, 1966).

34. Arthur Eddington, 1927 Gifford Lectures. *The Nature of the Physical World* (Ann Arbor: University of Michigan Press, 1974).

36. David Cline, Alfred Mann, and Carlo Rubbia, "The Search for New Families of Elementary Particles," *Scientific American* 234:1 (1976).

40. Eddington, *Nature of Physical World*.

48. R. R. Wilson, private letter to I. James Pikl, University of Wyoming, March 1972.

50. Wilson, *Perspectives*.

59. Nuel Pharr Davis, *Lawrence and Oppenheimer* (New York: Simon and Schuster, 1968).

64. R. R. Wilson, in *Alamogordo Plus Twenty-five Years*, ed. Richard S. Lewis and Jane Wilson (New York: Viking Compass Press, 1971).

66. Editors of *International Science and Technology* magazine, *The Way of the Scientist* (New York: Simon and Schuster, 1966).

69. Editors of *International Science and Technology* magazine, *Way of the Scientist*.

70. R. R. Wilson, in *All in Our Time*, ed. Jane Wilson (New York: Bulletin of the Atomic Scientists, 1974).

73. Herbert Anderson, in *All in Our Time*.

Pages

74. Wilson, in *Alamogordo*.

75–76. Wilson, in *Alamogordo*.

77. I. I. Rabi, quoted in Davis, *Lawrence and Oppenheimer*.

86. R. R. Wilson, Richtmeyer Memorial Lecture.

92. R. R. Wilson, "Physics and the Human Spirit," Oppenheimer Memorial Lecture, November 22, 1976.

106. James D. Watson, *Molecular Biology of the Gene* (Menlo Park, Calif.: W. A. Benjamin, 1977).

118. Richard Dawkins, *The Selfish Gene* (New York: Oxford University Press, 1976).

121. Horace Freeland Judson, *The Eighth Day of Creation* (New York: Simon and Schuster, 1979).

124. Ruth Moore, *The Coil of Life* (New York: Alfred A. Knopf, 1974).

124–25. François Jacob, *The Logic of Life* (New York: Vintage Books, 1976).

136. Editors of *International Science and Technology* magazine, *Way of the Scientist*.

142–43. Judson, *Eighth Day*.

152. Nicholas Wade, *The Ultimate Experiment* (New York: Walker, 1977).

152. Michael Rogers, *Biohazard* (New York: Avon, 1979).

152–53. Rogers, *Biohazard*.

179. Michael VerMeulen, "Harvard Passes the Buck," *TWA Ambassador* magazine, January 1982.

198–99. Joseph Weizenbaum, *Computer Power and Human Reason* (San Francisco: W. H. Freeman, 1976).

211. Philip and Emily Morrison, *Charles Babbage and His Calculating Engines* (New York: Dover, 1961).

212. Sara Turing, *Alan M. Turing* (Cambridge, England: W. Hefner and Sons, 1959).

214. Jeremy Bernstein, *The Analytical Engine* (New York: Morrow Quill Paperbacks, 1981).

216. John Kemeny, *Man and the Computer* (New York: Charles Scribner's Sons, 1972) .

217. Bernstein, *Analytical Engine*.

237. Margaret Boden, *Artificial Intelligence and Natural Man* (New York: Basic Books, 1977).

239. Herbert Simon and Allen Newell, *Operations Research* #6 (January–February 1958).

240. Donald G. Fink, *Computers and the Human Mind* (New York: Doubleday Anchor, 1966).

Pages

240. Roger Lind, "Here Come the Robots," *Oui* magazine, 1976.

241–42. Weizenbaum, *Computer Power*.

243–44. R. D. Rosen, "Computer Therapy," *New Times* magazine, 1976.

244. Weizenbaum, *Computer Power*.

247. A. M. Turing, in *Computers and Thought*, ed. Edward Feigenbaum and Julian Feldman (New York: McGraw-Hill, 1963).

252. David Marr, "Artificial Intelligence: A Personal View," M.I.T. Artificial Intelligence Laboratory Memo number 355, 1976.

252. Terry Winograd, *Understanding Natural Language* (New York: Academic Press, 1976).

253. Winograd, *Understanding Natural Language*.

263–64. Kemeny, *Man and the Computer*.

274. John McCarthy, "Ascribing Mental Qualities to Machines," unpublished manuscript, 1977.

274. McCarthy, "Ascribing Mental Qualities."

278. John McCarthy, in *Information: A Scientific American Book* (San Francisco: W. H. Freeman, 1966).

278–79. Thomas Whiteside, *The New Yorker*, August 22 and 29, 1977.

282. Ben Bagdikian, *The Information Machines* (New York: Harper Torchbooks, 1971).

283. McCarthy, *Information*.

Index

Tobacco mosaic disease, 109–10
Tolkien, J. R. R., 225, 267
Toohig, Father Timothy, 92–93, 94
Top quark, 39
Turing, Alan Mathison, 211–14, 215, 216, 221, 227, 234, 246–248, 255–56
Turing Test, 247, 255, 257
Typhus, 110

United Nations, 75
U. S. Department of Defense, 266
U. S. Department of State, 141
University of California at Berkeley, 46–47, 48, 64, 86, 87, 88, 162
University of California at Los Angeles (UCLA), 234
University of California at San Francisco, 146, 177
University of Illinois, 266
University of Indiana, 152
University of Minnesota, 113
University of Oregon, 116–17
University of Wisconsin, 25
   computer center bombing, 279
Up quark, 39
Uranium, 72, 73, 76
   isotope separator, 32, 68, 71, 96
   neutrons, 65
   separation problem, 66–69
Uranium 235, 32, 65–66, 68, 69, 72
Uranium 238, 66, 67

Vasopressin, 170
Velucci, Alfred, 108, 155–58, 159, 160
VerMeulen, Michael, 179
Vietnam War, 117, 140–41, 142, 155, 163, 224, 279
Viruses, 109–10
"Vital force," 106
Vitalism, 106, 107, 171, 174, 206

Wald, George, 155, 157
Ward, Judy, 29, 31
Watson, James, 106, 111, 117, 128, 129, 130, 139, 152, 167, 187
Watson, Vera, see McCarthy, Mrs. Vera
Weizenbaum, Joseph, 198–99, 241–44, 255
Wells, H. G., 73
Whitehead, Alfred North, 228
Whitehead family, 182
Whiteside, Thomas, 278–79, 280
Whitney and Company (J. H.), 180
Wigner, Eugene, 65
William the Conqueror, 97
Wilson, Mrs. Jane, 41, 52, 68, 71, 83, 88
Wilson, Jonathan, 78–79
Wilson, Platt, 45–46
Wilson, Robert, 17–99
   attic experiments, 43–45, 89
   birth of, 41
   boldness reputation, 29
   childhood, 41–44
   in China, 23
   colleague opinions, 29–30, 82–83
   congressional testimony, 97–98
   cowboy reputation, 27–28, 52
   dislike of phones, 31–32
   education of, 41, 42, 46–47
   entry into physics, 48–52
   Los Alamos project, 69, 70–79, 83, 89
   office (at Fermilab), 28–29, 31, 48, 59
   proton problems, 80–82
   Rome conference, 83–84, 86
   shyness of, 29, 32
   similarity between Lawrence's machine building and Wilson's, 61
   uranium work, 32, 66–69
   vacuum in a bottle device, 44
   See also Fermi National Ac-

LA DIETA
CONTRA LA INFLAMACIÓN

La **Dama** de los **Jugos**
PRESENTA

LA DIETA
CONTRA LA INFLAMACIÓN

Cherie Calbom, MC

con la CHEF ABBY FAMMARTINO

CASA
CREACIÓN

La mayoría de los productos de Casa Creación están disponibles a un precio con descuento en cantidades de mayoreo para promociones de ventas, ofertas especiales, levantar fondos y atender necesidades educativas. Para más información, escriba a Casa Creación, 600 Rinehart Road, Lake Mary, Florida, 32746; o llame al teléfono (407) 333-7117 en Estados Unidos.

La dieta contra la inflamación de la Dama de los Jugos
por Cherie Calbom con Abby Fammartino
Publicado por Casa Creación
Una compañía de Charisma Media
600 Rinehart Road, Lake Mary, Florida 32746
www.casacreacion.com

Traducido por: www.pica6.com (con la colaboración de Salvador Eguiarte D.G. y Yanzi E. Ferrer G.)
Diseño de la portada: Justin Evans
Director de diseño: Justin Evans

Originally published in the U.S.A. under the title:
The Juice Lady's Anti-Inflammation Diet
Published by Siloam, a Charisma Media Company,
Lake Mary, FL 32746 USA
Copyright © 2015 Cherie Calbom

Visite la página web de la autora: www.juiceladycherie.com

Library of Congress Control Number: 2015949865
ISBN: 978-1-62998-824-5
E-book: 978-1-62998-836-8

Impreso en los Estados Unidos de América
15 16 17 18 19 * 5 4 3 2 1

CONTENIDO

2. ALIMENTOS Y FACTORES QUE CONTRIBUYEN CON LA INFLAMACIÓN............ 17

4. RECETAS Y PLAN DE ALIMENTACIÓN DE VEINTIOCHO DÍAS PARA UNA SALUD LLENA DE VIDA 61

INFORMACIÓN DE CHERIE CALBOM.............. 235

INFORMACIÓN SOBRE LA CHEF ABBY FAMMARTINO Y LA MESA DE ABBY................ 239

RECETAS

Jugos

Batidos

Tés

Desayuno/Desayuno-almuerzo

Almuerzo/Comida

Pollo

Pescados y mariscos

Cena

Pollo

Pescados y mariscos

Vegetariano/vegano

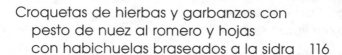

Ensaladas

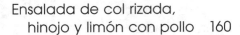

Sopas

Guarniciones

Aderezos, marinadas, salsas y condimentos

Refrigerios

Postres

Introducción

SU PLAN DIETÉTICO PARA UNA
SALUD LLENA DE VIDA

La primera riqueza es la salud.[1]
—RALPH WALDO EMERSON

H AY MUCHOS FACTORES en nuestro estilo de vida moderno que nos alejan de la salud que queremos: la salud que necesitamos para cumplir nuestro propósito. En este libro usted leerá acerca de varios factores que contribuyen con la enfermedad y la inflamación. De todos ellos, la dieta es sin duda el número uno para la mayoría de las personas de los países occidentales. Como nuestra comida ha cambiado tan drásticamente en décadas recientes, muchas personas ya no comen alimentos frescos, locales, orgánicos de temporada servidos con cariño y cuidado en su preparación. Vamos volando por el carril rápido de la vida tomando en el camino alimentos ya preparados. El resultado es una larga lista de padecimientos que afectan a nuestra nación. Estos alimentos rápidos y convenientes están provocando inflamación crónica: el factor presente en la raíz de varias enfermedades. Está destruyendo la salud y la vida de muchas personas. Como la inflamación es un desafío importante, he dedicado este libro para abordar este problema crónico y el estilo de vida para vencerlo. *La dieta contra la inflamación de La Dama de los Jugos* le brinda cuatro semanas de recetas sabrosas que no solamente combaten la inflamación, sino que también están diseñadas para alimentarlo y traerle deleite a usted, a su familia y a sus amigos.

Una nota personal de Cherie

Muchas personas me preguntaban qué deberían comer además de sus jugos y batidos verdes. Con frecuencia les respondía: "Una dieta contra la inflamación". Ellos casi siempre me preguntaban dónde podían encontrarla. Por otro lado, me di cuenta de que es imperativo que las personas que padecen inflamación cuenten con un buen plan de alimentos con recetas para aprender a comer este tipo de dieta y recuperarse. Así fue como nació la inspiración para este libro.

Probablemente usted o un ser querido hayan tenido que enfrentar dolor, eccema, obesidad, trastorno por déficit de atención con hiperactividad (TDAH), neuropatía periférica, diabetes, cardiopatías, embolia, migraña, problemas tiroideos, problemas dentales, cáncer u otras enfermedades o padecimientos. Si es así, usted ha estado tratando con la inflamación. Una de las maneras importantes para sanar el cuerpo, sin importar lo que pueda estar padeciendo, es comer una dieta que no promueva la inflamación además de llevar a cabo cambios en su estilo de vida como la reducción del estrés, mantener una actitud positiva y practicar el amor y el agradecimiento.

¿Dónde podría comenzar para llevar a cabo cambios dietéticos que traigan sanidad? Escoja alimentos no procesados que no promuevan la inflamación, cultivados localmente, sin pesticidas y preparados en casa. Probablemente requiera un poco de práctica aprender cómo hacer buena comida, pero vale la pena todo el esfuerzo. Y una vez que comience a dominarlo, preparar alimentos deliciosos le traerá mucho placer.

Primero me enamoré de preparar alimentos no procesados cuando era niña. Una de las grandes alegrías en la vida de mi padre era cocinar. Se emocionaba por la comida que hacía. Con frecuencia reunía a todos los niños de nuestra parentela en la cocina durante los días festivos para probar el pavo y el aderezo que había cocinado antes de llevarlo a la mesa. Yo disfrutaba completamente preparar los alimentos a su lado y jamás perdí el gusto por cocinar. Posiblemente esa sea la razón por la que terminé cocinando con la Parrilla George Foreman durante trece años en QVC y demostrando el extractor de jugos Juiceman en todo Estados Unidos.

Mi abuela me inculcó el amor por la tierra y por cultivar cosas. Ella tenía un jardín abundante que atendió con amor y orgullo hasta bien entrada en sus ochentas. Entonces a eso simplemente se le llamaba *comer alimentos cultivados en casa*. Ahora el término popular es *del huerto a la mesa*. En los días de mis padres o abuelos no era nada sofisticado o exótico; simplemente era la manera en que la gente comía...alimentos reales sin procesar, sin químicos o sin alimentos transgénicos, cosechados frescos o enlatados para el invierno y preparados en la cocina. Esa era la única manera en la que la mayoría de la gente comió durante siglos. El deseo de cultivar alimentos está en lo profundo de mi alma, y por eso es que siempre cultivo tomates y hierbas en macetas durante el año.

Pero en la adolescencia perdí el camino, lo cual continuó en mis veintes. Cuando se trataba de elegir qué comer comencé a consumir cantidades industriales de comida rápida y dulces; y no me gustaban las verduras. Mi salud se fue en picada, y terminé con síndrome de fatiga crónica y fibromialgia. Los médicos no me daban esperanza de recuperarme y sabía que tenía que encontrar mi propio camino. Mi viaje a la sanidad comenzó con un ayuno de jugos de verduras de cinco días y con un verano de tomar estrictamente jugos, verduras y arroz integral. Logré estar completamente bien en tres meses. Me recuperé porque le di a mi cuerpo lo que necesitaba para sanar y desintoxicarse. Por eso es que me apasiona tanto ayudarlo a que también usted encuentre el camino a la buena salud.

Comenzamos a perder nuestro camino como nación en la década

de 1950. El atractivo de los electrodomésticos y las fascinación con la televisión abrió el camino para los platos precocinados de Gerry Thomas para cenar frente al televisor. Más de 10 millones de platos precocinados para comer frente al televisor Swanson fueron vendidos durante el primer año de distribución nacional. Si no hubiera sido por Julia Child quien revolucionó la manera en que las mujeres consideraban la cocina, muchos de nosotros no hubiéramos comido ninguna otra cosa que platos precocinados para comer frente al televisor y alimentos precocinados empacados. No obstante, el concepto de la comida rápida había llegado para quedarse. La inteligente comercialización hizo que las mujeres creyeran que no tenían tiempo de preparar una comida completa, y que tenían que encontrar comida que fuera rápida de elaborar o de llevar a casa. Esa era introdujo la resbalosa cuesta abajo de alimentos refinados y mala salud. La comida se enfocó en la tarea más que en la nutrición.

Después de muchas horas en mi práctica de nutrición de aconsejar a la gente con una variedad de enfermedades y padecimientos—todos con el factor de la inflamación en su raíz—yo sabía que necesitaba un plan dietético sanador y recetas interesantes que la gente siguiera. Pero también me di cuenta de que muchas personas no se sienten cómodas en la cocina y que necesitan ayuda para aprender algunos principios básicos para hacer buena comida. Pensé en Abby, quien durante años me envió hermosos planes de menús y recetas a través de su boletín electrónico "La Mesa de Abby" [Abby's Table]. Conocí por primera vez a Abby cuando hizo una hermosa presentación de alimentos en una de mis fiestas de alimentos crudos en mi casa. Las recetas que ha creado son deliciosas. Las fotografías de sus alimentos son hermosas.

La invité a ser coautora de este libro. Hicimos equipo para traerle una amplia variedad de deliciosas recetas saludables y planes de menús diseñados con su salud y sanidad en mente. He escrito los capítulos de apertura para darle información sobre la inflamación, los factores que contribuyen con ella y los alimentos que pueden ayudarlo a mantenerla bajo control o evitar que aparezca en primer lugar. Me complace presentarle nuestro plan de veintiocho días que incluye jugos, batidos verdes y una gran variedad de recetas que mejoran la salud completas con fotografías encantadoras y listas de compras.

Espero que cada comida lo inspire y que disfrute los beneficios de comer alimentos saludables; comida que lo ame de vuelta.

—CHERIE CALBOM
LA DAMA DE LOS JUGOS
SALUD, SANIDAD Y RESTAURACIÓN

Una nota personal de la chef Abby

Mis recetas son un trampolín para aprender técnicas de cocina útiles y saludables para todo tipos de comensales. A lo largo de los últimos diez años y contando, he dedicado mi vida a elaborar comida inspiradora que el cuerpo ame. He estado encargada de un club de cenas, he creado una línea comercial de salsas, he cocinado en un barco durante cuarenta días, he cocinado para individuos en su casa, impartido clases de todo tipo para niños y adultos, y he cocinado para cientos de celebraciones de vida, amor y trabajo duro. También he dedicado varias cenas, cátedras y clases para compartir alimentos que se ajusten a las temporadas, enseñándole a la gente las maravillas (y la facilidad cotidiana) de tratar los alimentos como medicina. En la escuela de gastronomía aprendimos mucho acerca de la teoría china de Cinco Fases en la forma en cómo se relaciona con la comida de temporada para una salud óptima. Sobre todo, mi misión es desarrollar la comunidad alrededor de alimentos intensos que den vida. Al traer las necesidades de salud de todos a la mesa, me esfuerzo por hacer que la comida saludable sea divertida y práctica para la vida diaria.

Todas mis recetas son naturalmente libres de gluten, lácteos y soya y son apropiadas para una dieta contra la inflamación. A través de reducir el consumo de alimentos comunes que causan alergia y alimentos que favorecen la inflamación, usted le hace un favor a su cuerpo. La sensibilidad a los alimentos, al igual que las alergias de temporada, pueden ser mantenidas a raya si su nivel de consumo general es bajo y no experimenta reacciones que pongan en peligro su vida.

Imagínese un vaso de agua; a medida que llena el vaso con más agua, en cierto punto el vaso comienza a rebosar y a derramarse en la mesa. En una manera similar, cuando su cuerpo está sobrecargado con alimentos que causan inflamación (tales como el azúcar refinada, el trigo o los lácteos) usted comienza a sentir los síntomas. El letargo, la mente nublada, la distensión abdominal y la depresión se pueden reducir grandemente a través de disfrutar una dieta que consista principalmente en alimentos naturales no procesados libres de alérgenos. Afortunadamente para nosotros la dieta basada en alimentos no procesados rica en frutas y verduras de temporada, carne de alta calidad y pescado silvestre brindan inspiración infinita y un sabor que satisface.

En mi trabajo me encanta reunir a las personas alrededor de la mesa para celebrar la buena comida. Para mis eventos del club de cenas, comensales de todo tipo disfrutan una comida estilo familiar juntos donde ninguno es la persona rara por comer los alimentos que apoyan su salud. He organizado estos eventos en lugares interesantes de Portland y ahora en todo el país. También imparto lecciones privadas de cocina para grupos de amigos, familiares o compañeros de trabajo en la comodidad de su hogar. Allí es donde nace la verdadera confianza en la cocina: en la cocina de la casa. En estas lecciones mi meta es conectar a los cocineros con la manera en que los alimentos mantienen la vida en general y lo importante (¡y divertido!) que es traer a los seres queridos alrededor de la mesa para este propósito.

Para verdaderamente cosechar los beneficios de una dieta naturalmente saludable es crucial meterse a la cocina y simplemente comenzar a cocinar. Encuentre maneras para cocinar todos los días. Entre más practique, más divertido y relajante será.

—ABBY

Capítulo 1

LA INFLAMACIÓN: AMIGA O ENEMIGA

*La inflamación crónica es la madre malvada de la
mayoría de las enfermedades prevalentes y devastadoras
que rutinariamente matan a los estadounidenses.[1]*

—Dr. Barry Sears

De pronto la inflamación se ha convertido en uno de los mayores intereses de la investigación médica. Apenas pasa una semana sin que otro estudio revele una nueva manera en que la inflamación crónica daña el organismo. Los depósitos de colesterol se encuentran desestabilizados en las arterias coronarias, llevando a ataques cardiacos y derrames cerebrales potenciales. Devora las neuronas del cerebro de las víctimas de Alzheimer. Puede fomentar la proliferación de células anormales y facilita su transformación en cáncer. La inflamación crónica puede ser el motor que impulse la mayoría de las enfermedades más temidas de la mediana edad y la vejez.

Aunque quizá no tenga un sentimiento cálido o emotivo con respecto a ella, la inflamación es una respuesta natural al trauma, la infección, la enfermedad y otros ataques físicos. Ayuda al cuerpo a deshacerse de bacterias y toxinas. También "barre" con células y tejidos muertos.

Sin inflamación, los tejidos dañados no sanarían y las infecciones se propagarían sin control.

No obstante, la inflamación crónica no es una buena respuesta. Es una respuesta inflamatoria inmune de duración prolongada que con el tiempo lleva al daño de los tejidos. Es de bajo nivel y sistémica. Puede tener un efecto dominó que dañe seriamente su salud. La causa raíz de muchas enfermedades es la inflamación crónica: una respuesta inmune permanente provocada por una dieta pobre, reacciones alérgicas, estrés, toxinas y problemas psicológicos. Si se deja sin supervisión puede dañar muchos sistemas importantes, incluyendo los sistemas endocrino (hormonas), inmunológico, digestivo, cardiovascular y respiratorio.

Una de las moléculas inflamatorias más destructivas, llamada el factor nuclear kappa B, es una pequeña molécula que genera daños significativos en el cuerpo. El estrés emocional, las toxinas, los radicales libres y los alimentos tóxicos, inflamatorios o alergénicos pueden activarla. Cuando es lanzada, puede soltar la producción de numerosas moléculas inflamatorias: una aplanadora de inflamación que afecta todo el cuerpo. Podría aparecer en la articulación de un dedo, en sus rodillas, sus arterias o su corazón.

Se estima que más de la mitad de todos los estadounidenses están inflamados, y la mayoría de ellos ni siquiera están conscientes de ello. La mayoría de los padecimientos están asociados con la inflamación crónica como la cardiopatía, lupus, artritis reumatoide, fibromialgia, arterioesclerosis, enfermedad inflamatoria del intestino, pancreatitis crónica y hepatitis crónica. Las nuevas investigaciones también vinculan a la obesidad con la inflamación. Tener sobrepeso promueve la inflamación y la inflamación promueve la obesidad; un ciclo continuo y frustrante.

Estas condiciones y muchas más surgen de un sistema inmune que está fuera de control y lo afecta a nivel celular. Incluso la mitocondria puede estar inflamada. Cuando los síntomas de la inflamación no remiten, el mensaje es que su sistema inmune está atorado en la posición de "encendido" incluso cuando usted no se encuentra en peligro inminente. Cuando se perturba el ritmo del sistema inmune, cambia a un estado de alarma continuo, y la inflamación se esparce rápidamente a lo largo del cuerpo. Cuando la "alarma" de la inflamación suena en el corazón, genera cardiopatías; en el cerebro, demencia o enfermedad de Alzheimer; en los ojos, desórdenes como degeneración macular; y en las células grasas, obesidad. También es un contribuyente importante para la obesidad.

Nuestros cuerpos no fueron diseñados para un aluvión diario de toxinas, agentes infecciosos, alimentos transgénicos, alimentos rociados con pesticidas, alimentos refinados o estrés intenso y prolongado. Este tipo de demanda requiere apoyo significativo para mantener la resiliencia del sistema inmune. Nuestro estilo de vida tan acelerado no tiende hacia el apoyo del sistema inmune a menos que le prestemos atención particular a todo lo que hacemos: a lo que respiramos, comemos, bebemos, pensamos y sentimos.

Mientras que la incidencia de la inflamación y la enfermedad inflamatoria está elevándose en todos los países desarrollados, no estamos condenados a este escenario. Tenemos la opción de escoger la manera en la que respondemos a lo que genera tensión en nuestra vida, lo que decidimos comer y beber y cómo pensamos. Algunas de nuestras respuestas son comportamientos aprendidos de nuestros primeros días. Sin embargo, cambiar nuestras respuestas hacia lo que genera tensión en la vida y hacia lo que comemos y bebemos está bajo nuestro control. Podemos tener respuestas positivas y tomar decisiones positivas.

COLESTEROL, INFLAMACIÓN Y CARDIOPATÍAS

¿Alguna vez se ha preguntado si la acumulación de placa en el sistema circulatorio es el verdadero culpable de las cardiopatías siendo que las personas están tomando medicamentos que reducen el colesterol como si fueran dulces y las cardiopatías siguen siendo el asesino número uno? Más que ser el villano, el colesterol es el agente sanador que el cuerpo envía a los sitios para cubrir las lesiones de los vasos sanguíneos que han sido causadas por la inflamación. Si usted tiene demasiado colesterol acumulado en sus arterias, el problema es demasiada inflamación

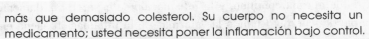

más que demasiado colesterol. Su cuerpo no necesita un medicamento; usted necesita poner la inflamación bajo control.

"Es la inflamación en los vasos lo que inicia la lesión —dice la Dra. Beverly Teter, una bioquímica de lípidos de la Universidad de Maryland quien ha estado investigando las grasas y su efecto en el cuerpo humano durante muchos años—. El cuerpo entonces envía al colesterol como una costra para cubrirlo con el fin de proteger el sistema circulatorio y la pared vascular de un daño mayor".[2]

Los estadounidenses han sido engañados para tomar medicamentos que reducen el colesterol y evitar grasas de alta calidad como el aceite de coco para su propio daño, mientras engullen aceites vegetales oxidados, grasas trans, azúcar, granos y comida chatarra baja en grasas: los verdaderos contribuyentes con la inflamación y las cardiopatías.

¿Está su sistema atorado en "fuego lento" o en "hervor"?

Con la inflamación incrementando el calor dentro de su cuerpo, podría desarrollar una multitud de síntomas como triglicéridos altos, alto colesterol, piel seca, tejidos y articulaciones inflamadas, aumento de peso y respuestas agitadas a los desafíos y tensiones de la vida.

Muchas personas en este país experimentan inflamación prolongada "a fuego lento": una importante condición para problemas de salud. Tenemos índices a la alza de cardiopatías, cáncer, alergias, asma, diabetes, obesidad, síndrome del intestino irritable (SII) y dolor crónico solamente por nombrar algunas de las condiciones causadas por la inflamación. Hay un incremento tan alto en los síntomas inflamatorios que se está convirtiendo en la norma más que en la excepción. Algunas personas tienen una inflamación tan rampante que están en un "hervor". Pero hay buenas noticias. Una vez que entendemos lo que la causa y que vemos lo rápido que nuestras acciones pueden atizar la llama o apagar el fuego interno, podemos tomar mejores decisiones cada día que nos lleven de vuelta al equilibrio.

NO ES SABIO DEPENDER DE SUSTANCIAS NO ESTEROIDEAS ANTIINFLAMATORIAS

Esto es lo que está asociado con los medicamentos no esteroideos antiinflamatorios:

- 3300 muertes al año.
- 41 000 hospitalizaciones al año.
- Hemorragia gastrointestinal (GI).
- Riesgo cardiovascular.
- Lleva a la disbiosis intestinal, que empeora la inflamación.[3]

Un intestino infeliz

Los bebés que no nacen por cesárea y que son amamantados tienen una flora intestinal más saludable. Muchas personas no fueron amamantadas y como consecuencia tienen más desafíos de salud. Además, tomar antibióticos mata las bacterias buenas y lo coloca en posición de un crecimiento más abundante de las levaduras y otros patógenos. Los azúcares alimentan la levadura, llevándola a crecer fuera de control.

Los problemas usualmente comienzan en el intestino—distensión, ataques frecuentes de diarrea o constipación, gases, eructos, pirosis y reflujo ácido—todo lo cual indica un tracto digestivo inflamado. El sistema inmune entra en acción cuando comemos alimentos inflamatorios porque fue diseñado para buscar y destruir sustancias amenazadoras como virus, parásitos y bacterias en nuestros alimentos. Nuestro sistema digestivo tiene que extraer los nutrientes de la materia inflamatoria e inútil que comemos y luego deshacerse del resto o almacenarlo.

La mayoría de la gente del hemisferio occidental sobretrabaja su sistema digestivo a causa de que una gran porción de lo que come es inflamatorio para el tracto digestivo. Nuestros ancestros cazaban y recolectaban sus alimentos: comida real, sin procesar, que el cuerpo podía usar. Hoy consumimos grandes cantidades de alimentos de conveniencia, refinados y rápidos que abruman al cuerpo y crean un intestino dañado.

PADECIMIENTOS Y ENFERMEDADES QUE TIENEN QUE VER CON INFLAMACIÓN*	
Acné	Acrodermatitis
Amiloidosis	Anemia falciforme
Arterioesclerosis (endurecimiento de las arterias)	Artritis
Artritis juvenil	Artritis psoriática
Artritis reactiva	Artritis reumatoide
Artrosis	Bursitis
Cáncer	Cáncer de la piel
Candidiasis	Cardiopatía isquémica
Cardiopatía reumática	Cardiopatías
Cardiopatías inflamatorias	Celíaca
Celulitis	Cervicitis
Cistitis	Colitis
Colitis ulcerosa	Condiciones inflamatorias de la piel
Dermatomitosis	Derrame cerebral
Diabetes mellitus	Dolor de la articulación sacroilíaca
Eccema	Eccema seborreico
Eccema varicoso	Enfermedad cerebrovascular
Enfermedad de Alzheimer	Enfermedad de Crohn
Enfermedad de Grave	Enfermedad de Parkinson
Enfermedad de Still	Enfermedad inflamatoria del intestino
Enfermedad pélvica inflamatoria	Enfermedades de transmisión sexual
Enfermedades inflamatorias de las articulaciones	Enfermedades inflamatorias sistémicas
Enfermedades neurodegenerativas	Enfermedades vasculares inflamatorias
ERGE	Esclerosis múltiple
Espondilitis anquilosante	Estenosis espinal lumbar
Estomatitis herpética	Fascitis necrotizante
Gastritis	Gota

PADECIMIENTOS Y ENFERMEDADES QUE TIENEN QUE VER CON INFLAMACIÓN*	
Hemangioma de la piel	Hepatitis
Herpes zóster	Hipohidrosis
Ictiosis común	Impétigo
Infecciones virales neurotró-picas	Liquen plano
Lupus	Nefritis
Onicomicosis	Osteoporosis
Pitiriasis versicolor	Prostatitis
Psoriasis	Queratosis actínica
Queratosis seborreica	Quiste pilonidal
Resfriado común	Rosácea
Sarcoidosis	Sarcoma de caposi
Síndrome de fatiga crónica	Síndrome metabólico
Síndrome SAPHO	Síndromes paraneoplásticos
Sinusitis	Tendonitis
Úlceras por presión	Urticaria
Vaginitis	Vasculitis sistémica
VIH/SIDA	Vitíligo

* Esta no es una lista exhaustiva, sino que tiene el propósito de darle una idea de todas las enfermedades en las que la inflamación está involucrada.

Un estilo de vida inflamatorio

Los individuos que de otro modo serían saludables pueden ser expuestos a través de su estilo de vida o el ambiente a sustancias que el cuerpo percibe como irritantes, como infecciones, virus, parásitos o bacterias, alérgenos alimentarios, toxinas y alimentos inflamatorios como el azúcar, los edulcorantes artificiales, el alcohol, los aceites oxidados, el gluten, los lácteos y el glutamato monosódico. Las causas de la inflamación crónica pueden variar de una persona a otra, pero incluyen presentar sobrepeso, experimentar estrés, comer mala comida y respirar aire contaminado. Las elecciones de estilo de vida como fumar o la falta de ejercicio también contribuyen. Un estilo de vida sedentario y la falta de sueño también pueden incrementar la

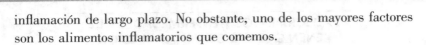

inflamación de largo plazo. No obstante, uno de los mayores factores son los alimentos inflamatorios que comemos.

Factores que contribuyen con la inflamación crónica

Factores psicológicos

¿Alguna vez ha visto una película de terror con su corazón latiendo aceleradamente? Las reacciones como esta, iniciadas por una amenaza percibida (real o ficticia) dilatan sus vasos sanguíneos, al igual que la inflamación. Capilares más anchos significa que más sangre y más nutrientes llegan a sus órganos para ayudarlo a combatir un ataque o tratar con una amenaza. Esta es la reacción de "pelear o huir". Esto dispara la secreción de cortisol, la hormona del estrés, desde sus glándulas suprarrenales con una cascada de otras hormonas del estrés, incluyendo adrenalina y norepinefrina.

Un pato podría estar cruzando un lago y encontrarse con una situación amenazadora. Grazna, se sale del lago, aletea con sus alas y se aleja volando. El estrés terminó. Probablemente una persona esté a punto de tener un accidente conduciendo de casa al trabajo, y los efectos de la tensión pueden durar un par de días antes de poderlo soltar y seguir adelante. Cuando uno no suelta un problema, el cuerpo continuamente secreta cortisol día tras día, semana tras semana. Demasiado cortisol puede suprimir el sistema inmune, incrementar la presión sanguínea, elevar el azúcar en la sangre, reducir la libido, producir acné, depositar grasa en su sección abdominal, mantenerlo despierto en la noche y contribuir con la obesidad. El cortisol tiene una función directa en la inflamación crónica.

¿Cuántas veces ha visto esta respuesta en su vida? Trabaja horas interminables preparándose para una prueba, una exposición o sus vacaciones y luego se enferma. Su cuerpo es bueno para mantener las cosas bajo control durante un rato, pero no lo puede hacer para siempre. Tratar con el estrés persistente perjudica su sistema inmune, sus glándulas suprarrenales y tiroides, su sistema nervioso central . . . y todo su cuerpo.

Las investigaciones han vinculado la depresión y el estrés con un aumento en los marcadores inflamatorios como la proteína C-reactiva (PCR). Este es un análisis que mide la concentración en el suero sanguíneo de un tipo especial de proteína producida en el hígado que se eleva durante los episodios de inflamación o infección agudas. Un resultado en los análisis de una PCR elevada es un indicador de inflamación aguda. Este es un indicador principal de un riesgo potencial para las cardiopatías (no el colesterol alto). Aproximadamente el mismo número de personas muere de ataques al corazón con colesterol bajo que alto.

Su cuerpo reacciona a lo que genera estrés en una manera general sin importar qué sea. Entre más seria parece ser la amenaza, más dramática será la respuesta. Con la inflamación, las experiencias emocionales dolorosas son tan dañinas como el estrés físico o los alimentos inflamatorios. Considere una condición como el asma. Un ataque emocional puede disparar un ataque de asma en algunas personas con tanta rapidez como el ejercicio físico o un alérgeno. Los pensamientos y los sentimientos son poderosos. Se manifiestan a sí mismos físicamente con síntomas inflamatorios. El estrés emocional puede provocar que su piel se abra y que su tracto intestinal se descontrole. Pero hay buenas noticias: sus emociones y su mente pueden ser sus aliados en el proceso de sanidad también. Todo depende de la manera en que usted decide reaccionar en varias situaciones.

Usted puede deshacerse de emociones tóxicas como el enojo, el resentimiento, el rechazo de otros, el autorechazo, la preocupación, el temor y la amargura. Puede entrar a un remanso de paz para usted mismo y los demás. Esto es tan importante como comer una dieta contra la inflamación si quiere deshacerse de la inflamación crónica.

Sus expresiones diarias podrían contener algunas claves hacia su mundo interno de emociones. ¿Con cuánta frecuencia usted utiliza palabras como *furioso, agotado, harto, cansado, sumamente preocupado* o *temo que no va a resultar*? Los conflictos dentro de su cuerpo y su alma sueltan poderosas hormonas inflamatorias, ácido en su estómago, dolor en su cabeza, articulaciones y músculos. Están allí para decirle que hay un problema. La solución es dejar ir las emociones y los pensamientos negativos, haciendo la paz con usted mismo y los demás y escoger el gozo, la paz, el amor, la confianza y la aceptación. También, un programa de ejercicio físico que produce endorfinas que lo hacen sentir bien ayudará a su cuerpo a controlar la inflamación.

Manejar el dolor emocional a menudo se pasa por alto, pero es un componente importante que usted puede abordar al aliviar la inflamación. Esto también puede contribuir grandemente para restaurar el equilibrio de sus sistema inmune.

Las investigaciones muestran que la oxitocina reduce los niveles de radicales libres y la inflamación, además de que desacelera el envejecimiento y la enfermedad en su raíz. La oxitocina es una hormona neurohipofisial que es secretada por la porción posterior de la glándula pituitaria. Actúa principalmente como un neuromodulador cerebral. Los actos de bondad con frecuencia son acompañados por calidez emocional, y la calidez emocional produce oxitocina en el cerebro y a lo largo del cuerpo. También, hay referencias en las revistas científicas que indican un fuerte vínculo entre la compasión y la actividad del nervio vago. El nervio vago controla los niveles de inflamación del cuerpo.[4]

Estrés

Cuando enfrenta una labor de limpieza de la casa interminable porque están por llegar visitas importantes o fechas límite que parecen imposibles de cumplir, usted tiene que tomar una decisión. Puede permitirse a sí mismo entrar en un frenesí, o puede escoger relajarse incluso en medio de la refriega. Usted puede dejar ir. Créame, lo sé de primera mano. Solía alterarme mucho por las fechas de entrega de los libros y ni siquiera podía dormir por la noche. He escrito veintiséis libros, así que he pasado algunas noches sin dormir. Esto retrasaba mi trabajo significativamente. Las respuestas estresantes no tienen resultados positivos. Usted puede escoger trabajar lo más eficientemente posible y confiar en que todo saldrá bien.

A medida que aprenda a relajarse y dejar ir el estrés, puede vivir armoniosamente a pesar de lo que lo estresa. Esto puede ayudarlo a trabajar y a interactuar con más personas creativa y eficientemente. Este es un gran factor en manejar el estrés. "Querer" más que "deber" o "tener que" es un gran reductor del estrés también. *Los deberías* no funcionan en ninguna manera; solamente contribuyen con el estrés. Cuando usted quiere hacer algo, cuando siente que tiene una opción en el asunto y en la manera en que diseña su tiempo, usted tiene más control y menos estrés.

El estrés es un factor inmenso de contribución con la inflamación. Es responsable de la secreción de sustancias dañinas que inundan su cuerpo. Las hormonas del estrés son ácidas, lo cual daña sus células. El estrés también afecta sus neurotransmisores cerebrales, provocando que sus transmisores excitadores como la norepinefrina se eleve y que los transmisores relajantes como la serotonina caigan. Entonces su mente comienza a conversar en la noche cuando usted necesita dormir y lo puede mantener despierto la mitad de la noche. Una discusión exhaustiva sobre el estrés va más allá de la temática de este libro, pero es extremadamente importante explorarla. Si usted hablara con mi marido que es psicoterapeuta, le diría que es un importante factor que contribuye con la inflamación y la enfermedad. Esta breve sección no resolverá sus problemas con el estrés, pero espero inspirarlo a buscar ayuda con su estrés y ponerlo bajo control.

El estrés siempre será una parte de la vida. No podemos evitarlo. Pero si destruye nuestra vida o no depende completamente de nuestra respuesta a él.

Falta de sueño

Los que sufren de insomnio secretan citocinas inflamatorias a un ritmo más alto en comparación con los que no. Durante el sueño el cuerpo se regenera, se sueltan hormonas de sanidad y el sistema inmune se calma y es capaz de rejuvenecer. La falta de un sueño restaurador es un promotor importante de la inflamación. La gente que sufre dolor conoce esto de primera mano porque la falta de sueño debido al

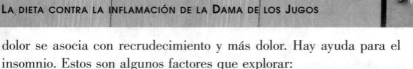

dolor se asocia con recrudecimiento y más dolor. Hay ayuda para el insomnio. Estos son algunos factores que explorar:

- *Desequilibrio suprarrenal.* Para determinar su nivel de estrés suprarrenal, puede tomar mi Cuestionario de Salud Suprarrenal en http://www.juiceladycherie.com/Juice/do-you-have-adrenal-fatigue/. Si usted tiene un puntaje alto, le recomiendo mi libro *The Juice Lady's Remedies for Stress and Adrenal Fatigue* [Los remedios para el estrés y la fatiga suprarrenal de La Dama de los Jugos]. Si sus suprarrenales están bajas, esto podría mantenerlo despierto por la noche. También puede solicitar el análisis de saliva para determinar qué tan estresadas están sus glándulas suprarrenales en www.neurogistics.com. Utilice mi código de médico SLEEP (en mayúsculas).
- *Ansiedad, preocupación o pensamientos tormentosos.* Debe encontrar una manera de sacar todo esto de su mente y alma por la noche, o no va a dormir bien. Nuevamente, esto va más allá del tema de este libro, pero es extremadamente importante abordarlo.
- *Desequilibrio en los neurotransmisores cerebrales.* El programa de aminoácidos con el que trabajo para balancear la química cerebral ha sido sumamente útil para muchas personas, junto con la reducción del estrés. Usted puede solicitar un análisis de orina que le dará un informe impreso del estado de sus neurotransmisores y una recomendación de los aminoácidos que lo ayudarán a ponerlos en equilibrio. Usted puede solicitar el análisis de orina en www.neurogistics.com. Utilice mi código de médico SLEEP (en mayúsculas).
- *Desequilibrios en nutrientes.* Quizá tenga deficiencia de magnesio. Si este mineral es bajo, puede hacer que se despierte por la noche. Si el calcio es bajo, puede evitar que se duerma. También consumir dulces, cafeína o beber demasiado alcohol puede perturbar su sueño.

Toxicidad ambiental

Lo sintético, el látex, los pegamentos, los tintes, los adhesivos, los plásticos, los aromatizantes y los productos de limpieza tóxicos representan en conjunto sustancias químicas a las que estamos expuestos con frecuencia. Muchos de nosotros trabajamos en edificios de oficinas, plantas o aviones con aire recirculado que solamente incrementa nuestra exposición a las toxinas ambientales.

¿Alguna vez ha escuchado acerca del "síndrome del edificio enfermo"? Este término es utilizado para describir a los ocupantes de un edificio que experimentan problemas agudos de salud y bienestar que están vinculados con el tiempo invertido en edificios tóxicos, y así como los edificios enfermos enferman a la gente, también los pesticidas, la contaminación y los metales pesados como el plomo, el cadmio y el mercurio. Estos metales pesados solamente son tres de más de dos docenas de metales pesados en nuestro ambiente de los que nuestros cuerpos deben tratar de desintoxicarse. Las toxinas están en todas partes: nuestra agua potable, nuestros alimentos, nuestro aire e incluso en la leche materna. Muchas de estas sustancias son liposolubles, lo cual significa que se almacenan en espacios de las células y tejidos grasos hasta que alcanzan niveles dañinos.

La sensibilidad química no es el único resultado de esta mezcla nociva de sustancias dañinas. La exposición constante a los químicos tóxicos e irritantes en el aire, incluso en dosis bajas, hacen que su sistema inmune pierda el control. Algunas personas se desintoxican mejor que otras y pueden resistir más exposición antes de mostrar síntomas. Otros necesitan soporte de salud temprano en sus vidas. Aprenda todo lo que pueda acerca de los productos de belleza, limpieza y jardinería que usa; el edificio en el que trabaja; la casa en la que vive; y el agua que bebe. Deshacerse de la toxicidad en todos los frentes es crucial para combatir la inflamación. Hacer limpiezas periódicas de sus órganos de eliminación puede hacer una diferencia enorme para reducir la inflamación. Usted puede tomar mi cuestionario "¿Qué tan tóxico es usted?" [How Toxic Are You?] en http://www.juiceladycherie.com/Juice/toxic-take-the-quiz/. Si obtiene una puntuación alta, es sumamente importante que limpie su cuerpo. Obtenga mi libro: *Juicing, Fasting, and Detoxing for Life* [Hacer jugos, ayunar y desintoxicarse para vivir]. Comience con la limpieza de colon, luego con la de hígado/vesícula, riñón/vejiga, pulmón, sistema linfático, piel y sangre. Va a encontrar kits de limpieza en mi sitio web para ayudarlo en su proceso de limpieza.

Síndrome de intestino con fugas

Cuando su cortisol es elevado debido al estrés, o bien sus niveles de hormonas tiroideas y suprarrenales fluctúan debido al estrés o a quemar el aceite de media noche, su recubrimiento intestinal se vuelve más permeable. Cuando usted come durante este tiempo, el alimento parcialmente no digerido, las toxinas, los virus, la levadura y las bacterias tienen la oportunidad de pasar a través de la pared intestinal y tener acceso al torrente sanguíneo. Este es el síndrome de intestino con fugas. Cuando el revestimiento intestinal es dañado repetidamente debido a las hormonas del estrés y una dieta que favorece la inflamación las células dañadas son incapaces de hacer bien su trabajo. Los intestinos son incapaces de absorber nutrientes y enzimas apropiadamente que son vitales para una digestión adecuada. Con el tiempo la digestión queda atrofiada y la absorción de nutrientes es afectada. A medida que este escenario progresa, su cuerpo inicia un ataque sobre los invasores extraños. Responde con inflamación, reacciones alérgicas y varios síntomas relacionados con una variedad de enfermedades. Incluso puede encenderse por sí solo si la persona es diagnosticada con una enfermedad autoinmune.

Inactividad

La falta de ejercicio puede llevar directamente a inflamación de bajo nivel. Según la Western Washington University: "Los músculos esqueléticos actúan como un órgano endocrino a través de influenciar el metabolismo y modificar la producción de mensajes del sistema inmune en otros tejidos incluyendo tejidos endoteliales y adiposos. A medida que los músculos esqueléticos realizan un trabajo, producen y liberan sustancias antiinflamatorias en la sangre".[5] Cuando uno está activo los marcadores de la inflamación como la proteína C-reactiva se reducen. Si usted se sienta a un escritorio una buena porción del día es importante levantarse y moverse tanto como sea posible. Levántese cuando hable por teléfono. Cuando tome un descanso realice algunos estiramientos o flexiones. Camine en su hora del almuerzo. Camine después de la cena o de su comida principal. Estacione el coche un poco más lejos de lo usual para que pueda caminar algunos pasos más. Monte su bicicleta fija mientras habla por teléfono o ve las noticias de la noche. Hágase miembro de un gimnasio y ejercítese tres veces a la semana. Continuamente piense en maneras de hacer más movimientos en su vida.

Obesidad

Las células grasas de hecho desempeñan su parte para promover la inflamación. La inflamación de bajo nivel del tejido adiposo (graso) puede resultar por la activación crónica del sistema inmune innato. Las investigaciones han mostrado una relación entre las citocinas inflamatorias y las proteínas y la función del tejido adiposo.[6] Las personas obesas tienen niveles más altos de proteína C-reactiva.[7]

MUJERES EN CLIMATERIO, TERAPIA DE REEMPLAZO HORMONAL (TRH) Y LA INFLAMACIÓN VASCULAR

La terapia de reemplazo hormonal (TRH) tiene un efecto de inflamación vascular y puede llevar a un riesgo mayor de enfermedades cardiovasculares.[8] La información de la Women's Health Initiative (Iniciativa de Salud Femenina) mostró que los niveles elevados de proteína C-reactiva y la interleucina-6 (IL-6) es al mismo tiempo proinflamatoria y antiinflamatoria. Cuando se encuentra fuera de equilibrio, estimula los procesos inflamatorios y de enfermedad. La PCR y la IL-6 elevadas estaban relacionadas con el uso de la TRH, pero no eran tan significativas en las mujeres que se ejercitaban al tomar terapia de reemplazo hormonal (TRH). Los niveles de proteína C-reactiva eran significativamente más altos en las usuarias de TRH.[9] Este estudio brinda evidencia de que el ejercicio puede ser benéfico para contrarrestar los impactos negativos de la TRH. No obstante, es mucho mejor utilizar hormonas de origen vegetal y también ejercitarse.

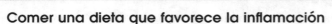

Comer una dieta que favorece la inflamación

Nuestra dieta occidental cargada de alimentos refinados, azúcares, aditivos y rellenos, contribuye con la inflamación especialmente en las células de los vasos sanguíneos así como a lo largo de todo el cuerpo. Los siguientes dos capítulos están dedicados a la dieta contra la inflamación porque muchos profesionales de la salud creen que nuestra dieta es el contribuyente principal para la inflamación.

ALIMENTOS Y FACTORES QUE CONTRIBUYEN CON LA INFLAMACIÓN

La salud es como el dinero, nunca tenemos una
verdadera idea de su valor hasta que la perdemos.[1]

—JOSH BILLINGS

NOS HEMOS DESLIZADO en un círculo destructivo consumiendo la dieta estadounidense que pone el énfasis en los alimentos que contribuyen directamente con la inflamación. Esta dieta genera la producción de cortisol y contribuye con elevados niveles de estrés. Los elementos básicos de una dieta estadounidense típica—azúcar, almidón, maíz, soya y granos (gluten)—son indudablemente los mayores contribuyentes para la inflamación crónica. Del desayuno a la cena los estadounidenses se sirven alimentos que avivan el fuego inflamatorio en el cuerpo. A continuación se encuentran los alimentos que usted debe evitar para poner la inflamación bajo control y disfrutar una salud intensa.

Evite el azúcar y los edulcorantes artificiales y bajos en calorías

A Estados Unidos le encanta su azúcar. La mayoría de nosotros somos bebés de azúcar; hemos sido criados con estas cosas. Desde los refrigerios y los refrescos a los cereales del desayuno y los postres, no podemos tener suficiente de ella. Pero el lado dulce tiene un lado negativo. Nuestra adicción a lo dulce nos está matando lentamente. Somos seducidos con azúcar añadida en los alimentos procesados, las salsas, los aderezos, los refrigerios y las bebidas. Lo cual está duplicando nuestras probabilidades de muerte prematura relacionada con el corazón, el cáncer, la diabetes y la obesidad.

El azúcar y otros alimentos con alto valor glucémico disparan los niveles de insulina y ponen al sistema inmune en gran alerta. Cuando el nivel de azúcar en sangre se dispara, tenemos antojo de más dulces, almidón, alimentos con harina refinada, sal y comida chatarra. Como respuesta a una dieta inflamatoria, el cuerpo produce más cortisol, que provoca más inflamación, más producción de cortisol, niveles más altos de insulina, más antojos; y una y otra vez se repite un ciclo interminable.

Como resultado, los altos niveles de insulina activan las enzimas que elevan el ácido araquidónico en nuestra sangre. El ácido araquidónico es un ácido graso natural en ciertos alimentos y que también es elaborado en el cuerpo. Es esencial para la vida en pequeñas cantidades, pero también es uno de los componentes para elaborar hormonas inflamatorias. No lo queremos en abundancia.

Consumir grandes cantidades de azúcares, fructosa, edulcorantes artificiales y edulcorantes bajos en calorías como los alcoholes de azúcar pueden llevar a que sus bacterias se adapten en una manera que interfiera con sus señales de saciedad y el metabolismo, según un informe publicado en *Obesity Reviews*.[2] Las bacterias adaptadas a los edulcorantes proliferan y se vuelven más eficientes en procesar grandes cantidades de azúcares y a su vez producen más y más ácidos grasos de cadena corta. Los ácidos grasos de cadena corta promueven la inflamación en el revestimiento intestinal.

Un estudio de mujeres saludables de mediana edad mostró que las altas cargas glucémicas estaban relacionadas con altos niveles de proteína C-reactiva, independientemente del peso y de la ingesta total calórica.[3]

Algunas veces la inflamación puede estar presente y usted ni siquiera saber que está allí. Este tipo de inflamación crónica de bajo nivel es conocida como la inflamación silenciosa, y sabemos por estudios que el exceso en la ingesta de azúcar está asociado con el tipo silencioso de inflamación.

Para romper este ciclo es imperativo evitar azúcar, fructosa, edulcorantes artificiales, edulcorantes bajos en calorías, jarabe de maíz, dextrosa, jarabe para panqueques, maltosa, sorgo y sacarosa. Muchas personas son adictas a los edulcorantes, así que les toma un poco de esfuerzo evitar los dulces. Aliente su corazón. Después de dos semanas los antojos se van.

Esto es lo que hay que evitar:

- Cereales empacados y barras para desayunar.
- Bebidas de café con jarabe endulzado.
- Alimentos elaborados comercialmente con edulcorantes añadidos; lea las etiquetas.
- Barras de energía.
- Galletas, magdalenas, postres, dulces.
- Proteína en polvo con azúcares añadidos.
- Botanas y comida chatarra.
- Refrescos, bebidas de frutas, ponche (una Coca-Cola es igual a tomar alrededor de diez cubos de azúcar).

TODA LA VERDAD SOBRE LOS REFRESCOS DE DIETA

Los edulcorantes artificiales son cientos de miles de veces más dulces que el azúcar regular, lo cual activa la preferencia de la persona por más alimentos dulces sobre cualquier otra sustancia. Engañan a su metabolismo haciéndolo pensar que está consumiendo azúcar. Esto lleva a su organismo a secretar insulina, la hormona que almacena grasa, lo cual promueve grasa abdominal que se pega como caramelo sobre una manzana.

También confunde y desacelera su metabolismo; usted quemará menos calorías. Esto lo hace tener más hambre, y a usted se le antoja más azúcar y almidón como el pan y la pasta. En estudios con animales las ratas que consumían más edulcorantes artificiales comían más, su metabolismo se desaceleraba y ganaban 14% más grasa corporal en solamente dos semanas, a pesar de que comían menos calorías. En estudios poblacionales hubo un incremento de 200% del riesgo de obesidad en los que toman bebidas dietéticas.[4]

Dígale "no" a los granos refinados

Los granos refinados están vacíos de fibra y vitamina B y cargados de almidón. Esto los hace similares a los azúcares refinados; ambos son calorías vacías. Al igual que los azúcares refinados, también tienen un índice glucémico más alto que los granos no procesados. Al ser consumidos consistentemente, pueden acelerar la aparición de inflamación y enfermedades degenerativas como el cáncer, la cardiopatía coronaria y la diabetes.

Deshágase del trigo

El principal problema con el trigo es el gluten. Las gliadinas, los componentes del gluten, son proteínas que se encuentran en el trigo (duro, escanda, espelta, farina, farro y kamut), centeno, cebada y triticale; son responsables por la textura elástica de la masa. A partir de la década de 1960, hemos estado manipulando el trigo para obtener pan más esponjoso. Algunas variedades de trigo contienen más gluten, así que por eso lo manipulan para obtener más gluten. *Gluten* proviene de la palabra latina para pegamento. Sus propiedades adhesivas mantienen unido el pan. No obstante, este pegamento interfiere con la descomposición y absorción de nutrientes, incluyendo nutrientes de otros alimentos en la misma comida. Como resultado obtenemos una mezcla "pegada" que constipa el intestino en lugar de una comida nutritiva de fácil digestión. El gluten no digerido entonces dispara al sistema inmune para atacar el revestimiento del intestino delgado y provoca síntomas como diarrea, constipación, náusea, distensión

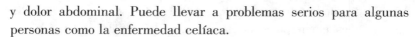
y dolor abdominal. Puede llevar a problemas serios para algunas personas como la enfermedad celíaca.

Comemos demasiado gluten actualmente. Solamente échele un vistazo a la dieta estadounidense típica: un bagel o un pan tostado para desayunar, un sándwich o una hamburguesa para almorzar, y bollos, pizza o pasta para cenar o para la comida principal. Eso es muchos granos (y gluten) en solo un día. Incluso se consumen cantidades mayores si tomamos en cuenta los refrigerios comunes como las galletas y frituras hechas a base de granos y los postres como las galletas y las tortas. Adicionalmente, los productos comerciales basados en granos que llenan los estantes de las tiendas y que se sirven en los restaurantes como panes y rellenos son comunes. Estos productos producen moco, elevan los niveles de azúcar en sangre e incrementan la inflamación. Además, los panes con frecuencia son adicionados con ingredientes que no son alimento, como la sustancia azodicarbonamida que también se utiliza en la elaboración de tapetes de yoga, piel sintética y suelas de zapatos, junto con acondicionadores de masa como el bromato de potasio (que interfiere con la absorción de yodo), saborizantes o colorantes artificiales, transgénicos y L-cisteína, un aminoácido que extiende la caducidad y con frecuencia se elabora a partir del cabello que se recoge del piso de las peluquerías chinas.

El gluten y la inflamación tiroidea

Aunque existen ciertas investigaciones que vinculan la enfermedad celíaca y la enfermedad de Hashimoto, el impacto que tiene el gluten en la función tiroidea todavía no se ha aceptado ampliamente como un hecho. No obstante, un número cada vez mayor de médicos están compartiendo su experiencia y éxito al utilizar una dieta libre de gluten para aliviar un poco los síntomas de desequilibrios tiroideos. Según el Dr. Datis Kharrazian: "Como la estructura molecular del gluten es tan semejante a la de la glándula tiroides, el problema puede ser de una confusión de identidad. Cada vez que el gluten sin digerir por error entra al torrente sanguíneo, el sistema inmune responde a través de destruirlo para removerlo".[5] Con el tiempo el cuerpo pierde el control.

A causa de que la estructura molecular del gluten se asemeja tanto a la de la tiroides, el cuerpo comienza a atacar a la tiroides: un caso de confusión de identidad. Una vez que el ataque es puesto en marcha, no hay manera de apagarlo. Una persona con tiroides autoinmune de Hashimoto debe llevar una dieta libre de gluten. Si usted come gluten, puede afectarlo durante seis meses. La gente con una tiroides baja también se puede beneficiar grandemente de una dieta libre de gluten.[6]

Los que tienen condiciones tiroideas a menudo preguntan acerca de los alimentos bociógenos (que significan bloqueadores de yodo) los cuales incluyen a la soya, los cacahuetes, el mijo y las verduras crucíferas: brócoli, coles de bruselas, coliflor, repollo y col rizada. Estas verduras maravillosas no están en la lista de alimentos que contribuyen con la inflamación; más bien, combaten la inflamación, el cáncer y una horda de padecimientos. Pero están en la lista de cosas a evitar por los que tienen hipotiroidismo o tiroiditis de Hashimoto. Usted quizá pueda incluirlos crudos (algunos pueden; otros no), pero no todos los días. Principalmente debería cocinarlos, ligeramente al vapor o fermentarlos lo cual desactiva los glucosinolatos, reduciendo así su actividad bociogénica.

Siempre es mejor rotar sus verduras verdes. El Dr. Craig Maxwell alienta a sus pacientes con problemas tiroideos a que incluyan verduras crucíferas. Él dice: "En mi experiencia, los valores de laboratorio (TSH, T3 libre y T4 libre) utilizados para evaluar la función tiroidea han permanecen en el mismo rango sea que los pacientes los consuman o no".[7] Si tiene problemas de tiroides, debería definitivamente evitar los otros alimentos bociógenos: cacahuetes y mantequilla de maní, mijo y todos los productos de soya (la soya bloquea la actividad de la enzima TPO). El aceite de canola (colza) también es bociógeno y debería ser eliminado. Es altamente procesado y además es elaborado de cultivos modificados genéticamente.

Evite la sal refinada de mesa

La sal de mesa es una forma de sodio manufacturado llamado cloruro de sodio. Es una sustancia altamente refinada hecha por el hombre que se produce a través de tomar ya sea sal natural o sobras de "hojuelas" de petróleo crudo que se cocinan a 1200°F [648,9°C]. Una vez que la sal se calienta a esta temperatura, pierde la mayoría de los minerales. Entonces se le añaden yodo y químicos dañinos como:

- Agentes antiaglutinantes
- Blanqueador
- Flúor
- Glutamato monosódico (GMS)
- Yoduro de potasio
- Aluminato de sodio y otros derivados del aluminio

Estos aditivos y preservadores de alimentos pueden contribuir con problemas serios de salud. Esta sal también es altamente ácida, lo cual puede contribuir con la inflamación crónica. Usted solamente debería utilizar sal marina natural, sal gris o sal rosa del Himalaya.

Olvídese de las carnes de lote de engorda

Los animales engordados comercialmente son alimentados principalmente con granos, frijol de soya y maíz: una dieta que es alta en ácidos grasos omega-6 que favorecen la inflamación y baja en grasas omega-3 que combaten la inflamación. Los ácidos grasos omega-6 favorecen la inflamación porque son descompuestos por el cuerpo y convertidos en prostaglandinas y otras proteínas inflamatorias. Estas proteínas causan inflamación. Los animales se mantienen en condiciones de vida de hacinamiento donde ganan exceso de peso. Esto genera grasa altamente saturada. Para forzarlos a crecer más rápido y evitar que se enfermen se les inyectan hormonas y antibióticos. Los alimentos animales incluyendo res, cordero, aves y huevos han sido consumidos en una manera segura por miles de años sin generar problemas. Las enfermedades contemporáneas asociadas con la dieta occidental incluyen comer grandes cantidades de carne barata desarrollada en lotes de engorda que es alta en ácido araquidónico y grasas omega-6 que disparan dolor en las articulaciones e inflamación. Lo mismo sucede con los pollos y los huevos criados en jaulas o encierros con alimento convencional. La mayoría de los productos animales en los supermercados y restaurantes provienen de granjas con lotes de engorda. Evítelos por completo.

Aléjese de los aceites poco saludables

Elimine todos los aceites hidrogenados y parcialmente hidrogenados, las grasas trans y los aceites vegetales poliinsaturados, incluyendo cártamo, girasol, maíz y soya junto con el de canola o colza (un cultivo bastante transgénico). La dieta estadounidense está cargada de aceites omega-6 y deficiente en aceites omega-3 antiinflamatorios que se encuentran en las verduras; semillas como la linaza, el cáñamo y la chía; así como las nueces; además de pescado graso de agua fría. Demasiado omega-6 proveniente de aceites vegetales refinados da como resultado sustancias químicas inflamatorias que circulan en el cuerpo, las cuales reducen la habilidad de nuestras células para funcionar normalmente. También, los aceites poliinsaturados se oxidan con facilidad, lo cual significa que reaccionan con el oxígeno y forman un óxido. Al calentarse, los aceites vegetales pueden oxidarse rápidamente y causar daño por los radicales libres; a altas temperaturas forman grasas trans que generan todavía más radicales libres, los cuales pueden dañar células saludables, disparar la inflamación y los niveles de LDL (colesterol malo). Los aceites parcialmente hidrogenados, como la margarina, son igualmente dañinos.

Los aceites poco saludables están en la mayoría de los aderezos de ensalada, mayonesa, alimentos empacados y alimentos de conveniencia. Cuando sale a comer, su comida es muy probable que haya sido preparada con estos aceites, a menos que coma en un restaurante orientado a la salud o pida alimentos que hayan sido asados y aceite de oliva y vinagre para su ensalada.

Haga a un lado los lácteos

Los lácteos (y el trigo) se encuentran entre los alimentos más irritantes para nuestros sistemas ya que alientan la producción de moco (flema) en el cuerpo. En la medicina china es conocido como "humedad". El moco lleva a la inflamación y a una multitud de síntomas comunes como baja energía, poco sueño y digestión atrofiada. Los lácteos también son un alérgeno común que puede disparar respuestas inflamatorias como incomodidad estomacal, constipación, diarrea, sarpullido, acné, urticaria y dificultades respiratoria en las personas susceptibles. El Dr. David Ludwig y el Dr. Walter Willett de Harvard (publicado en la revista de la Asociación Médica Estadounidense, *Journal of the American Medical Association*) no encontraron datos que le den soporte a la aseveración de que el consumo de lácteos lleve a mejores huesos, pérdida de peso o una salud mejorada. También encontraron algunos riesgos vinculados con el consumo de lácteos, incluyendo subir de peso, incremento en el riesgo de cáncer e incremento en el riesgo de fracturas. ¡Resulta que la leche no desarrolla huesos fuertes! También descubrieron que los lácteos pueden producir otros problemas como la constipación, síndrome de intestino irritable, distensión, gases, diarrea, alergias, eccema y acné.[8]

Reduzca la ingesta de cafeína

Un estudio publicado en 2004 en la revista médica *American Journal of Clinical Nutrition* encontró una relación entre el consumo moderado a alto de café y el incremento en la inflamación, tanto en hombres como mujeres que bebían café. La interleucina-6 y la proteína C-reactiva (marcadores de inflamación) fueron significativamente más altos que en los que no bebían café. Esta relación podría explicar, en parte, el efecto negativo de incrementar la ingesta de café en el sistema cardiovascular.[9] Observe que la cafeína también se encuentra en el té negro y en los refrescos (una bebida todavía más inflamatoria que el café).

Tenga cuidado con las mentiras sobre el alcohol

La cerveza, la sidra, el aguardiente, el licor y el vino promueven la inflamación. Se ha llegado a conocer que el consumo regular de alcohol causa irritación e inflamación del esófago, la laringe y el hígado. El consumo excesivo de alcohol puede incrementar la respuesta inflamatoria del cuerpo de la cabeza a los pies. La inflamación crónica promueve el crecimiento de tumores y cáncer en los sitios de irritación repetida. Según el Dr. Mark Hyman, usted debería tomar un descanso de seis a ocho semanas de beber alcohol; luego no regrese a beber todos los días. Dice que dos o tres porciones de alcohol es lo máximo que usted debería ingerir a la semana. El tamaño de una porción es:

- 12 onzas [354,9 ml] de cerveza.
- 4 a 5 onzas [118,3 a 147,9 ml] de vino (escoja orgánico; las uvas son rociadas [con pesticidas] abundantemente).
- 1,5 onzas [44,36 ml] de licores.

Si bebe más de esto en una semana se está exponiendo a serios riesgos de salud incluyendo demencia, depresión y un mayor riesgo de diabetes tipo 2 que puede contribuir con una amplia variedad de condiciones de salud incluyendo hipertensión y cardiopatías.[10]

Evite los alimentos irradiados

La irradiación de los alimentos ha estado llevándose a cabo en verduras, carnes y otros productos no orgánicos convencionales durante años. Mata los insectos que se podrían haber trepado en los alimentos antes de enviarlos a la tienda. Las frutas y verduras cultivadas convencionalmente, desde las manzanas a la calabaza italiana son irradiadas rutinariamente. Al principio podría parecer que la irradiación de alimentos para matar bacterias e insectos en las verduras convencionales y carnes debería ser una práctica común. Después de todo, la espinaca irradiada para eliminar salmonella es una espinaca feliz, ¿no? No necesariamente.

La irradiación de alimentos tiene que ver con exponer la comida a altos niveles de radiación para matar insectos, bacterias, hongos y moho y para darle una caducidad más larga. Aunque la idea de irradiar la comida suena bastante poco apetitosa, ha sido practicada en Estados Unidos desde la década de 1960, cuando la FDA aprobó la

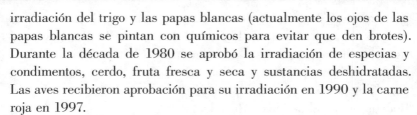

irradiación del trigo y las papas blancas (actualmente los ojos de las papas blancas se pintan con químicos para evitar que den brotes). Durante la década de 1980 se aprobó la irradiación de especias y condimentos, cerdo, fruta fresca y seca y sustancias deshidratadas. Las aves recibieron aprobación para su irradiación en 1990 y la carne roja en 1997.

Compre solamente frutas y verduras orgánicas. Lo único bueno es que en Estados Unidos, los cultivadores y fabricantes de alimentos se supone deben etiquetar los alimentos que han sido irradiados; por lo cual, es posible evitar los alimentos irradiados si uno compra con cuidado. Desde 1986 todos los productos irradiados deben llevar al símbolo internacional llamado radura, que es una flor dentro de un círculo y es similar al símbolo de la Agencia de Protección Ambiental. No obstante, yo no he visto el símbolo de radura todavía en las frutas o las verduras donde compro.

Dígale "no" a los transgénicos

¿Qué tienen en común los totopostes, la leche de soya y el aceite de canola? Están hechos a partir de los cultivos más transgénicos de América del Norte. Alrededor de 85% del maíz cultivado en EE. UU. está modificado genéticamente para producir insecticidas o para sobrevivir a la aplicación de herbicidas. Y entre 91% y 93% de todos los frijoles de soya están modificados genéticamente para sobrevivir dosis masivas del herbicida Roundup.[11]

Es probable que ni siquiera desee comprar muchos de estos productos, pero cuando se trata de ciertas verduras, a menos que compre las cultivadas orgánicamente, es bastante probable que esté comiendo alimentos transgénicos. Y eso lo debería preocupar bastante. Somos los "conejillos de Indias" humanos cuando se trata de los alimentos transgénicos o modificados genéticamente (MG). Los estudios en ratas han mostrado que los alimentos MG promueven tumores e indican que deberíamos estar sumamente preocupados por comer alimentos transgénicos. Un estudio francés—la evaluación de seguridad transgénica más exhaustiva jamás aplicada—destaca esa preocupación. Tenía que ver con doscientas ratas y duró dos años, que es la expectativa de vida de la especie de ratas utilizadas. Los investigadores dicen que sus resultados muestran "severos efectos adversos a la salud, incluyendo tumores mamarios y daño a los riñones y al hígado, lo cual llevó a muerte prematura" a causa del maíz listo para Roundup y por el herbicida Roundup.[12]

Algunos cálculos dicen que tanto como treinta mil diferentes productos en los estantes de las tiendas han sido modificados genéticamente, lo cual se debe principalmente porque muchos alimentos procesados contienen alguna forma de soya o de maíz.

Al tratar de evitar estos cultivos principales transgénicos, tendrá que vigilar no consumir maltodextrina, lecitina de soya, aceite de soya, proteína vegetal texturizada (soya), aceite de canola, productos de maíz y jarabe de maíz de alta fructosa. Otros cultivos transgénicos que evitar incluyen algunas variedades de calabaza italiana, calabazas amarillas de cuello curvado, papayas de Hawái, leche que contenga BST, cuajo (que contenga enzimas transgénicas) utilizado para elaborar quesos duros y aspartame (NutraSweet).

Deje atrás los alimentos preparados en el microondas

Cocinar en un microondas no se recomienda ya que genera productos secundarios tóxicos como d-Nitrosodietanolamina (un reconocido agente que provoca cáncer) en los alimentos cocinados. También genera alteraciones en la descomposición de los elementos glusocisa y galatosida en las frutas congeladas al ser desongeladas en un horno de microondas, y se forman radicales libres que causan cáncer dentro de ciertas formaciones moleculares de minerales traza en plantas, especialmente en verduras crudas. Yo (Cherie) ni siquiera uso el microondas para calentar agua; es así de destructivo. Esa agua puede matar plantas.

Culpables poco conocidos que contribuyen con la inflamación

Verduras solanáceas

El vínculo entre la familia de las solanáceas, el dolor crónico y la inflamación no es muy conocido por muchas personas. Aunque esto no les sucede a todos, esta familia de alimentos se cree que provoca síntomas de inflamación y artritis en alrededor de 30% de la población. Las solanáceas pertenecen a la familia de los alimentos más populares que consumimos, como los tomates, las papas y todo tipo de pimientos (tanto los chiles como los pimientos morrones; no la pimienta negra ni los granos enteros de pimienta), y la berenjena. Aunque no son realmente solanáceas, los arándanos azules, las moras negras, los licios y la bufera comparten los mismos alcaloides. No obstante, no son problemáticos para la mayoría de la gente. Los glicoalcaloides en las papas se sabe que contribuyen con el síndrome de intestino irritable (SII) y afectan negativamente la permeabilidad intestinal. Según el Dr. Marvin Childers: "Cuando estos inhibidores se acumulan en el cuerpo, solos o con otros inhibidores de la colinesterasa como la cafeína o impurezas alimenticias que contengan pesticidas inhibidores sistémicos de la colinesterasa, el resultado puede ser un espasmo muscular semejante a la parálisis, dolencias, dolores, blandura, inflamación y movimientos corporales rígidos".[13]

Muchas personas que padecen artritis o una enfermedad relacionada con la artritis como el lupus, el reumatismo y otros trastornos musculoesqueléticos dolorosos han descubierto que consumir alimentos de la familia de las solanáceas es un factor importante en su mala salud.

La mejor manera de determinar si usted es sensible a la familia de las solanáceas es realizar la eliminación de solanáceas y luego hacer pruebas de reto. Esto es similar a la dieta de eliminación. Usted omite todos los alimentos con solanáceas durante tres meses. Usted debe leer las etiquetas y buscar cualquier cosa como almidón de papa o alguna forma de estos alimentos. También esté al tanto de que pueden aparecer en medicamentos de venta libre o por prescripción. Después de tres meses introduzca un alimento de solanáceas a la vez. Si experimenta dolencias, dolores, rigidez, pérdida de energía, dolores de cabeza o problemas respiratorios quizá sea sensible a esta familia de alimentos. Esté al tanto de que podría tener una reacción retardada un par de días después; no todas las personas reaccionan inmediatamente después de haber ingerido ciertos alimentos. También, observe que la salsa de soya hecha en Estados Unidos suele elaborarse con frijoles de soya transgénicos (OMG) que son combinados con la planta solanácea petunia.

Cítricos: Para algunos no

La mayoría de las personas no son sensibles a las frutas cítricas. No obstante, para los que tienen sensibilidad a los cítricos, estas frutas pueden provocar inflamación y contribuir con el desarrollo de rigidez, artritis y enfermedades crónicas. Si la sensibilidad a los cítricos lo afecta, pruebe las cerezas ácidas o guindas en su lugar, que tienen el contenido antiinflamatorio más alto de cualquier alimento, según las investigaciones de la Oregon Health and Science University.[14]

Alérgenos alimentarios

Los alérgenos alimentarios pueden provocar o contribuir con el proceso inflamatorio a lo largo del cuerpo. Los alérgenos comunes como la caseína (en los lácteos) y el gluten (en el trigo, cebada, centeno, espelta y avena) pueden encender una cascada inflamatoria. Todos los que sufren la enfermedad celíaca conocen acerca de la inflamación en el intestino provocada por el gluten. Cuando una persona ingiere alimentos a los que es sensible, su ritmo cardiaco se eleva dieciséis latidos por minuto o más. Hay una aplicación que se ha desarrollado para ayudarlo a detectar las sensibilidades alimentarias a través de medir su pulso en la mañana y luego antes y después de comer. Esto es lo último en tecnología de detección de sensibilidad alimentaria de SweetWater Health.[15]

Capítulo 3

¡CAMBIE SU DIETA; CAMBIE SU VIDA!

Que la comida sea su medicina y la medicina sea su alimento.[1]

—HIPÓCRATES

HE AYUDADO A miles de personas de todo el mundo con su salud y su nutrición. Cuando han estado dispuestos a cambiar su dieta y hacer jugos todos los días, su salud y de hecho su vida entera ha cambiado. La inflamación se controla. Las dolencias y los dolores desaparecen como neblina al sol de la mañana. Todo tipo de padecimientos son sanados. Disfrutan energía para hacer muchas cosas que jamás podrían haber hecho antes.

Como usted aprendió en la introducción, hacer jugos y una dieta de alimentos saludables no procesados cambió mi vida. Había sufrido del síndrome de fatiga crónica y fibromialgia durante varios años hasta que avanzó al punto en que ya no podía ir a trabajar. Busqué respuestas porque nadie en la profesión médica me podía ayudar. Fue entonces cuando descubrí los jugos y el poder de una dieta contra la inflamación con alimentos no procesados. Corté todo lo que no era un alimento que diera vida y bebía alrededor de un cuarto (aprox. 1 l) de jugo fresco de verduras al día.

En tres meses todo mi dolor, fatiga, mente nublada y síntomas semejantes al resfriado se fueron. Me sentí como una persona completamente nueva.

LOS CAMBIOS EN LA DIETA LE DIERON UNA NUEVA VIDA

He andado un largo camino de que me hayan dicho que soy prediabética y que tengo colesterol alto. Había estado luchando con subir unas cortas escaleras. Ahora estoy disfrutando la vida. Hago senderismo, bailo toda la noche, escalo rocas, patino y esquío sobre agua. Todo esto por haber cambiado mis hábitos alimenticios y tomar jugos.

—Iris

La dieta moderna nos ofrece una proporción inversa de ácidos grasos (omega-3, -6 y -9), demasiada azúcar y carbohidratos, y una abundancia de trigo, lácteos, soya y otros alimentos alergénicos inflamatorios comunes. "Lo que usted come y cuánto se ejercite son los factores más importantes que gobiernan la inflamación", dice Mark Hyman, MD.[2] La mayoría de los factores para deshacerse de la inflamación se encuentran bajo su control. Usted tiene el poder de cambiar y sanar su cuerpo. Comienza con lo que usted escoge comer cada día.

Escoja alimentos reales sin procesar

Con frecuencia escuchamos el término *alimentos reales* o *alimentos no procesados*, que tiene el propósito de contrarrestar sustancias hechas por el hombre, preparadas en fábricas y terminadas en formas que son cualquier cosa excepto reales o sin procesar. Estos alimentos se han convertido en la base de la dieta estadounidense, pero no deberían ser llamados alimentos. Están procesados y vaciados de sus nutrientes naturales y llenados con sustancias químicas para promover una caducidad más duradera, facilidad de transporte y almacenamiento más largo. Están diseñados con una sola cosa en mente: el sabor que le va a gustar y las sustancias correctas para volverlo adicto a ese producto. A pesar de una variedad de sabores, texturas y formas, la mayoría de estos productos son elaborados de los mismos elementos mono-cultivados: trigo, maíz, soya y papas. Están vacíos de nutrientes debido a su crecimiento en ambientes de alta densidad y suelos agotados, mientras que al mismo tiempo son saturados con fertilizantes basados en petróleo. Se encuentran entre los cultivos más transgénicos de Estados Unidos. Debido a esta situación de crecimiento estresado, son susceptibles a las plagas. La agricultura comercial trata con esta susceptibilidad a través de rociarlos con altas cantidades de insecticidas o mediante producir "frankenplantas" transgénicas que tienen los pesticidas integrados en la planta como la alfalfa y el maíz Roundup Ready [listos para Roundup] de Monsanto. Esto presenta amenazas alarmantes a nuestra salud, nuestro ecosistema y nuestro abasto de alimentos a largo plazo.

Los valores nutritivos de las plantas son disminuidos todavía más en el curso del procesamiento y el almacenamiento, de modo que los alimentos procesados son fortificados con vitaminas y minerales sintéticos. Se les añaden saborizantes para mejorar el sabor porque les queda muy poco sabor. Estos alimentos son adictivos, carcinógenos e inflamatorios, mientras que son carentes de los nutrientes necesarios para la función celular. Suministran calorías vacías que se almacenan como grasa porque el cuerpo no las puede usar para la mayoría de sus funciones.

Los alimentos reales son los alimentos que han sido menos procesados. Son más cercanos a su forma natural y, por lo tanto, retienen la mayor parte de su valor nutricional y brindan los más altos beneficios a la salud. Son ricos en sabor. Retienen la diversidad natural de sabores. Tienen un alto contenido en nutrientes y antioxidantes. Y si son alimentos cultivados orgánicamente, de temporada y locales, son las opciones más saludables posibles.

Un milagro delante de nuestros ojos

En 1991 a Lois le diagnosticaron artritis reumatoide (AR) por la Clínica Mayo. Fue sanada poco tiempo después. En 1992 ella y su marido regresaron al campo misionero donde trabajaron hasta abril de 2011. Habían volado a Polonia y estaban esperando una camioneta a las 11:30 p.m. cuando su marido tuvo un ataque cardiaco. Murió allí en la acera de una calle extranjera. Lois estaba en choque. Dijo que sintió como si fuera un mal sueño. Tuvo que esperar ocho días en Polonia antes de poder traer su cuerpo a casa.

Después de este trauma la AR volvió. Para el verano de 2013 ella sufría una AR paralizante y estaba postrada en cama, solamente era capaz de utilizar la silla de ruedas o una andadera ocasionalmente. Oró y oró por sanidad pero su enfermedad progresaba. A principios de marzo de 2014 recibió un diagnóstico médico sumamente desalentador: su hinchazón e infección en la sangre era alta. Justo después de eso, ella vio *It's Supernatural!*, donde fui entrevistada por Sid Roth. El programa le dio esperanza. Su hija, Rudina, visitó mi sitio web y se enteró de nuestro retiro.

Lois llegó con una gran cantidad de dolor con los pies muy hinchados de haber estado sentada muchas horas en el coche en el viaje de Chicago a Glorieta, Nuevo México. Se le dificultó entrar a los edificios. Pero las cosas comenzaron a cambiar para ella más bien rápidamente. La dieta contra la inflamación de jugos de verduras, batidos verdes y alimentos crudos cambiaron su fisiología. El dolor comenzó a reducirse. Las clases de desintoxicación emocional y mental de mi marido la ayudaron a identificar el pesar, el choque y el trauma que habían afectado su cuerpo en una manera adversa con las sustancias tóxicas que las emociones generan. El miércoles por la tarde tuvo la oportunidad de dejar ir esas emociones en nuestro servicio Taizé. La oración matutina alimentó su espíritu.

La tarde del miércoles de vuelta en su habitación, solo cuatro días después de su llegada, Lois le dijo a su hija que pensaba que podía caminar y le mostró a Rudina que podía dar pasos sin la andadera. Para el jueves estaba derecha de pie. Rudina a menudo le había dicho a su mamá que se parara derecha, pero ella no podía porque el dolor era demasiado intenso. El jueves por la tarde ella sintió que tenía que decirme lo que había sucedido, pero yo estaba siempre rodeada de personas. Entonces de pronto todos se fueron de la sala de conferencias y nos quedamos solas.

Ella me dijo: "Cherie, tengo algo que te quiero enseñar". Su hija hizo a un lado algunas sillas, y Lois comenzó a caminar por el lugar sin ayuda. ¡Qué milagro! Cuando ella y Rudina entraron al salón comedor, ella iba empujando su andadera frente a ella y entonces caminó sin ella. ¡Toda la sala irrumpió en ovaciones y lágrimas!

Lois no es única. Usted puede encontrar sanidad y salud abundante también. Esto es lo que puede escoger para promover su programa contra la inflamación de salud llena de vida.

Verduras, frutas, germinados y jugos de verduras

Estos son los alimentos más alcalinizadores; y también son superantiinflamatorios. Su meta es equilibrar el pH de su cuerpo. Para la buena salud y para mantener la inflamación bajo control, nuestro cuerpo necesita estar levemente alcalino con un pH entre 7,35 y 7,45. Suena como algo muy sencillo, ¿no? Bueno, estas no son matemáticas regulares basadas en aritmética; el pH opera en una escala logarítmica en múltiplos de diez. Una unidad de reducción en pH significa un incremento ácido de diez veces. Por ejemplo, la diferencia entre un alimento clasificado como cuatro y otro clasificado como cinco significa que el cuatro es diez veces más ácido. La mayoría de los alimentos que se comen en Estados Unidos forman ácidos en su descomposición final en el cuerpo. Estos alimentos incluyen carne, aves, pescado, lácteos, granos, algunas leguminosas, azúcar, café, té negro, refresco, alcohol y comida chatarra. Los alimentos con base alcalina son las verduras, las frutas, los jugos, los brotes, las gramíneas como el pasto de trigo y la cebadilla ratonera, las semillas (la quinoa es una semilla) y las nueces. Como puede ver, los alimentos estadounidense típicos están enfocados principalmente en los alimentos que forman ácido.

La mejor manera de neutralizar ácidos en el cuerpo es a través de los alimentos que comemos. Como requieren un equilibrio delicado, necesitamos comer una dieta sumamente rica en alimentos alcalinos para lograr este balance y promover la buena salud. Las frutas y las verduras son nuestras mejores amigas cuando se trata de alcalinidad. Contienen poderosos antioxidantes para reforzar el sistema inmune

35

y prevenir la inflamación crónica. Además, las frutas y las verduras son altas en antioxidantes y fitonutrientes como los bioflavonoides que mejoran la fuerza de los vasos sanguíneos y reducen la tendencia de los capilares a fugar fluidos. Para cambiar el cuerpo en dirección del equilibrio alcalino, haga que los alimentos alcalinos constituyan 75% de su dieta. Para ayudarlo a alcanzar esta meta hemos incluido abundantes recetas de jugos, batidos y verduras deliciosos en la dieta contra la inflamación.

Esto es lo que usted debería enfatizar.

Verduras y frutas ricas en antioxidantes

Los antioxidantes son compuestos que se encuentran especialmente en las verduras y las frutas de colores brillantes. Incluyen las vitaminas A, C y E; glutatión; beta-caroteno; licopeno; coenzima Q [ubiquinona]$_{10}$; y el mineral traza selenio. Un estudio de 2009 con seres humanos y ratones demostró que los antioxidantes reducen la inflamación.[3]

¿Cuántas porciones de verduras y frutas debería comer?

El estudio basado en la Encuesta de Salud de Inglaterra descubrió que las personas que comían siete o más porciones al día de frutas y verduras tenían una probabilidad 42% menor de morir prematuramente.[4] Cuando los investigadores combinaron los descubrimientos de estudios de Harvard con varios otros estudios de largo plazo en los Estados Unidos y Europa, y consideraron las cardiopatías coronarias y los derrames cerebrales por separado, encontraron un efecto protector similar: los individuos que comían más de cinco porciones de frutas y verduras tenían aproximadamente 20% menos riesgo de cardiopatías coronarias y derrames cerebrales en comparación con los individuos que comían menos de tres porciones al día.[5]

- *Batidos verdes.* Dependiendo de la cantidad de verduras y frutas, esto podría sumar de una a dos porciones.
- *Frutas y verduras orgánicas.* Coma de seis a nueve porciones al día (una porción es una taza y media cocida y una taza cruda).

- *Jugos de verduras.* Beba de uno a tres vasos de jugo de verduras recién hecho cada día. Esto puede ayudar significativamente a alcalinizar su cuerpo y brinda una abundancia de antioxidantes para neutralizar radicales libres. Hacer jugos es la cosa más importante que puede hacer para apagar la inflamación (una taza y media de jugo equivale a una porción). Un estudio de 2006 de la Universidad Vanderbilt descubrió que las personas que consumían tres o más porciones de jugos de frutas y verduras cada semana parecían 76% menos propensos a desarrollar señales de Alzheimer a lo largo de diez años que los que bebían menos de una porción a la semana.[6]

Batido poder antioxidante

Las moras ayudan a prevenir los efectos dañinos de los radicales libres y la inflamación al apagar las señales de inflamación disparadas por las citocinas y la COX-2, convirtiéndolas en una parte ideal de su dieta.

1 taza de leche de cáñamo, coco o almendra sin edulcorar
½ taza de arándanos azules
1 pera
½ taza de hojas tiernas de espinaca
1 cucharada de extracto indio de uva crispa (opcional)*
1 cucharada de linaza
Cubos de hielo (opcionales dependiendo de lo frío que le gustaría su batido)

Añada todos los ingredientes a la licuadora y procese hasta que quede suave.

*A 3277 umol TE/100 g, las uvas crispas tienen una capacidad de absorción de radicales de oxígeno (ORAC, por sus siglas en inglés) comparable al de las grosellas rojas (3387 umol TE/100 g), lo cual se encuentra entre los valores más altos de ORAC.

Cerezas para el dolor en articulaciones y artritis

Las cerezas ácidas pueden ayudar a reducir la inflamación crónica, especialmente en las personas que sufren de dolor en las articulaciones y artritis según las investigaciones. Los investigadores sugieren que las cerezas ácidas tienen el "contenido antiinflamatorio más alto de cualquier alimento" y pueden ayudar a las personas con artrosis a manejar su enfermedad. Un estudio de la Universidad de California en Davis descubrió que el consumo regular de cerezas durante veintiocho días producía una reducción en las señales bioquímicas de la inflamación en sangre, incluyendo una reducción de 25% en la proteína C-reactiva (PCR), el marcador de la inflamación más ampliamente estudiado. La elevación de la PCR en sangre se asocia con incremento en el riesgo de cardiopatías y derrame cerebral.[7]

Licuado de cereza con chocolate

1 cucharada de cacao en polvo sin edulcorar y sin procesar
½ taza de cerezas negras congeladas, sin semilla
1 taza de leche de coco, almendra o linaza
½ cucharadita de extracto puro de vainilla
Varias gotas de stevia líquido (se sugiere de la marca Sweet Leaf sabor Vanilla Crème)
Cubos de hielo al gusto

Coloque todos los ingredientes en la licuadora y procese hasta que quede suave.

Semillas y nueces

Las nueces y semillas crudas, especialmente las almendras, nueces, nueces de la India, semillas de girasol, linaza, ajonjolí y semillas de calabaza son una fuente rica en lignanos. Los lignanos son polifenoles únicos relacionados con la fibra que nos brindan beneficios antioxidantes, beneficios semejantes a los de la fibra y también actúan como fitoestrógenos.

Entre todos los alimentos que se consumen comúnmente, los investigadores clasifican a la linaza como la fuente número uno de lignanos. La linaza contiene una combinación de ácidos grasos omega-3,

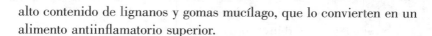

alto contenido de lignanos y gomas mucílago, que lo convierten en un alimento antiinflamatorio superior.

Alimentos silvestres

Los alimentos silvestres como las hojas de diente de león, ortigas, pamplina de canarios, acedera de madera, hojas de ensalada silvestres y la alforja nos ofrecen nutrientes que no se encuentran en otra parte de la naturaleza. Como la gente se ha adaptado a comer plantas silvestres por varios cientos de miles de años, surgen problemas cuando tratamos de comer frutas y verduras híbridas y modificadas genéticamente. Nuestra fisiología no está programada para manejar esto. Incluya más alimentos silvestres en su dieta, lo cual enviará el antiguo mensaje de vida a sus células hambrientas.

Batido salvaje dulce

1 pera (asiática o Bartlett)
½ manzana verde
1 puñado grande de hojas de diente de león* u otras hojas verdes silvestres
1 taza de leche de coco
El jugo de ½ limón (amarillo)
¼ taza de linaza
1 cucharadita de cúrcuma
6 cubos de hielo (opcionales)

Coloque todos los ingredientes en una licuadora y procese hasta obtener un batido cremoso. Rinde 2 porciones.

*El diente de león ha sido usado como un remedio tradicional para tratar los problemas del hígado, infecciones, hinchazón, retención de agua, problemas de mama, problemas de vejiga, neumonía y virus. Los estudios han mostrado que estimula el flujo de la bilis y que tiene un suave efecto diurético.

Verduras que tienen propiedades antiinflamatorias especiales

- El espárrago contiene saponinas: fitonutrientes que repetidamente ha sido demostrado que tienen propiedades antiinflamatorias y anticáncer. Su ingesta también ha sido asociada con una presión sanguínea mejorada, regulación del azúcar

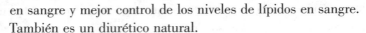
en sangre y mejor control de los niveles de lípidos en sangre. También es un diurético natural.

- La remolacha contiene fitonutrientes llamados betalaínas. La betanina y la vulgaxantina son dos de las betalaínas más estudiadas de la remolacha. Cada una ha demostrado brindar efectos antioxidantes, antiinflamatorios y de desintoxicación. Las remolachas también han demostrado reducir la presión sanguínea.

EL DOLOR DE JANET SE FUE

Sé con toda seguridad que los jugos han sanado mi artritis y mi codo de tenista. También las articulaciones de mi dedo estaban sumamente hinchadas y ahora están normales como las de mi marido. Mi marido no ha tomado medicamentos desde su ataque cardiaco. Mi amiga también ha sido sanada de su dolor. Un médico general que conozco está sumamente interesado ahora. Creo que el jugo de raíz de remolacha es muy sanador. Cherie, es simplemente sorprendente. Sé que Dios nos ha dado estos alimentos con toda seguridad. Es tan emocionante.

- La zanahoria tiene propiedades que contrarrestan la inflamación y brinda beneficios antiinflamatorios que son significativos incluso al compararlos con sustancias antiinflamatorias como la aspirina, el ibuprofeno, el naproxeno y el celebrex.
- El apio es una buena fuente de vitamina C, beta-caroteno, sodio y manganeso, los cuales son antioxidantes fenólicos que se ha demostrado reducen la inflamación. Si está sufriendo de dolores articulares, infecciones pulmonares, asma o acné, comer y hacer más jugo de apio traerá el muy necesitado alivio. También ayuda a calmar y a aliviar el estrés. Los minerales en el apio, especialmente el magnesio, reconfortan el sistema nervioso. Si usted disfruta el apio en la noche, podría dormir mejor. También el jugo de apio reduce su presión sanguínea. Un estudio de veinte años en animales descubrió

que el 3-n-butileftalida, un extracto que se encuentra en el apio, reduce la presión sanguínea y los niveles de colesterol. La dosis diaria necesaria para obtener este beneficio al parecer es de cuatro tallos, lo cual explica por qué uno preferiría hacerlo jugo.[8]

- El hinojo es rico en el fitonutriente anetol. Este nutriente ha mostrado repetidamente reducir la inflamación y ayudar a prevenir la ocurrencia de cáncer.

- Col rizada. Las investigaciones han identificado más de cuarenta y cinco flavonoides diferentes en la col rizada. Con el kaemferol y la quercetina al principio de la lista, los flavonoides de la col rizada y sus antioxidantes tienen beneficios antiinflamatorios que ayudan a apagar la inflamación crónica y el estrés oxidativo.

- Espinaca. El ácido glucurónico, un nutriente de la espinaca, puede ayudar a proteger el revestimiento del tracto digestivo especialmente del daño relacionado con la inflamación.

Fruta antiinflamatoria

- Los aguacates contienen grasas sumamente importantes, a saber los fitoesteroles, que dan cuenta de la mayor porción de su grasa. Las grasas del aguacate son soportes clave de nuestro sistema inflamatorio y ayudan a mantener la inflamación bajo control.

- Las moras o frutas del bosque contienen antioxidantes que pueden ayudarle a su cuerpo a combatir el estrés oxidativo causado por los radicales libres. Las moras contienen compuestos de polifenol que han demostrado tener actividad antiinflamatoria en los humanos. Entre los polifenoles más notables de las moras están las antocianinas, responsables por sus colores distintivos de rojo, azul y púrpura. Las moras han sido estudiadas ampliamente por sus propiedades antioxidantes; los datos sugieren efectos importantes en los canales inflamatorios.[9] Comer una dieta rica en antioxidantes puede ayudar a proteger su piel y su cabello y combatir la inflamación.

- La papaya tiene varias enzimas únicas para la digestión de proteína, incluyendo la papaína y la quimopapaína, que han demostrado ayudar a reducir la inflamación.

- Los duraznos contienen compuestos fenólicos que previenen la oxidación del colesterol de lipoproteína de baja densidad (LDL). (Es el LDL oxidado (oxLDL) el que es peligroso; la mayoría de los análisis sanguíneos no lo distinguen del LDL no oxidado). Estos compuestos fenólicos pueden ayudar a combatir la inflamación asociada con el síndrome metabólico: una combinación de desórdenes médicos que incrementan el riesgo de obesidad, diabetes tipo 2 y enfermedades cardiovasculares.

- Las peras contienen fitonutrientes que han mostrado brindar beneficios antiinflamatorios. Han sido asociadas con un riesgo menor de varias enfermedades comunes asociadas con inflamación crónica y estrés oxidativo excesivo.

Los beneficios increíbles de los ácidos grasos omega-3

Los omega-3 son ácidos grasos esenciales que ayudan a reducir la inflamación en todo su cuerpo, incluyendo su cerebro. Un desequilibrio inadecuado de ácidos grasos (demasiado omega-6; muy poco omega-3) contribuye con el desarrollo de la inflamación y la enfermedad, mientras que un equilibrio apropiado mantiene la inflamación bajo control y mejora la salud. Una dieta saludable debería consistir en aproximadamente dos a cuatro veces más ácidos grasos omega-3 que grasas omega-6. La dieta estadounidense típica tiende a contener catorce a veinticinco veces más grasas omega-6. Muchos investigadores creen que este desequilibrio es un factor significativo en el incremento del índice de desórdenes inflamatorios en los Estados Unidos.

Para incrementar sus grasas omega-3 escoja trucha silvestre

y salmón capturado silvestre de Alaska lo cuales son analizados regularmente y no se ha descubierto que contengan niveles significativos de la radiación de Fukushima (usted debería evitar otros pescados en este momento debido a la contaminación por radiación). También incluya aceite de kril, aceite de hígado de bacalao, linaza, cáñamo, semillas de chía y nueces.

Utilice solamente aceites saludables

El infarto al miocardio (IAM) era casi inexistente en 1910 y provocaba no más de 3000 muertes al año en 1930. Para 1960 hubieron por lo menos 500 000 muertes por IAM al año en EE. UU. ¿Qué cambios en el estilo de vida causaron este incremento? Uno de los cambios más importantes en este país fue la introducción al público de aceites para cocinar poliinsaturados en la década de 1940. Hasta la Segunda Guerra Mundial no eran utilizados popularmente. Pero cuando los barcos no podían transportar aceite de coco de Asia y del Pacífico Sur a causa de la guerra, la industria del aceite vegetal incrementó su producción.[10]

Hay una correlación entre los aceites poliinsaturados para cocinar y el auge de las cardiopatías y el LDL oxidado (oxLDL), que se forma cuando los lípidos de las partículas de LDL reaccionan con oxígeno y se descomponen. Esto les sucede específicamente a las grasas insaturadas del LDL, porque las grasas saturadas por su naturaleza química, son sumamente resistentes al daño por oxidación. Las grasas poliinsaturadas son mucho más susceptibles al daño oxidativo que las grasas saturadas o monoinsaturadas. El ácido linoleico (el ácido graso omega-6 que se encuentra abundantemente en los aceites industriales de semillas) ese el principal ácido graso poliinsaturado en el LDL.[11]

Es imperativo evitar el aceite de cártamo, girasol, soya, maíz y canola (la canola porque es un gran cultivo transgénico). Escoja sus aceites para cocinar de la lista siguiente. Selecciónelos según su punto de humo para la receta que esté preparando. Usted no quiere sobrecalentar su aceite ya que si lo hace se va a oxidar, lo cual quiere decir que está generando radicales libres que contribuirán con la inflamación de su cuerpo. El punto de humo significa

43

la temperatura en la que el aceite comienza a producir humo y a oxidarse. Escoja solamente aceites orgánicos sin refinar de alta calidad prensados en frío.

- El aceite de almendra es apropiado para cocinar con un alto grado de calor ya que tiene un punto de humo de 420°F [215,6°C].

- El aceite de aguacate tiene un punto de humo medio entre los 375°F [190,6°C] y los 400°F [204,4°C].

- El aceite de coco virgen ha sido utilizada como remedio natural para muchos padecimientos y es considerada que cuenta con propiedades que combaten la inflamación. Ha recibido una prensa negativa durante varias décadas, lo cual estaba completamente infundado y basado en esquemas de comercialización de la industria de los aceites de semillas y aceites vegetales. Utilice solamente aceite de coco orgánica virgen porque es procesada en una manera que preserva sus cualidades saludables. Es buena para cocinar a temperaturas medias con un punto de humo de 350°F [176,7°C].

- Aceite de oliva virgen extra. El aceite de oliva contiene un compuesto especial conocido como oleocantal que ayuda a prevenir la producción de las enzimas COX-1 y COX-2 que favorecen la inflamación. Así que cuando el aceite de oliva se usa para preparar los alimentos, ayuda a reducir el dolor y la inflamación. El aceite de oliva es buena para cocinar a temperatura media y tiene un punto de humo de alrededor de 375°F [190,6°C]. La oxidación de las sustancias que se encuentran en el aceite de oliva virgen extra, así como la formación de acrilamida puede suceder a temperaturas más altas.

- Ghee (mantequilla clarificada, que es aceite de mantequilla) tiene un punto de humo de 485°F [251,7°C].

- El aceite de semilla de uva también es apropiado para cocinar con un alto grado de calor con un punto de humo de 420°F [215,6°C].

ADVERTENCIA PARA EL COMPRADOR

Solía ser que la sustitución con aceite de soya y girasol era el fraude de la industria de aceite de oliva. Pero uno de los mayores problemas ahora es lo que han llamado aceite desodorizada: aceite que ha sido hecha de aceitunas no comestibles, aceitunas que barren del piso con lo que parecen escobas para la calle. Si usted asiste a las ferias agrícolas del sur de España podrá ver un amplio rango de estos diferentes recolectores de aceitunas; excepto que están recogiendo aceitunas que han estado tiradas en el suelo durante un largo tiempo.

Entonces las someten a un proceso de refinamiento sumamente ligero y delicado que no deja muchas huellas químicas, por lo que es muy difícil para las autoridades detectarlo con las pruebas de calidad estándar. Ellos venden ese aceite mezclado con aceite de oliva virgen extra verdadera para darle el sabor de virgen extra. Eso es porque no hay requerimientos químicos para que el aceite sea virgen extra, pero también hay requisitos de sabor; tiene que tener cierto sabor afrutado, y no puede tener defectos. Ese aceite desodorizado, por lo menos en las primeras semanas es libre de defectos. Pero rápidamente se deteriora y se vuelve rancio.[12]

Cinco consejos para reconocer aceite de oliva virgen extra verdadera:

- Sospeche de cualquier aceite de oliva virgen extra que cueste menos de diez dólares el litro.
- Busque un sello del Consejo Oleícola Internacional (COI).
- Busque la fecha de la cosecha en la etiqueta.
- Cualquier cosa que tenga en la etiqueta ligero, puro o una mezcla no tiene calidad virgen.[13] El Grupo Dr. Weston Price recomienda el aceite de oliva virgen extra Bariani.

- El aceite de palma roja ha demostrado poseer actividades potentes antioxidantes, anticáncer y de reducción del colesterol. Es rico en tocotrienol (una forma única de vitamina E) y tiene una potente actividad antiinflamatoria a través de

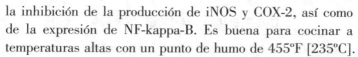

la inhibición de la producción de iNOS y COX-2, así como de la expresión de NF-kappa-B. Es buena para cocinar a temperaturas altas con un punto de humo de 455°F [235°C].

- El aceite de salvado de arroz tiene un punto de humo de 490°F [254,4°C] y con frecuencia es utilizado para altas temperaturas como las del wok y para saltear al estilo chino.

- El aceite de nuez es antiinflamatorio con sus omega-3, tiene un bajo punto de humo de 320°F [160°C].

Directrices adicionales

- Utilice solamente edulcorantes saludables: stevia (la marca Sweet Leaf sabor Vanilla Crème es muy buena), azúcar de coco y néctar de coco, xylitol hecho de corteza de abedul (pero no el que es producto secundario de la industria de la pulpa de madera, que son la mayoría) y pequeñas cantidades de miel cruda o jarabe de arce puro.

- Limite los alimentos que forman ácidos. Alrededor de 25% de su dieta debería ser de alimentos que forman ácido (75% debería ser alkalina): 1) granos integrales: arroz integral, quinoa, mijo, espelta, amaranto y kamut; 2) proteína animal: pescado, pollo, pavo y carne roja; 3) leguminosas: frijoles, lentejas y guisantes cortados.

- Solamente coma carne y aves limpias. No toda la carne muscular es creada igual. Además de tener un contenido más alto de grasas omega-3 y ácidos linoléicos conjugados (CLA), la carne de animales alimentados con pasto es también más alta en vitamina E. De hecho, los estudios muestran que la carne de ganado de pastura es cuatro veces más alta en vitamina E que la carne del ganado de lote de engorda, y, en una manera interesante, casi lo doble que la carne de lote de engorda a la que se le dan suplementos de vitamina E. Las aves de campo alimentadas con pastura muestran beneficios similares.

- Pescado saludable. Escoja solamente pescado silvestre. Sus opciones están limitadas a trucha silvestre y salmón capturado silvestre de Alaska, que es analizado regularmente y no se ha descubierto que contenga niveles significativos de la radiación de Fukushima. Evite el pescado de criadero. Se les dan antibióticos y hormonas y se les alimenta con alimentos sumamente tóxicos que pueden incluir retardantes de fuego.
- Agua. Beba por lo menos sesenta y cuatro onzas [1893 ml] de agua purificada para sacar nuestras toxinas y auxiliar al metabolismo celular.

Sopa sanadora de soya verde

Los granos mung brindan beneficios antiinflamatorios al inhibir la secreción de la proteína (HMGB1), que regula la respuesta inflamatoria. En la medicina aiurvédica, la sopa de soya verde es conocida porque ayuda a equilibrar el cuerpo. Sus especias y hierbas penetrantes son la fuerza impulsora que ayudan al cuerpo a deshacerse de toxinas y moco que se aloja allí con el tiempo debido a una mala dieta, falta de ejercicio y un estilo de vida poco saludable. Esta sopa ayuda a descomponer el moco y sacarlo del cuerpo.

Tiempo de preparación: 45 minutos

1 taza de granos de soya verde mung
2 tazas de agua purificada con ½ cucharadita de sal marina (para cocer los granos)
1 cucharada de aceite de coco, aceite de oliva virgen extra o ghee
½ cucharadita de semillas de mostaza
¼ de cucharadita de hing (especia oriental); opcional 1 hoja de laurel
½ cucharadita de cúrcuma
½ cucharadita de comino
1–2 cucharaditas de cilantro en polvo
2 tazas de agua purificada, para la sopa
2 cucharaditas de jengibre finamente picado
1 cucharadita de ajo, finamente picado
Pimienta negra recién molida, al gusto
1 cucharadita de sal marina
2 cucharaditas de jugo de limón fresco

Remoje los granos de soya verde toda la noche en agua purificada. Tire el agua de los granos y enjuáguelos 2 veces, y cocine en una olla de presión u olla para sopa con las dos tazas de agua hasta que estén suaves. Se requieren

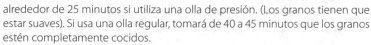

alrededor de 25 minutos si utiliza una olla de presión. (Los granos tienen que estar suaves). Si usa una olla regular, tomará de 40 a 45 minutos que los granos estén completamente cocidos.

Caliente el aceite o el ghee en una olla grande y profunda para sopa y añada las semillas de mostaza. Cuando las semillas de mostaza crujan, añada el hing—si lo está usando—y el laurel, la cúrcuma, el comino, el cilantro, el jengibre, el ajo y una pizca de pimienta negra. Mezcle bien, saltee y no permita que se queme.

Ponga los granos cocidos, el agua y la sal en la olla de la sopa con las hierbas y especias. Llévela a hervir y luego déjela en fuego lento unos 15 minutos. Añada limón, remueva el laurel ¡y disfrute!

(Adaptado del Dr. Oz: http://www.doctoroz.com/recipe/green-mung-bean -soup).

Por qué debe escoger orgánico

La popularidad de los alimentos orgánicos ha aumentado dramáticamente en los últimos años y sigue creciendo en popularidad. Las ventas de los alimentos orgánicos alcanzan los millardos de dólares cada año y continúan aumentando anualmente. Hay un número de personas siempre creciente que quieren evitar los millardos de libras o más de pesticidas y herbicidas que se les rocían o se les añaden a nuestros cultivos anualmente. ¡Y es por una buena razón! Se estima que solamente alrededor de 2% de esta cantidad realmente combate a los insectos y a las hierbas, mientras que el resto es absorbido por las plantas y la tierra y se propaga a nuestro aire, tierra y agua.

Cuando usted compra sus frutas y verduras de granjeros orgánicos certificados o de granjeros locales que venden frutas y verduras no rociados, pero que están trabajando sin certificación, usted no va a recibir fertilizantes sintéticos, cieno de drenaje, organismos modificados genéticamente ni radiación por ionización. Comprar sus verduras de una fuente local también es la mejor manera de asegurar su frescura. Tenga en mente que entre más frescas son las verduras, más biofotones (rayos de luz de energía) estará recibiendo. Muchos granjeros locales le entregarán una caja de verduras orgánicas cada semana en su hogar por un precio razonable.

Según los resultados de un estudio de $25 millones de dólares de alimentos orgánicos, el más grande de su tipo a la fecha, los productos orgánicos eclipsan totalmente a los cultivados convencionalmente en contenido nutricional. Un estudio de cuatro años financiado por la Unión Europea en 2007 descubrió que las verduras y frutas orgánicas contienen hasta 40% más antioxidantes. Tienen niveles más altos de minerales beneficiosos tales como hierro y zinc. La leche de manadas orgánicas contenía hasta 90% más antioxidantes. Los investigadores obtuvieron sus resultados después de cultivar frutas y verduras y criar ganado en sitios orgánicos e inorgánicos adyacentes vinculados con la Newcastle University. Según el profesor Carlos Leifert, coordinador del proyecto, comer alimentos orgánicos incluso puede ayudar a aumentar la ingesta de nutrientes de las personas que no consumen la cantidad recomendada de porciones de frutas y verduras al día.[14]

EVITE LA "DOCENA SUCIA"

Si usted no puede darse el lujo de comprar productos orgánicos, todavía podría evitar los alimentos que más son rociados al utilizar solamente las frutas y verduras cultivadas orgánicamente de la lista de las mejores doce. La organización de investigación sin fines de lucro Environmental Working Group (EWG) reporta periódicamente sobre los riesgos de salud que presentan los pesticidas en las frutas y verduras. El grupo dice que usted puede recortar su exposición a los pesticidas casi en 90% simplemente evitando las doce frutas y verduras cultivadas convencionalmente que se han descubierto son las más contaminadas. Se ha descubierto que comer las doce frutas y verduras más contaminadas expondrá a una persona, en promedio, a alrededor de catorce pesticidas al día. Comer las doce frutas y verduras cultivadas convencionalmente menos contaminadas expondrá a la persona a menos de dos pesticidas al día. Esta es la docena sucia actual más dos:

1. Manzana
2. Pimiento morrón
3. Apio
4. Tomate cherry
5. Pepino
6. Uva
7. Col rizada/Hojas de berza
8. Nectarina (importada)

9. Durazno	14. Papa
10. Pepino	15. Espinaca
11. Uva	16. Fresa/frutilla
12. Col rizada/Hojas de berza	17. Calabaza de verano
13. Chile	

La lista cambia cada año. Para obtener la clasificación actual, vaya a www.ewg.org.

Recomendaciones de nutrientes

Los antioxidantes son poderosos para combatir radicales libres. Los radicales libres, producidos como parte del proceso inflamatorio, son moléculas inestables que dañan las células. Las células dañadas entonces se vuelven fuentes de todavía más radicales libres y se pone en movimiento una reacción en cadena. Los nutrientes antioxidantes se combinan con los radicales libres, evitando que dañen el tejido saludable y reduciendo así el proceso de inflamación. Los siguientes antioxidantes son bastante útiles para mantener la inflamación a raya:

- El cobre se ha demostrado que reduce la inflamación en animales de laboratorio. Las mejores fuentes de cobre incluyen: ostión, nuez de Brasil, almendra, guisante seco, trigo sarraceno, jengibre, nabo, perejil, ajo, zanahoria, espinaca, repollo, lechuga y pepino. Usted no debería necesitar tomar suplementos adicionales de cobre, excepto por lo que viene en una cápsula multivitamínica.

- La quercetina se encuentra en muchas frutas y verduras. Puede ser tan útil como los medicamentos de venta libre para inhibir la liberación de histamina y estabilizar los mastocitos pero sin efecto secundarios como la somnolencia. Al inhibir la liberación de la histamina desde el inicio, la quercetina queda en contraste directo contra muchos medicamentos que tratan de nulificar los efectos de la histamina después de que ha sucedido una reacción alérgica. Al combinarse con la ortiga, la quercetina es útil para prevenir o reducir el estornudo, la comezón y la inflamación de las vías nasales. También ayuda a prevenir la disminución de vitamina C. Para una dosis suplementaria para ayudar a reducir la inflamación, usted debería tomar de 500 mg al día hasta 2000 mg al día.

- El selenio es un poderoso antioxidante. Las mejores fuentes de selenio incluyen acelga, nabo, ajo, rábano, zanahoria, repollo, vinagre de sidra de manzana y nuez de Brasil (una de las mejores fuentes). Cuatro nueces de Brasil le aportan casi 400 mcg de selenio. Para una dosis suplementaria, usted debería tomar hasta 400 mcg.

- La vitamina A y el beta-caroteno son potentes antioxidantes. El beta-caroteno se convierte en vitamina A en el cuerpo según se necesite. Las mejores fuentes de carotenos en general incluyen zanahoria, col rizada, perejil, espinaca, acelga, hojas de remolacha, berro, brócoli y lechuga romana; el aceite de hígado de bacalao se encuentra entre las mejores fuentes. No necesita tomar suplementos de vitamina A si toma aceite de hígado de bacalao o come una dieta rica en verduras y frutas.

- La vitamina C y los bioflavonoides ambos inhiben la liberación de histamina, una sustancia que se libera como respuesta a las infecciones y las alergias. Además, la vitamina C estabiliza las membranas celulares y los bioflavonoides mejoran la acción de la vitamina C. Las mejores fuentes de vitamina C incluyen col rizada, perejil, brócoli, coles de bruselas, berro, coliflor, repollo, espinaca, limón, lima, nabo y espárrago. Las mejores fuentes de bioflavonoides incluyen pimiento morrón, moras o frutas del bosque (arándano azul, zarzamora y arándano rojo), limón, lima, brócoli, repollo, perejil y tomate. La dosis suplementaria recomendada de vitamina C es alrededor de 2000 mg al día, pero podría variar dependiendo de la edad, salud (¿está combatiendo una enfermedad?) y qué tantos alimentos ricos en vitamina C ingiere.

- Se considera que la vitamina E es un antioxidante antiinflamatorio. Las mejores fuentes de vitamina E incluyen almendra, aceite de oliva, espinaca, berro, espárrago, zanahoria y tomate. La dosis suplementaria recomendada es de 400 UI diariamente.

- El cinc promueve la actividad antiinflamatoria. Las mejores fuentes de cinc incluyen ostión, jengibre, carne de res, cordero, pollo, nabo, perejil, ajo, zanahoria, uva, espinaca, repollo, lechuga y pepino. La dosis suplementaria recomendada es no más de 100 mg. No recomendaría tomar cinc adicional más allá del que está en su cápsula multivitamínica/multimineral, excepto cuando tiene un resfriado, ya que el uso a largo plazo durante diez años o más incrementa el riesgo de cáncer de próstata.

Recomendaciones de hierbas y especias

- La bufera es una hierba adaptogénica que tiene actividad anitoxidante y también ha demostrado actividad antiinflamatoria. La dosis diaria recomendada es de 500 mg al día.

- La boswelia (incienso), cuando se toma una dosis de 300 mg, tres veces al día, actúa como un poderoso suplemento antiinflamatorio.

- La bardana es una hierba digestiva maravillosa que apoya la función y la desintoxicación del hígado, reduce la inflamación del hígado, sana las células hepáticas en la enfermedad de hígado graso y estimula la producción de ácido gástrico. La raíz de bardana es una medicina nutritiva de sabor suave y acción lenta. Así es cómo puede incluir más raíz de bardana en su dieta: corte camotes, zanahorias, remolachas, colinabo y bardana en pedazos del tamaño de un bocado y colóquelos en una plancha para galletas. Sumérjalas en aceite de oliva o aceite de coco y rocíelas con sal de ajo y una combinación de especias como Spike [mezcla de 39 hierbas diferentes con sal].

Hornee a 375°F [190,6°C] durante unos 45 minutos. También lo puede saltear al estilo chino con brócoli y cebolla como guarnición. O puede agregar bardana picada al chili, a la carne de res o el estofado de cordero.[15] Usted también puede hacerla jugo en sus recetas favoritas de jugo.

- La curcumina, un componente de la cúrcuma, tiene efectos contra la inflamación. Tradicionalmente ha sido utilizada en heridas, desgarres y articulaciones inflamadas para reducir la inflamación. Es tan eficaz como algunos medicamentos de prescripción en aliviar la hinchazón y la rigidez asociada con la artritis. La curcumina está disponible en forma de suplemento. También puede cocinar con cúrcuma (que contiene curcumina), añadírsela al té de especias con un poco de ghee y combinarla en un batido.

- El diente de león mejora el flujo de la bilis. También reduce y previene la inflamación en el hígado y la vesícula. Usted puede hacer té de diente de león a través de derramar una taza de agua hirviendo sobre una o dos cucharaditas de hojas secas de diente de león o cueza las hojas al vapor y añádaselas a una tortilla de huevo o a un batido. Tiene un sabor amargo, así que es probable que tenga que experimentar con lo que le funcione. Pero no las deje fuera de su dieta; tienen muchos beneficios.

- La garra del diablo es similar en sus efectos antiinflamatorios a la cortisona. También ayuda a aliviar el dolor.

- Ajo. Hay evidencia de que algunos aspectos inflamatorios de la obesidad se pueden alterar por los compuestos presentes en el ajo que contienen azufre.

- El jengibre es un poderoso antiinflamatorio. Los estudios identifican al jengibre como un producto herbolario medicinal que comparte propiedades farmacológicas con medicamentos no esteroideos antiinflamatorios. El jengibre suprime la síntesis de prostaglandina a través de la inhibición de la ciclooxigenasa-1 y ciclooxigenasa. También puede proteger el estómago de los efectos de los medicamentos no esteroideos antiinflamatorios. El jengibre fresco tiene un sabor excelente en casi cualquier receta de jugo o batido.

Té chai

2 cucharaditas de jengibre molido
2 cucharaditas de canela molida
1 cucharadita de clavo molido
1 cucharadita de cardamomo molido
1 cucharadita de nuez moscada
1 cucharadita de pimienta dulce
¼ de cucharadita de pimienta blanca

Mezcle bien todos los ingredientes y mantenga en un contenedor tapado. Mezcle ½ a 1 cucharadita de la mezcla de especias con 8 onzas [236,6 ml] de agua caliente. Añada 1 cucharadita de ghee y revuelva. Este es un té que hace entrar bastante en calor en otoño y en invierno.

- Hibisco. Cuando se trata del contenido antioxidante, el hibisco tiene más poder antioxidante que el té verde. El hibisco ayuda a reducir la presión sanguínea, reduce los niveles de ácido úrico en los que padecen gota y mejora los niveles de colesterol y triglicéridos en prediabéticos y diabéticos. Puede tomar té helado de hibisco a lo largo del día. También actúa como diurético.

Té helado poder jamaiquino

Flores de hibisco picadas (pídalas en Amazon) o 5 bolsas de té herbal de hibisco*
12 hojas de menta (opcional)
El jugo de 1 lima [limón verde] (opcional)
2 cuartos [1893 l] de agua purificada

Sumerja el té de hibisco o las flores en agua. Póngalo todo en la nevera. En una hora aproximadamente tendrá té helado.

*Recomiendo el té de hibisco o "Back on Tract"—hibisco con arándano rojo—ambos de Traditional Medicinals (visite su sitio web en www .traditionalmedicinals.com).

- El regaliz inhibe la fosfolipasa A, una enzima que, como factor activador de las plaquetas, inicia reacciones inflamatorias. Utilice el extracto de regaliz para desórdenes inflamatorios. No utilice dulce de regaliz. Utilice DGL (no contiene glicirricina) si usted padece hipertensión, enfermedad de los riñones o del hígado, diabetes o cardiopatías, y no lo utilice por más de seis semanas. Utilice el regaliz si tiene suprarrenales con bajo funcionamiento. Me encanta el té de regaliz de Traditional Medicinals.

- Extracto de magnolia. La corteza de magnolia contiene dos sustancias antiinflamatorias, magnolol y honokiol, que se piensa inhiben la activación de NF-KB, un mediador clave en los procesos inflamatorios y de envejecimiento. La dosis diaria recomendada es de 200 mg al día.

- El perejil contiene flavonoides—especialmente luteolina— que se ha demostrado se combinan con moléculas altamente reactivas que contienen oxígeno (radicales de oxígeno) y ayudan a evitar el daño basado en el oxígeno a las células. Esto significa reducción de la inflamación.

- El aceite esencial de piperita actúa como descongestionante, y ciertas sustancias en la piperita contienen componentes antiinflamatorios y antibacteriales suaves.

- La rhodiola (raíz del ártico) es considerada una hierba adaptogénica, lo cual significa que actúa en maneras no específicas para incrementar la resistencia al estrés sin perturbar las funciones biológicas normales. La evidencia sugiere que actúa como un antioxidante y que mejora la función del sistema inmune. La investigación clínica ha mostrado que la rhodiola mejora la congición, la memoria y el aprendizaje, reduciendo grandemente el estrés y la fatiga, estimula el sistema inmune, incrementa el metabolismo, auxilia la función tiroidea protege el sistema cardiovascular, fortalece la fertilidad y la función sexual y mejora el humor. Produce un té rosado cuyo aroma y sabor recuerda el de los pétalos de la

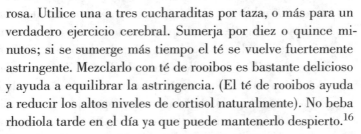

rosa. Utilice una a tres cucharaditas por taza, o más para un verdadero ejercicio cerebral. Sumerja por diez o quince minutos; si se sumerge más tiempo el té se vuelve fuertemente astringente. Mezclarlo con té de rooibos es bastante delicioso y ayuda a equilibrar la astringencia. (El té de rooibos ayuda a reducir los altos niveles de cortisol naturalmente). No beba rhodiola tarde en el día ya que puede mantenerlo despierto.[16]

- Corteza de sauce blanco. En combinación con los poderosos compuestos vegetales antiinflamatorios de la hierba (flavonoides), se cree que la salicina es responsable por sus efectos analgésicos y antiinflamatorios. En los 1800 la salicina fue usada para desarrollar la aspirina. El sauce blanco parece traer alivio del dolor más lentamente que la aspirina, pero sus efectos pueden durar más tiempo.

Otros suplementos que ayudan

- La amilasa es una enzima digestiva que descompone carbohidratos complejos en azúcares simples. También está presentes en la saliva. Así que mientras masticamos nuestros alimentos, trabaja en los carbohidratos. Por eso es que se recomienda que mastiquemos cada bocado de alimentos unas treinta veces.
- El páncreas elabora la amilasa. Y la amilasa es abundante en las semillas que contienen almidón. (Usted puede hacer jugo la mayoría de las semillas de las frutas y las verduras). Su uso terapéutico es en la regulación de la histamina que es producida como respuesta a invasores conocidos del cuerpo. La histamina es una respuesta de las reacciones alérgicas como la fiebre del heno y es lo que causa la urticaria; ojos llorosos con comezón; estornudos; y flujo nasal. La amilasa descompone la histamina producida por el cuerpo como respuesta a alérgenos como el polen o los ácaros. Algunos profesionales de la salud creen que puede ayudar al cuerpo a identificar que el alérgeno no es tan dañino de modo que no

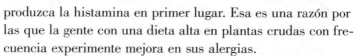

produzca la histamina en primer lugar. Esa es una razón por las que la gente con una dieta alta en plantas crudas con frecuencia experimente mejora en sus alergias.

- Para el acercamiento más eficaz a incrementar las enzimas como la amilasa, quizá quiera tomar un suplemento de enzimas. A mí me gusta especialmente una fórmula de enzimas que se toma entre comidas. Limpia todas las partículas de alimentos no digeridas que flotan en el sistema y mejora grandemente la digestión. ¡Un beneficio secundario popular es que su cabello se vuelve más grueso y sus uñas se fortalecen!

- El aceite de onagra es un ácido graso que es una buena fuente de ácido gamma-linolénico (GLA), que puede ayudar a mantener saludables las articulaciones a través de modificar la inflamación.

- Probióticos: La toxicidad de su intestino puede fluir a lo largo de su cuerpo hasta su cerebro donde puede causar síntomas de autismo, TDAH, dislexia, dispraxia, depresión, esquizofrenia y otros trastornos mentales. Reducir la inflamación de su intestino es imperativo. Hipócrates dijo que todas las enfermedades comienzan en el intestino. La parte principal de su sistema inmune se encuentra en su intestino. El tracto gastrointestinal tiene un papel vital en su salud, incluyendo la digestión, la absorción de nutrientes, la defensa en contra de patógenos invasores, metabolismo hormonal, desintoxicación y eliminación, así como producción de energía. Natasha Campbell-McBride, MD, desarrolló la Dieta GAPS en su esfuerzo por sanar eficazmente trastornos relacionados con el intestino. Enfatizó la importancia de desintoxicar el tracto digestivo, sanar el intestino a través de alimentos densos en nutrientes y sellar o proteger el intestino mediante establecer niveles saludables de bacterias benéficas, utilizando alimentos y bebidas fermentados tradicionales. Si sana su intestino tomará un gran paso hacia apagar la llama de la inflamación en su cuerpo. Consuma solamente probióticos de cepa humana.

- El prebiótico es una fibra vegetal especializada que se puede encontrar en los alimentos vegetales que nutre en una manera benéfica a las bacterias benignas del colon. El cuerpo no digiere estas fibras vegetales; más bien, las fibras actúan como un fertilizante para promover el crecimiento de muchas bacterias benignas en el intestino. Estas, a su vez, brindan muchos beneficios digestivos. Añadir alimentos con contenido prebiótico no digerible genera cambios positivos en el perfil de las bacterias intestinales. Reducen la inflamación, la endotexemia, la resistencia a la insulina, el apetito, la masa de grasa, la glucemia, los lípidos, la inflamación hepática e incrementa la tolerancia a la glucosa.

PRINCIPALES ALIMENTOS PREBIÓTICOS[17]

1. Espárrago (crudo), 5%
2. Banana (cruda), 1%
3. Raíz de achicoria (cruda) 64,6%
4. Hojas de diente de león (crudas), 24,3%
5. Ajo (crudo), 17,5%
6. Alcachofa Jerusalén (cruda), 31,5%
7. Puerro (crudo), 11,7%
8. Cebolla (cruda), 8,6%
9. Cebolla cocida, 5%
10. Salvado de trigo (crudo), 5%

Desintoxique su cuerpo

Usted puede tomar medicamentos contra la inflamación, tragar aceite de pescado diariamente, ingerir suplementos fielmente y masticar pedazos de cacao todo el año, pero si no se deshace de los alimentos que favorecen la inflamación y las toxinas que contribuyen con su inflamación, simplemente estará echando cosas buenas sobre su inflamación impulsada por los alimentos y las toxinas.

Usted necesita llevar a cabo una desintoxicación completa. Es imperativo controlar parásitos, hongos, levaduras, bacterias y virus. Estos patógenos pueden ser fuentes escondidas de inflamación. Es beneficioso realizar una limpieza periódica de *candida albicans* y de parásitos. Desintoxicar su cuerpo es un aliado excelente para eliminar la inflamación. Consulte mi libro *Juicing, Fasting and Detoxing for Life* [Hacer jugos, ayunar y desintoxicarse para vivir] para programas completos de desintoxicación.

Coma, beba y esté bien

Ahora que sabe todo acerca de los alimentos que quiere incluir en su dieta y los alimentos que quiere evitar, es tiempo de poner en práctica las recetas de las páginas que siguen. Usted está por recibir un verdadero agasajo con veintiocho días de alimentos hermosos, deliciosos y nutritivos. Mi oración es que al final de su delicioso viaje, se sienta renovado, lleno de alegría y saludable. Esto va para comer bien *y* vivir bien.

Capítulo 4

RECETAS Y PLAN DE ALIMENTACIÓN DE VEINTIOCHO DÍAS PARA UNA SALUD LLENA DE VIDA

El médico del futuro no prescribirá medicamentos, sino que hará
que sus pacientes se interesen en el cuidado de la constitución
humana, la dieta y en la causa y prevención de las enfermedades.[1]

—THOMAS EDISON

¿SABE QUÉ ES lo que está matándonos a la mayoría de nosotros en Estados Unidos? El desayuno, el almuerzo y la cena. ¡Así es! Es lo que estamos comiendo todos los días lo que está causando tantas enfermedades y padecimientos en nuestra sociedad de comida rápida y de comer de paso. Pero la situación está cambiando a su favor. Usted está aprendiendo cómo tomar las decisiones más sabias posibles al mismo tiempo de disfrutar lo que come. La mitad de la batalla es planificar por adelantado y tener recetas que disfrute.

Su plan de menús de veintiocho días de este capítulo no solamente lo ayudará a planear con anticipación con deliciosas recetas, sino que también lo ayudará a reducir la inflamación y a promover una salud llena de vida. Usted puede entrar de lleno y comenzar su programa tan pronto como desee. No tiene que hacer nada especial para empezar. Su dieta contra la inflamación lo ayudará a suavemente desintoxicar su cuerpo. Lo animamos a seguir el plan de menús de cada semana tanto como sea posible. Hemos preparado una lista de compras para ayudarlo a recolectar todo lo que necesita para la semana. Cada semana usted puede sacarle una copia a la lista de compras. Está completa con recuadros para marcar los artículos una vez que los haya recolectado el sábado, el domingo o el día que sea que haga sus compras de la semana. Si no desea hacer todas las recetas, también viene una lista de compras debajo de cada receta. Esto le facilitará ajustar el plan a sus necesidades.

También le recomendamos que compre frutas y verduras locales siempre que sea posible. A finales de la primavera, en verano y otoño encontrará una abundancia de frutas y verduras locales y con frecuencia orgánicas en los mercados de granjeros. Esta es la elección más fresca y saludable que puede tomar. Es vigorizante para su alma y su cuerpo, ya que usted estará relacionándose con los agricultores locales que cultivaron los alimentos y que los presentan con orgullo. Esto también lo ayudará a comer de acuerdo con la temporada; otra manera excelente de promover la buena salud. Además de los mercados de granjeros, busque en las tiendas locales que tienen frutas y verduras orgánicas e ingredientes saludables como hierbas y especias orgánicas, néctar de coco y sal marina.

Prepárese para el éxito en la cocina

De la chef Abby

Hay varias maneras de ahorrar tiempo al preparar múltiples recetas. Primero, vea las recetas de la semana y observe qué artículos puede preparar en una sola vez. Por ejemplo, remuévale el tallo a todas sus verduras de hoja, límpielas y téngalas listas para picar en su nevera colocadas sobre toallas para mantenerlas secas y frescas. Pique en trozos una cabeza de ajo o un pedazo de jengibre, y manténgalos frescos en su nevera mediante cubrirlos con aceite de oliva. Pique las verduras macizas de raíz como las zanahorias, los camotes o las chirivías, y cúbralas en agua en su nevera para que estén listas para cocerlas a media semana. Como Cherie también mencionará, es una buena idea escoger un día a la semana para cocinar lo que va a usar en la semana ¡para prepararse a sí mismo para tener éxito! Una vez que comience a cortar y a limpiar las frutas y verduras, descubrirá que ahorra tiempo al hacerlo todo al mismo tiempo.

Lo mismo va para las compras. Tome su lista de compras y planifique uno (o dos) viajes para comprar lo de toda la semana. Limpie todas sus frutas y verduras cuando regrese para que esté un paso más cerca de cocinar cuando sea el momento correcto. Estas son habilidades de vida que beneficiarán su salud y su relación con la cocina mucho tiempo después de que termine con este plan de menús de veintiocho días.

UNA NOTA CON RESPECTO A CIERTOS INGREDIENTES DE LAS RECETAS

Sal

La sal marina es nuestra sal preferida. Está menos procesada que la sal de mesa regular y con frecuencia contiene minerales y elementos traza que son benéficos para la salud en general. Mi recomendación personal es que utilice sal marina gris, sal marina celta, sal marina Real o sal rosada. Personalmente utilizo una marca de Utah llamada sal Real. Probablemente necesite comprar un molino de sal si escoge utilizar una versión de grano grueso de cualquiera de estas sales. Pero también hay variedades finas. No recomendamos que utilice la sal marina Morton's porque se le añade yodo, y está fuertemente procesada.

Pimienta

También le recomiendo que compre granos completos de pimienta negra y los muela (o quiebre) frescos para cada receta utilizando un molino de pimienta. La pimienta fresca es desintoxicante. La capa externa del grano de pimienta estimula la descomposición de las células grasas. La pimienta estimula el HCl (ácido clorhídrico), que ayuda con la digestión en general.

Aceite de oliva

Hay diferencias entre los distintos tipos de aceite de oliva. Le sugiero que encuentre un aceite de oliva virgen extra para los aderezos de las ensaladas, y que use aceite de oliva regular para guisar.

Por último, considere el poder de un equipo. Convenza a su mejor amigo o a su cónyuge, a su hermana o a su madre de participar en el programa de veintiocho días con usted. Aparte algunos días al mes para cocinar con ellos, preparando platillos juntos o compartiendo la cocina. Usted se sentirá más responsable de terminar todo el programa, y también se encontrará disfrutando estas recetas para más años por venir, ya que las asociaciones positivas con amigos y familiares alrededor de la mesa desarrollarán su compromiso con el plan. El sistema de amigos siempre funciona.

¡Haga arreglos para el dominio de los jugos y los batidos!

De Cherie

Fotografía por Sika Stanton

Quizá quiera escoger el sábado o el domingo como el día de preparación para los jugos y los batidos. Hay cosas que puede hacer con anticipación para que sea más fácil comer bien durante la semana. Por ejemplo, muchas personas encuentran difícil hacer jugos todos los días, pero se vuelve algo factible cuando hacen todos los jugos en el fin de semana y los congelan en contenedores individuales. Deje un poco de espacio en la parte superior del envase para expansión del líquido, si no sus frascos se romperán. Hay recetas diferentes de jugos o batidos cada día de la semana. Esto es para darle una variedad de opciones. Sin embargo, no tiene que hacer un jugo o un batido distinto cada día. Puede preparar sus favoritos y mantenerlo simple.

Planifique con anticipación con Cherie y Abby

Cuando planee sus compras, es probable que también quiera duplicar o incluso triplicar las cantidades si usted tiene una familia grande o está preparando un platillo para una convivencia o una reunión familiar. Si está cocinando solo para usted mismo, quizá quiera cortar las cantidades por la mitad. O probablemente quiera hacer la cantidad completa y congelar una porción para tener comidas listas para los días ajetreados. Hemos diseñado algunas recetas para esa opción ya con alimento extra para que lo pueda usar al día siguiente en una receta. Otros días hay alimento extra que puede congelar para comidas futuras. Al cambiar la manera en que come es importante que planee con anticipación para que no se atore en los momentos ajetreados con nada qué comer y sin tiempo de preparar algo. Allí es cuando la mayoría de nosotros nos metemos en problemas. Nos dirigimos a la comida rápida en una forma u otra. Además, queremos que tenga un descanso de vez en vez para que no tenga que pasar tanto tiempo en la cocina. Si puede hacer una ensalada rápida y sacar una sopa congelada u otro plato del congelador, obtiene una comida fácil. Comience a pensar en la manera en que va a hacer que eso suceda regularmente.

La lógica para el plan de menús era darle lineamientos con el fin de mostrarle cómo debe lucir una dieta contra la inflamación además de darle recetas que disfrutara. Nunca sienta que no puede aprovechar el programa porque hay un alimento o receta que no le gusta o que no puede comer. Por ejemplo, si es alérgico al huevo, utilice un sustituto de huevo o prepare otra receta. Si no le gusta un ingrediente en una receta o no lo puede encontrar, sustitúyalo por algo más. Ambas hemos escuchado de demasiadas personas que se rinden porque hay un alimento en una receta o plan de menús que no pueden comer o que no les gusta. Este es el momento de ser creativos. Si no se le puede ocurrir con qué sustituir un ingrediente, intente hacer una búsqueda en línea para encontrar sustitutos. Si la receta suena poco apetitosa, busque una que parezca apetitosa y que se mantenga dentro de los lineamientos contra la inflamación. Haga que cocinar y preparar sea una aventura divertida. Se sorprenderá de lo innovador que usted puede ser.

¿Qué hay para desayunar? Tenemos una variedad de recetas intercaladas a lo largo del plan de menús. Quizá solamente quiera un vaso de jugo o un batido para desayunar. Pero probablemente también necesite un poco de comida adicional o proteína extra para comenzar su día. Busque recetas que le funcionen. También tenemos algunas ideas divertidas para desayunar los fines de semana como panqueques libres de gluten y croquetas de camote. Para los refrigerios y postres saludables, vea las secciones al final de la semana cuatro. Queremos asegurarnos de que tenga abundantes ideas para refrigerios y postres que no provoquen inflamación en su cuerpo.

Estamos muy emocionadas de compartir nuestras recetas con usted no solo porque creemos que las va a disfrutar, sino porque también sabemos que promueven una buena salud.

¡Disfrute!

—Cherie y chef Abby

Consejos de cocina de la chef Abby que ahorran tiempo

Pique mientras tanto

Cuando me tomo el tiempo de limpiar y picar cualquier verdura, siempre preparo más de la que necesito. Ahorro tiempo al estar en la "mentalidad" de picar y solamente necesito limpiar la encimera y la tabla de picar una vez para muchas frutas y verduras. Al mismo tiempo de afinar sus habilidades con el cuchillo, usted puede adelantar trabajo.

- Pique ajo adicional y manténgalo fresco para la semana a través de cubrirlo con aceite de oliva y colocarlo en la nevera.

- Pique verduras de raíz adicionales (zanahoria, camote, nabicol, calabaza) y manténgalas cubiertas en agua en un cuenco de vidrio en la nevera para que estén listas para sacarlas, hervirlas y asarlas en cualquier momento.
- Remueva los tallos de sus verduras de hoja.
- Limpie sus espinacas y sus lechugas y manténgalas secas con toallas entre las capas.

Estos pasos hacen que sea sencillo armar rápidamente una comida para una noche entre semana en muy poco tiempo.

Designe su día de compras general

Un día a la semana (suele ser el lunes para mí) cocino en grande. Esta no es una idea nueva, pero es una idea excelente que hace que algunos ingredientes básicos estén listos para trabajar en la semana. Estos son algunos elementos básicos personales:

- Caldo de pollo (utilizando un pollo asado completo que hayamos comido ese fin de semana).
- Una cantidad grande de quinoa o arroz integral.
- Verduras asadas o escaldadas (de muchos tipos, manténgalo distinto cada semana).
- Un frasco de aderezo de ensalada.
- Una sopa o estofado (con frecuencia usando el caldo y las verduras que acabo de preparar, o las últimas verduras que se necesitan utilizar antes de hacer el viaje semanal a la tienda).

Si tiene tiempo, haga una ensalada robusta (como una ensalada de col rizada curada a mano) que también pueda servir como la guarnición sencilla de una comida a media semana. Una vez que inicie, descubrirá que cocinar en grande no le tomará tanto tiempo como cree, ya que aprovecha que está haciendo algo para preparar más cosas.

Termine y asómbrese delante de su nevera llena y felicítese por el tiempo que ahorrará toda la semana por los esfuerzos de este día.

Use sus mitades de inmediato

Lo admito, yo también cortó mitades de verduras y las dejo en la nevera pensando que serán usadas dentro de algunos días. Algunas veces esto simplemente no sucede, y esa mitad de camote o de cebolla o puñado de hojas de mostaza que pensé que podría usar se ha pasado. La solución: utilícelas de inmediato.

Ejemplo:

- Si usted está usando la mitad de una calabaza y la mitad de una cebolla para hacer una sopa, eche la otra mitad (sin siquiera quitarle las semillas o cortarla) en el horno a 325°F [162,8°C], boca abajo, para asarla con un poco de aceite de oliva y la cebolla picada a su alrededor. ¡Voilà! Una vez horneada, remueva las semillas y tendrá otra guarnición lista para una comida, y no tuvo que utilizar tiempo adicional para prepararla.

Cocine a menudo para que compre lo correcto

Este consejo proviene de mi maravilloso esposo, Eric, quien señaló que cuando uno cocina regularmente, como nosotros lo hacemos, uno sabe exactamente lo que necesita al hacer el viaje a la tienda. Usted sabe que ya utilizó su última porción de col rizada, y que nada se va a desperdiciar en su nevera ya que se tomó el precioso tiempo de hacer una sopa para la semana. Esta es una adición sumamente perceptiva a esta lista, ya que simplemente significa que va a ahorrar dinero al no dejar marchitar buenas frutas y verduras (involuntariamente) debido al tiempo.

Fotografía por David Reamer Photography

Lista de compras de la semana uno

Vino y vinagre para cocinar

- ❑ Vinagre de manzana
- ❑ Vinagre balsámico
- ❑ Vinagre de mirin o de vino de arroz
- ❑ Vinagre de vino tinto
- ❑ Vinagre de arroz

Lácteos y huevo

- ❑ 1½ docena de huevo

Fruta seca

- ❑ 2½ tazas de arándano rojo seco sin edulcorar
- ❑ Grosella seca
- ❑ 4 higos misión secos

Hierbas y especias secas

- ❑ Hojas de laurel
- ❑ Granos de pimienta negra (o pimienta negra molida)
- ❑ Pimienta de Cayena
- ❑ Sal de apio
- ❑ Canela en rajas
- ❑ Semillas de cilantro
- ❑ Albahaca seca
- ❑ Orégano seco
- ❑ Semillas de hinojo
- ❑ Canela molida
- ❑ Clavo molido
- ❑ Comino molido
- ❑ Jengibre molido
- ❑ Nuez moscada molida
- ❑ Cúrcuma molida
- ❑ Polvo de mostaza
- ❑ Páprika
- ❑ Pimienta blanca

Artículos secos o enlatados para la despensa

- ❑ Alcaparras
- ❑ Aminoácidos de coco o salsa de soya
- ❑ 2 latas de leche de coco (15 oz. [443,6 ml])
- ❑ Mostaza Dijon
- ❑ Migajas de pan libre de gluten (o 1 paquete de galletas saladas de arroz)
- ❑ Pasta de curry verde (opcional)
- ❑ Miel cruda
- ❑ Jarabe de arce (maple)
- ❑ Aceitunas negras
- ❑ Proteína en polvo
- ❑ Sal marina
- ❑ Extracto de vainilla
- ❑ Vino blanco seco (opcional)
- ❑ Levadura nutricional

Hierbas y especias frescas

- 16 hojas de laurel fresco
- 1 manojo de cilantro
- 2 manojos de perejil rizado
- 3 manojos de perejil de hoja plana
- 7 pulgadas [17,78 cm] de jengibre
- ¼ de taza de hierbas frescas de su elección
- 1 manojo de menta
- 1 manojo de estragón
- 2 ramitas de tomillo fresco

Pescado, aves, carnes

- 1 pollo entero de campo u orgánico
- 1½ lb. [680,4 g] de pechuga de pollo, deshuesada, sin piel
- ½ lb. [226,8 g] pulpa de cangrejo fresca en trozo
- 2 lb. [907,2 g] de filete de salmón silvestre sin piel
- ½ lb. [226,8 g] de salmón ahumado
- 1½ lb. [680,4 g] de camarón (o más pechuga de pollo deshuesada, sin piel)
- 1½ lb. [680,4 g] de filetes de lenguado silvestre (petrale o dover)

- 1½ lb. [680,4 g] de medallones de atún silvestre

Harinas

- ½ taza de harina de almendra o harina de arroz
- Harina de arrurruz o tapioca
- Harina libre de gluten

Granos y leguminosas

- Quinoa
- 2 tazas de lentejas rojas
- 1 taza de arroz basmati integral
- 1 taza de arroz integral de grano corto
- 8 tazas de hojuelas de avena (libres de gluten)
- ½ taza de alubias

Nueces y semillas

- 1 taza de almendras
- 1 cuarto [946,4 ml] de leche de almendras
- ½ taza de nueces de la India
- 1 cucharada de semillas de chía
- ½ taza + 1 cucharada de semillas de linaza
- 4 tazas de avellanas, pacanas, o almendras

- ¼ de taza de ajonjolí
- ¼ de taza de semillas de girasol

Aceites

- Aceite de coco
- Aceite de oliva virgen extra
- Aceite de semilla de uva
- Aceite de ajonjolí sin refinar

Frutas y verduras

Frutas

- 4 aguacates
- 3 manzanas de su elección
- 3 manzanas verdes
- 2 plátanos
- 12 limones [amarillos] (o 1 cuarto [946,4 ml] de jugo de limón)
- 1 lima [limón verde]
- 1 naranja
- 1 pera
- 1 piña
- 1 pinta seca [551 ml] de moras o frutas del bosque

Verduras

- 3 manojos de espárragos
- 14 tazas de hojas tiernas de espinaca (1¼ lb. [567 g])
- 6 remolachas (con las hojas que las coronan)
- 1 tallo de brócoli

- 5 lb. [2268 g] zanahorias
- 2 cabezas de coliflor
- 2 pencas de apio
- 1 manojo de hojas de berza
- 6 pepinos
- 3 cabezas de hinojo
- 4 cabezas de ajo
- 1 taza de habichuelas (o 1 manojo de espárragos)
- 7 manojos de col rizada
- 1 colinabo con hojas
- ½ taza de champiñones (¼ lb. [113,4 g])
- 4 tazas de brotes de guisantes o rúcula (¼ lb. [113,4 g])
- 1 cabeza de radicchio
- 2 manojos de rábanos
- 1 cabeza de repollo morado
- 2 cebollas rojas pequeñas
- 1 lechuga romana grande
- 4 lb. [1814 g] de nabicol
- 1 repollo chino o repollo Savoy
- 8 cebollas amarillas
- 10 manojos grandes de mezcla de hojas verdes para ensalada
- 2 manojos de cebolletas
- 1 chalota mediana
- 3 tazas de arvejas chinas (½ lb. [226,8 g])

- ❑ 1 pinta seca [551 ml] de germinados
- ❑ 6 tazas de verduras: bok choy, zanahorias, cebolletas, hongo shiitake, brócoli, arvejas chinas, hojas de mostaza

Caldos

- ❑ 5 cuartos [4762 ml] de caldo de pollo o caldo de verduras (¡hecho en casa es mejor!)

Menús y recetas de la semana uno

Desayuno del lunes

Coctel antiinflamatorio   Rinde 2 porciones

Hinojo: Antiinflamatorio, antihistamínico, analgésico y antioxidante.

Manzana: Inhibe el desarrollo de alergias; rica en quercetina que reduce la histamina.

Pepino: Analgésico (reductor del dolor); antioxidante que previene la síntesis del compuesto inflamatorio, prostaglandina.

Brócoli: Anticarcinógeno, previene el daño de la mucosa gástrica (sugiere una acción potencial de reducción de la histamina).

Jengibre: Tan eficaz como un medicamento de prescripción antagonista del receptor H2.

1 manzana verde
½ hinojo grande con sus frondas
1 trozo de 1 pulgada [2,54 cm] de raíz de jengibre
1 tallo de brócoli grande
3 hojas de col rizada
½ pepino, pelado si no es orgánico

Corte la fruta y la verdura para que quepa en el tubo de alimentación de su extractor de jugos. Comience por la manzana y termine con el pepino. Beba tan pronto como sea posible.

Lista de compras

1 brócoli
1 manojo de col rizada
1 pepino
1 bulbo de hinojo con sus frondas
1 trozo de 1 pulgada [2,54 cm] de raíz de jengibre
1 manzana verde

73

Almuerzo del lunes

Verduras de verano picadas y curadas a mano con quinoa básica   Rinde 4–6 porciones

Verduras de verano picadas y curadas a mano

Esta receta se mantiene bien de 4 a 5 días en la nevera, así que haga una gran cantidad y disfrútela como una guarnición crujiente con cualquier comida. Utilice las verduras de temporada para hacer de esta receta un elemento básico de todo el año.

1 aguacate, rebanado
1 cabeza (o 4 tazas) de repollo chino o repollo Savoy, rebanado en delgados
    bocados
2 tazas de arvejas chinas
1 taza de habichuelas, rebanadas sesgadas [a 45°] en tercios
1–2 tazas de rábanos, en cuartos
2 dientes de ajo, picados
2 tazas de col rizada, cortadas en pedazos pequeños
1 trozo de 1 pulgada [2,54 cm] de jengibre, picado (opcional)
1 cucharadita de sal marina

Combine todos los ingredientes en un cuenco grande. Con las manos limpias masajee las verduras como si las estuviera exprimiendo. Trabaje con las verduras por lo menos 15 veces, luego coloque un plato sobre la boca del cuenco. Añada peso sobre el plato y ponga un temporizador a contar 10 minutos.

Después de 10 minutos use el plato para mantener las verduras en el cuenco e inclínelo para dejar escapar el exceso de líquido en la pila. Trabaje con las verduras otras 15 veces y pruebe. Termine la receta en este punto, o coloque el plato sobre la boca del cuenco 1 vez más. Añada peso y establezca el temporizador para que cuente 10 minutos.

Repita el proceso de escurrido y pruebe las verduras. Disfrute muchas variaciones sobre este mismo tema.

Los tomates no son una buena verdura para este tipo de ensalada, ya que se ponen pastosos al trabajarlos con las manos. Si usa pepinos, primero remueva las semillas.

Variaciones:
    *Añada ajonjolí al final, o nueces de la India en trozos para que quede crujiente.
    *Reduzca la sal marina a ½ cucharadita y añada 1 cucharadita de pasta de ciruela umeboshi.

Quinoa básica

Combine 1 taza de quinoa, 2 tazas de agua y ¼ de cucharadita de sal en una olla mediana. Llévelo a que hierva sobre fuego medio. Una vez que la quinoa hierva, cubra y disminuya el calor a bajo. Cocine a fuego lento durante 15 minutos. Apague el calor, manténgalo tapado y déjelo al vapor 5 minutos más. Rinde 6 porciones.

Lista de compras

1 aguacate
1 repollo chino o repollo Savoy
1 cabeza de ajo
1 trozo de 1 pulgada [2,54 cm] de
   jengibre
1 taza de habichuelas
1 manojo de col rizada
Quinoa
1 manojo de rábanos
2 tazas de arvejas chinas

Revise la despensa

Sal marina

Cena del lunes

Piccata de lenguado silvestre y espárragos asados con una ensalada simple
Rinde 4 porciones

Piccata de lenguado silvestre

Esta es una rica receta tradicional italiana que es ligera y refrescante para el almuerzo o la cena. Utilice harina de almendra para hacerla 100% libre de granos.

½ taza de harina de almendra o harina de arroz
¼ de taza de levadura nutricional
½ cucharadita de sal marina, o más al gusto
½ cucharadita de pimienta fresca negra molida 1½ lb.
   [680,4 g] de filetes de lenguado silvestre (petrale
   o dover)
¼ de taza de aceite de oliva virgen extra
¼ de taza de aceite de coco
¼ de taza de vino blanco seco (o caldo)
¼ de taza jugo de limón [amarillo] recién exprimido

¼ de taza de alcaparras en salmuera, escurridas
½ taza de perejil fresco, cortado en trozos
Limones adicionales para adornar y servir
1 manojo grande de espárragos, con las puntas ásperas removidas
6 puñados de mezcla de hojas verdes para ensalada

Vinagreta básica

1 cucharada de aceite de oliva virgen extra
2 cucharadas de vinagre de vino tinto (o 1 limón [amarillo])
1 diente de ajo
1 cucharadita de mostaza Dijon
½ cucharadita de miel cruda
Sal marina, al gusto
Pimienta negra recién molida, al gusto

En un cuenco mezcle el harina, la levadura nutricional, la sal y la pimienta. Si está usando harina de almendra, mezcle el harina de almendra, la levadura, la sal y la pimienta juntas. Extienda la mezcla en un plato grande.

Enjuague el lenguado en agua y sacuda el exceso. Enharine 1 filete a la vez en la mezcla de harina, presionando la mezcla suavemente sobre el lenguado. Vaya colocándolas en un plato aparte mientras enharina el resto de las piezas.

Caliente un sartén grande a fuego medio. Añada el aceite de oliva y 2 cucharadas de aceite de coco. Una vez que el aceite esté caliente, coloque 2–3 filetes de lenguado preparados en el sartén; ¡no llene demasiado su sartén! Cocine de 2–3 minutos o hasta que el primer lado esté bien dorado. Voltee y cocine de 2–3 minutos del otro lado. Pase el lenguado cocinado a un plato para servir limpio y cúbralo con papel aluminio para mantenerlo caliente. También puede colocar el plato en un horno tibio. Repita el procedimiento con las piezas restantes.

Añada el vino (o el caldo) y el jugo de limón al sartén. Raspe el sartén para incorporar todos los pedazos dorados que quedaron de cocinar el pescado. Añada las alcaparras y cocine hasta que la salsa se reduzca a la mitad. Debería tener la consistencia de jarabe de arce ligero. Revuelva las 2 cucharadas restantes de aceite de coco, hasta que se derrita y añada el perejil. Derrame la salsa sobre el pescado, y sirva con rebanadas o gajos de limón.

Espárragos asados y una ensalada simple

Caliente el horno a 425ºF [218,3ºC]. Mezcle los espárragos con aceite de oliva para cubrirlos. Espolvoréelos con sal y pimienta, y añada un toque de vinagre balsámico. Ase durante 10 minutos. Mezcle la vinagreta con las hojas de las ensalada en un cuenco, añadiendo lo suficiente para cubrir bien las hojas. ¡Y listo!

Lista de compras

½ taza de harina de almendra o harina de arroz
1 manojo grande de espárragos
1 diente de ajo
Jugo de limón [amarillo] (2 limones o ¼ de taza de jugo)
11 manojos de perejil rizado
6 puñados de mezcla de hojas verdes para ensalada
½ lb. [226,8 g] de filetes de lenguado silvestre (petrale o dover)

Revise la despensa

Granos de pimienta negra
Alcaparras en salmuera
Aceite de coco
Mostaza Dijon
Vino blanco seco (o caldo)
Aceite de oliva virgen extra
Levadura nutricional
Miel cruda
Vinagre de vino tinto (o jugo de limón [amarillo])
Sal marina

Desayuno del martes

Tornado de jengibre   Rinde 1 porción

Se ha demostrado en estudios científicos que el jengibre posee propiedades antiinflamatorias.

1 puñado de perejil
½ limón [amarillo], pelado si no es orgánico
4 zanahorias, bien fregadas, sin hojas o tallos y con ambos extremos recortados
1 trozo de 1 pulgada [2,54 cm] de raíz de jengibre

Corte la fruta y/o la verdura para que quepa en el tubo de alimentación de su extractor de jugos.

Lista de compras

4 zanahorias
1 trozo de 1 pulgada [2,54 cm] de raíz de jengibre
1 limón [amarillo]
1 manojo de perejil

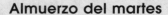

Almuerzo del martes

Ensalada de atún y aceitunas negras con vinagreta Dijon Rinde 4 porciones

Esta es una "ensalada compuesta" en un sentido tradicional, así que tómese el tiempo de hacer que cada elemento sea delicioso y arréglela hermosamente. ¡Vale la pena el esfuerzo!

Vinagreta Dijon

2 cucharadas de jugo de limón [amarillo]
2 cucharadas de mostaza Dijon
1 cucharada de miel
2 cucharadas de vinagre de manzana
1 chalota mediana, picada
1 diente de ajo, finamente picado
¾ de taza de aceite de oliva virgen extra
Sal marina
Pimienta negra recién molida, al gusto

Bata todos los ingredientes excepto el aceite en un cuenco mediano. Bata el aceite añadiéndolo gradualmente. Sazone al gusto con sal y pimienta.

Ensalada de atún y aceitunas negras

¾ lb. [340,2 g] de nabicol, fregado y cortado en cuñas de dos pulgadas [5,08 cm]
Sal marina
2 cucharadas de aceite de oliva virgen extra
1 cabeza grande de lechuga romana, con las hojas lavadas, enjuagadas y
     cortadas en pedazos del tamaño de un bocado
1 taza de habichuelas o espárragos, sin tallo y cortados a la mitad
Pimienta negra recién molida
1½ lb. [680,4 g] de medallones de atún silvestre (omítase en la opción vegana)
½ cebolla morada pequeña, rebanada muy delgada
3 huevos cocidos, pelados y en cuartos
¼ de taza de aceitunas negras
1 cucharada de alcaparras, enjuagadas

En una olla grande, cubra el nabicol con 2–3 pulgadas [5,08–7,62 cm] de agua. Añada 1 cucharada de sal y cocine hasta que esté tierno, aprox. 8 minutos. Conserve aparte el agua donde lo cocinó. Transfiera el nabicol a un cuenco mediano y mezcle con unos toques de aceite de oliva. Ponga aparte.

Mientras se está cociendo el nabicol, coloque la lechuga en platos para servir (o en un contenedor de vidrio para empacar su almuerzo).

Lleve nuevamente el agua que reservó a hervir y cocine las habichuelas (o espárragos) 2 minutos hasta que estén tiernos. Escúrralos y sumérjalos en agua helada unos minutos. Sáquelos y séquelos dándoles palmadas con una toalla y eche las judías en 1 cucharada de vinagreta, añadiendo sal y pimienta al gusto. Acomode las habichuelas en un montón en la orilla de la cama de lechuga.

Caliente un sartén grande en fuego medio-alto y cocine los filetes de salmón o los medallones de atún de 3–4 minutos por lado hasta que queden cocidos a término medio. Remuévalos del sartén, y cuando estén listos para manejarse, rebane el pescado y cúbralo con más de la vinagreta. Acomode el pescado sobre la lechuga.

Coloque la cebolla morada en un cuenco y rocíe con un poco de vinagreta. Acomódela cerca de las habichuelas.

Finalmente rebane los huevos cocidos y acomódelos sobre la lechuga y añada las aceitunas y las alcaparras sobre la ensalada.

Lista de compras

¾ lb. [340,2 g] de nabicol
1½ lb. [680,4 g] de medallones de atún silvestre (omítase en la opción vegana)
1 cabeza grande de lechuga romana
1 cebolla morada pequeña, rebanada muy delgada
3 huevos
1 taza de habichuelas o 1 manojo de espárragos
1 limón [amarillo]
1 chalota mediana
1 diente de ajo

Revise la despensa

Vinagre de manzana
Granos de pimienta negra
Alcaparras
Mostaza Dijon
Miel
Aceite de oliva virgen extra
Aceitunas negras
Sal marina

Fotografía por Polara Studio

Cena del martes

Salteado al estilo chino asiático básico con arroz integral horneado con cilantro   Rinde 4 porciones

Salteado al estilo chino asiático básico

Haga esta receta con una variedad de combinaciones de verduras y proteínas. Esta es verdaderamente una receta con la cual jugar. Hágala una vez a la semana para una merienda sencilla. ¡Manténgala colorida!

1½ lb. [680,4 g] de pollo deshuesado/camarón
5–6 tazas de verduras rebanadas delgadas, como zanahorias, bok choy, hojas
    de mostaza, hongo shiitake, raíz de bardana, calabaza cocida, arvejas chinas,
    cebolletas, brócoli y tallos de brócoli
2 cucharadas de aceite de coco
1–2 dientes de ajo picados
½ pulgada [1,27 cm] de jengibre picado
4 cucharadas de caldo (de verduras o de pollo)

Marinada asiática básica

1–2 cucharadas de aminoácidos de coco (o salsa de soya)
2 cucharaditas de arrurruz (o harina de tapioca)
2 cucharadas de vinagre de mirin (o vinagre de vino de arroz)

Si usa una proteína, corte la carne o el ave en tiras largas de 2 pulgadas [5,08 cm] y menos de ½ pulgada [1,27 cm] de ancho. Mezcle la marinada en un cuenco con un batidor para integrarla. Marine el pollo o el camarón durante 10–20 minutos.

Corte las verduras en pedazos pequeños (rebane sesgado). Caliente el aceite de coco en un sartén grande o en un wok sobre una flama muy alta. Cuando el aceite comience a formar ondas introduzca la carne o los mariscos, dejando la marinada en el cuenco para un uso posterior. Cuando la carne comience a dorar, añada el ajo y el jengibre durante 15 segundos, luego añada las verduras.

Rápidamente revuelva las verduras y el pollo/camarón hasta que ambos estén cocidos, alrededor de 3-5 minutos solamente. Escurra el exceso de aceite del fondo del sartén y agregue el caldo revolviendo. Caliente a fuego lento 30 segundos solamente. Añada 1 cucharada de la marinada a la mezcla, revolviendo unos 30 segundos más. Sazone con aminoácidos de coco o salsa de soya para un sabor más salado.

Añadiduras opcionales: 1 cucharadita de aceite de ajonjolí, 2 cucharaditas de miel cruda, 2 cucharaditas de jugo de lima [limón verde], 1 cucharadita de aceite de chile picante, ¼ de taza de nueces de la India. Añada estos ingredientes al terminar de cocinar en el momento de añadir el caldo o el agua.

Lista de compras

1½ lb. [680,4 g] de pollo deshuesado o de camarón
½ cabeza de ajo
1 pulgada [2,54 cm] de jengibre
Hojas de mostaza
6 tazas de verduras: bok choy, zanahorias, cebolletas, hongo shiitake, brócoli, arvejas chinas

Revise la despensa

6 tazas de agua (4 tazas para remojar el arroz)
2 tazas de arroz basmati integral (o arroz integral de grano corto)
2 cucharadas de semillas de cilantro (o 1 raja de canela, o condimento preferido)
¾ de cucharadita de sal marina

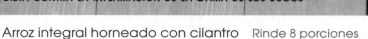

Arroz integral horneado con cilantro   Rinde 8 porciones

Esta es una manera excelente de hacer arroz aromático sin manos, utilizando el horno en lugar de una olla o arrocera eléctrica. ¡Mi versión favorita incluye un par de rajas de canela y semillas de cilantro! Hornear el arroz le infunde al grano un aroma de nueces. Si remoja el arroz, reduzca el agua en esta receta a 4 tazas y siga el tiempo de cocción más corto que se menciona más adelante.

6 tazas de agua (4 tazas para remojar el arroz)
2 tazas de arroz basmati integral (o arroz integral de grano corto)
2 cucharadas de semillas de cilantro (o 1 raja de canela,
o condimento preferido)
¾ de cucharadita de sal marina

Precaliente el horno a 375ºF [190,6ºC].

Lleve el agua a hervir en una olla en la estufa. Utilice aceite de oliva para cubrir un molde para hornear. Una vez que el agua hierva, añádala al molde para hornear, luego mezcle el arroz, los condimentos y la sal. Cubra con papel aluminio o con una tapa que cierre herméticamente (se recomienda el papel aluminio).

Hornee durante 50 minutos (arroz basmati) o 60–75 minutos para el arroz integral. Si el arroz fue remojado, hornee durante 50–60 minutos. De no ser así, hornee durante 75 minutos.

Remuévalo del horno para que se cueza al vapor entre 3–5 minutos. ¡Pruebe y sirva!

Lista de compras

2 tazas de arroz basmati integral (o arroz integral de grano corto)

Revise la despensa

Semillas de cilantro o canela en rajas
Sal marina

Desayuno del miércoles

Enverdeciente   Rinde de 1 a 2 porciones

¡La col rizada está llena de calcio en una forma que es asimilada por el cuerpo mucho mejor que el calcio de los productos lácteos, y eso es una gran ventaja para sus huesos!

1–3 hojas de col rizada
1–3 hojas de colirrábano
2 pencas de apio
1 pepino, pelado si no es orgánico
3 zanahorias
1 pera
½ limón [amarillo], pelado si no es orgánico

Coloque algunas de las hojas verdes en el extractor; alterne las hojas con el apio seguido del pepino, la zanahoria, la pera y el limón. Revuelva el jugo y beba tan pronto como sea posible.

Lista de compras

1 remolacha con hojas (utilice la raíz de la remolacha para algo más)
1 manojo de col rizada
1 manojo de apio

3 zanahorias
1 pepino
1 limón [amarillo]
1 pera

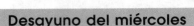

Desayuno del miércoles

Muesli remojado por la noche con plátano
Rinde 4–6 porciones

La inspiración para esta receta proviene de Jamie Oliver, una de mis heroínas gastronómicas personales. Esta es una receta excelente para prepararla con los niños, especialmente porque toda la preparación sucede la noche anterior y es fácil y satisfactorio terminar rápidamente en la mañana.

8 tazas de hojuelas de avena orgánica
½ taza de linaza, entera o molida
2 tazas de pasas sin edulcorar, cerezas secas o grosellas
2 tazas de su nuez preferida en trozos (tostada)
1 cucharadita de canela molida
3–4 tazas de leche de almendra o de coco, para cubrir el avena
2–3 manzanas
2 plátanos
Miel cruda (aderezo opcional)
Moras (frutas del bosque) frescas (aderezo opcional)

Coloque todos los ingredientes secos en un vaso grande, en un recipiente plástico de tapa hermética o en una bolsa de un galón [3,785 l] para combinarlos.

La noche antes de que quiera comer el muesli, coloque sus porciones deseadas de la mezcla de avena en un cuenco con leche de almendra o de coco.

Ralle ½ manzana por persona. Revuelva de inmediato para evitar que la manzana se oscurezca.

Tápelo y colóquelo en la nevera toda la noche.

En la mañana cuando vaya a comérselo, rebane o haga puré ½ plátano por persona, mézclelo con la avena reblandecida y añada más leche de almendras. Opcionalmente agregue encima miel cruda al gusto.

Es excelente servido con moras (frutas del bosque) surtidas frescas.

Lista de compras

3–4 tazas de leche de almendra o
    de coco, para cubrir el avena
2–3 manzanas
2 plátanos
Moras (frutas del bosque) frescas
    (aderezo opcional)

Revise la despensa

Canela
Linaza, entera o molida
Nueces al gusto
Hojuelas de avena orgánica
Miel cruda
Pasas, cerezas secas o grosellas sin
    edulcorar

Almuerzo del miércoles

Crema de zanahoria con onigiri de arroz integral y nori tostada   Rinde 4–6 porciones

Crema de zanahoria

Esta es una receta que adapté de mi escuela de cocina (The Natural Gourmet Institute of Food and Health in Manhattan). Me encanta la técnica de añadir grano cocido a la sopa para darle una consistencia más cremosa. ¡Añada el doble de jengibre si a usted, como a mí, le encanta un sabor intenso en su sopa!

2 cucharadas de aceite de oliva virgen extra
1 cebolla amarilla, cortada en trozos medianos
¾ de cucharadita de sal marina
2 lbs. [907,2 g] de zanahorias cortados en piezas de ½ pulgada [1,27 cm]
5 tazas de caldo de verduras
¼ de taza de arroz cocido o nueces de la India crudas, remojadas 30 minutos
1 pieza de 2 pulgadas [5,08 cm] de jengibre, pelado y cortado
1 cucharada de jugo de limón [amarillo]
Pimienta negra recién molida, al gusto

Caliente una olla con caldo sobre fuego medio y agregue el aceite de oliva. Añada las cebollas y la sal, salteando durante 5 minutos. Agregue las zanahorias y cubra. Deje cocer durante otros 5 minutos sobre fuego medio. Añada el caldo de verduras y el arroz cocido o las nueces de la India a la olla y caliéntelo hasta que hierva. Una vez que la sopa comience a hervir, reduzca el calor y cocine a fuego lento durante 25 minutos.

En la licuadora haga puré la mezcla en lotes, teniendo cuidado de no llenar de más la licuadora (¡podría suceder un desastre caliente!). Agregue el jengibre recién cortado a la sopa conforme la va haciendo puré. Mezcle el jugo de limón y sazone con sal y pimienta al gusto.

Nota: Añada más caldo si prefiere su sopa más líquida (añádalo al final).

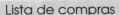

Lista de compras

2 lb. [907,2 g] de zanahorias
1 pieza de 2 pulgadas [5,08 cm] de jengibre
1 limón [amarillo] (por el jugo)
2 cuartos [1893 ml] de caldo de verduras

Revise la despensa

Granos de pimienta negra
Arroz integral o nueces de la India
Aceite de oliva virgen extra
Sal marina
Cebolla amarilla

Onigiri de arroz integral y nori tostada   Rinde 6–8 porciones

¡No se intimide por la cantidad de pasos! Una vez que domine cómo hacer arroz pegajoso, el resto es pan comido. Excelentes para llevar, los onigiri se sirven tradicionalmente en Japón como un almuerzo sencillo o una comida portátil. Hágalos con anticipación y sírvalos con muchos tipos de comidas.

1 taza de arroz integral de grano corto, remojada 4 horas o durante la noche
2¼ de tazas de agua filtrada
½ cucharadita de sal marina
¼ de taza de vinagre de arroz
1 cucharada de aceite de ajonjolí
¼ de taza de ajonjolí (opcional)
½ taza de nueces de la India crudas en trozos
2 piezas de nori tostada, cortada en piezas de ½ pulgada por 4 pulgadas [1,27 x 10,16 cm]
¼ de taza de ciruelas umeboshi enteras, sin hueso (opcional)

Enjuague el arroz remojado 3 veces, primero drenando el líquido para remojo y llenando la olla con el arroz con suficiente agua para cubrirlo, frotando bien el arroz con sus manos para que el líquido se vuelva de un color almidonado. Tire el agua mediante inclinar la olla, ¡con cuidado de no perder el arroz! Llene la olla de agua y repita dos veces más. Estos pasos hacen que el arroz se vuelva pegajoso y limpio en un sentido tradicional.

Ahora está listo para cocinar el arroz: añada 2¼ tazas de agua al arroz remojado y enjuagado (asegúrese de que no le quede agua (y agregue la sal). Llévelo a hervir, tape y luego reduzca el calor para cocerlo a fuego lento durante 35 minutos. Apague el calor y permita que el arroz continúe cociéndose al vapor durante 5 minutos.

Extienda el arroz en una plancha para hornear para que se enfríe rápido, lo suficiente como para que pueda trabajar con él con sus manos. Rocíe el arroz uniformemente con vinagre de arroz y aceite.

Muela las nueces de la India en un procesador de alimentos dando impulsos cortos hasta que queden molidas uniformemente y espolvoree sobre el arroz. Coloque el resto del vinagre de arroz en un cuenco pequeño para que pueda usarlo para mantener sus manos húmedas para enrollar.

Tome un poco de sal marina en sus manos y frótelas. Tome alrededor de 1/3 de la mezcla de arroz, y amásela en pequeñas bolas de arroz, humedeciendo sus manos según sea necesario con el vinagre a medida que avanza para evitar que se le peguen. Añada más sal cuando así lo desee. Repita hasta que se termine el arroz. Espolvoree la parte superior con ajonjolí y envuelva la nori a lo largo del diámetro de la bola de arroz, colocando la parte que se traslapa boca abajo hasta que se vaya a comer. Puede rellenar el onigiri con ingredientes opcionales como ciruelas umeboshi en conserva, o bien, mezcle pedazos de las ciruelas con el arroz antes de hacer las bolitas. Sirva a temperatura ambiente o enfríe y disfrútelos directamente salidos de la nevera. ¡Deliciosos!

Lista de compras

1 taza de arroz integral de grano corto

Revise la despensa

Piezas de nueces de la India crudas
Vinagre de arroz
Sal marina
Ajonjolí (opcional)
Aceite de ajonjolí sin refinar

Cena del miércoles

Pollo cubierto de nueces con coliflor asada entera y ensalada de repollo y cebolleta   Rinde 4 porciones

Pollo cubierto de nueces

Esta receta satisface el deseo de comida frita dorada crujiente sin todos los aceites malos y la harina blanca. Yo vivo en Oregón, así que las avellanas son mi opción de nueces favorita. Las pacanas y las almendras también son fabulosos en esta receta.

2 tazas de su nuez preferida, finamente picadas
1 cucharadita de sal marina
¼ de cucharadita de pimienta negra recién molida
2 cucharaditas de hierbas/especias de su elección (cebolla en polvo, ajo en polvo, páprika, orégano, etc.)
4 pechugas de pollo de campo, sin hueso, sin piel, cortadas en tiras cortas delgadas
2 huevos grandes, batidos

Añada una taza de nuez picada a un cuenco. Agregue sal, pimienta y suficientes condimentos hasta que le agrade el sabor. Sumerja las piezas de pollo en el huevo batido. Siguiente, cubra ligeramente con la mezcla de nueves y condimentos.

Ase a fuego alto durante 7 minutos, luego voltee y ase durante otros 5 minutos, o hasta que los jugos salgan transparentes y no tenga una apariencia rosada en el centro.

Lista de compras

4 pechugas de pollo grandes, sin hueso, sin piel
2 huevos
2 tazas de nueces de su elección (avellana, pacana o almendra)

Revise la despensa

Granos de pimienta negra
Hierbas/especias de su elección
Sal marina

Coliflor entera asada   Rinde 4 porciones

2 cabezas completas de coliflor, cortadas por la mitad
¼ de taza de aceite de semilla de uva
½ cucharadita de sal marina

Precaliente el horno a 350ºF [176,7ºC].

Coloque las mitades de coliflor en una plancha para hornear ligeramente engrasada. Frote el aceite restante en las coliflores y espolvoree con sal marina.

Ase en el horno durante 1 hora. Sirva caliente o enfríe y use en una ensalada.

Lista de compras

2 cabezas de coliflor

Revise la despensa

Aceite de semilla de uva
Sal marina

Ensalada de repollo y cebolleta   Rinde 4–6 porciones

1 cabeza de repollo morado, sin corazón y en rebanadas delgadas
3 zanahorias, cortadas en juliana
¼ de manojo de perejil, menta o cilantro
1 manojo de cebolletas, rebanadas delgadas
1 pieza de jengibre de 1 pulgada [2,54 cm] o 1 diente de ajo, picado
¼ de taza de vinagre de manzana o jugo de limón [amarillo]
½ cucharadita de sal marina
1 cucharada de aceite de oliva virgen extra (opcional)
Pimienta negra recién molida o pimienta de Cayena al gusto (opcional)

Combine los ingredientes en un cuenco. Con las manos limpias masajeé la ensalada firmemente, apretando en puñados a la vez. Repita 20 veces en total. La ensalada debería reducirse en tamaño y quedar cubierta uniformemente por el aderezo.

Pruebe y ajuste los condimentos al gusto. Añada miel cruda para reducir la acidez, añada varias especias para variedad, añada vinagre o sal para una ensalada más brillante. Puede mantenerla en la nevera hasta por 5 días.

Lista de compras

3 zanahorias
1 trozo de 1 pulgada [2,54 cm] de
    jengibre o 1 diente de ajo
1 manojo de menta, cilantro o
    perejil
1 cabeza de repollo morado
1 manojo de cebolletas

Revise la despensa

Vinagre de manzana
Granos de pimienta negra o
    pimienta de Cayena
Aceite de oliva virgen extra
Miel cruda
Sal marina

Desayuno del jueves

El asombroso batido verde de Cherie   Rinde 2 porciones

Las investigaciones han identificado más de 45 flavonoides diferentes en la col rizada. Con el kaemferol y quercetina al principio de la lista, los flavonoides de la col rizada y sus antioxidantes tienen beneficios antiinflamatorios que nos ayudan a evitar la inflamación crónica y el estrés oxidativo.

1 aguacate, pelado, sin semilla y cortado en cuartos
1 taza de hojas tiernas de espinaca
2 hojas de col rizada
½ pepino, pelado y cortado en trozos
El jugo de 1 lima [limón verde]
1 cucharada de suplemento alimenticio de verduras en polvo de su elección (opcional)
2–3 cucharadas de almendra molida (opcional)

Combine todos los ingredientes en una licuadora y procese hasta obtener un batido suave. Espolvoree la almendra molida sobre él, al gusto.

Lista de compras

1 aguacate
1 manojo de col rizada
1 manojo de espinaca
1 lima [limón verde]
1 pepino orgánico

Revise la despensa

Almendra (si la usó)

Almuerzo del jueves

Wrap de salmón ahumado y berza con zanahorias a la miel   Rinde 4 porciones

Wrap de salmón ahumado y berza

1 manojo grande de hojas de berza (8 hojas)
1 aguacate, machacado
3 cucharadas de jugo de limón [amarillo], al gusto
½ lb. [226,8 g] de salmón ahumado, rebanado en hojuelas
1 taza de germinado
1 taza de pepino, en rebanadas delgadas
½ taza de estragón o perejil, picado
Sal marina, al gusto
Pimienta negra recién molida, al gusto

Arme el wrap como sigue: Remueva los tallos de las hojas de berza para re-mover el tallo central duro de modo que cada hoja de berza rinda 2 piezas para envolver.

Coloque las 8 piezas de hoja de berza en una fila y añada aguacate macha-cado y rocíe limón a cada pieza. Añada el salmón ahumado repartiéndolo uni-formemente sobre el aguacate Añada el germinado, el pepino y el estragón (o el perejil) sobre el salmón. Enrolle cada pieza hacia afuera (alejándolo de usted), coloque con cuidado el final de la hoja boca abajo, y repita. Fije con un palillo hasta que se vayan a servir.

Lista de compras

1 aguacate
1 manojo de hojas de berza
1 pepino
1 manojo de perejil o estragón
½ lb. [226,8 g] de salmón ahumado
1 taza de germinados (alfalfa o su favorito)

Revise la despensa

Granos de pimienta negra
Jugo de limón [amarillo]
Sal marina

Zanahorias a la miel   Rinde 4 porciones

1½ lb. [680,4 g] de zanahorias rebanadas a la "faux tourné"
½ cucharadita de sal marina
¼ de cucharadita de pimienta recién molida
½ taza de miel cruda
2 cucharadas de aceite de coco

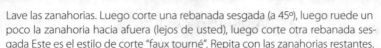

Lave las zanahorias. Luego corte una rebanada sesgada (a 45º), luego ruede un poco la zanahoria hacia afuera (lejos de usted), luego corte otra rebanada sesgada Este es el estilo de corte "faux tourné". Repita con las zanahorias restantes.

Coloque las zanahorias en un sartén y añada agua para cubrir hasta la mitad de la altura del sartén. Tape y ponga a fuego alto al vapor hasta que la mayor parte del agua se haya evaporado y las zanahorias estén casi cocidas al vapor; alrededor de 5–7 minutos.

Añada los ingredientes restantes y baje el fuego a medio-bajo, cociendo a fuego lento por unos 5–10 minutos más hasta que las zanahorias queden hermosamente caramelizadas. Rinde 4 porciones.

Lista de compras

1½ lb. [680,4 g] de zanahorias

Revise la despensa

Granos de pimienta negra
Aceite de coco
Miel cruda
Sal marina

Cena del jueves

Sopa de lentejas y limón con ensalada verde simple y aderezo balsámico de higos   Rinde 6–8 porciones

Sopa de lentejas y limón

Esta es una de mis sopas más populares. Es sazonada brillantemente con mucho limón y cúrcuma, convirtiéndola en una opción antiinflamatoria predilecta. Adapté esta receta de la escuela de cocina donde aprendí muchas recetas que apoyan una buena salud. Sírvala con una generosa porción de yogur de coco y pistou de cilantro (vea la receta abajo).

3 cucharadas de aceite de coco o aceite de oliva virgen extra
3 dientes de ajo medianos, picados
1–2 zanahorias, finamente picadas
4 tallos de apio, finamente picados
¼ cucharadita colmada de clavo molido
1½ cucharadita colmada de comino molido
1–2 cucharadas de cúrcuma
2 tazas de lentejas rojas, lavadas y escurridas
7 tazas de agua o caldo de verduras
2 hojas de laurel
1 pulgada [2,54 cm] de ralladura de limón [amarillo], cortada en tiras delgadas, como unas 4 piezas
¾ de taza de jugo de limón [amarillo], o más al gusto

2 cucharaditas de sal marina
½ manojo de cilantro, cortado en trozos grandes

En una cacerola mediana, caliente el aceite de oliva sobre fuego medio-alto y saltee la cebolla, el ajo, la zanahoria y el apio hasta que este suave, unos 5 minutos. Añada el clavo molido y el comino; saltee durante 1 minuto más. Agregue las lentejas, el agua/caldo, las hojas de laurel y las tiras de ralladura de limón. Llévelo a hervir, tape, baje el fuego y cueza a fuego lento durante 45 minutos a 1 hora, hasta que las lentejas estén tiernas pero no reblandecidas. Añada el jugo de limón y la sal marina. Revuelva y cocine durante 3 minutos.

Adorne con cilantro picado. Como una alternativa, en el procesador de alimentos pique con impulsos breves el cilantro con ¼ de cucharadita de sal marina para crear un aderezo de "pistou" para su sopa. Rinde 6–8 porciones.

Lista de compras

2 zanahorias
½ penca de apio
1 manojo de cilantro
3 dientes de ajo (½ cabeza)
4 limones [amarillos]
2 tazas de lentejas rojas
2 cuartos [1893 ml] de caldo de verduras
3 cebollas amarillas

Revise la despensa

Hojas de laurel (frescas)
Aceite de coco o aceite de oliva virgen extra
Clavo molido
Comino molido
Cúrcuma molida

Ensalada verde simple y aderezo balsámico de higos Rinde 4 porciones

1 cabeza de lechuga de hoja verde o 4 puñados de hojas tiernas de espinaca
½ taza más 2 cucharadas de aceite de oliva virgen extra
½ taza de vinagre balsámico
4 higos secos, sin tallos
½ cucharadita de sal marina
¼ de cucharadita de pimienta negra recién molida
1–2 dientes de ajo

Mezcle todos los ingredientes en una licuadora o procesador de alimentos hasta que quede suave. Sazone al gusto y añada suficiente aderezo para cubrir ligeramente la ensalada. Rinde 4 porciones.

Lista de compras

2 dientes de ajo
1 cabeza de lechuga de hoja verde
   o 4 puñados de hojas tiernas de
   espinaca
4 higos misión secos

Revise la despensa

Vinagre balsámico
Granos de pimienta negra
Aceite de oliva virgen extra
Sal marina

Desayuno del viernes

Jugo matutino de buen humor   Rinde 1–2 porciones

El jugo de hinojo se ha utilizado como tónico tradicional para ayudar al cuerpo a liberar endorfinas, que son los péptidos que nos hacen "sentir bien", desde el cerebro al torrente sanguíneo. Las endorfinas ayudan a disminuir la ansiedad y el miedo y generan un sentimiento de euforia.

4–5 zanahorias, bien fregadas, sin hojas o tallos y con ambos extremos
   recortados
3 tallos de hinojo; incluya las hojas y las flores
½ pepino
½ manzana (la verde es más baja en azúcar)
1 puñado de espinaca
1 trozo de 1 pulgada [2,54 cm] de raíz de jengibre

Corte la fruta o la verdura para que quepa en el tubo de alimentación de su extractor de jugos. Procese primero la manzana y siga con los demás ingredientes. Revuelva y sirva en un vaso; beba tan pronto como sea posible.

Lista de compras

4–5 zanahorias
1 pepino
1 bulbo de hinojo

1 trozo de raíz de jengibre
1 manzana verde
1 manojo de espinaca

Almuerzo del viernes

Ensalada básica cruda de col rizada con crema de espárragos   Rinde 4–6 porciones

Ensalada básica cruda de col rizada

1 taza de zanahoria rallada, o arvejas chinas (cuando sean de temporada)
2 tazas de rábanos, rebanados
1 diente de ajo, picado
6 tazas de col rizada, cortados en pedazos pequeños (2 manojos)
1 pieza de 1 pulgada [2,54 cm] de jengibre, picada (opcional)
Sal marina, al gusto
2 cucharadas de jugo de limón [amarillo]
1 cucharadas de aceite de oliva virgen extra

Combine todos los ingredientes en un cuenco grande. Con las manos limpias masajee las verduras como si las estuviera exprimiendo. Trabaje las verduras por lo menos 15 veces. Diez minutos después, trabaje las verduras otras 15 veces. ¡Sazone al gusto y disfrute muchas variaciones de este tema!
    Variaciones divertidas:
    *Añada ajonjolí y aceite de ajonjolí al final, o nueces de la India en trozos para que sea crujiente.
    *Reduzca la sal marina a ½ cucharadita y añada 1 cucharadita de pasta de ciruela umeboshi.
    *¡Añada pasas doradas sumergidas en jugo de manzana y semillas de calabaza para una "granola" de col rizada!

Lista de compras

1 diente de ajo
1 pulgada [2,54 cm] de jengibre
2 manojos grandes de col rizada
    (verde, roja o lacinato)
1 limón [amarillo]
1 manojo grande de rábanos
1 taza de arvejas chinas o 3
    zanahorias

Revise la despensa

Aceite de oliva virgen extra
Sal marina

Crema de espárragos   Rinde 6 porciones

¼ de taza de aceite de oliva virgen extra
2 dientes de ajo, picado
½ taza de cebolla picada
½ cucharada de pasta de curry verde (opcional)
5 tazas de espárragos frescos, cortados en piezas de 1 pulgada [2,54 cm]
    (2 manojos)
4 tazas de nabicol, cortados en trozos de 1 pulgada [2,54 cm]
4 tazas de caldo de verduras, para cubrir
¼ de manojo de perejil, cortado en trozos grandes
1½ cucharaditas de sal marina (o más al gusto)
Pimienta negra recién molida, al gusto
1–2 tazas de leche de coco, o al gusto
Agua fresca, según se necesite

Caliente el aceite de oliva en una olla para sopa grande sobre fuego medio y revuelva el ajo, la cebolla y la pasta de curry (esto sazona el aceite). Añada los espárragos cortados y el nabicol. Agregue *solamente* suficiente caldo para cubrir las verduras; no demasiado, siempre puede adelgazar la sopa con agua más tarde si lo necesita.

Agregue el perejil cortado. Sazone con sal marina y pimienta fresca, al gusto. Lleve las verduras a hervir a fuego alto. Tape la olla, y reduzca el calor a fuego mediano. Cocine durante 20 minutos o más, hasta que el nabicol este tierno al tenedor.

Remueva la olla del calor. Utilice una licuadora de inmersión para hacer puré la sopa. Regrese la olla a la estufa y añada la leche de coco. Revuelva y caliente suavemente (no hierva la sopa hecha puré). Pruebe y ajuste los condimentos.

Sirva con un toque de perejil fresco picado o una cucharada de yogur vegano natural o crema agria.

Lista de compras

2 manojos de espárragos
2 dientes de ajo, picados
1 cebolla amarilla mediana
1 manojo de perejil
3 lb. [1361 g] de nabicol

Revise la despensa

Granos de pimienta negra
Aceite de coco
Aceite de oliva virgen extra
Pasta de curry verde (opcional)
Sal marina
Caldo de verduras

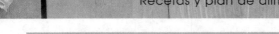

Cena del viernes

Ensalada de alubias con radicchio y aderezo balsámico de miel con remolachas asadas con limón a la griega   Rinde 4 porciones

Ensalada de alubias con radicchio

Esta es una ensalada preferida que es una comida completa. Calentar el aderezo es una excelente técnica del otoño y el invierno para quitarle el toque crudo a las verduras robustas y reblandecer ligeramente las hojas sin cocerlas.

½ lb. [226,8 g] de alubias secas, remojadas durante la noche
2 hojas de laurel
3 granos de pimienta negra
¼ cabeza de hinojo (reserve las frondas)
2 dientes de ajo, picado
½ cebolla amarilla, picada en trozos pequeños
½ cabeza de radicchio, en rebanadas delgadas
2 tazas de germinado de guisantes (use rúcula, en caso de no encontrarlo)
1 puñado de albahaca fresca
Un puñado pequeño de piñones

Aderezo balsámico de miel

½ taza de vinagre balsámico
½ taza de aceite de oliva virgen extra
1 cucharadita de albahaca seca
2 cucharadas de miel
½ cucharadita de sal marina
Pimienta negra recién molida, al gusto

Escurra y enjuague las alubias remojadas. Cueza las alubias al dente: Cubra las alubias con agua fresca; añada las hojas de laurel, los granos de pimienta, las frondas de hinojo (no el hinojo picado). Lleve las alubias a hervir, remueva la espuma con una cuchara. Reduzca el calor a bajo, y cocine a fuego lento durante 30 minutos.

Mientras tanto, pique su ajo, su cebolla y su hinojo. Ponga aparte. Rebane el radicchio en rebanadas delgadas, y corte el germinado de guisantes en trozos grandes. Colóquelo en un cuenco grande para mezclar. Rebane la albahaca en chifonada y póngala aparte en un cuenco pequeño (enrolle las hojas de albahaca y corte en rebanadas muy delgadas para hacer tiras largas). Bata el aderezo y condimente al gusto.

Una vez que las alubias estén cocidas al dente, cuidadosamente cuele el agua y remueva los condimentos. Esparza las alubias en una plancha para hornear para acelerar el tiempo de enfriamiento (5–10 minutos).

Derrame el aderezo en un sartén amplio, y llévelo a hervir a fuego lento. Agregue el ajo, la cebolla y el hinojo y cocine a fuego lento entre 3–4 minutos. Añada las alubias enfriadas al radicchio y el germinado de guisante. Agregue el aderezo encima y mezcle para cubrir, sazonando con sal y pimienta al gusto. Añada la albahaca fresca, y adorne con los piñones.

Lista de compras

- 1 cabeza de hinojo
- 2 dientes de ajo
- 1 cebolla amarilla
- 2 tazas de germinado de guisante o rúcula
- 1 cabeza de radicchio
- ½ taza de alubias secas

Revise la despensa

- Vinagre balsámico
- Albahaca, seca
- Hojas de laurel
- Granos de pimienta negra
- Aceite de oliva virgen extra
- Miel
- Sal marina

Remolachas asadas con limón a la griega
Rinde 4 porciones

La exvoluntaria de una cocina, Annalise, me compartió una receta que encontró en un periódico para Patatas Caramelizadas a la Griega "al estilo iglesia". Yo la adapté, reemplazando la papa blanca promedio, con la esplendida y hermosa remolacha. El resultado es esta fantástica receta con limón que recuerda la remolacha en conserva, sin azúcar añadida.

3 lb. [1361 g] de remolacha roja
½ de taza de aceite de oliva virgen extra
½ taza de jugo de limón [amarillo]
2 cucharadas de mostaza Dijon
1½ cucharaditas de sal marina
2 cucharadas de orégano fresco o tomillo
1½ cucharaditas de orégano seco
½ cucharadita de pimienta negra recién molida
Agua

Corte la remolacha en cuartos (córtela en 6–8 piezas si es grande). En un cuenco mezcle el aceite de oliva, el jugo de limón, la mostaza, la sal, el orégano y la pimienta.

Coloque la remolacha con el lado cortado hacia arriba en un molde para hornear grande. Derrame la mezcla uniformemente sobre la remolacha. Añada suficiente agua al molde para casi cubrir la remolacha (deje alrededor de ¼ de la remolacha sin cubrir).

Tape con papel aluminio y horneé a 425ºF [218,3ºC] durante 1 hora. Destape y regrese la remolacha al horno para seguir horneando durante 30 minutos para glasear, revolviendo solo una vez. Sirva caliente o fría con hierbas frescas adicionales añadidas, al gusto.

Lista de compras

6 remolachas
4 limones [amarillos]
2–3 ramilletes de orégano o tomillo

Revise la despensa

Granos de pimienta negra
Mostaza Dijon
Orégano seco
Aceite de oliva virgen extra
Sal marina

Desayuno del sábado

Chía Mía   Rinde 2 porciones

La combinación de ácidos grasos omega-3, alto contenido de lignano y gomas mucílago en las semillas de linaza la convierten en un excelente alimento antiinflamatorio.

10 almendras crudas
1 cucharada de semillas de girasol crudas
1 cucharada de semillas de chía
1 cucharada de ajonjolí
1 cucharada de semillas de linaza
1 piña o 1 taza de jugo sin edulcorar
1 taza de perejil picado
½ taza de leche de almendras
½ cucharadita de extracto de vainilla puro
1 cucharada de proteína en polvo (opcional)
6 cubos de hielo

Coloque las nueces, las semillas y el jugo de piña en un cuenco. Cubra y deje remojar durante la noche. Coloque la mezcla de nueces y semillas con el jugo en una licuadora y añada el perejil, la leche, la vainilla, la proteína en polvo (si la está usando) y los cubos de hielo. Procese en alta velocidad hasta obtener un batido suave. Esta bebida será un poco espesa debido a las nueces y las semillas.

Nota: Para matar el moho, agregue ½ cucharadita de ácido ascórbico al jugo, después agregue las nueces y remoje toda la noche.

Lista de compras

10 almendras
Leche de almendras sin edulcorar
1 paquete de semillas de chía o 1
    cucharada de semillas de chía
1 paquete de semillas de linaza,
    dorada o marrón, o 1 cucharada
    de semillas de linaza
1 manojo de perejil
1 piña o 1 taza de jugo sin edulcorar
1 paquete de ajonjolí o 1
    cucharada de ajonjolí
1 paquete de semillas crudas
    de girasol o 1 cucharada de
    semillas de girasol

Revise la despensa

Extracto de vainilla puro
Proteína en polvo (opcional)

Almuerzo del sábado

Salmón silvestre escalfado sobre ensalada de espinaca   Rinde 6 porciones

Líquido para escalfar

3 tazas de agua
3 ramas de perejil fresco
1 cucharada de semillas de hinojo
2 hojas de laurel (fresco o seco)
1 copa de vino blanco seco (Pinot Grigio o Sauvignon Blanc)
4 granos de pimienta negra
¾ de cucharadita de sal marina
2 lb. [907,2 g] de filete de salmón silvestre sin piel
½ taza de vinagre balsámico
½ de taza de aceite de oliva virgen extra
Pimienta negra recién molida, al gusto
8 tazas de hojas de espinaca
1 remolacha amarilla, cortada en juliana
½ taza de grosella seca
¼ de taza de semillas de girasol

Lleve el agua a hervir en una olla o sartén profundo. Añada el perejil, el hinojo y las hojas de laurel. Remueva del fuego y cubra para remojar durante 10 minutos. Añada el vino, los granos de pimienta y la sal.

Quite las espinas del salmón (del frente a dos tercios del salmón) y remueva la grasa. Corte el pescado en 4 porciones.

Regrese el líquido a fuego lento, y deslice con cuidado los filetes de pescado en la olla. Eleve el calor a fuego medio-bajo para mantener el líquido justo debajo del hervor. El líquido para escalfar debería apenas cubrir el salmón (añada más agua, si no es así). Cocine el pescado suavemente, sin tapar, durante 8–10 minutos. Levante las piezas de pescado del líquido con una espátula perforada y transfiera a un plato para servir.

Haga la ensalada: en un frasco agite el vinagre balsámico y el aceite de oliva con algunas pizcas de sal y pimienta. Junte todas las verduras preparadas, la fruta seca y las semillas; luego aderece la ensalada, al gusto.

Sirva con el salmón escalfado encima de la ensalada, añadiendo más aderezo sobre el pescado, a su elección.

Lista de compras

1 remolacha amarilla
1 manojo de perejil
2 lb. [907,2 g] de filete de salmón silvestre sin piel
8 tazas de hojas de espinaca

Revise la despensa

Vinagre balsámico
Hojas de laurel
Granos de pimienta negra
Grosella seca
Aceite de oliva virgen extra
Semillas de hinojo
Sal marina
Semillas de girasol
Vino blanco

Cena del sábado

Tortas de cangrejo con "aioli" de limón y col rizada con cebollas caramelizadas   Rinde de 10–12 tortas

Tortas de cangrejo con "aioli" de limón

Nota adicional para la cena del sábado: Si no come cangrejo, puede usar la misma cantidad de salmón crudo, por peso, y utilice un procesador de alimentos para obtener una consistencia uniforme. Otra alternativa es utilizar alubias en lugar de cangrejo, machacándolas para hacer una pasta antes de continuar con la receta.

Variedad vegana: Use alubias cocidas en lugar del cangrejo para una versión deliciosa.

Con anticipación: Remoje las nueces de la India durante la noche o durante un mínimo de 4 horas.

½ taza de aioli de limón (vea la receta más adelante)
½ manojo de cebolletas, en rebanadas delgadas
¼ de taza de cebollas picadas
1 huevo grande, ligeramente batido (o sustituto de huevo marca Ener-G Egg Replacer)
1 cucharada de mostaza Dijon
1 cucharada de jugo fresco de limón [amarillo], más los gajos para adornar
½ taza de apio, finamente picado en cubos
3 cucharadas de condimento "Laurel Antiguo" hecho en casa (vea la receta más adelante)
½ lb. [226,8 g] de pulpa de cangrejo fresca, revisada y limpia
½ taza de migajas de pan libre de gluten (o 1 paquete de galletas saladas de arroz, trituradas hasta hacerlas semejantes a las migajas de pan)
¼ de taza de harina libre de gluten marca Bob's Red Mill All-Purpose Gluten-Free Flour
2 cucharadas de aceite de oliva virgen extra
½ cucharadita de sal marina, o más al gusto
¼ de cucharadita de pimienta negra recién molida, o más al gusto
½ taza de aceite de coco, para freír

Bata los primeros 8 ingredientes en un cuenco (del aioli de limón a las 3 cucharadas de condimento "Laurel Antiguo"). Añada el cangrejo, envolviéndolo para mezclarlo. Añada las migajas de galleta, el harina, el aceite de oliva, la sal y la pimienta. Divida la mezcla de cangrejo en tortas de 1 pulgada [2,54 cm] de ancho (utilice una cuchara medidora de ¼ de taza). Refrigere por lo menos durante 40 minutos.

Caliente ¼ de taza de aceite de coco en un sartén a fuego medio-alto, añadiendo suficiente aceite para cubrir generosamente el fondo del sartén.

Fría las tortas hasta que queden doradas, 3–4 minutos por lado. Coloque las tortas cocidas en una plancha para hornear y manténgalas calientes en el horno a 350ºF [176,7ºC] hasta que sea el momento de servirlas. Sirva adornándola con los gajos de limón y más aioli (receta más adelante).

Fotografía por Ben Garvey Photography

Condimento "Laurel antiguo" hecho en casa

2 cucharaditas de sal de apio
1 cucharadita de mostaza en polvo
½ de cucharadita de pimienta negra recién molida
½ cucharadita de páprika
½ cucharadita de pimienta blanca
½ cucharadita de jengibre molido
¼ de cucharadita de nuez moscada molida

Combine todos los ingredientes y mezcle hasta que quede bien integrado.

"Aioli" de limón   Rinde 2 tazas

2 tazas de nueces de la India, remojadas 4 horas o más
¼ de taza de ralladura de limón [amarillo]
3 cucharadas de jugo de limón [amarillo]
3 dientes de ajo picados
¼ de taza de agua
1 cucharada de vinagre de manzana
½–1 cucharadita de sal marina, al gusto

Combine los ingredientes en una licuadora de alta velocidad y procese hasta que quede muy suave. Condimente al gusto.

Lista de compras

2 tazas de pedazos de nueces de la India crudas sin sal
½ lb. [226,8 g] pulpa de cangrejo fresca en trozo, revisada y limpia
½ penca de apio
1 huevo
3 dientes de ajo
1 limón [amarillo]
1 manojo de cebolletas
1 cebolla amarilla pequeña

Revise la despensa

Vinagre de manzana
Granos de pimienta negra
Sal de apio
Aceite de coco
Mostaza Dijon
Harina libre de gluten
Migajas de pan libre de gluten o galletas de arroz
Jengibre molido
Nuez moscada molida
Mostaza en polvo
Páprika
Sal
Pimienta blanca

Col rizada con cebollas caramelizadas   Rinde 4 porciones

¼ de taza de aceite de coco
¼ de taza de aceite de oliva virgen extra
2 cebollas amarillas, rebanadas
½ cucharadita de sal marina
2 manojos de col rizada, sin tallos y picados

Caliente el aceite en un sartén pesado mediano sobre fuego medio-alto. Añada la cebolla rebanada y la sal. Dore las cebollas durante 5–7 minutos, revolviendo ocasionalmente. Reduzca a fuego lento y caramelice las cebollas durante 20–30 minutos más, revolviendo ocasionalmente. Añada la col rizada y ⅓ de taza de agua. Suba el fuego a alto y tape el sartén para cocer la col rizada al vapor. Sazone con unas pizcas de sal y pimienta, al gusto.

Lista de compras	Revise la despensa
2 manojo de col rizada	Aceite de coco
2 cebollas amarillas	Aceite de oliva virgen extra
	Sal marina

Desayuno-almuerzo dominical

Verde de moras   Rinde 1 porción

Los antioxidantes de las moras o frutas del bosque pueden ayudarle a su cuerpo a combatir el estrés oxidativo causado por los radicales libres. Comer una dieta rica en antioxidantes puede ayudarlo a mejorar su salud, proteger su piel y su cabellos y combatir la inflamación.

1 manzana verde
½ limón [amarillo], pelado si no es orgánico
1 taza de moras o frutas del bosque, frescas o descongeladas si estaban
    congeladas
1 puñado de espinaca
2 hojas de col rizada
½ pepino

Corte la fruta o la ver-
dura para que quepa en
el tubo de alimentación
de su extractor de jugos.
Procese la ½ manzana y
el limón en su extractor.
Apague la máquina y

añada las moras, luego tápelo con el émbolo. Vuelva a encender la máquina y empuje las moras; añada las hojas, el pepino y la manzana restante. Revuelva el jugo y vierta en un vaso; sirva helado.

Lista de compras

Alrededor de 1 taza de hojas tiernas de espinaca	1 manzana verde
1 taza de moras o frutas del bosque de su elección	1 manojo de col rizada
	1 limón [amarillo]

Tortilla española con ensalada simple con vinagreta de arce y naranja   Rinde 4–6 porciones

Tortilla española

Mi mamá solía hacer tortilla español (muy semejante a la de esta receta) casi todos los domingos para el almuerzo con una gran ensalada fresca. Aprendí muchas recetas excelentes de mi mamá, y esta es una que adapté removiéndole los lácteos. Es una comida fácil de un solo plato. ¡Gracias, Mamá!

12 huevos orgánicos grandes
½ taza de leche de coco
½ cucharadita de sal marina, o más al gusto
2 cucharadas de aceite de coco o aceite de oliva virgen extra
1 cebolla morada pequeña, cortada en pedazos pequeños
½ taza de champiñones salteados o verduras favoritas de su elección
1 taza de espinaca o rúcula

Precaliente el horno a 375ºF [190,6ºC].

En un cuenco mediano bata los huevos y la leche de coco con 2 pizcas de sal. Ponga aparte.

En un sartén de 4-6 pulgadas [10,16 a 15,24 cm] o en un sartén para tortilla de huevo sobre fuego medio-alto añada el aceite de coco, la cebolla morada y otra pizca de sal. Saltee, revolviendo ocasionalmente hasta que la cebolla se vuelva traslúcida, unos 3 minutos. Añada los champiñones o las verduras de su elección y saltee hasta que esté suave.

Fotografía por Polara Studio

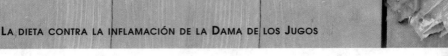

Agregue la espinaca y envuelva en la mezcla vegetariana justo hasta que se cueza. Remueva las verduras del sartén. Ponga aparte.

Baje el fuego a bajo, y añada un poco más de aceite de coco si es necesario. Utilizando el mismo sartén, añada los huevos, sacudiendo para distribuir la mezcla uniformemente. Cocine sobre fuego medio-bajo durante 5 minutos, utilice una espátula para extender los huevos de las orillas al centro hasta que las orillas ya no presenten líquidos. Acomode la mezcla de verduras sobre la tortilla uniformemente.

Transfiera el sartén a un horno caliente a 375ºF [190,6ºC] y cocine durante 5 minutos hasta que esté listo y ligeramente dorado. Sáquelo del horno. ¡Cuidado con el mango caliente!

Para terminar, usando guantes para horno coloque un plato grande sobre el sartén y, sujetando los dos juntos, inviértalos para que la tortilla parcialmente cocida caiga en el plato. Deslice la tortilla de regreso al sartén para que el lado parcialmente cocido quede hacia arriba. Meta de nuevo el sartén en el horno para cocerla 3 minutos más.

Corte en rebanadas triangulares (com o tarta) y sirva.

Lista de compras

1 docena de huevo
½ taza de champiñones
1 cebolla morada pequeña
2 tazas de espinaca o rúcula

Revise la despensa

Leche de coco
Aceite de coco o aceite de oliva
    virgen extra
Sal marina

Ensalada simple con vinagreta de arce y naranja
Rinde 4 porciones

Esta es una receta que soñé para una noche temática de "desayuno para la cena" en nuestro restaurante. Cada semana servimos cenas de cuatro tiempos, y con frecuencia escogemos un tema étnico, preparando ingredientes de temporada con un giro internacional. El desayuno para la cena fue una desviación de nuestro menú normal, ya que la variedad es la clave de la vida. Me encanta enseñar esta receta para nuestras clases prácticas de desayuno-almuerzo (*brunch*).

Ingredientes de la vinagreta:

½ de taza de aceite de oliva virgen extra
⅓–½ taza de vinagre de manzana (ajuste al gusto)
⅓ de taza de jarabe de arce
1½ cucharaditas de ralladura de naranja
El jugo de 1 naranja
1 cucharadita de tomillo fresco, finamente picado
¾ de cucharadita de sal marina
Pimienta negra recién molida, al gusto

En un cuenco combine los ingredientes y bata para combinarlos bien. Manténgalo en refrigeración y agite o bata nuevamente antes de aderezar su ensalada. Rocíe 4 puñados de hojas de ensalada grandes con aderezo justo antes de servir y revuelva.

Lista de compras

1 naranja
4 puñados grandes de hojas de
    ensalada (una por persona)
2 ramitas de tomillo fresco

Revise la despensa

Vinagre de manzana
Granos de pimienta negra
Aceite de oliva virgen extra
Jarabe de arce
Sal marina

Cena del domingo

Pollo asado al laurel con zanahorias asadas y col rizada con aderezo balsámico de higos
Rinde 4–6 porciones

Pollo asado al laurel

Encuentre hojas de laurel frescas en la sección refrigerada de su tienda; ¡son la base de esta receta! Hágalas crujir una vez para que suelten el asombroso aroma que sazona el pollo. Yo siempre sazono debajo de la piel cuando aso pollo con hueso.

3½–4 lb. [1588–1814 g] de pollo de
    campo u orgánico
12 hojas de laurel frescas,
    quebradas
4 dientes de ajo, cortados en
    rodajas
Sal marina
2 cucharadas de aceite de oliva
    virgen extra
Pimienta negra recién molida
½ taza de vino blanco seco

Precaliente el horno a 475ºF [246,1ºC]; (su horno podría producir humo; ¡asegúrese de encender el extractor de la campana!). Coloque la bandeja en el centro del horno. Limpie el pollo

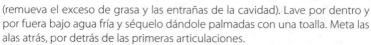

(remueva el exceso de grasa y las entrañas de la cavidad). Lave por dentro y por fuera bajo agua fría y séquelo dándole palmadas con una toalla. Meta las alas atrás, por detrás de las primeras articulaciones.

Utilice las yemas de sus dedos para aflojar la piel de la carne, comenzando desde la pechuga hacia el muslo en cada lado.

Coloque 2 hojas de laurel en la cavidad del pollo. Inserte las hojas restantes debajo de la piel, distribuyéndolas uniformemente en toda la pieza con las rodajas de ajo (2 por muslo, 3 por pechuga). Sale ligeramente debajo de la piel. Amarre las piernas con un cordel.

Coloque la pechuga del pollo viendo hacia arriba en el molde para asar. Frote aceite de oliva sobre la piel y añada sal y pimienta. Ase todo el ave entre 50–60 minutos, hasta que la piel esté hermosamente dorada y los jugos salgan transparentes, y que no tenga un aspecto rosado al hacer un corte en la pierna. Asegúrese de cubrir el pollo una vez con los jugos del molde. Déjelo reposar 10 minutos antes de cortarlo.

Opcional: caliente los jugos del molde en la estufa, y añada el vino blanco para crear una salsa rápida para el pollo.

Lista de compras

12 hojas de laurel frescas
1 pollo entero de campo u
    orgánico
4 dientes de ajo

Revise la despensa

Granos de pimienta negra
Aceite de oliva virgen extra o
    aceite de cártamo
Sal marina
Vino blanco seco (opcional)

Zanahorias asadas   Rinde 4 porciones

6 zanahorias grandes
½ cucharadita de sal marina
3 cucharadas de aceite de semilla de uva o aceite de coco
¼ de taza de hierbas frescas (estragón, romero, etc.)

Precaliente el horno a 400ºF [204,4ºC].

Coloque las zanahorias en una olla y cubra con agua. Sale el agua, suba el calor a fuego alto y tape hasta que el agua comience a hervir. Hierva durante 2 minutos, luego escurra.

Coloque las zanahorias sancochadas en un cuenco con aceite, sal y hierbas frescas de su elección, picadas. Distribuya en una plancha para hornear.

Horneé durante 20–25 minutos o hasta que estén doradas y completamente cocidas. Voltéelas una vez durante el tiempo de cocción para dorar ambos lados.

Lista de compras

5 zanahorias
¼ de taza de hierbas frescas de su elección

Revise la despensa

Aceite de semilla de uva o aceite de coco
Sal marina

Col rizada con aderezo balsámico de higos
Rinde 4 porciones

2 manojos de lacinato o col rizada negra, sin tallos y cortada en pedazos
2 cucharadas de aceite de oliva virgen extra
1–2 manojos de hojas de nabo o de rábano (1–2 tazas)
½ cucharadita de sal marina
¼ de taza de aderezo balsámico de higo (ver semana uno: Almuerzo del jueves)
½ taza de arándano rojo seco sin edulcorar (opcional)
Pimienta negra recién molida, al gusto

Caliente un sartén grande a fuego medio-alto. Una vez caliente, añada el aceite de oliva, luego la col rizada y la mitad de la sal para comenzar. Utilizando tenazas, cubra las hojas con el aceite hasta que se reblandezcan (agregue el arándano rojo opcional en este momento).

Añada el aderezo balsámico de higo, revolviendo suavemente para cubrir las hojas. Pruebe y sazone con más vinagreta o sal, al gusto.

Termine con pimienta negra quebrada, al gusto.

Lista de compras

2 manojo de lacinato o col rizada negra
1–2 manojos de hojas de nabo o de rábano

Revise la despensa

Vinagre balsámico
Granos de pimienta negra
Arándano rojo seco
Aceite de oliva virgen extra
Sal marina

Lista de compras de la semana dos

Vino y vinagre para cocinar

- ❏ 1 taza de sidra de manzana
- ❏ Vinagre de manzana
- ❏ Vinagre balsámico añejado
- ❏ Vinagre de vino tinto
- ❏ Vinagre de arroz
- ❏ Vino blanco seco (o más caldo)

Lácteos y huevos

- ❏ 12 huevos orgánicos grandes

Hierbas y especias secas

- ❏ Raíz de astralagus (opcional)
- ❏ Clavo
- ❏ Vainas de cardamomo
- ❏ Chile molido (opcional)
- ❏ Canela en raja
- ❏ Jengibre en polvo
- ❏ Cardamomo molido
- ❏ Canela molida
- ❏ Cilantro molido
- ❏ Comino molido
- ❏ Cúrcuma molida
- ❏ Orégano seco

Artículos secos o enlatados para la despensa

- ❏ Extracto de almendra
- ❏ Leche de almendras (8 oz. [236,6 ml])
- ❏ Polvo para hornear
- ❏ Migajas de pan libre de gluten o harina de almendra
- ❏ Miso de garbanzo
- ❏ Aminoácidos de coco o salsa de soya
- ❏ 2 latas de leche de coco (15 oz. [443,6 ml])
- ❏ Azúcar de coco
- ❏ Mostaza Dijon
- ❏ Salsa de pescado o vinagre de umeboshi
- ❏ Miel cruda
- ❏ Jarabe de arce o jarabe de dátil
- ❏ Sal marina
- ❏ Stevia líquida (se sugiere usar stevia marca Sweet Leaf sabor Vanilla Crème)
- ❏ Extracto de vainilla
- ❏ Wasabi en polvo

Harinas

- ❏ Arrurruz/Harina de tapioca
- ❏ Harina libre de gluten

❏ ¾ de cucharadita de xantano

Hierbas y especias frescas

❏ 1 manojo de albahaca
❏ 3 manojos de cilantro
❏ 11 pulgadas [27,94 cm] de jengibre
❏ 2 cucharadas de lavanda fresca (opcional)
❏ 3 manojos de menta
❏ 2 manojos de perejil
❏ 2 ramitas de romero

Pescado, aves, carnes

❏ 6 piernas enteras de pollo, de campo
❏ 5 muslos o pechugas de pollo, deshuesado
❏ 1½ lb. [680,4 g] de pollo deshuesado
❏ 1½ lb. [680,4 g] de rockfish
❏ 1½–2 lb. [680,4–907,2 g] de salmón silvestre
❏ 1½ lb. [680,4 g] de camarón silvestre, pelado y desvenado (o pollo)

Granos y leguminosas

❏ 1 taza de frijol negro
❏ 2 tazas de garbanzo seco
❏ 3 tazas de quinoa
❏ 1 taza de arroz integral

❏ 2 paquetes de fideos delgados de arroz

Nueces y semillas

❏ 2 tazas de leche de almendras o leche de coco
❏ 1 taza de nueces de la India
❏ Coco rallado
❏ ½ taza de avellanas
❏ ½ taza de semillas de calabaza
❏ 3 tazas de nueces

Aceites

❏ Aceite de coco
❏ Aceite de oliva virgen extra
❏ Aceite de semilla de uva
❏ Aceite de ajonjolí sin refinar

Frutas y verduras

Frutas

❏ 7 manzanas
❏ 1 manzana verde
❏ 3 aguacates
❏ 6 limones [amarillos]
❏ 7 limas (verdes)
❏ 1 mango
❏ 1 papaya
❏ 2 peras
❏ Piña fresca o congelada (suficiente para ½ taza)

❏ ½ pinta seca [275,3 ml] de fresas

❏ 2 lb. [907,2 g] de frutas de drupa (ciruelas, nectarinas, duraznos)

Caldos

❏ 3 cuartos [2839 ml] de caldo de pollo

❏ 2 cuartos [1893 ml] de caldo de verduras

Verduras

❏ 2 manojos de espárragos

❏ 5 tazas de rúcula o berro (¼–½ lb. [113,4–226,8 g])

❏ Hojas tiernas de espinaca equivalente a 3 tazas

❏ 1 remolacha

❏ 1 cabeza de bok choy

❏ 1 cabeza de brócoli

❏ 3 lb. [1361 g] de calabaza moscada

❏ 6½ lb. [2,948 kg] zanahorias

❏ ½ cabeza de apio

❏ 1 cabeza de berza con sus hojas

❏ 4 pepinos

❏ 1 pepino holandés (sin semilla)

❏ 1½ cabeza de hinojo

❏ 2 cabezas de ajo

❏ 2 tazas de habichuelas

❏ 1 repollo verde pequeño

❏ 2 manojos de col rizada

❏ 1 pinta seca [550,6 ml] de germinado de soya mung

❏ 2 manojos de hojas de mostaza

❏ 1 cebolla morada pequeña

❏ 2 cabezas de lechuga romana (u hojas de su elección)

❏ 4 tazas de mezcla de hojas verdes para ensalada (¼ lb. [113,4 g])

❏ 3 manojos de cebolletas

❏ 2 chalotas

❏ 1 taza de hongo shiitake (opcional)

❏ 1 pinta seca [550,6 ml] de germinados de su elección

❏ 2 lb. [907,2 g] verduras de raíz (chirivías, nabicol)

❏ 3 lb. [1361 g] cebolla amarilla

Ensalada HUM de su elección (se necesitan 8 tazas en total):

❏ Rúcula

❏ Espárragos

❏ Remolacha

❏ Bok choy

❏ Zanahorias

❏ Apio

❑ Frijoles cocidos
❑ Rábano blanco
❑ Hojas de diente de león
❑ Haba
❑ Jícama
❑ Hojas de mostaza
❑ Nectarinas
❑ Duraznos
❑ Peras
❑ Radicchio
❑ Rábanos
❑ Cebolletas
❑ Fresas (frutillas)
❑ Acelga roja
❑ Nabo
❑ Berro

Menús y recetas de la semana dos

Desayuno del lunes

En el Green   Rinde 1–2 porciones

El perejil contiene miristicina, un aceite volátil que ha sido demostrado activa la enzima Glutatión S-transferasa (GST). Esta enzima ayuda a desactivar moléculas que de otro modo dañarían el cuerpo. Los aceites únicos del perejil lo hacen un alimento "quimioprotector", lo cual significa que es un alimento que puede neutralizar cierto tipo de carcinógenos que pueden provocar cáncer.

1 pepino, pelado si no es orgánico y picado
½ taza de col rizada picada
½ taza de perejil picado
½ taza de piña congelada en trozos
1 cucharada de aceite de coco orgánico virgen
6–8 cubos de hielo

Combine todos los ingredientes en una licuadora y procese hasta obtener un batido suave y cremoso. Vierta en un vaso y sirva helado.

Lista de compras

1 pepino
1 manojo de col rizada
1 manojo de perejil
1 piña fresca pequeña o 1 bolsa de
    piña congelada en trozos

Revise la despensa

Aceite de coco virgen

Almuerzo del lunes

Ensalada de cinta de espárrago con pollo
rebanado   Rinde 4 porciones

Los espárragos son altos en vitaminas B y ayuda a equilibrar niveles de azúcar en sangre saludables. El berro y la rúcula son hojas de sabor acre y ayuda a expulsar las toxinas del cuerpo. Esta es una ensalada saludable, hermosa que vale la pena el esfuerzo de pelar los espárragos en cintas. Añada flores comestibles si las tiene a la mano.

1 manojo de espárragos frescos, enjuagados, con los tallos y las puntas removidas
3 tazas de rúcula o berro
1 chalota, finamente picada
¼ de taza jugo de limón [amarillo] recién exprimido
¼ de taza de aceite de oliva virgen extra
2 pechugas de pollo cocidas, rebanadas
2 cucharadas de miel
Sal marina
Pimienta negra recién molida
¼ de taza de avellanas, asadas y picadas en trozos

Enjuague las verduras. Pique la chalota y póngala aparte. Exprima el jugo de limón fresco. Remueva las puntas de los espárragos. Utilice un pelador para rallar los espárragos en cintas. Coloque las espigas de espárragos en sentido horizontal y pele, volteando cuando un lado se adelgace demasiado. Repita. Corte a mano las últimas piezas de espárrago a la mitad y agréguelos a la ensalada. Aparte los espárragos en un cuenco.

Aderezo

Bata el jugo de limón, la miel y la chalota en un cuenco. Rocíe el aceite de oliva a la mezcla y bata constantemente. Añada la sal y la pimienta, al gusto. Revuelva los espárragos con el aderezo para cubrirlos. Déjelo reposar 15 minutos.

Tueste las avellanas en un sartén hasta que suelten su aroma. Añada la rúcula/berro y el pollo a los espárragos marinados, y sazone al gusto. Recubra la ensalada con capas de avellanas tostadas. Corone con pimienta fresca.

Lista de compras

1 manojo de espárragos frescos
3 tazas de rúcula o berro
1 limón [amarillo]
¼ de taza de avellanas
1 chalota

Revise la despensa

Granos de pimienta negra
Aceite de oliva virgen extra
Miel cruda
Sal marina

Cena del lunes

Croquetas de hierbas y garbanzos con pesto de nuez al romero y hojas con habichuelas braseadas a la sidra   Rinde 4 porciones

Croquetas de hierbas y garbanzos

1½ taza de garbanzos, cocidos
⅓ de taza de aceite de oliva virgen extra, para batir
1 taza de quinoa cocida
½ taza de chalota, en cubos
2 dientes de ajo, picados
½ taza de apio, picado en cubos
½ cucharadita de orégano seco
½ cucharadita de sal marina
1 cucharada de mostaza Dijon
1¼ de tazas de harina de almendra o migajas de pan libre de gluten
⅓ de taza de harina libre de gluten
Aceite de coco o aceite de semilla de uva, para freír en sartén

Procese los garbanzos y el aceite de oliva juntos en el procesador de alimentos con impulsos breves, o machaque en un cuenco con un utensilio. Combine todos los ingredientes en un cuenco y añada los garbanzos machacados y el aceite. Pruebe para revisar el sabor y déjelo descansar 10 minutos. Si la masa parece seca, agregue más aceite de oliva hasta que pueda formar fácilmente una bolita en su mano. Forme bolitas no mayores a 2 pulgadas de diámetro [5,08 cm].

Caliente un sartén con ¼ de taza de aceite de coco a fuego medio-alto hasta que esté muy caliente. Fría las croquetas 2 minutos por lado, y si es necesario colóquelas en una plancha para hornear y termine de cocinarla en el horno a 350°F [176,7°C] hasta que estén doradas y crujientes en el exterior pero no secas, unos 5-10 minutos.

Reponga el aceite según sea necesario, cambiando el aceite si se forman pedazos color marrón (escurra el aceite en un cuenco recubierto con un colador para que pueda utilizar el aceite una vez más para freír en el sartén).

116

Lista de compras

½ taza de apio
2 dientes de ajo
½ taza de chalotas

Revise la despensa

Garbanzos
Aceite de coco o de semilla de uva
Mostaza Dijon
Orégano seco
Aceite de oliva virgen extra
Harina libre de gluten o migajas de
    pan libre de gluten
Harina de almendra
Quinoa
Sal marina

Pesto de nuez al romero   Rinde 2 tazas

El pesto en nuestra cocina toma muchas formas diferentes a través de las temporadas. Esta es una receta de invierno que nos encanta; ¡pruébela con col rizada en lugar de perejil! Llegado el verano, sustituya la albahaca o el cilantro con el romero (alrededor de ½ taza) para mantener esta receta actual con la temporada.

1 manojo de perejil
2 ramitas de romero
1 diente de ajo
1 taza de nueces
⅓ de taza de garbanzos o miso blanca
¾ de cucharadita de sal marina, al gusto
1 de taza de aceite de oliva virgen extra

Combine los primeros 6 ingredientes en un procesador de alimentos, derramando lentamente el aceite de oliva. Ajuste el sabor y la consistencia como desee. ¡Añada el jugo de medio limón para un toque alcalino adicional!

Lista de compras

1 diente de ajo
1 manojo de perejil
2 ramitas de romero

Revise la despensa

Garbanzos o miso blanca
Aceite de oliva virgen extra
Avellana
Sal marina

Hojas con habichuelas braseadas a la sidra
Rinde 4 porciones

1 taza de sidra de manzana
¼ de taza de aceite de coco
1 cucharadita de sal marina
1 cabeza de hojas de berza, sin tallo y picadas
2 tazas de habichuelas, sin tallo y picadas
1 cucharada de vinagre de manzana

Caliente la sidra de manzana en un sartén mediano sobre fuego alto. Permita que la sidra se reduzca en un rápido hervor durante 5 minutos, o hasta que se reduzca a la mitad.

Añada el aceite y la sal y revuelva para combinar. Añada las hojas de berza, las habichuelas y el vinagre de manzana y continúe hirviendo.

Baje el calor a bajo y dore durante 5–7 minutos. Pruebe y sirva.

Lista de compras

1 taza de sidra de manzana
1 cabeza de hojas de berza
2 tazas de habichuelas

Revise la despensa

Vinagre de manzana
Aceite de coco
Sal marina

Desayuno del martes

Energía matutina   Rinde 1–2 porciones

La remolacha contiene fitonutrientes únicos llamados betalaínas, que han demostrado brindar efectos antioxidantes, antiinflamatorios y desintoxicantes.

1–2 zanahorias, bien fregadas, sin hojas o tallos y con ambos extremos recortados

½ remolacha pequeña, con hojas

1 pepino, pelado si no es orgánico

1 puñado de espinaca o varias hojas de acelga

½ limón [amarillo], pelado

1 trozo de 1 pulgada [2,54 cm] de raíz de jengibre, fregado, pelado si ya tiene tiempo

Corte la fruta o la verdura para que quepa en el tubo de alimentación de su extractor de jugos. Procese los ingredientes en su extractor y revuelva. Sirva en un vaso y beba tan pronto como sea posible.

Lista de compras

1 taza de hojas tiernas de espinaca o 1 manojo de acelga

1 remolacha con hojas

1–2 zanahorias

1 pepino

1 trozo de 1 pulgada [2,54 cm] de raíz de jengibre

1 limón [amarillo]

Omelet sencillo con hojas y albahaca   Rinde 4 porciones

Esta es una manera excelente de practicar cómo hacer omelets. Asegúrese de mantener el calor en fuego medio y disminuya la flama si los huevos comienzan a dorarse. Enrollar los omelets los hace especialmente elegantes. ¡Sin importar lo elegantes, son fáciles de hacer!

8 huevos orgánicos grandes
¼ de cucharadita de sal marina
2 cucharadas de aceite de oliva virgen extra
2 puñados grandes de rúcula o espinaca
½ taza de hojas de albahaca
1½ cucharadas de vinagre balsámico añejado
Pimienta negra recién molida, al gusto

Precaliente el horno a 300ºF [148,9ºC].

Nota: Usted llevará a cabo todo este proceso dos veces para elaborar 2 omelets grandes para cortarlos por la mitad, para 4 porciones. Si su sartén es pequeño, repita 4 veces, haciendo 1 omelet por persona.

Bata los huevos y la sal en un cuenco pequeño, hasta que los huevos tengan un color uniforme.

Caliente un sartén antiadherente mediano a grande a fuego medio. Con una brocha aplique ligeramente el aceite de oliva y derrame la mitad de la mezcla de huevo (para 2 omelets grandes, o ¼ de la mezcla de huevo para 4 omelets).

Incline el sartén para que el huevo se distribuya uniformemente a lo largo del sartén en una capa muy delgada. Déjelo cocer (2–3 minutos). Meta una espátula por debajo del omelet y deslícelo fuera del sartén en una plancha para hornear recubierta con papel pergamino para cocinar.

Añadas las hojas y la albahaca al interior del omelet y enróllelo hacia afuera. Corte a la mitad y caliente ligeramente en el horno para suavizar las hojas y cocer el huevo del centro.

Dele el toque final con una rociada de vinagre balsámico o pimienta, al gusto.

Lista de compras

2 puñados grandes de rúcula o
    espinaca picada
½ taza de hojas de albahaca
8 huevos orgánicos grandes

Revise la despensa

Vinagre balsámico añejado
    (opcional)
Pimienta negra en granos
Aceite de oliva virgen extra
Sal marina

Almuerzo del martes

Ensalada de quinoa tropical con nueces de la India y frituras de zanahoria   Rinde 4 porciones

Ensalada de quinoa tropical con nueces de la India

1 taza de quinoa seca, bien enjuagada
½ cebolla morada, finamente picada
1 taza de manzana o zanahoria, finamente picada
Jugo de 1 lima [limón verde]
2 cucharaditas de miel o agave
1 cucharada de aceite de oliva virgen extra
1 mango grande, picado *(no demasiado maduro)*
¼ de taza de menta, finamente picada
½ taza de cilantro, finamente picado
1 cucharadita de sal marina, al gusto
Pimienta negra recién molida, al gusto
1 pieza de ½ pulgada [1,27 cm] de jengibre, finamente picada
1 aguacate, picado o en rebanadas delgadas
1 taza de nueces de la India, picadas en trozos grandes
3 tazas de lechuga romana (u hojas de su elección), cortada en pedazos

Cocine la quinoa: Lleve a hervir 2 tazas de agua en un sartén mediano, añada la quinoa, y hierva a fuego lento tapado durante 15–20 minutos. Aparte y deje enfriar (extiéndala para mejores resultados).

En un cuenco grande ponga la cebolla morada picada y la manzana/zanahoria. Bata juntos el jugo de lima [limón verde], miel y aceite de oliva. Añada al cuenco. Agregue la quinoa cocida y enfriada junto con el mango al cuenco y revuelva bien. Mezcle la menta, el cilantro, el jengibre y la sal y pimienta, al gusto.

Adorne con rebanadas de aguacate y nueces de la India. Con una cuchara ponga la mezcla sobre las hojas y sirva helado o a temperatura ambiente.

Fotografía por Polara Studio

121

Frituras de zanahoria   Rinde 4 porciones

Esta es una alternativa encantadora a las patatas fritas. ¿A quién no le gustan las papas a la francesa? En serio. Hay muchas alternativas de verduras de raíz a las "papas a la francesa" que son mejores para el cuerpo y que no contribuyen con la inflamación como las papas. Así, que ¡hela aquí! Una divertida receta de frituras horneadas: ¡pruébela con chirivías o nabicol, o incluso con remolacha!

2 grandes puñados de zanahorias (8 más o menos)
3 cucharadas de aceite de semilla de uva (más otras 2 para el sartén)
2 cucharaditas de cúrcuma molida
Algunas pizcas de sal marina

Precaliente el horno a 425ºF [218,3ºC] y engrase una plancha para hornear. Rebane las zanahorias en tiras de ¼ de pulgada [6,35 mm] (piense en papas a la francesa). En un cuenco grande coloque las zanahorias con el aceite, la cúrcuma y la sal.

Alinee las rodajas en una sola capa en una plancha para hornear engrasada y hornee hasta que estén doradas, unos 12–15 minutos, volteándolas dos veces. Asegúrese de darle espacio a las frituras (utilice dos planchas si hizo muchas).

Remuévalas del horno, déjelas enfriar y disfrute. ¡Trate de no comérselas todas de una vez!

Lista de compras

1 manzana o ½ pinta seca [275,3 ml] de fresas (escoja lo que esté de temporada)
1 aguacate
8 zanahorias
1 manojo de cilantro
1 lima [limón verde]
1 mango
1 manojo de menta
1 cebolla morada pequeña
1 cabeza de lechuga romana (u hojas de su elección)

Revise la despensa

Granos de pimienta negra
Nueces de la India
Aceite de oliva virgen extra
Aceite de semilla de uva
Cúrcuma molida
Quinoa
Miel cruda
Sal marina

Cena del martes

Piernas de pollo asadas con camotes asados y una ensalada simple con aderezo Dijon   Rinde 4–6 porciones

Piernas de pollo asadas

6 piernas de pollo completas (muslo y pierna), de pollo de campo
4 dientes de ajo, cortados en rodajas
2 cucharadas de aceite de semilla de uva
Sal marina
Pimienta negra recién molida
½ taza de vino blanco seco

Precaliente el horno a 475ºF [246,1ºC]. Coloque la bandeja en el centro del horno. Limpie el pollo (remueva el exceso de grasa). Lave por dentro y por fuera bajo agua fría y séquelo al contacto con una toalla.

Utilice las yemas de sus dedos para aflojar la piel de la carne, e introduzca el ajo debajo de la piel; trate de no romper la piel mientras hace esto.

Coloque el pollo en un sartén para asar. Frote aceite sobre la piel, y generosamente espolvoree con sal y pimienta. Ase durante 30 minutos, hasta que la piel esté hermosamente dorada y los jugos salgan transparentes, y que no tenga un aspecto rosado al hacer un corte en la pierna. Déjelo reposar 10 minutos antes de cortarlo para servirlo.

Opcional: caliente los jugos restantes que quedaron en el sartén, y añada vino blanco para crear una salsa rápida para el pollo.

Lista de compras

6 piernas enteras de pollo, de
    campo
4 dientes de ajo

Revise la despensa

Pimienta negra en granos
Vino blanco seco (opcional)
Aceite de semilla de uva
Sal marina

Camotes asados

2 camotes grandes
3 cucharadas de aceite de girasol o de aceite de semilla de uva
½ cucharadita de sal marina

Precaliente el horno a 400ºF [204,4ºC].

Corte los camotes en piezas grandes con forma de cuña de 1–2 pulgadas [2,54–5,08 cm] de grosor. Coloque las piezas de camote en un cuenco con aceite y sal, y luego distribuya en una plancha para hornear. Horneé durante

30–35 minutos o hasta que estén doradas. Voltéelas una vez durante el tiempo de cocción para dorar ambos lados.

Lista de compras

2 camotes grandes

Revise la despensa

Sal marina
Aceite de girasol o aceite de
semilla de uva

Ensalada simple con aderezo Dijon

2 cucharadas de mostaza Dijon
3 cucharadas de vinagre de manzana
⅓ de taza de aceite de oliva virgen extra
4 puñados de mezcla de hojas verdes para ensalada
½ taza de semillas de calabaza
Sal marina, al gusto
Pimienta negra recién molida, al gusto

Combine la mostaza Dijon, el vinagre y el aceite en un frasco y agite hasta que se combinen. Mezcle con las hojas y las semillas de calabaza en un cuenco, añadiendo sal y pimienta, al gusto.

Lista de compras

4 puñados de mezcla de hojas
verdes para ensalada

Revise la despensa

Vinagre de manzana
Granos de pimienta negra
Mostaza Dijon
Aceite de oliva virgen extra
Semillas de calabaza
Sal marina

Desayuno del miércoles

Leche helada de papaya   Rinde 1 porción

La papaya tiene dos enzimas únicas para la digestión de proteínas, la papaína y la quimopapaína, que han demostrado ayudar a reducir la inflamación.

1 taza de leche de almendras sin edulcorar
1 papaya, cortada en trozos y congelada (unas 1½ tazas)
½ taza de perejil de hoja plana picado
1½ cucharaditas de piel de limón [amarillo] orgánico, recién rallada
1 cucharadita de extracto de vainilla puro

Coloque todos los ingredientes en una licuadora y procese hasta obtener un batido suave y cremoso. Vierta en un vaso y sirva helado.

Lista de compras

1 envase de leche de almendras
   sin edulcorar
1 manojo de perejil de hoja plana
1 limón [amarillo]
1 papaya

Revise la despensa

Extracto de vainilla puro

Almuerzo del miércoles

Ensalada de col rizada y ajonjolí con manzana y bisque de calabaza moscada   Rinde 4–6 porciones

Ensalada de col rizada y ajonjolí con manzana

2 tazas de manzana, rebanada o rallada
1 diente de ajo, picado
6 tazas de col rizada, cortada en pedazos pequeños
1 pieza de 1 pulgada [2,54 cm] de jengibre, picada (opcional)
1 cucharadita de sal marina
2 cucharadas de jugo de limón [amarillo]
1 cucharada de aceite de oliva virgen extra
½ cucharada de aceite de ajonjolí

Combine todos los ingredientes en un cuenco grande. Con las manos limpias masajee las verduras como si las estuviera exprimiendo. Trabaje las verduras por lo menos 15 veces.

Después de 10 minutos use un plato para mantener las verduras en el cuenco e inclínelo para escurrir en la pila el exceso de líquido. Trabaje con las verduras otras 15 veces.

Si prefiere una ensalada más salada o con un sabor más encurtido repita el proceso 1–2 veces más.

¡Disfrute muchas variaciones sobre este mismo tema!

Lista de compras

2 manzanas
1 diente de ajo
1 trozo de 1 pulgada [2,54 cm] de
   jengibre
2 manojos de col rizada
1 limón [amarillo]

Revise la despensa

Aceite de oliva virgen extra
Sal marina
Aceite ajonjolí

125

Bisque de calabaza moscada   Rinde 8 porciones

3 lb. [1361 g] de zanahorias o batatas, peladas y cortadas en piezas de ¾ de pulgada [1,9 cm]

3 lb. [1361 g] de calabaza moscada, pelada, con la semilla removida, y picada en cubos

2 lb. [907,2 g] de cebolla amarilla, picada

2 cucharadas de aceite de semilla de uva

Sal marina, al gusto

Pimienta negra recién molida, al gusto

6 tazas de caldo de verduras

1 taza de leche de coco

1 cucharadita de cardamomo molido (o canela)

Precaliente el horno a 425º F [218,3ºC]. Sumerja las zanahorias, la calabaza y las cebollas en aceite y distribuya las verduras en una plancha de hornear grande (o en dos planchas pequeñas). Sazone con sal y pimienta, entonces dore durante 20 minutos hasta que estén tiernas, revolviendo una o dos veces.

Remueva del horno y transfiéralas directamente a una olla. Añada el caldo, la leche de coco y el cardamomo/canela. Déjelo hervir a fuego lento durante 10 minutos.

Trabajando con cuidado por porciones, haga puré la sopa en una licuadora o procesador de alimentos hasta que esté suave y sazónela al gusto con sal hasta que alcance el sabor deseado.

Tres ideas como variación: Agregue ½ taza de sidra de manzana. Añada ½ taza de jugo de limón [amarillo]. Póngale ¼ de taza de jugo de lima [limón verde].

Lista de compras

3 lb. [1361 g] de calabaza moscada
3 lb. [1361 g] de zanahorias
2 lb. [907,2 g] de cebollas amarillas (alrededor de dos)

Revise la despensa

Granos de pimienta negra
Leche de coco
Aceite de semilla de uva
Cardamomo molido o canela
Sal marina
Caldo de verduras

Cena del miércoles

Rockfish salteado al estilo chino con hojas de mostaza sobre puré de camote   Rinde 4 porciones

Rockfish salteado al estilo chino con hojas de mostaza

1½ lb. [680,4 g] de rockfish, cortado en piezas de 1–1½ pulgadas [2,54–3,81 cm]
Una pieza de jengibre de 2 pulgadas [5,08 cm], picada
2 dientes de ajo, picados
1 cucharada de salsa de pescado o vinagre de umeboshi
½ taza de coco rallado (opcional)
2 tazas de hojas de mostaza, en chiffonade
2 cucharada de aceite de coco para freír
1 manojo de cebolletas, en rebanadas delgadas
½ cucharadita de sal marina, al gusto
2 cucharadas de salsa de soya o aminoácidos de coco
2 cucharadas de jugo de lima [limón verde]
½ taza de cilantro, picado
¼ de taza de menta, picada

Marine el pescado con el jengibre picado, el ajo picado, la salsa de pescado, y hojuelas de coco opcionales, revolviendo para cubrirlo uniformemente. Déjelo reposar 20 minutos. Coloque las hojas de mostaza en un cuenco y póngalas aparte.

Caliente el aceite de coco en un wok hasta que esté sumamente caliente; añada las cebolletas y una pizca de sal, sacudiendo el sartén para cocer uniformemente. Dore bien las cebolletas y remuévalas del sartén. Añada el pescado al sartén y no lo toque durante 2 minutos.

Sacuda el sartén y haga que se volteé el pescado con cuidado (¡sin tenazas!) para que se cueza uniformemente, añadiéndole salsa de soya y jugo de lima [limón verde]. Cueza 2–4 minutos o más o hasta que quede cocido. Remueva del sartén y colóquelo en el cuenco con las hojas de mostaza rebanadas en chiffonade, revolviendo para combinar y ablandar ligeramente las hojas.

Revuelva el cilantro y la menta con la mezcla del salteado estilo chino, y agregue las cebolletas fritas como adorno de la ensalada. Sirva con un chorrito de lima [limón verde].

Sirva sobre camotes asados o machacados.

Lista de compras

1 manojo de cilantro
2 dientes de ajo
2 pulgadas [5,08 cm] de jengibre
2 cucharadas de jugo de lima
[limón verde]
¼ de taza de menta
1 manojo de hojas de mostaza
1½ lb. [680,4 g] de rockfish
1 manojo de cebolletas

Revise la despensa

Aceite de coco
Salsa de pescado o vinagre de
umeboshi
Sal marina
Coco rallado
Salsa de soya o aminoácidos de
coco

Camotes asados (vea semana dos: Cena del martes) o puré de camote   Rinde 4 porciones

2 lb. [907,2 g] de camotes
¼ de taza de aceite de oliva virgen extra
¾ de cucharadita de sal marina, o más al gusto
¼ de taza de leche de coco
Pimienta negra recién molida

Pele los camotes y córtelos en pedazos de tamaño mediano. Colóquelos en una cacerola (1 galón [3,785 l]) llenando la cacerola con agua fría. Cubra las verduras por 2 pulgadas [5,08 cm].

Lleve las verduras a hervir, tapadas, sobre fuego alto. Siga hirviendo hasta que sean perforadas fácilmente con un tenedor, alrededor de 15–20 minutos. Escurra y ponga aparte.

Ponga las verduras en un cuenco grande con el aceite de oliva y el aceite de coco, la leche de coco y la sal. Machaque con un machacador de papas hasta que quede cremoso, añadiendo más sal si así desea.

Opción para después: mantenga las verduras machacadas calientes a través de mantenerlas tapadas en un cuenco de metal sobre un sartén de agua hirviendo a fuego lento hasta por una hora (baño maría).

Lista de compras

2 lb. [907,2 g] de camotes

Revise la despensa

Granos de pimienta negra
Leche de coco
Aceite de oliva virgen extra
Sal marina

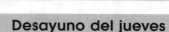
Desayuno del jueves

Coctel "Eres amado"   Rinde 1–2 porciones

El apio es una buena fuente de vitamina C, beta-caroteno y manganeso: antioxidantes que han demostrado brindar beneficios contra la inflamación.

3 zanahorias, bien fregadas, sin hojas o tallos y con ambos extremos recortados
2 pencas de apio con hojas
1 pepino, pelado si no es orgánico
1 puñado de espinaca
1 limón [amarillo], pelado si no es orgánico
½ remolacha, bien fregada, con tallos y hojas

Corte la fruta o la verdura para que quepa en el tubo de alimentación de su extractor de jugos. Procese los ingredientes en su extractor y revuelva. Sirva en un vaso y beba tan pronto como sea posible.

Lista de compras

1 remolacha con hojas	1 pepino
3 zanahorias	1 limón [amarillo]
2 pencas de apio	1 puñado de espinaca

Almuerzo del jueves

Ensalada HUM con aguacate y garbanzos

HUM significa "hágala-usted-mismo". Aquí es donde sucede la magia de las ensaladas: improvisar en su cocina con las frutas y verduras que usted tiene a la mano, para hacer una ensalada fresca sobre la marcha que sirva como una comida completa o como guarnición. Piense más allá de la típica lechuga; pique cualquier cosa colorida y fresca para su ensalada, y experimente con hierbas frescas para realmente hacer que las cosas brillen. Pique las verduras en pedazos que pueda comer de un bocado, especialmente si son verduras firmes como la remolacha o las zanahorias. Complemente su ensalada con aguacate y garbanzos hoy para convertirla en una comida completa.

Aquí esté una lista de ingredientes de inicio para hacer ensaladas. ¡Lo animo a que encuentre todavía más ingredientes para hacer que sus ensaladas sean fantásticas!

Manzanas
Rúcula
Espárragos
Aguacate
Frijoles cocidos
Remolacha
Bok choy
Zanahorias
Apio
Garbanzos cocidos
Rábano blanco (daikon)
Hojas de diente de león
Habas
Ajo
Jengibre
Hierbas frescas (albahaca, menta, cilantro, romero)

Jícama
Col rizada
Hojas de mostaza
Nectarinas
Nueces/semillas
Duraznos
Peras
Radicchio
Rábanos
Cebolletas
Fresas (frutillas)
Acelga roja
Nabos
Berro

Lista de compras

Su elección de la lista anterior, unas 2–3 tazas por persona

Fotografía por Polara Studio

Cena del jueves

Albahaca salteada al estilo chino con pollo
Rinde 4 porciones

Servida con quinoa básica (semana uno: Almuerzo del lunes)
Las hojas de albahaca fresca hacen que esta receta sea fresca y colorida. Utilice menta completa para una variación divertida.

1 lb. [453 g] de pollo deshuesado (o tofu)
2 cucharadas de aceite de semilla de uva o de aceite de coco
1 pieza de jengibre de 1 pulgada [2,54 cm], picada
2 dientes de ajo, picados
2 tazas de zanahorias, rebanadas sesgadas
1 cabeza de brócoli, cortada en grumos
1 cabeza de bok choy, rebanada sesgada
½ taza de hojas de albahaca completa, apretada (remueva los tallos largos)
4 cucharadas de caldo (pollo) o agua

Marinada

1–2 cucharadas de salsa de soya (o aminoácidos de coco)
1 cucharada de arrurruz (o harina de tapioca)
2 cucharadas de vinagre de arroz

Corte el pollo en piezas de 2 pulgadas [5,08 cm] de menos de ½ pulgada [1,27 cm] de ancho. Mezcle la marinada en un cuenco con un batidor para integrarla. Marine el pollo durante 10–20 minutos.

Caliente el aceite en un sartén grande o en un wok sobre una flama muy alta. Cuando el aceite comience a formar ondas, introduzca la carne revolviendo, dejando marinada en el cuenco para un uso posterior. Cuando la carne comience a dorar, añada el ajo y el jengibre durante 15 segundos, luego añada las verduras. Rápidamente revuelva las verduras y el pollo hasta que ambos estén cocidos, alrededor de 3–5 minutos solamente. Agregue revolviendo el caldo o el agua con la marinada restante. Cocine a fuego lento durante 1–2 minutos más.

Complementos opcionales: 1 cucharadita de aceite de ajonjolí, 2 cucharadas de néctar de agave, 2 cucharadas de vinagre de arroz, 1 cucharada de aceite de chile picante, ¼ de taza de nueces de la India.

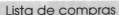

Lista de compras

Albahaca
1 cabeza de bok choy
1½ lb. [680,4 g] de pollo deshuesado
Brócoli
6 zanahorias
Ajo
Jengibre
Cebolletas

Revise la despensa

Harina de arrurruz o tapioca
Caldo de pollo
Aminoácidos de coco o salsa de
    soya
Aceite de coco
Vinagre de mirin o vino de arroz
Quinoa

Desayuno del viernes

Licuado de coco   Rinde 1–2 porciones

En estudios científicos se ha descubierto que el aceite de coco tiene propiedades antiinflamatorias y analgésicas.

1 taza de leche de coco
1 cucharada de aceite de coco virgen
1 cucharada de semillas de linaza molidas
1 cucharadita de extracto de vainilla puro
¼ de cucharadita de extracto de almendras
Varias gotas de stevia líquida
8–10 cubos de hielo

Coloque todos los ingredientes, excepto el hielo, en una licuadora y procese a alta velocidad hasta que quede bien combinado. Añada el hielo después de que licúe el aceite de coco para que no se apelmace. Usted puede utilizar más o menos hielo, dependiendo de qué tan frío prefiera su licuado.

Lista de compras

1 envase o lata de leche de coco
1 paquete de semillas de linaza

Revise la despensa

Extracto de almendras
Stevia líquida
Extracto de vainilla puro
Aceite de coco virgen

Almuerzo del viernes

Bisque de calabaza moscada con ensalada HUM

¡Agasájese por sus esfuerzos esta semana! Descongele su sopa y haga una nueva versión de una ensalada HUM con los ingredientes que tenga a la mano. ¡Esta combinación le hará ahorrar tiempo y lo pondrá en posición de disfrutar un excelente fin de semana con nuevas recetas por venir!

Bisque de calabaza moscada.— semana dos: Almuerzo del miércoles

Ensalada HUM.— semana dos: Almuerzo del jueves

Cena del viernes

Ensalada de fideos asiáticos con camarón silvestre con vinagreta de wasabi a la lima   Rinde 4–6 porciones

Ensalada de fideos asiáticos con camarón silvestre

½ lb. [226,8 g] de fideos de arroz
1½ lb. [680,4 g] de camarón silvestre, pelado y desvenado
2 cucharadas de aceite de ajonjolí
4 zanahorias rayadas
1 pepino holandés (sin semillas), con las semillas removidas y rallado
2 tazas de germinado de frijol de soya mung, enjuagado y escurrido
1 manojo de cebolletas, en rebanadas delgadas
½ manojo de hojas de su elección (mostaza, bok choy, etc.)
2 tazas de nueces tostadas
¼ de taza de cilantro o menta frescos, cortados en trozos grandes

Vinagreta de wasabi a la lima

2 cucharadas de wasabi en polvo (preparado con 2 cucharadas de agua tibia, déjelo reposar 10 minutos antes de usarlo)
½ de taza de jugo de lima [limón verde].
⅓ de taza de aceite de oliva virgen extra
½ cucharadita de sal marina
1 pieza de 1½ pulgadas [3,81 cm] de jengibre, pelada y picada
1 cucharada de aceite de ajonjolí

Fotografía por Polara Studio

Mezcle los ingredientes de la vinagreta y ponga aparte en un cuenco.

133

Hierva agua en una olla y sumerja los fideos. Apague el fuego y suavice los fideos durante 10 minutos.

Cocine el camarón en un sartén mediano mediante agregar ½ taza de agua al sartén. Llévelo a hervir, añada el camarón y tápelo hasta que quede opaco y esté bien cocido, unos 5–6 minutos.

Escurra los fideos y colóquelos en un cuenco con los ingredientes restantes. Añada la ½ taza de vinagreta de wasabi a la lima, para cubrir bien, añadiendo más al gusto. Acomode el camarón sobre los fideos, o mézclelos.

Este plato es excelente servido a temperatura ambiente o helado con un poco de salsa extra como complemento.

Lista de compras

4 zanahorias
1 pepino holandés (sin semilla)
1 manojo de hojas de su elección
½ taza de jugo de lima [limón verde].
1 manojo de menta fresca o cilantro
2 tazas de germinado de frijol de soya mung
1 manojo de cebolletas
1½ lb. [680,4 g] de camarón silvestre, pelado y desvenado

Revise la despensa

Aceite de oliva virgen extra
Fideos de arroz
Sal marina
Aceite de ajonjolí
Nueces, tostadas
Wasabi en polvo

Desayuno del sábado

Refrescante de menta   Rinde 1–2 porciones

El hinojo es rico en el fitonutriente anetol. En estudios de animales, este nutriente ha mostrado repetidamente reducir la inflamación y ayudar a prevenir la ocurrencia de cáncer.

2 tallos de hinojo con sus hojas
½ pepino, pelado si no es orgánico
½ manzana verde como la Granny Smith o la Newton Pippin
1 pequeño puñado de menta
1 pieza de 1 pulgada [2,54 cm] de raíz de jengibre, fregada o pelada si está vieja

Corte la fruta o la verdura para que quepa en el tubo de alimentación de su extractor de jugos. Procese los ingredientes en su extractor y revuelva. Sirva en un vaso y beba tan pronto como sea posible.

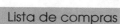

Lista de compras

1 pepino
1 bulbo de hinojo
1 trozo de 1 pulgada [2,54 cm] de
    raíz de jengibre

1 manzana verde
1 manojo de menta

Almuerzo del sábado

Rollitos primavera vegetarianos con salsa de jengibre y menta   Rinde 4 porciones

Rollitos primavera vegetarianos

Estos rollitos de ensalada lo van a hacer querer moverse. El jengibre, la menta y las hojas de mostaza son estimulantes para el cuerpo, y ayudan con la concentración y la digestión. Las peras nutren los pulmones y también ayudan a remover el exceso de moco o flema del cuerpo. ¡Salga a jugar!

½ manojo de hojas de mostaza
½ manojo de lechuga
1 zanahoria rayada
1 pera rebanada
1 manojo de cebolletas
1 aguacate
½ taza de germinado

½ manojo de cilantro
½ manojo de albahaca
Fideos de arroz cocidos (opcional)
Hongo shiitake (opcional)
Papel de arroz comestible (hojas
    grandes)

Fotografía por Polara Studio

135

Salsa de jengibre y menta

¼ de taza de menta, finamente
   picada
3 cucharadas de jengibre, picado
½ taza de vinagre de arroz
⅓ de taza de aceite de oliva
   virgen extra

1 cucharada colmada de miel
2 pizcas de sal marina
Chiles secos tailandeses
   (opcional)

Combine todos los ingredientes, bátalos juntos y póngalos aparte.

Para los rollitos primavera: Reúna sus ingredientes. Limpie bien sus frutas y verduras. Remueva los tallos de las hojas y la lechuga. Ralle la zanahoria. Rebane la pera y las cebolletas en rebanadas delgadas. Rebane el aguacate. Prepárese para enrollar.

Llene un cuenco grande con agua tibia. Sumerja el papel de arroz en el agua tibia y revuelva, 10 segundos.

Coloque una hoja de papel de arroz en la tabla para picar, con el lado áspero hacia abajo. Corónelo con las hojas de mostaza, la lechuga y los fideos y los hongos opcionales. Coloque un poco de cada ingrediente restante en el tercio inferior del wrap. Doble el lado más cercano a usted sobre los ingredientes, luego doble ambos extremos hacia adentro. Enrolle hacia adelante para terminar y colóquelo con el extremo del rollo hacia abajo. Repita hasta que utilice todos los ingredientes. Luego acomode en un plato y sirva con la salsa de jengibre y menta.

Lista de compras

1 aguacate
1 manojo de albahaca, otro de
   cilantro y otro de menta
1 zanahoria
1 pulgada [2,54 cm] de jengibre
1 cabeza de lechuga
1 manojo de hojas de mostaza
1 pera
1 paquete de hojas de papel de
   arroz comestible
1 manojo de cebolletas
1 taza de hongos shiitake (opcional)
1 pinta seca de germinados
2 chiles tailandeses (secos,
   opcionales)

Revise la despensa

Aceite de oliva virgen extra
Miel cruda
Fideos de arroz (vermicelli)
Vinagre de arroz
Sal marina

Cena del sábado

Salmón y espárrago asados con chutney de fruta de drupa y lavanda   Rinde 4–6 porciones

Piense en duraznos, ciruelas y nectarinas maduras. Piense en asados. ¡Piense en el verano! Esta es una receta por completo de verano y se disfruta mejor al exterior. Yo añado un toque de lavanda al chutney por diversión, pero no es esencial.

Salmón y espárrago asados
1½–2 lb. [680,4–907,2 g] de salmón silvestre
2 manojos de espárragos
2 cucharadas de aceite de oliva virgen extra
Sal marina, al gusto
Pimienta negra recién molida, al gusto

Prepare el asador para calor alto
Cubra el salmón con aceite de oliva por ambos lados con una brocha. Añada sal y pimienta al salmón liberalmente.

Añada aceite ligeramente a los espárragos y sazone con sal y pimienta. Coloque los espárragos en el asador y ase entre 5–7 minutos o hasta que se tornen verde brillante y se glaseen.

Ase el salmón con el lado de la piel hacia abajo durante 5 minutos. Voltee y siga cocinando de 4–5 minutos o hasta que quede cocido. Remueva el salmón del asador y corone con el chutney.

Fotografía por Polara Studio

137

Chutney de fruta de drupa y lavanda

2 lb. [907,2 g] de fruta de drupa, picada en cubos pequeños
1 cebolla grande, finamente picada
Ralladura de 1 limón [amarillo] o 1 lima [limón verde]
2 cucharadas de ajo, finamente picado
¼ de cucharadita de chile seco molido (opcional)
⅓ de taza de vinagre de vino tinto
¾ de taza de miel cruda o agave
¾ de cucharadita de sal marina
2 cucharadas de lavanda fresca (o use albahaca o menta; utilice solamente 1
   cucharadita de lavanda seca si no puede encontrarla fresca)

En una cacerola combine todos los ingredientes preparados excepto las hierbas. Llévelo a hervir. Continúe cociendo en un hervor, 15 minutos. Revuelva ocasionalmente. Mezcle las hierbas frescas o lavanda al final.

Lista de compras

2 manojos de espárragos
2 dientes de ajo
2 cucharadas de lavanda, albahaca
   o menta fresca
1 limón [amarillo] o lima [limón
   verde]
1½–2 lb. [680,4-907,2 g] de salmón
   silvestre
2 lb. [907,2 g] de frutas de drupa
1 cebolla amarilla

Revise la despensa

Granos de pimienta negra
Chile seco molido (opcional)
Aceite de oliva virgen extra
Miel cruda o agave
Vinagre de vino tinto
Sal marina

Desayuno del domingo

Chai verde dulce Rinde 2 porciones

La espinaca contiene ácido lipoico, que ayuda a las vitaminas C y E a regenerarse y tiene efectos contra la inflamación.

1 taza de leche de almendras
1 pera, cortada en trozos
1 taza de hojas tiernas de espinaca
½ cucharadita de canela molida
⅛ de cucharadita de cardamomo molido
⅛ cucharadita de cilantro molido
⅛ cucharadita de clavo molido
⅛ de cucharadita de pimienta negra recién molida
5–6 gotas de stevia
6 cubos de hielo (o 6 cubos de té chai verde congelado)

Combine todos los ingredientes en una licuadora y procese hasta obtener un batido cremoso. Sírvalo frío.

Lista de compras	Revise la despensa
Leche de almendras	Granos de pimienta negra
1 taza de hojas tiernas de espinaca	Cardamomo
1 pera	Canela
	Cilantro
	Clavo molido
	Stevia

Desayuno-almuerzo dominical

Panqueques de manzana con canela
Rinde 4–6 porciones

Los panqueques ocasionales son una manera genial de iniciar un fin de semana. Involucre a uno de sus seres queridos para que le ayude a rallar las manzanas o a voltear los panqueques mientras usted limpia las manchas que hayan causado los ingredientes al repartir la mezcla. ¡Estos panqueques son una manera refrescante y gratificante de comenzar una mañana de otoño con los niños!

2 huevos de gallina libre, bien batidos
1½ tazas de leche de almendra o de coco
2 tazas de harina libre de gluten
¾ de cucharadita de xantano
1 cucharadita de polvo para hornear
½ cucharadita de sal marina
¼ de taza de azúcar de coco
4 manzanas medianas, ralladas
Ralladura de 1 limón [amarillo]
1 cucharadita de canela
½ cucharadita de extracto de vainilla
⅓ de taza de aceite de coco, para cocinar
⅓ de taza de jarabe de dátil, jarabe de arce o miel cruda (como aderezo opcional)

Mezcle el huevo con la leche en un cuenco grande.

En un cuenco mediano cierna el harina, el xantano, el polvo para hornear, la sal marina y el azúcar.

Combine los ingredientes húmedos y secos, y añada revolviendo las manzanas ralladas, la ralladura de limón, la canela y el extracto de vainilla.

Caliente una capa delgada de aceite de coco en un sartén grande a fuego medio. Vierta grandes cucharadas de la mezcla en el sartén, aplanando un poco con el reverso de la cuchara. Cocine hasta que quede dorado por debajo. Voltee, presione con la espátula y cocine unos dos minutos más o hasta que quede completamente cocido.

Sirva de inmediato con el jarabe de su elección. ¡Mantenga los panqueques calientes en el horno mientras termina de hacer el resto!

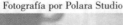

Fotografía por Polara Studio

Lista de compras

4 manzanas medianas
2 huevos de gallina libre
1 limón [amarillo]

Revise la despensa

Leche de almendra o de coco
Polvo para hornear
Canela
Aceite de coco
Azúcar de coco
Jarabe de dátil, jarabe de arce o
    miel (elija su favorita para los
    panqueques)
Harina libre de gluten
Sal marina
Extracto de vainilla
Xantano

Almuerzo del domingo

Sopa asiática de pollo   Rinde 8 porciones

Esta es una nutritiva sopa de origen sureño. Yo la hago en mi cocina con frecuencia, y la disfruto como un almuerzo o cena ligero en cualquier momento en que siento que mi sistema inmune necesita un refuerzo. La riqueza de la miso de garbanzo (¡libre de soya!) le añade profundidad. Agregue raíz de astragalus si puede encontrarla.

¼ de taza de aceite de ajonjolí refinado
8 rebanadas de jengibre pelado
2 cebollas amarillas, rebanadas
5 muslos o pechugas de
    pollo, deshuesados o
    con la carne rebanada
    sin hueso
4 tazas de verduras de raíz
    (zanahoria, nabo, nabicol,
    bardana) picadas
½ cucharada de pimienta
    negra recién molida
1 cucharadita de sal, al gusto
2–3 cuartos [1893-2839 ml]
    de caldo de pollo
⅓ de taza de pasta miso
1–2 tazas de arroz integral
    cocido (opcional, añada
    al final)

Photo by Polara Studio

141

Especias

½ cucharada de jengibre en polvo
4 vainas verdes de cardamomo
1 raja de canela
1 trozo de raíz de astragalus (opcional)

Saltee la cebolla y el jengibre en el aceite de ajonjolí. Cuando esté ligeramente dorado, añada el pollo y saltee unos 5 minutos más. Agregue las verduras de raíz y las especias. Luego añada el caldo y llévelo a hervir. Reduzca a fuego medio-bajo y cocine durante 45 minutos a una hora.

Diez minutos antes de terminar, revuelva la pasta miso mezclada con un poco de caldo en un cuenco pequeño, luego agrégueselo a la sopa. Añada sal y pimienta, al gusto. Agregue arroz cocido, si así lo desea.

Lista de compras

5 muslos o piernas de pollo,
   deshuesado
4 pulgadas [10,16 cm] de jengibre
4–5 verduras de raíz
2 cebollas amarillas

Revise la despensa

Raíz de astragalus (opcional)
Granos de pimienta negra
1–2 tazas de arroz integral cocido
   (opcional)
Vainas de cardamomo
Caldo de pollo
Canela en raja
Jengibre en polvo
Pasta miso
Aceite de ajonjolí refinado
   (apropiado para cocinar)
Sal marina

Cena del domingo

Hamburguesa de frijoles negros con arroz integral horneado y ensalada de zanahorias ralladas
Rinde 6–8 porciones

Hamburguesa de frijoles negros

¿Olvidó remojar los frijoles? Está bien; usted puede eliminar este paso mediante utilizar kombu fresco, un alga utilizada en la cocina japonesa. El kombu desactiva la enzima inhibidora del ácido fítico que nos hace sentirnos distendidos si no remojamos los frijoles. Corte un pedazo de 3 pulgadas [7,62 cm] de kombu y cubra los frijoles con agua, llévelo a hervir durante 5 minutos, luego apague el fuego. Escurra 2 horas después y proceda a cocinar los frijoles con el kombu.

2 tazas de frijoles negros cocidos (conserve el líquido donde los coció)
¼ de taza de aceite de oliva virgen extra y un poco más para engrasasar la
    plancha para hornear
¾ de taza de harina libre de gluten
1 pizca de sal marina
¼ de taza de miso de garbanzo
2 cucharadas de aceite de coco
1 taza de cebollas amarillas, finamente picadas
2 dientes de ajo, finamente picados
2 cucharaditas de comino molido
1 cucharadita de cúrcuma molida
1 cucharadita de cilantro molido
2 cucharadas de jugo de lima [limón verde]
¼ de taza de cilantro, finamente picado
1 cucharadita de sal marina, al gusto

Previamente: cocine los frijoles, cubriéndolos con 1–2 pulgadas [2,54–5,08 cm] de agua sobre el nivel de los frijoles. Lleve los frijoles a hervir, remueva la espuma con una cuchara de madera. Reduzca el fuego y cocine a fuego lento durante 45 minutos a una hora y media, hasta que los frijoles estén suaves.

Precaliente el horno a 350°F [176,7°C]. Ligeramente engrase una plancha para hornear con aceite de oliva. En un cuenco mediano, machaque los frijoles negros hasta que queden densos y

Fotografía por Ben Garvey Photography

143

pastosos. Añada revolviendo ¼ de taza de harina, aceite de oliva, una pizca de sal y el miso. Ponga aparte.

En un sartén, caliente el aceite de coco a fuego medio-alto. Saltee las cebollas durante 5 minutos, revolviendo frecuentemente. Añada el ajo y las especias. Agregue el jugo de lima [limón verde], el cilantro picado y la sal; revuelva bien. Quite del fuego.

Añada las cebollas sazonadas y salteadas a los frijoles machacados, agregue algunas cucharadas del agua donde se cocieron los frijoles de ser necesario para lograr una consistencia más suave. Mezcle el ¼–½ de taza de harina restante y mezcle con las manos hasta que se integre y la mezcla sea homogénea y no se separe.

Divida la mezcla en 6–8 tortas del tamaño de una hamburguesa. Acomode las hamburguesas en la plancha para hornear engrasada y hornee durante unos 20 minutos, volteándolas una vez. Sirva sobre bollos libre de gluten. Congele el sobrante.

Lista de compras

1 manojo de cilantro
2 dientes de ajo
1 lima [limón verde]
1 cebolla amarilla

Revise la despensa

Arroz integral
Miso de garbanzo
Aceite de coco
Frijol negro seco
Aceite de oliva virgen extra
Harina libre de gluten
Cilantro molido
Comino molido
Cúrcuma molida
Sal marina

Arroz integral horneado (vea la semana uno: Cena del martes al final)

Ensalada de zanahorias ralladas   Rinde 4–6 porciones

5 zanahorias grandes
1 bulbo de hinojo grande
½ cabeza de repollo verde
¼ taza de jugo de limón [amarillo]
¼ de taza de vinagre de manzana
⅓ de taza de aceite de oliva virgen extra
Sal marina, al gusto
Pimienta negra recién molida, al gusto
Complementos opcionales: ¼ de taza de perejil picado, 1 cucharadita de comino molido, 2 cucharadas de ajonjolí blanco, 1 cucharada de miel cruda.

Corte las zanahorias en juliana a mano o con una mandolina (en juliana). Pique finamente las frondas del bulbo de hinojo. Corte en rebanadas delgadas el bulbo de hinojo y el repollo con una mandolina (o pique finamente con el cuchillo del chef). Mezcle todas las verduras.

Bata juntos los ingredientes del aderezo, pruebe y ajuste. Mezcle el aderezo con la ensalada y sazónela al gusto con sal y pimienta.

Refrigere durante una hora antes de servir.

Lista de compras	Revise la despensa
½ cabeza de repollo	Vinagre de manzana
5 zanahorias	Granos de pimienta negra
1 bulbo de hinojo	Aceite de oliva virgen extra
1 limón [amarillo] (jugo de limón [amarillo])	Sal marina

Lista de compras de la semana tres

Utensilios de cocina

- ❏ Brochetas de metal o bambú
- ❏ Papel pergamino para cocina

Vino y vinagre para cocinar

- ❏ Vinagre de manzana
- ❏ Vinagre balsámico añejado
- ❏ Vinagre de vino tinto
- ❏ Vinagre de arroz
- ❏ Vinagre de umeboshi
- ❏ Vino blanco seco (o más caldo)

Lácteos y huevos

- ❏ 1 docena huevos

Fruta seca

- ❏ 3 dátiles grandes
- ❏ 1½ tazas de higos frescos o secos

Hierbas y especias secas

- ❏ Granos de pimienta negra
- ❏ Pimienta de Cayena
- ❏ Clavo molido (opcional)
- ❏ Canela molida
- ❏ Canela en raja
- ❏ Cilantro molido

- ❏ Comino molido
- ❏ Garam masala
- ❏ Nuez moscada molida
- ❏ Orégano seco
- ❏ Hojuelas de chile seco molido (opcional)
- ❏ Cúrcuma molida

Artículos secos o enlatados para la despensa

- ❏ 1 lata de corazones de alcachofa
- ❏ Miso de garbanzo
- ❏ Aminoácidos de coco o salsa de soya
- ❏ 2 latas de leche de coco (tamaño regular)
- ❏ Azúcar de coco
- ❏ Hojuelas de alga dulse (opcional)
- ❏ Salsa de pescado (o vinagre de umeboshi)
- ❏ Miel cruda
- ❏ 1 paquete de kelp (kombu)
- ❏ 1 bolsa de fideos de kelp (12 onzas [340,2 g]) (Los encuentra en la sección de refrigerados de la tienda)
- ❏ Jarabe de arce
- ❏ Melaza
- ❏ 1 taza de puré de calabaza

❏ Pasta de curry rojo
❏ Sal marina
❏ Frasco pequeño de pasta de tamarindo
❏ Pasta de ciruela umeboshi
❏ Levadura nutricional

Extractos y edulcorantes

❏ Extracto de almendras
❏ Stevia líquido (sugerimos la stevia líquida de la marca Sweet Leaf sabor Vanilla Crème)

Pescado, aves, carnes

❏ 5 lb. [2268 g] de pechuga de pollo o muslo, deshuesado y sin piel
❏ 1 lb. [453 g] de fletán, sin espinas y cortado en dos partes
❏ 4 piezas de salmón de 6 onzas [170,1 g] cada una (1½ lb. [680,4 g])

Harinas

❏ Harina de arrurruz/harina de tapioca
❏ Harina libre de gluten

Hierbas frescas y especias

❏ 4 hojas de laurel
❏ 3 manojos de albahaca

❏ 1 manojo de cebollín
❏ 2 manojos de cilantro
❏ 1 manojo de eneldo
❏ 4 pulgadas de jengibre
❏ 2 manojos de menta
❏ 4 manojos de perejil
❏ 2 ramitas de romero
❏ 1 manojo de tomillo

Granos y leguminosas

❏ 1 lata de judías adzuki (o ½ taza de judías adzuki cocidas y drenadas)
❏ 1 taza de amaranto seco
❏ 1 taza de arroz integral
❏ 3 tazas de garbanzos cocidos
❏ 2 tazas de quinoa
❏ 2 tazas de lentejas rojas
❏ 1 lata de alubias (o ½ taza de alubias, cocinadas)
❏ ⅓ lb. [151,2 g] de alubias secas

Nueces y semillas

❏ 3 cucharadas de almendras
❏ 4 tazas de leche de almendras
❏ ½ taza de nueces de la India
❏ ½ taza de hojuelas de coco rallado (sin edulcorar)

- ❏ ¾ de taza de leche de coco
- ❏ ¾ de taza de nueces

Aceites

- ❏ Aceite de coco
- ❏ Aceite de oliva virgen extra
- ❏ Aceite de semilla de uva
- ❏ Aceite de ajonjolí sin refinar

Frutas y verduras

Frutas

- ❏ 3 manzanas
- ❏ 2 manzanas verdes
- ❏ 3 aguacates
- ❏ 1 taza de arándanos azules
- ❏ 11 limones [amarillos]
- ❏ 1 taza de jugo de limón [amarillo] (o 4-5 limones más)
- ❏ 6 limas [limón verde]
- ❏ 1 naranja
- ❏ 2 peras

Verduras

- ❏ 4 remolachas (1 lb. [453 g])
- ❏ 1 cabeza de bok choy
- ❏ 4 tazas de mezcla de hojas para dorar a fuego lento (¼ lb. [113,4 g])
- ❏ 3 lb. [1361 g] de brócoli
- ❏ 18 zanahorias (4 lb. [1814 g])
- ❏ 2 pencas de apio + 3 tallos

- ❏ 7 pepinos
- ❏ 1 pepino holandés
- ❏ 4 cabezas de hinojo
- ❏ 3 cabezas de ajo
- ❏ 1 hojas de lechuga verde oscuro (usted puede usar lechuga de hoja morada; véase abajo)
- ❏ 1 manojo de col rizada, acelga o berzas (a su elección)
- ❏ 5 manojos de col rizada
- ❏ 2 lb. [907,2 g] de chirivía
- ❏ 1 manojo de rábanos
- ❏ 1 cabeza de repollo rojo
- ❏ 2 cabezas de lechuga de hoja morada
- ❏ 2 cebolla morada
- ❏ 12 tazas de mezcla de hoja verdes para ensalada (¾ lb. [340,2 g])
- ❏ 5 manojos de cebolletas
- ❏ 4 chalotas
- ❏ 1 calabaza espagueti grande
- ❏ 1 lb. [453 g] de espinacas
- ❏ 4 camotes
- ❏ 6 tazas de nabos
- ❏ 2 lb. [907,2 g] de verduras de raíz de su elección (chirivía, nabicol, nabo, etc.)
- ❏ 1 manojo de berro
- ❏ 5 cebollas amarillas grande

❑ 2 calabazas italianas

Caldos

❑ 5 cuartos [4732 ml] de
caldo de verduras o de pollo

Menús y recetas de la semana tres

Desayuno del lunes

Giro Waldorf   Rinde 1 porción

Las manzanas Granny Smith contienen un poco más de potasio que el resto de las manzanas. El potasio mantiene equilibrados los fluidos alrededor y dentro de las células, lo cual es vital para el intercambio eléctrico diario en nuestro cuerpo. Si no se consume diariamente suficiente potasio, usted posiblemente termine teniendo un latido del corazón irregular.

1 manzana verde
3 tallos de apio orgánico con sus hojas
1 Limón [amarillo], pelado si no es orgánico

Corte la fruta y la verdura para que quepa en el tubo de alimentación de su extractor de jugos. Procese los ingredientes y revuelva. Vierta en un vaso y beba tan pronto como sea posible.

Lista de compras

1 manzana verde   1 Limón [amarillo]
1 manojo de apio

Almuerzo del lunes

Ensalada mediterránea de quinoa con frituras de chirivía   Rinde 4 porciones

Ensalada mediterránea de quinoa

1 taza de quinoa seca
6 cebolletas, rebanadas finamente
2 tazas de perejil de hoja plana, finamente picado
3 tazas de menta fresca, finamente picada
2 pepinos, sin semillas y finamente picados
2 tazas de hojas tiernas de espinacas
½ taza de aceite de oliva virgen extra
½ taza de jugo de limón [amarillo]
½ cucharadita de sal marina (o más si hace falta)
1 cucharadita de comino molido
1 taza de garbanzos cocidos
2 pechugas de pollo, cocidas y rebanadas (opcional)

Ponga a hervir 2 tazas de agua con la quinoa, sin tapar. Coloque la tapa, baje el fuego y hierva a fugo lento durante 15 minutos. Apague el fuego y permita que la quinoa se mantenga cociéndose al vapor durante 5 minutos. Destape y esponje la quinoa con un tenedor.

Mientras tanto, pique las verduras de la ensalada y cocine el pollo, algunas opciones pueden ser: escalfarlo, cocerlo al vapor o asarlo

Combine los ingredientes de la ensalada con la quinoa en un cuenco y sírvalo inmediatamente o bien mantenga en la nevera; ¡es excelente frío como una sola comida en una ensalada sencilla!

Lista de compras

2 pechugas de pollo
2 pepinos
1 manojo de menta
1 puñado de perejil
1 manojo de cebolletas
2 tazas de espinacas

Revise la despensa

Garbanzos
Comino molido
Aceite de oliva virgen extra
Jugo de limón [amarillo]
Quinoa
Sal marina

Fritura de chirivía

Sustituya las zanahorias por chirivía en la receta de "Frituras de zanahoria" (semana dos: Almuerzo del martes).

Cena del lunes

Camarón asado al ajo y brócoli servido con quinoa y cebolleta   Rinde 4 porciones

2 lb. [907,2 g] de brócoli, cortado en pequeños grumos
3 dientes de ajo, picados finamente
2 lb. [907,2 g] de camarones silvestres, pelados y desvenados
2 cucharadas de vinagre de umeboshi
2 cucharadas de aminoácidos de coco o salsa de soya
2 cucharadas de harina de tapioca
¾ cucharadita de sal marina
½ cucharadita de pimienta negra recién molida
⅓ taza de aceite de coco fluidificado
2 tazas de quinoa cocida
1 manojo de cebolletas, rebanadas finamente de manera sesgada
Unas gotitas de limón [amarillo] (opcional)

Precaliente el horno a 425ºF [218,3ºC].

Revuelva el brócoli, el ajo, 2 cucharadas de aceite y la mitad de la sal y la pimienta. Extienda el brócoli en una plancha para hornear y ase durante 10

151

minutos. Mientras tanto, en un cuenco mezcle juntos el sobrante del aceite, la sal y la pimienta, el vinagre de umeboshi, los aminos o tamari y el harina de tapioca, agitando hasta mezclar completamente. Enjuague bien los camarones y métalos en la mezcla.

Añada los camarones a la plancha para hornear (o en una plancha nueva si necesita más espacio) y ase durante 10 minutos más, dele vuelta a los camarones a la mitad del tiempo de cocción para asegurar que estén completamente cocinados.

Sazone los camarones y el brócoli con unas gotas de jugo de limón si lo desea. Sírvalo aún caliente con la quinoa cocinada y las cebolletas.

Para cocinar la quinoa: Combine 2 tazas de agua con 1 taza de quinoa seca y póngalas al fuego hasta que suelten el hervor. Tape y deje cocinar a fuego lento durante 20 minutos. Mezcle con las cebolletas picadas y sirva acompañando los camarones y el brócoli.

Lista de compras

2 lb. [907,2 g] de brócoli
1 limón [amarillo] (opcional)
1 manojo de cebolletas
1 lb. [453 g] de camarones
    silvestres, pelados y
    desvenados

Revise la despensa

Granos de pimienta negra
Aminoácidos de coco o salsa de
    soya
Ajo
Aceite de semilla de uva Quinoa
Sal marina
Vinagre de umeboshi

Desayuno del martes

Batido matutino de Cherie   Rinde 2 porciones

El apio reduce la inflamación. Si usted está padeciendo de dolor en las articulaciones, infección en los pulmones, asma, o acné, comer más apio le traerá un muy necesario alivio. También ayuda a tranquilizarse y aliviar el estrés. Los minerales del apio, especialmente el magnesio, y sus aceites esenciales tranquilizan el sistema nervioso. Si le gusta comer apio por la tarde, usted dormirá mejor.

4–5 zanahorias, bien fregadas, sin hojas o tallos y con ambos extremos recortados
4 hojas verde oscuro, como el acelga, la col rizada o las berzas
2 tallos de apio con hojas
1 pepino grande, pelado si no es orgánico
1 limón [amarillo] pelado, si no es orgánico
1 trozo de 1 pulgada [2,54 cm] de raíz de jengibre

Corte la fruta y la verdura para que quepa en el tubo de alimentación de su extractor de jugos. Proceso los ingredientes y revuelva. Vierta en un vaso y beba tan pronto como sea posible.

Lista de compras

4–5 zanahorias
2 tallos de apio con hojas
1 pepino grande
1 trozo de 1 pulgada [2,54 cm] de raíz de jengibre

4 hojas verde oscuro, como acelga, col rizada o berzas
1 limón [amarillo]

Almuerzo del martes

Cuscús de nabo con dal de lentejas y pepino encurtido   Rinde 4 porciones

Cuscús de nabo

6 tazas de nabos, picados en cubos de 1 pulgada [2,54 cm]
½ taza de nueces de la India
1 cucharada más 1 cucharadita de sal marina
2 cucharadas de vinagre de arroz

Coloque los nabos y las nueces de la India en un procesador de alimentos y pique con impulsos breves hasta tener los ingredientes del tamaño de granos de arroz. Hágalo por partes si es necesario.

Presione el "arroz" en un colador sobre un cuenco para eliminar cualquier exceso de líquido.

Combine el "arroz" con sal y vinagre y revuelva. Extienda una capa delgada sobre una plancha para hornear y hornee a la temperatura más baja del horno, 150ºF [65,66ºC] o menos. Deshidrátelo si es una opción para usted.

Para hornear en horno convencional: 30–45 minutos (hasta que esté ligeramente seco).

Para el deshidratador (115ºF [46,11ºC]): 1½–2 horas.

Dal de lentejas

1 cebolla amarilla grande, picada en pequeños cubos
2 dientes de ajo, finamente picados
1 trozo de 2 pulgadas [5,08 cm] de jengibre, finamente picado (¼ de taza)
3 cucharadas de aceite de semilla de uva
1 taza de lentejas rojas, enjuagadas y drenadas
6 tazas de agua o caldo de verduras
2 hojas de laurel
1 raja de canela completa
1 taza de cilantro, picado
¾ de taza de jugo de limón [amarillo]
1½–2 cucharaditas de sal marina
½ lb. [226,8 g] de espinacas

Especias

2 cucharadas de cúrcuma molida
1 cucharada de garam masala
¼ de cucharadita de clavo molido (opcional)

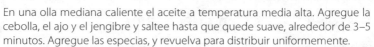
En una olla mediana caliente el aceite a temperatura media alta. Agregue la cebolla, el ajo y el jengibre y saltee hasta que quede suave, alrededor de 3–5 minutos. Agregue las especias, y revuelva para distribuir uniformemente.

Añada las lentejas, el agua o caldo, las hojas de laurel y la raja de canela entera. Mezcle y deje hervir. Reduzca el fuego, tape, deje hervir a fuego lento durante 20–25 minutos hasta que las lentejas estén tiernas, pero no pastosas.

Remueva la canela en raja y las hojas de laurel. Agregue el cilantro picado, el jugo de limón [amarillo] y la sal. Incorpore las espinacas y compruebe el sazón, si desea añada un poco más de jugo de limón y sal.

Pepino encurtido

¼ taza de vinagre de manzana
2 pepinos, sin semilla y picados en trozos pequeños
¼ cucharadita de sal marina

Combine todos los ingredientes y sazone al gusto. Añada semillas de comino y pimienta de Cayena, si lo desea más condimentado.

Lista de compras	Revise la despensa
1 manojo de cilantro	Vinagre de manzana
2 dientes de ajo	Hojas de laurel
2 pepinos	Nueces de la India
1 trozo de 2 pulgadas [5,08 cm] de jengibre	Garam masala
	Aceite de semilla de uva
½ lb. [226,8 g] de espinacas	Clavo molido (opcional)
6 tazas de nabos	Jugo de limón [amarillo]
1 cebolla amarilla grande	Lentejas rojas
	Vinagre de arroz
	Sal marina
	Cúrcuma
	Agua o caldo de verduras
	Canela en raja entera

Cena del martes

Sopa toscana de alubias y col rizada con frituras de kelp   Rinde 6 porciones

Sopa toscana de alubias y col rizada

Esta sopa en una versión de la clásica ribollita que tradicionalmente contiene tomates, panceta y queso. A mi familia le encanta esta versión vegetariana, es un elemento básico en mi cocina durante el invierno.

⅓ lb. [151,2 g] de alubias secas, remojadas durante toda la noche (o remojadas rápidamente)
2 cucharadas de aceite de oliva virgen extra
1½ tazas de cebolla amarilla picada
4 dientes de ajo finamente picados
1 taza de hinojo picado
1 taza de apio picado
2 cucharaditas de sal marina, o más al gusto
¾ cucharadita de pimienta negra recién molida
2 cucharaditas de orégano seco
6 tazas de col rizada picada (2 manojos)
¼ taza de albahaca fresca picada
4 tazas de caldo, de preferencia hecho en casa
⅓ de taza de miso de garbanzo
3 cucharadas de levadura nutricional

Drene las alubias remojadas y colóquelas al fuego en una olla grande con 8 tazas de agua, y deje hervir. Baje el fuego y deje hervir a fuego lento sin tapar durante 40 minutos. Añada 1 cucharadita de sal y continúe hirviendo a fuego lento durante 10 minutos, hasta que las alubias estén tiernas. Retire del fuego y permita que las alubias se enfríen en su propio líquido.

Mientras tanto, caliente el aceite en una olla grande. Añada las cebollas y el ajo y cueza a fuego medio-bajo durante 7–10 minutos, hasta que las cebollas estén translucidas. Agregue el hinojo, el apio, 2 pizcas de sal, la pimienta y el orégano. Cocine a fuego medio-bajo durante 7–10 minutos, hasta que las verduras estén tiernas. Añada la col rizada, y la albahaca y cocine a fuego medio-bajo moviendo ocasionalmente, durante otros 7–10 minutos.

Drene las alubias, reserve el líquido donde se cocieron. En el cuenco del procesador de alimentos adaptado con las aspas de acero, haga puré la mitad de las alubias con un poco del líquido donde se cocieron. Añádalo a la olla, junto con el resto de las alubias enteras. Mida 4 tazas del líquido donde se cocieron las alubias, y agréguelas a la sopa junto con 4 tazas de caldo. Deje hervir. Reduzca el fuego y cocine a fuego lento durante 20 minutos.

Disuelva el miso en una pequeña cantidad de agua caliente, después añádalo a la sopa con levadura nutricional. Pruebe y sazone.

Lista de compras

2 manojos de albahaca
1 penca de apio
1 cabeza de hinojo
½ cabeza de ajo
2 manojos de col rizada
4 tazas de caldo
⅓ lb. [151,2 g] alubias secas
1 cebolla amarilla grande

Revise la despensa

Granos de pimienta negra
Miso de garbanzo
Orégano seco
Aceite de oliva virgen extra
Levadura nutricional
Sal marina

Fritura de kelp   Rinde 4 porciones

El kelp es una maravillosa fuente de oligoelementos y de iodo, como todos los vegetales del mar. Nos puede ayudar a proteger el cuerpo de la radiación y mantiene las glándulas suprarrenales. ¡He aquí una manera crujiente y sabrosa de consumir vegetales del mar en tu dieta semanal!

6 trozos de 6 pulgadas [15,24 cm] de kelp (conocida también como kombu)
⅓ taza de aceite de semilla de uva o aceite de coco

Remueva el exceso de sal del kelp limpiándolo rápidamente con una toalla de papel ligeramente húmeda. ¡No deje que el kelp se humedezca demasiado! Con tijeras corte el kelp en piezas de 2 pulgadas [5,08 cm] por 1 pulgada [2,54 cm]. Deberá tener aproximadamente 20 piezas.

Caliente el aceite a fuego alto hasta que esté muy caliente. Añada las tiras de kelp al aceite caliente, y fríalas durante 3 minutos, de un lado y del otro hasta que el color cambie a café dorado profundo y el kelp se rice y quede crujiente.

Remueva y escurra en una toalla de papel. Repita con todas las tiras hasta terminar. Para mejores resultados, cómalas el mismo día que las preparó. Pruebe usarlas con un aderezo o acompañando una ensalada.

Lista de compras

1 paquete de kelp (kombu)

Revise la despensa

Aceite de semilla de uva o aceite de coco

Desayuno del miércoles

Batido de pera y col rizada Rinde 2 porciones

La col rizada es rica en una forma de calcio que el cuerpo puede asimilar mucho mejor que el calcio que contienen los productos lácteos; y eso es una gran recompensa para sus huesos. Los productos lácteos son alimentos proinflamatorios para muchas personas, de ahí la importancia de comer abundantes hojas verdes que nos proporcionen calcio.

1 pepino, pelado si no es orgánico
1 taza de col rizada picada
2 peras (asiáticas o Bartlett)
1 aguacate
6 cubos de hielo

Pique el pepino, la col rizada y las peras, y colóquelos en la licuadora. Procese hasta que quede suave. Añada el aguacate y el hielo y licue hasta que tenga consistencia cremosa.

Lista de compras

1 aguacate
1 pepino

1 manojo de col rizada
2 peras (asiática o Bartlett)

Desayuno del miércoles

Gachas de calabaza y amaranto Rinde 4 porciones

El amaranto al igual que la quinoa es uno de los "supergranos", ya que contiene un grupo completo de nutrientes y muchas proteínas. Aquí está acompañado de calabaza para hacerlo un cremoso y abundante desayuno de gachas. ¡Disfrútelo!

1 taza de amaranto seco
½ cucharadita de nuez moscada
1 cucharadita de canela
⅓ de taza de hojuelas de coco rallado
¼ de taza de azúcar de coco
2 cucharadas de jarabe de arce
2 cucharadas de aceite de coco
¼ de cucharadita de sal marina
1 taza de puré de calabaza
2½ tazas de leche de almendras
1 taza de agua (omítase si se hacen "tortas", véase abajo)

Precaliente el horno a 400ºF [204ºC].

Ponga todos los ingredientes a cocinar a fuego medio, revuelva para combinarlos (esto llevará aproximadamente 10 minutos). Una vez que la mezcla comience a hervir ligeramente, apague el fuego y cubra con una tapa que ajuste bien o con papel aluminio. Colóquelo en el horno.

Hornee durante 45–60 minutos. Use guantes para horno para sacar la olla del horno. Agite bien, ya que el líquido se queda en la parte superior. Sirva inmediatamente o enfríe y recaliente por la mañana.

Para recalentar usamos un molde para horno de vidrio o cerámica, lo metemos al horno a 425ºF [218,3ºC] durante 25 minutos, para una manera de disfrutar un desayuno caliente de temporada sin meter las manos.

Para hacer "tortas" de amaranto para el desayuno:

Siga esta receta, pero omita el agua y reduzca la leche de almendras a solo 2 tazas. Enfríe completamente la mezcla en la nevera. En un sartén con divisiones fría lo equivalente a ¼ de taza de la mezcla en aceite de coco muy caliente, presionando un poco para formar pequeñas "tortas". Dore durante 2–3 minutos de cada lado y rocíe con jarabe de arce. Si las tortas se separan, intente agregando 1 huevo (o 1 cucharada de linaza) y ½ taza de harina libre de gluten. ¡Disfrútelas!

Lista de compras

Leche de almendras
Canela
Aceite de coco
Azúcar de coco
Amaranto seco

Jarabe de arce
Nuez moscada
Puré de calabaza
Sal marina
Hojuelas de coco rallado

Almuerzo del miércoles

Ensalada de col rizada, hinojo y limón con pollo
Rinde 4 porciones

1 taza de rábanos, cortados con mandolina o finamente rebanados
2 tazas de hinojo, cortados con mandolina o finamente rebanados
1 diente de ajo, finamente picado
6 tazas de col rizada, picada en trozos medianos (2 manojos)
La ralladura de 1 limón [amarillo]
1 cucharadita de sal marina
El jugo de 1 limón [amarillo]
1 cucharadas de aceite de oliva virgen extra
1 lb. [453 g] de pechuga de pollo, limpia
4 tazas de agua o caldo
4 granos de pimienta negra entera
Tallos y hojas de hinojo (de la parte superior del hinojo)

En un cuenco grande combine los primeros 8 ingredientes. Con las manos limpias, dé un masaje a las verduras como si quisiera extraerles el agua. Trabaje con las verduras por lo menos 15-20 veces hasta que se reduzcan en tamaño y estén completamente impregnadas. Aparte y deje reposar durante 20–30 minutos antes de consumirlas.

Mientras tanto cocine el pollo: Ponga agua o caldo a hervir a fuego lento con los granos de pimienta y el hinojo. Añada unas pizcas de sal, y ponga el pollo a escaldar durante 12–15 minutos, o hasta que esté completamente cocido.

Rebane el pollo y sirva encima de la ensalada de col rizada.

Lista de compras

1 lb. [453 g] de pechuga de pollo
2 cabezas de hinojo
1 diente de ajo
2 manojos de col rizada
1 limón [amarillo]
1 manojo de rábanos

Revise la despensa

Granos de pimienta negra
Aceite de oliva virgen extra
Sal marina
Agua o caldo

Cena del miércoles

Salmón empapelado con limón y juliana de verduras con raíz de apio asada y nabicol   Rinde 4 porciones

Salmón empapelado con limón y juliana de verduras

¡Una gran receta para recibir invitados! Cada miércoles por la noche solía ser anfitriona de una cena para aproximadamente 45 personas (donde cada comensal se sirve de los platos que se presentan en la mesa) y me sigue gustando recibir invitados a cenar a la mitad de semana. Haga los paquetes de papel pergamino con anticipación y métalos al horno un poco antes de la hora de la cena. Asegúrese de que los paquetitos estén a temperatura ambiente antes de cocinar, haga esto con anticipación (15–20 minutos antes es suficiente).

4 hojas de papel pergamino para hornear
4 piezas de salmón o bacalao silvestre de 6 onzas [170,1 g] cada una, sin espinas
2 cucharadas de aceite de oliva virgen extra
1 limón [amarillo], rebanado finamente
½ taza de eneldo
1 chalota, cortada en juliana (3½ pulgadas [8,89 cm] de largo por ¼ de pulgada [0,635 cm] de ancho, más o menos)
1 zanahoria grande, cortada en juliana
1 calabaza italiana, cortada en juliana
Sal marina, al gusto
Pimienta negra recién molida, al gusto

Fotografía por Chris Lang

Precaliente el horno a 425ºF [218,3ºC]. Corte cada hoja de papel pergamino en un gran corazón a través de doblar la hoja por la mitad y cortar la forma de un corazón utilizando la mayor parte del papel. Coloque abierto el corazón en una tabla de picar asegurándose de que el lado externo vea hacia arriba, de modo que el doblez forme una especie de carpa. Barnice con aceite de oliva el lado derecho del corazón.

Coloque el pescado en el lado engrasado del corazón y agregue sobre él un poco de la sal, la pimienta, las rebanadas de limón y las hierbas de su elección. Añada un poco de las verduras cortadas en juliana encima de las hierbas y después rocíe cada paquete con aceite de oliva y otra pizca de sal y pimienta.

Doble el papel nuevamente sobre sí mismo para cubrir el pescado y volver a formar el medio corazón. Enrolle las orillas hacia adentro bien apretadas, sellándolo bien para asegurarse que se cocine al vapor. Repita el procedimiento con cada porción.

Coloque los paquetitos en una plancha para hornear. Hornee durante 10–12 minutos, hasta que los paquetes resoplen.

Remueva los paquetes usando una espátula de metal. Sirva directo en los platos y permita que los invitados abran su propio paquetito en la mesa. ¡Elegante y sencillo!

Lista de compras

1 zanahoria grande
1 manojo de eneldo
1 Limón [amarillo]
Papel pergamino para cocina (solo
    se necesitan 4 hojas)
4 piezas de salmón de 6 onzas
    [170,1 g] cada una, sin espinas
1 chalota mediana
1 calabaza italiana

Revise la despensa

Granos de pimienta negra
Aceite de oliva virgen extra
Sal marina

Raíz de apio asada y nabicol

1 raíz de apio grande (6 pulgadas de diámetro [15,24 cm])
1 nabicol grande
3 cucharadas de aceite de semilla de uva
½ cucharadita de sal marina

Precaliente el horno a 400ºF [204,4ºC].

Corte los extremos redondos de la raíz de apio para dejarlos planos, y crear una superficie estable para pelarla. Use un cuchillo filoso para seguir la forma de la raíz de apio, pelando hacia abajo hasta que quede sin cáscara. Córtela en piezas de 1–2 pulgadas [2,54–5,08 cm]. Pique el nabicol de manera similar, aunque no es necesario pelarlo.

Coloque las verduras picadas en una olla y cúbralas con agua. Cuando el agua esté muy caliente, agregue sal y tape hasta que el agua comience a generar vapor. Cocine al vapor durante 2 minutos, después cuele.

Mezcle la raíz apio precocida y el nabicol en un cuenco con aceite y sal, después extienda en una plancha para hornear.

Hornee durante 25 minutos o hasta que dore. Voltee durante el tiempo de cocción una vez para dorar por ambos lados.

Lista de compras

1 raíz de apio grande
1 nabicol grande

Revise la despensa

Aceite de semilla de uva
Sal marina

Desayuno del jueves

Pepino fresco   Rinde 4 porciones

Científicos de la Universidad de Ulster revelaron que comer berro diariamente puede reducir los daños del ADN en las células sanguíneas, lo cual es considerado como un fuerte detonador en el desarrollo del cáncer.

1 manojo de berro
1 hoja de lechuga verde oscuro
1 pepino, pelado si no es orgánico
½ bulbo de hinojo con sus hojas
1 limón [amarillo], pelado si no es orgánico
½ manzana verde

Corte la fruta y la verdura para que quepa en el tubo de alimentación de su extractor de jugos. Envuelva el berro en la hoja de lechuga y páselo lentamente por el extractor. Procese en su extractor los ingredientes restantes. Vierta en un vaso, revuelva, y beba tan pronto como sea posible.

Lista de compras

1 pepino
1 bulbo de hinojo con sus hojas
1 manzana verde
1 cabeza de lechuga verde oscuro
1 limón [amarillo]
1 manojo de berro

Almuerzo del jueves

Wrap de ensalada de salmón con salsa verde brillante   Rinde 4 porciones

Este es un fabuloso almuerzo de verano. Proceda con precaución, ya que es muy fácil que se ensucie comiéndolo, aunque siempre lo dejará satisfecho. Durante el verano cuando necesita refrescarse, pero desea algo más que una simple ensalada de lechuga, esta es una receta que puede salvar el día. Haga la salsa y úsela durante la semana con verduras, sobre pescado o en este wrap.

Wrap de ensalada de salmón

2 cucharadas de aceite de oliva virgen extra
¼ taza de vinagre de vino tinto
1 cucharadita de miel cruda
¼ de cucharadita de sal marina
Pimienta negra recién molida, al gusto
1¼ lb. [567 g] de salmón cocido, picado
3 tallos de apio, finamente picados
1 manzana, finamente picada
⅓ de taza de cebolla morada, picada
2 cabezas de lechuga de hojas moradas
2 zanahorias, ralladas
½ taza de salsa verde brillante (vea la receta)

En un cuenco pequeño incorpore rápidamente el aceite, el vinagre, la miel, la sal y la pimienta. Combine el salmón y los ingredientes de la ensalada con la vinagreta y mezcle para incorporar bien.

Coloque las hojas enteras de lechuga en una tabla para picar y rebane las hojas a lo largo por el centro, de manera que los wraps sean más fáciles de comer. Divida la zanahoria rallada en cantidades iguales para las hojas y coloque la zanahoria en el primer tercio de la hoja. A continuación añada la ensalada de salmón en cantidades iguales sobre la zanahoria, alrededor de 2–3 cucharadas por wrap. Añada una cucharada de salsa verde brillante sobre el salmón. Con mucho cuidado enrolle los wraps de lechuga hacia fuera, lejos de usted, y sujételos con un palillo si los servirá más tarde.

Sírvalos con un poco más de salsa verde brillante como guarnición. ¡Este plato puede ser difícil de comer sin ensuciarse, pero es muy sabroso!

Nota: Puede utilizar el salmón que preparó para la cena de la noche anterior ¡si aún le sobra algo!

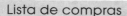

Lista de compras

1 manzana
2 zanahorias
3 tallos de apio
2 cabezas de lechuga de hoja
   morada
1 cebolla morada pequeña
1¼ lb. de salmón

Revise la despensa

Granos de pimienta negra
Aceite de oliva virgen extra
Miel cruda
Vinagre de vino tinto
Sal marina

Salsa verde brillante   Rinde 1 taza

Mezcle esta salsa con arroz integral, verduras salteadas o rocíela sobre un pescado blanco para darle un sabor distinguido e intenso. La pasta de ciruela umeboshi la puede encontrar en la sección internacional de la tienda de comestibles o en los mercados asiáticos. Con un poco es suficiente ¡no es necesario añadir sal cuando se usa esta maravillosa pasta!

1 manojo de cebolletas, picada
1 manojo de perejil, finamente picados
⅓ taza de aceite de oliva virgen extra
3 cucharadas de pasta de ciruela umeboshi
1 cucharadas de miso de garbanzo, al gusto
1 cucharadita de vinagre de manzana (opcional)
1 taza de agua

Pique en trozos grandes las cebolletas y el perejil, e introdúzcalos a la licuadora. Añada el resto de los ingredientes y procese hasta tener una consistencia cremosa.

Lista de compras

1 manojo de cebolletas
1 manojo de perejil

Revise la despensa

Vinagre de manzana
Miso de garbanzo
Aceite de oliva virgen extra
Pasta de ciruela umeboshi

Cena del jueves

Brochetas de pollo glaseadas con tamarindo con tortas de arroz integral y camote   Rinde 4 porciones

Brochetas de pollo glaseadas con tamarindo

Prepare con anticipación: Remoje los palos de bambú durante aproximadamente 1 hora para prevenir que se incendien durante el cocimiento del pollo. Si utiliza brochetas de metal, cúbralas con aceite de oliva y apártelas.

Marinado

1 cucharada de comino
½ cucharada de garam masala
¼ de taza de aceite de oliva virgen extra
2 dientes de ajo
1½ cucharadita de sal marina
½ cucharadita de pimienta negra recién molida

Glasé de tamarindo

1½ lb. [226,8 g] [680,4 g] de pechuga de pollo deshuesada, sin piel, limpia sin grasa
3 cucharadas de pasta de tamarindo
⅓ de taza de jugo de naranja
¼ de taza de melaza
¼ de taza de miel
¼ de cucharadita de hojuelas de chile seco molido (opcional)
2 cucharadas de jugo de lima [limón verde]
¼ de taza de picado menta
12–15 brochetas de bambú o de metal
1½ tazas de higos frescos o secos, partidos en mitades verticalmente y sin tallos

Para hacer el marinado: El pollo ya sin grasa, córtelo en cubos de 1–2 pulgadas [2,54–5,08 cm]. Sumerja las piezas de pollo en el marinado, cubra con una película plástica y refrigere durante toda la noche. Si no tiene el tiempo para hacerlo déjelo a temperatura ambiente durante 1–1½ horas y prepárese para cocinarlo al instante.

Para hacer el glasé: En una cacerola ponga a hervir la pasta de tamarindo, el jugo de naranja, la melaza, el agave o la miel, y de manera opcional el chile seco.

Reduzca el fuego y cocine a fuego lento hasta que el líquido se reduzca a 1 taza, revuelva ocasionalmente, alrededor de 8 minutos. Quite del fuego. Agregue mezclando 3 cucharadas de jugo de lima y ¼ taza de menta picada. Mantenga aparte.

Para hacer las brochetas: Inserte las brochetas directamente en el centro del pollo y de los higos. Deberá ensartar alrededor de 3–4 piezas de pollo por brocheta. Barnice las brochetas con la mitad del glasé. Deseche el marinado que sobra.

Hornee las brochetas en el horno en una plancha para hornear previamente engrasada hasta que el pollo quede completamente cocido, aproximadamente 10–12 minutos. Finalice barnizando las brochetas con el glasé sobrante.

Lista de compras

1½ lb. [226,8 g] [680,4 g] deshuesada, sin piel pechuga de pollo
1½ tazas de higos frescos o secos
2 dientes de ajo
1 lima [limón verde]
1 manojo de menta
1 naranja
Un frasco pequeño de pasta de tamarindo

Revise la despensa

Agave o Miel cruda
Granos de pimienta negra
Hojuelas de chile seco molido (opcional)
Aceite de oliva virgen extra
Comino molido
Garam masala molido
Melaza
Sal marina

Tortas de arroz integral y camote

1½ tazas de camote cocido machacado
2½ tazas de arroz cocido
1½–2 cucharadita de sal marina
⅔ taza de aceite de oliva virgen extra
½ taza de cebolla picado en cubos muy pequeños
1 taza de harina libre de gluten (o ⅔ taza de harina de arroz integral y ⅓ de harina de tapioca)
½ taza de aceite de coco, para freír

Combine todos los ingredientes y revuelva bien. Pruebe hacer una torta usando una taza medidora de ¼ en un sartén: cubra un sartén pequeño para

freír con una capa ligera y uniforme de aceite de coco y póngalo a fuego alto (aproximadamente ¼ taza de para iniciar).

Agregue más tortas (no ponga demasiadas en el sartén) y cocine durante 3 minutos de cada lado; no voltee las tortas hasta que las orillas estén doradas.

Use una espátula de metal para voltearlas. Vuelva a agregar aceite de coco a medida que lo necesite. Recaliéntelas en el horno si las elaboró con anticipación.

Una alternativa es engrasar una plancha para galletas con aceite de coco y hornearlas a 425ºF [218,3ºC], volteándolas una vez para que doren por ambos lados (aproximadamente 12 minutos en total). Rinde 32 tortas.

Nota: ¡Esta receta se congela bien!

Lista de compras

1 cebolla
2 camotes

Revise la despensa

Arroz integral
Aceite de coco
Aceite de oliva virgen extra
Harina libre de gluten
Sal marina

Desayuno del viernes

Delicia verde de coco   Rinde 1–2 porciones

El aguacate contiene importantes grasas, incluyendo los fitoesteroles, que dan cuenta de la mayor parte de la grasa del aguacate. Son clave para darle soporte a nuestro sistema de inflamación y nos ayudan a mantener la inflamación bajo control.

1 taza de espinacas crudas
1 aguacate
½ pepino holandés, pelado si no es orgánico, sin semillas y partido en cuartos
½–¾ de taza de leche de coco
El jugo de 1 lima [limón verde]
1 cucharada de suplemento alimenticio de verduras en polvo de su elección como el de hojas de cebada (opcional)
2–3 cucharadas de almendras molidas (opcional)

Combine todos los ingredientes, excepto las almendras en una licuadora hasta que tenga consistencia de batido. Espolvoree con almendras molidas, al gusto.

Lista de compras	Revise la despensa
1 aguacate	Almendras (opcional)
1 lata leche de coco	Suplemento alimenticio de
1 pepino holandés	verduras en polvo como el de
1 lima [limón verde]	hojas de cebada (opcional)
1 manojo de espinacas	

Almuerzo del viernes

Rica sopa de lentejas con cilantro y frituras de kelp   Rinde 4 porciones

Esta sopa adquiere su adorable profundidad de la capa de especias que se esparcen en ella antes de servir. Revuélvala rápido mientras sazona el aceite, ya que le infunde a la mezcla un intenso y delicioso sabor.

3 cucharadas de aceite de coco
1½ cucharadita de comino molido
2 cucharaditas de cilantro molido
1½ cucharaditas de garam masala
¼ de cucharadita de clavo molido
¾ de cucharadita de sal marina
3 dientes de ajo, finamente picados
2 cebolla amarillas, picadas en cubos
    medianos
½ penca de apio, picada en cubos medianos
5 zanahorias, picada en cubos pequeños
1 taza de lentejas rojas
2 hojas de laurel
8 tazas de caldo de verduras
¼ de taza de hierbas frescas de su elección
    (cilantro, albahaca, romero)
¼ de cucharadita de sal marina
1 cucharadita de cúrcuma molida
1 cucharadas de vinagre de vino tinto
    (opcional)

Caliente a fuego alto el aceite de coco en una olla. Agregue las especias para cocinar y la sal, y agite durante 15 segundos. Añada a la olla el

ajo, la cebolla, el apio y las zanahorias. Saltee las verduras durante 5–7 minutos o hasta que estén brillantes. Agregue las lentejas, las hojas de laurel y el caldo. Mueva para asegurarse de que las lentejas no se peguen a la olla, deje hervir. Baje el fuego y tape parcialmente la olla, y deje cocinar a fuego lento durante 30 minutos, revuelva ocasionalmente.

Añada la sal y la cúrcuma, y pruebe. Agregue el vinagre de vino tinto si lo desea, o sazone con más sal.

Disfrútela acompañada de frituras de Kelp (vea semana tres: Cena del martes).

Lista de compras

2 hojas de laurel
5 zanahorias
½ penca de apio
1 cabeza de ajo
Hierbas frescas de su elección
(cilantro, albahaca, romero)
8 tazas de caldo de verduras
2 cebolla amarillas

Revise la despensa

Aceite de coco
Clavo molido
Cilantro molido
Comino molido
Garam masala molido
Cúrcuma molida
Lentejas rojas
Vinagre de vino tinto (opcional)
Sal marina

Cena del viernes

"Pasta" de calabaza espagueti con salsa de alubias al limón y ensalada con aderezo "César" en crudo   Rinde 4 porciones

"Pasta" de calabaza espagueti

He aquí una versión de salsa "blanca" sin crema que no contiene cacahuetes ni soya. La receta de esta salsa usa alubias para simular la consistencia, acompañada de un brillante sabor a limón y un rico y sabroso miso de garbanzo. ¡Asar los ajos lleva esta receta al siguiente nivel!

Calabaza espagueti

1 calabaza espagueti grande (4 lb. [1814 g] o más)
3 cucharadas de aceite de semilla de uva
Sal marina, al gusto
Pimienta negra recién molida, al gusto

Precaliente el horno a 350ºF [176,7ºC].

Coloque la calabaza entera en el horno durante 20 minutos para suavizar la cáscara.

Una vez que la calabaza esté suficientemente fría para tomarla con las manos, corte a lo largo por la mitad y retire las semillas con una cuchara.

Frote el interior y el exterior de la calabaza con aceite, sazone con sal y pimienta y coloque ambas mitades boca abajo en una plancha para hornear.

Hornee durante 30–40 minutos o más, hasta que la cáscara quede suave al tacto y ligeramente dorada.

Una vez que se enfríe los suficiente para tomarla con las manos, con una cuchara retire la pulpa de la cáscara y ¡mezcle con la salsa de su elección!

Salsa de alubias al limón

3 dientes de ajo asados (o 1 diente crudo)
¼ de taza de levadura nutricional
2 cucharadas colmadas de miso de garbanzo
2 cucharadas de aceite de oliva virgen extra
1½ tazas de alubias cocidas
½ taza de agua
3 cucharadas de jugo de limón [amarillo]
1 cucharadita de sal marina

Para asar el ajo: corte la parte de arriba del ajo y remuévala. Rocíe el resto del ajo con aceite de oliva. Envuelva en papel aluminio y ase en el horno a 300ºF [148,9ºC] durante 35 minutos o hasta que se suavice.

Licúe todos los ingredientes juntos hasta que tenga consistencia de batido, si lo desea con una consistencia más ligera añada un poco de agua, hasta tener la consistencia deseada.

Lista de compras

1 cabeza de ajo
1 limón [amarillo]
1 calabaza espagueti grande
Una lata de 12 oz. [340 g] de
    alubias (o ½ taza de alubias
    cocidas)

Revise la despensa

Granos de pimienta negra
Miso de garbanzo
Aceite de oliva virgen extra
Aceite de semilla de uva
Levadura nutricional
Sal marina

Aderezo "César" en crudo

Nota: Es importante NO "acremar" las nueces con otros líquidos si usted desea que se mantenga la textura granulosa. Esto es lo que le dará un sabor parecido al queso. Si el aderezo necesita más sabor añada jugo de limón y sal marina.

¾ de taza de nueces, remojadas durante 1 hora
1 cucharada de aceite de oliva virgen extra
1½ cucharaditas de sal marina, o más si lo desea
⅓ de taza de aceite de oliva virgen extra
3 dátiles, sin hueso y remojados durante 10 minutos
1 diente de ajo grande
¼ de taza de jugo de limón [amarillo] (1 limón grande)
1 taza de agua
1 cucharada de miso de garbanzo
2 cucharaditas de hojuelas de alga dulse (opcional)

En el procesador de alimentos, procese con impulsos breves las nueces con 1 cucharada de aceite y sal hasta que tengan consistencia grumosa. No procese de más para mantener la textura. Remueva del procesador y colóquela en un cuenco pequeño. En la licuadora, coloque el resto de los ingredientes y licue hasta tener una consistencia de batido. Retire la mezcla y colóquela en el mismo cuenco donde se encuentran las nueces. Revuelva bien hasta incorporar las mezclas. Si desea una mezcla más ligera añada agua hasta que se obtenga el sabor y consistencia deseadas.

Para la ensalada (que acompaña a la calabaza espagueti): Mezcle ⅓ de taza del aderezo "César" con 4 tazas colmadas de hojas verdes, y sazone al gusto con más aderezo, sal marina y pimienta. Para hacer una variación añada, si lo desea verduras picadas.

Lista de compras

3 dátiles grandes
Hojuelas de alga dulse (opcional)
1 diente de ajo
4 manojos grandes de mezcla de
    hoja verdes para ensalada o
    lechuga
1 limón [amarillo] grande/
    2 limones [amarillos] pequeños
¾ de taza de nueces

Revise la despensa

Miso de garbanzo
Aceite de oliva virgen extra
Sal marina

Desayuno del sábado

Auxiliar de la visión   Rinde 1 porción

Las zanahorias son ricas en carotenos, los cuales son muy útiles para el fortalecimiento de los ojos y mejorar la visión. Los arándanos azules también ayuda a mejorar el alcance visual, y las manzanas ayudan a eliminar toxinas de los ojos.

3 zanahorias, bien fregadas, sin hojas o tallos y con ambos extremos recortados
1 pepino, pelado si no es orgánico
2 hojas de col rizada, acelga, o de berza
1 taza de arándanos azules, descongelados si eran congelados
½ manzana verde

Corte la fruta y la verdura para que quepa en el tubo de alimentación de su extractor de jugos. Procese las zanahorias, el pepino y la col rizada. Apague el extractor y añada los arándanos azules. Tape con el émbolo. Vuelva a encender el extractor y haga pasar las moras por el tubo de alimentación; después procese la manzana. Revuelva y vierta en un vaso. Beba tan pronto como sea posible.

Lista de compras

1 manzana verde
1 pinta seca [550,6 ml] de
    arándanos azules
3 zanahorias

1 pepino
1 manojo de hojas de col rizada,
    acelga o berza

Desayuno-almuerzo del sábado

Croqueta del desayuno con camote   Rinde 4 porciones

Use cualquier verdura asada que tenga en su nevera para crear muchas variantes de esta receta. De lo que se trata es de combinar verduras recién cocinadas con huevos ricos en proteínas para formar un paquete de poder para iniciar su mañana.

2 camotes grandes, picados en cubos (precocidos y primero asados en el sartén)
3 cucharadas de aceite de oliva virgen extra
1 cebolla pequeña picada en cubos (o 1 cebolla, caramelizada)
1–2 zanahorias o calabazas italianas, picadas en cubos
2 manojos de espinacas u hojas verdes, picadas
2 dientes de ajo
Una pizca de pimienta de Cayena (opcional)
¼ cucharadita de Sal marina más pimienta negra recién molida, al gusto
12 huevos
Hierbas frescas (perejil, orégano, albahaca, estragón) (opcional)

Precocine los camotes: Coloque los camotes picados en cubos en una olla y añada agua hasta cubrirlos. Agregue sal y tape para que comience a hervir. Hierva durante 2–3 minutos y escurra. Omita este paso si usted previamente asó los camotes o cualquier otra verdura que desea usar.

Añada aceite de oliva a un sartén y caliente a fuego medio alto. Agregue todas las verduras junto con sal y pimienta al gusto. Cocine durante 5–6 minutos, hasta que las verduras queden suaves.

Añada los huevos y la pimienta de Cayena, utilice una cuchara de madera para mezclar rápidamente los huevos en el sartén. Cocine durante 4 minutos, moviendo hasta que los huevos queden cocidos. Agregue de manera opcional hierbas frescas picadas.

¡Es estupendo servido con mostaza Dijon!

Lista de compras

1–2 zanahorias o calabaza italianas
12 huevos
2 dientes de ajo (opcional)
1 cebolla pequeña
2 manojos de espinacas u hojas verdes
2 camotes grandes
Hierbas frescas (perejil, orégano, albahaca, estragón) (opcional)

Revise la despensa

Granos de pimienta negra
Pimienta de Cayena
Aceite de oliva virgen extra
Sal marina

Almuerzo del sábado

Ensalada tibia con fideos de kelp con curry y judías adzuki   Rinde 4 porciones

Los fideos de kelp los encuentra en el área de refrigerados en la mayoría de las tiendas naturistas de alimentos, grandes y pequeñas. Estás se venden limpias y listas para comerse directo de la bolsa. El kelp tienen una textura estupenda y por ser algas marinas contienen ¡gran cantidad de nutrientes!

Salsa

2 cucharadas de vinagre de ciruela umeboshi
1 taza de leche de coco
1 cucharada de pasta de curry rojo
1 cucharada de azúcar de coco
⅓ taza de chalotas, finamente picadas

Ensalada

2 tazas de judías Adzuki, cocinadas y drenadas
1 bolsa de 12 oz. [340,2 g] de fideos de kelp, drenados
⅓ de taza de cilantro, picado
3 cebolletas, finamente rebanadas de manera sesgada
1 cabeza de bok choy grande, rebanada de manera sesgada a ½ pulgada [1,27 cm] de ancho.

Mezcle juntos los ingredientes de la salsa y cocínelos a fuego lento en una cacerola pequeña.

Mientras tanto, coloque las judías, los fideos de kelp y las verduras en un cuenco grande. Añada la salsa caliente hasta cubrir y sazone con el vinagre restante o con la pasta de curry al gusto.

Permita que la ensalada se marine en la salsa durante 10 minutos o más antes de comerla.

Lista de compras

1 lata judías Adzuki (o ½ taza de judías Adzuki secas)
1 cabeza de bok choy
1 manojo de cilantro
1 paquete de 12 oz. [340,2 g] de fideos de kelp, drenados
1 manojo de cebolletas
2 chalotas

Revise la despensa

Leche de coco
Azúcar de coco
Pasta de curry rojo
Vinagre de ciruela umeboshi

175

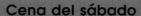

Cena del sábado

Pollo y alcachofas al limón con brócoli crujiente y puré de verduras de raíz   Rinde 4 porciones

2 pechugas de pollo libres de hormonas, enteras, deshuesadas, sin piel (4 mitades)
½ cucharadita de sal marina
½ taza de harina libre de gluten
½ cucharadita de pimienta negra recién molida
2 huevos para 4 mitades de pechugas de pollo
¼ de taza de aceite de oliva virgen extra
2 cucharadas de aceite de coco
3 cucharadas de vino blanco
⅓ de taza de jugo de limón [amarillo] recién exprimido (2 limones)
½ taza de corazones de alcachofa, picados (opcional)
¼ de taza de perejil fresco, picado

Coloque la media pechuga de pollo entre 2 piezas de papel pergamino para cocinar y golpéela con un mazo para carne (del lado plano) o con la parte de debajo de un sartén pesado hasta conseguir que quede de un ¼ de pulgada [0,635 cm] de espesor. Repita este procedimiento con las pechugas de pollo restantes. Espolvoree un ¼ de cucharadita de sal sobre ellas.

Añada el restante de sal y pimienta al harina y mezcle. Extienda la mezcla de harina sobre un plato grande. Bata los huevos en un cuenco. Sumerja cada pechuga de pollo en huevo y después cúbralos con el harina por ambos lados. Colóquela en un plato y prepare las otra pechugas.

Caliente un sartén grande a fuego medio-alto. Añada el aceite de oliva y el aceite de coco. Una vez que esté caliente coloque las pechugas de pollo en el sartén. Cocine durante 4 minutos por cada lado o hasta que queden bien doradas. Traslade las pechugas de pollo a un plato limpio y cúbralas hasta que queden todas la pechugas completamente cocidas y doradas por ambos lados.

Añada el vino y el jugo de limón al sartén. Raspe el sartén para incorporar todas la migajas. Agregue los corazones de alcachofa y el perejil, y cocine hasta que la salsa espese, aproximadamente 2 minutos. Vierta la salsa sobre las pechugas de pollo.

Lista de compras	Revise la despensa
1 lata pequeña de corazones de alcachofa 2 pechugas de pollo libres de hormonas, enteras, deshuesadas, sin piel (4 mitades) 2 limones (amarillos) 1 manojo de perejil	Granos de pimienta negra Aceite de coco Aceite de oliva virgen extra Harina libre de gluten Sal marina Vino blanco

Brócoli crujiente   Rinde 4 porciones

2 manojos de brócoli, picado en trozos de tamaño mediano
1–2 cucharadas de aceite de oliva virgen extra
Sal marina
Pimienta negra recién molida

Revuelva todos los ingredientes juntos, hasta que queden bien cubiertos. Ase en el horno a 425ºF [218,3ºC] hasta que queden crujientes, aproximadamente de 10–12 minutos.

Lista de compras	Revise la despensa
2 manojos de brócoli	Granos de pimienta negra Aceite de oliva virgen extra Sal marina

Puré cremoso de verduras de raíz   Rinde 4 porciones

El puré de verduras de raíz se puede convertir en un favorito de la casa en las comidas diarias así como en las celebraciones. ¡Sorpréndase con nuevas verduras! Intente con la raíz de apio (la más nudosa de las verduras de raíz) para una limpia y fresca perspectiva de esta receta.

2 lb. [907,2 g] de verduras de raíz (apio, nabos, chirivía, nabicol)
2 ramitas de tomillo fresco
2 cucharadas de aceite de oliva virgen además de 2 cucharadas de aceite de coco
¾ de cucharadita de sal marina, o más si lo desea
¾ de taza de leche de coco
1 cucharada de miel cruda (opcional)
Pimienta negra recién molida, al gusto

Pele las verduras y córtelas en trozos medianos. Colóquelas en una cacerola grande (1 galón [3785 ml]) y llene la cacerola con agua fría. La verduras deben quedar cubiertas por aproximadamente 2 pulgadas [5,08 cm]. Agregue tomillo fresco.

Deje que las verduras alcancen el hervor a fuego medio-alto. Continúe hirviendo las verduras hasta que queden tiernas al pinchar con un tenedor, alrededor de 25 minutos. Escurra y deje aparte.

En un cuenco grande mezcle las verduras con el aceite de oliva y de coco, la leche de coco, sal, y opcionalmente el edulcorante. Machaque con un triturador de papas hasta que obtenga una consistencia cremosa, añada más leche de coco si es necesario.

Para más adelante: Mantenga el puré caliente colocándolo en un cuenco de metal con tapa sobre una cacerola con agua hirviendo a fuego lento hasta por 1 hora (baño maría).

Lista de compras

1 manojo de tomillo
2 lb. [907,2 g] verduras de raíz de su elección

Revise la despensa

Granos de pimienta negra
Leche de coco
Aceite de coco
Aceite de oliva virgen extra
Miel cruda
Sal marina

Desayuno del domingo

Remolino de almendra   Rinde 2 porciones

Los duraznos contienen compuestos fenólicos que previenen la oxidación de las lipoproteínas de baja densidad (LDL por sus siglas en inglés) del colesterol. El colesterol oxidado es lo que daña nuestro cuerpo. Los compuestos fenólicos nos ayudan a combatir la inflamación asociada con el síndrome de metabólico, una combinación de desórdenes médicos que incrementa el riesgo de obesidad, de diabetes tipo 2 y problemas cardiovasculares.

1 taza de leche de almendras
2 duraznos maduros, sin hueso, cortados en trozos (si están fuera de temporada, use duraznos congelados)
½ taza de col rizada, picada
2–3 gotas de stevia, al gusto
1 cucharadita de extracto de vainilla puro
½ cucharadita de extracto puro de almendras
6 cubos de hielo

Combine todos los ingredientes en una licuadora y procese hasta tener un batido cremoso. Sirva bien frío.

Lista de compras

1 manojo de col rizada
2 duraznos maduros

Revise la despensa

Extracto de almendras
Leche de almendras
Extracto de vainilla puro
Stevia líquida (se sugiere con sabor crema de vainilla de la marca SweetLeaf)

Almuerzo del domingo

Ensalada de manzana con pollo tai y arroz tostado
Rinde 4 porciones

2 tazas de manzanas, sin corazón, finamente rebanadas, mezcladas con jugo de limón [amarillo]
2 chalotas, finamente picadas
8 tazas no muy apretadas de espinacas o mezcla de hojas verdes para ensalada
1 manojo de cebolletas, rebanadas
1 nabo, finamente rebanado
1 taza de zanahorias, cortadas en juliana
1 taza de albahaca fresca en trozos
¼ de taza de arroz integral sin cocer (opcional)
2 cucharadas de aceite de coco
1 lb. [453 g] de pechuga de pollo, rebanada
2 cucharadas de salsa de pescado libre gluten
2 cucharadas de néctar de agave o de miel
Sal marina, al gusto
Pimienta negra recién molida, al gusto

Aderezo

½ taza de jugo de lima [limón verde]
¼ de taza de azúcar de palma de coco
3 dientes de ajo, finamente picados
1 cucharadita de aceite de ajonjolí
2 cucharaditas de jengibre fresco, finamente picados

Fotografía por Polara Studio

Combine los ingredientes del aderezo en un cuenco.

Combine los ingredientes de la ensalada (hasta la albahaca) en un cuenco para ensaladas grande. Póngalo a un lado.

Tueste el arroz en una sartén seco a fuego medio-alto hasta que esté perfumado, aproximadamente 5 minutos, debe quedar con un color dorado ligero y comenzar a saltar. Traslade el arroz a una licuadora o a un mortero y muela el arroz para obtener un polvo grueso.

Caliente el aceite de coco en un sartén grande. Saltee al estilo chino el pollo hasta que se cocine, aproximadamente 8 minutos, gradualmente añada la salsa de pescado y el agave, 1 cucharada a la vez. Si el sartén se pone muy seco, añada un poco de agua y tape para cocinar al vapor.

Traslade el pollo al cuenco para ensalada con los ingredientes de la ensalada ya preparados, caliente el aderezo y mezcle todos los ingredientes. Decore con el arroz tostado molido y la albahaca deshojada. Agregue sal y pimienta al gusto.

Lista de compras

2 manzanas
1 manojo de albahaca
2 zanahorias
1 lb. [453 g] de pollo
3 dientes de ajo
1 trozo de 1 pulgada [2,54 cm] de jengibre
4 Lima (limón verde)
1 manojo de cebolletas
2 chalotas
8 tazas de espinacas o mezcla de hojas verdes para ensaladas
1 nabo

Revise la despensa

Arroz integral
Aceite de coco
Azúcar de palma de coco
Salsa de pescado libre de gluten
Miel cruda
Pimienta
Sal marina
Aceite de ajonjolí

Cena del domingo

Ensalada caliente de fletán y garbanzo con hierbas frescas y preparado de remolacha con alcaravea
Rinde 4 porciones

Ensalada caliente de fletán y garbanzo con hierbas frescas

1 lb. [453 g] de fletán, sin espinas, cortado en dos piezas
1 cucharadita de sal marina
Pimienta negra recién molida, al gusto
3 cucharadas de aceite de oliva virgen extra
2 cucharadas de vinagre de vino tinto
2 cucharadas de mostaza Dijon
¼ de taza de eneldo picado
½ taza de cebollín picado
4 manojos grandes de mezcla de hojas para estofar
2 tazas de garbanzos cocidos (o 1 lata de 15 oz. [425 g] de garbanzos, bien enjuagados)
1 aguacate, rebanado Granos de pimienta negra
Miso de garbanzo
Orégano seco
Aceite de oliva virgen extra
Levadura nutricional
Sal marina

Espolvoree el pescado con un ¼ de cucharadita de sal y pimienta al gusto. Coloque el pescado en un sartén mediano y añada agua hasta la mitad del pescado. Deje que comience a hervir a fuego medio-alto. Tape el sartén y cocine el fletán hasta que se opaque y esté tierno al tocarlo con un tenedor, aproximadamente 8 minutos.

Mezcle el aceite de oliva, el vinagre, la mostaza y el eneldo en un cuenco pequeño, y bata a mano para combinar completamente los ingredientes. Mezcle el aderezo con los ingredientes de la ensalada restantes en un cuenco y sazone con sal y pimienta al gusto.

Divida la ensalada en 2 cuencos y coloque encima el pescado. Una opción es enfriar en la nevera el pescado y después disfrutarlo sobre la ensalada.

Preparado de remolacha con alcaravea
Rinde 4 porciones

½ cabeza de repollo rojo, sin corazón y rebanado finamente
4 remolachas, cortadas en juliana
1 manzana pequeña, cortada en juliana (opcional)
¼ de manojo de perejil rizado, finamente picado
¼ de taza de chalota, finamente picada
¼ de taza de vinagre de manzana
½ cucharadita de sal marina
1 cucharada de aceite de oliva virgen extra (opcional)
1 cucharada de semillas de alcaravea tostadas (tuéstelas en un sartén a fuego
    medio-bajo hasta que perfumen)

Combine todos los ingredientes en un cuenco. Con las manos limpias, estruje el preparado firmemente, exprimiendo las verduras en puñados por vez. Repita el procedimiento 20 veces en toda la ensalada. La ensalada debe disminuir en tamaño y estar completamente cubierta de aderezo.

Pruebe y ajuste el sazón a su gusto. Manténgala en refrigeración hasta por 5 días.

Lista de compras

1 manzana pequeña (opcional)
1 aguacate, rebanado
4 remolachas
½ taza de cebollín picado
¼ de taza de eneldo picado
4 manojos grandes de mezcla de
    hojas para estofar
1 lb. [453 g] de fletán, sin espinas y
    partido en dos piezas
1 manojo de perejil
1 cabeza de repollo rojo
1 chalota

Revise la despensa

Vinagre de manzana
Granos de pimienta negra
Semillas de alcaravea
Garbanzos
Mostaza Dijon
Aceite de oliva virgen extra
Vinagre de vino tinto
Sal marina

Lista de compras de la semana cuatro

Utensilios de cocina

- ❏ Brochetas de metal o bambú
- ❏ Capacillos

Vino y vinagre para cocinar

- ❏ Vinagre de manzana
- ❏ Vinagre balsámico añejado
- ❏ Vinagre de vino tinto
- ❏ Vinagre de arroz
- ❏ Vinagre de umeboshi

Lácteos y huevos

- ❏ 1 docena de huevos grandes de gallina libre

Fruta seca

- ❏ ¼ de taza de grosella seca
- ❏ ½ taza de pasas, arándano rojo o grosellas

Hierbas y especias secas

- ❏ Granos de pimienta negra
- ❏ Pimienta de Cayena (opcional)
- ❏ Sal marina celta
- ❏ Curry en polvo
- ❏ Pimienta dulce molida
- ❏ Cardamomo molido
- ❏ Canela molida
- ❏ Cilantro molido
- ❏ Nuez moscada molida

Artículos secos o enlatados para la despensa

- ❏ Extracto de almendras
- ❏ 1 taza de leche de almendras
- ❏ 1 paquete de alga arame seca (1 taza)
- ❏ 1 frasco de corazones de alcachofa
- ❏ 1 hogaza de pan libre de gluten
- ❏ Migajas de pan libre de gluten (o harina de almendra)
- ❏ Miso de garbanzo
- ❏ Aminoácidos de coco o salsa de soya
- ❏ 4 latas de leche de coco
- ❏ Azúcar de coco
- ❏ Mostaza Dijon
- ❏ Salsa de pescado libre de gluten
- ❏ Miel cruda
- ❏ 1 frasco de aceitunas kalamata
- ❏ Kelp/kombu
- ❏ Jarabe de arce
- ❏ Mayonesa o aderezo libre de huevo marca Veganaise

- ❏ 1 paquete de hojas de nori
- ❏ Sal marina
- ❏ Tomatillo salsa (opcional)
- ❏ Extracto de vainilla

Pescado, aves, carnes

- ❏ 4 lb. [1814 g] de pechuga de pollo sin piel y deshuesada.
- ❏ 1½ lb. [680,4 g] de bacalao silvestre
- ❏ ½ lb. [226,8 g] de salmón ahumado
- ❏ 2¾ lb. [1021 g] de filete de salmón

Harinas

- ❏ 1 taza de harina de garbanzo
- ❏ Harina libre de gluten

Hierbas y especias frescas

- ❏ 5 manojos de cilantro
- ❏ 2 manojos de menta
- ❏ ½ manojo de orégano

Granos y leguminosas

- ❏ 3 tazas de arroz integral cocido
- ❏ 2 tazas de garbanzos cocido
- ❏ 1 taza de quinoa

Nueces y semillas

- ❏ 1 taza de almendra

- ❏ ½ taza de almendra fileteada
- ❏ ½ taza de nueces de la India
- ❏ 2 cucharadas de linaza molida
- ❏ 1½ tazas de pacanas
- ❏ 1 taza de semillas de calabaza
- ❏ ¼ de taza de ajonjolí
- ❏ ¼ de taza de ajonjolí negro
- ❏ 2½ tazas de nueces

Aceites

- ❏ Aceite de coco
- ❏ Aceite de oliva virgen extra
- ❏ Aceite de semilla de uva
- ❏ Aceite de ajonjolí sin refinar
- ❏ Aceite de girasol (para cocinar)

Frutas y verduras

Frutas

- ❏ 5 manzanas
- ❏ 6 aguacates
- ❏ 1 taza de moras de su elección
- ❏ 9 limones [amarillo]
- ❏ 4 limas [limón verde]
- ❏ 1 mango
- ❏ 3 peras
- ❏ 2 manzanas pippin o cualquier otra manzana verde

Verduras

- ❏ 2 tazas de rúcula
- ❏ ¼ lb. [113,4 g] hojas tiernas de espinaca
- ❏ 1 pinta seca [550,6 ml] de germinados de frijol
- ❏ 1 manojo de remolacha
- ❏ 1 cabeza de bok coy
- ❏ 3 lb. [1361 g] de brócoli
- ❏ 3 pulgadas [7,62 cm] de bardana (opcional)
- ❏ 3 lb. [1361 g] de calabaza moscada (completa)
- ❏ 16 zanahorias (3½ lb. [1588 g])
- ❏ 2 pencas de apio
- ❏ 1 manojo de hojas de berza
- ❏ 3 pepinos
- ❏ 1 cabeza de escarola
- ❏ 4 cabezas de ajo
- ❏ 1 repollo verde
- ❏ 3 tazas de guisantes verdes, frescos o congelados
- ❏ 4 tazas de mezcla de hojas verdes (¼ lb. [113,4 g])
- ❏ 2 batatas japonesa (o camotes)
- ❏ 2 jícamas medianas
- ❏ 2 hojas de col rizada + 1 hoja de lechuga verde
- ❏ 3 manojos de col rizada + 3 hojas

- ❏ 1–2 hojas de colinabo o cualquier otra hoja verde oscuro
- ❏ 2 tallos de citronela
- ❏ 1 manojo de hojas de mostaza
- ❏ 1 manojo de perejil
- ❏ 2 lb. [907,2 g] de raíz de apio
- ❏ 1 cabeza de radicchio
- ❏ 1 manojo de rábanos
- ❏ 2 cebollas moradas
- ❏ 1 cabeza de lechuga romana
- ❏ 5 manojos de cebolletas
- ❏ 3 tazas de hongo shiitake (¼–½ lb. [113,4-226,8 g])
- ❏ ½ lb. [226,8 g] espinaca
- ❏ 5 nabos
- ❏ 1 manojo de berro
- ❏ 1 cebolla amarilla
- ❏ 3 calabazas italiana medianas
- ❏ 1 manojo de cebollín
- ❏ 13 pulgadas [33,02 cm] de jengibre
- ❏ 1 manojo de estragón

Caldos

- ❏ 1 cuarto [946,4 ml] de caldo de verduras o de caldo de pollo

Menús y recetas de la semana cuatro

Desayuno del lunes

Fiesta de Newton Pippin Rinde 1 porción

Se ha demostrado la función antioxidante de los flavonoides que contiene el perejil—especialmente la luteolina que se combinan con moléculas altamente reactivas que contienen oxígeno (llamadas radicales de oxígeno) y ayudan a evitar el daño basado en el oxígeno a las células. La prevención de dicho daño es muy importante cuando se comienza a controlar la inflamación. No acostumbramos comer grandes cantidades de perejil, pero es fácil hacerlo jugo.

1 manojo pequeño de perejil
1 hoja verde de lechuga
3–4 zanahorias, bien fregadas, sin hojas o tallos y con ambos extremos recortados
2 tallos de apio con hojas
2 dientes de ajo
2 manzanas pippin

Corte la fruta o la verdura para que quepa en el tubo de alimentación de su extractor de jugos. Enrolle el perejil en la hoja de lechuga y métalas lentamente en el extractor. Procese el resto de los ingredientes y revuelva. Vierta en un vaso y beba tan pronto como sea posible.

Lista de compras

2 manzanas pippin o cualquier otra manzana verde
3–4 zanahorias
1 manojo de apio
1 cabeza de ajo
1 cabeza de lechuga de hoja verde oscuro
l manojo de perejil

Almuerzo del lunes

Sopa de calabaza italiana cruda y guisantes con fideos de nabo   Rinde porciones 4

Sopa de calabaza italiana cruda y guisantes

3 tazas de leche de coco
1 taza de agua filtrada
3 tazas de guisantes sin cáscara, recién cocidos al vapor o congelados
3 tazas de calabaza italiana, picada
½ taza de jugo de limón [amarillo]
3 dientes de ajo, finamente picados
2 cucharaditas de jengibre fresco, finamente picado
3 tazas de aguacate, machacados
½ taza de apio, picado
½ cucharadita de pimienta de Cayena
1 cucharada sal marina (o más, al gusto)
3 cucharadas de miel cruda
¼ de taza de menta, sin tallos

Fideos de nabo

2 nabos pequeños
Sal marina, al gusto

Ponga aparte una taza de guisantes. Combine el resto de los ingredientes en una licuadora y procese hasta obtener una mezcla suave. Agregue agua al gusto para hacer más ligera la textura de la sopa, hasta un máximo de 2 tazas de agua.

Vierta en tazones para servir. Agregue en la parte de arriba los guisantes que separó y los fideos de nabo como decoración.

Para hacer los fideos de nabo: emplee un rallador de verduras en espiral o un pelador de verduras para hacer largos listones de nabo. Sazone con sal y añádalos en la superficie de la sopa como adorno.

Sírvase fría o ligeramente caliente.

Lista de compras

2 aguacates grandes
2 tallos de apio
3 dientes de ajo
1 trozo de 1 pulgada [2,54 cm] de jengibre
3 tazas de guisantes verdes, frescos o congelados
½ taza de jugo de limón [amarillo]
1 manojo de menta
2 nabos pequeños
3 calabazas italianas medianas

Revise la despensa

Pimienta de Cayena
Leche de coco
Miel cruda
Sal marina

Cena del lunes

Bacalao silvestre asado con popurrí de verduras al olivo   Rinde 4 porciones

Bacalao silvestre asado

1½ lb. [680,4 g] de bacalao silvestre
2 cucharadas de aceite de semilla de uva
¼ de cucharadita de sal marina
Pimienta negra recién molida, al gusto
1 cucharadita de orégano seco, opcional
1 limón [amarillo]
3 cucharadas de aceite de oliva virgen extra
3 dientes de ajo, picados
2 nabos, picados en trozos medianos
2 cabezas de brócoli, los grumos se pican en trozos pequeños
½ manojo de col rizada, sin tallos y picados
2 zanahorias, rebanadas de manera sesgada
½ taza de salmuera de las aceitunas

Precaliente el horno a 425ºF [218,3ºC].

Remueva las espinas del bacalao y córtelo en cuatro porciones. Unte con una brocha el aceite de semilla de uva en el pescado, sazone espolvoreando sal, pimienta, y orégano. Cocine en el horno de 12–15 minutos o hasta que esté cocido completamente.

Para finalizar exprima sobre del limón [amarillo] y sirva inmediatamente.

Popurrí de verduras al olivo

Caliente el aceite de oliva a temperatura media baja en un sartén con tapa que ajuste bien. Añada el ajo y un ¼ de cucharadita de sal marina, 15 segundos.

Agregue las verduras y la salmuera de las aceitunas y agite el sartén ligeramente para distribuir uniformemente los líquidos en el fondo. Tape y cocine, moviendo una o dos veces.

Las verduras se dejan cocinar durante 5–7 minutos o hasta que estén completamente cocidas. Sazone con un poco más de la salmuera de las aceitunas o sal al gusto.

Lista de compras

2 cabezas de brócoli
2 zanahorias
1½ lb. [680,4 g] de bacalao
3 dientes de ajo
1 manojo de col rizada
1 limón [amarillo]
2 nabos

Revise la despensa

Granos de pimienta negra
Orégano seco
Aceite de oliva virgen extra
Aceite de semilla de uva
Salmuera de las aceitunas (del
    frasco de las aceitunas)
Sal marina

Desayuno del martes

Realmente verde   Rinde 1–2 porciones

Las peras contienen fitonutrientes que se han demostrado proveen beneficios antiinflamatorios. Los fitonutrientes se han asociado con la disminución del riesgo de muchas enfermedades relacionadas con la inflamación crónica y el excesivo estrés oxidativo.

2–3 hojas de colinabo
2 tallos de apio
1 pepino, pelado si no es orgánico
1 pera
½ limón [amarillo], pelado si no es orgánico

Coloque algunas de las hojas verdes en su extractor y procese; alterne hojas con apio siguiendo con pepino, pera, y limón [amarillo]. Revuelva el jugo y beba tan pronto como sea posible.

Lista de compras

1 colinabo con hojas (el bulbo
  picado puede usarse en una
  ensalada)
1 manojo de apio (use el sobrante
  en otra receta)

1 pepino
1 pera
1 limón [amarillo]

Almuerzo del martes

Quinoa con mango y menta con garbanzos sazonados al curry   Rinde 4 porciones

1 lima [limón verde], rallada y exprimida
¼ de taza de cilantro fresco, picado
½ cucharadita de sal marina
½ cucharadita de pimienta negra molida en grano grande
1 taza de quinoa seca
1 pepino, sin semillas y picado en cubos
1 manojo grande de menta, finamente picado
1 mango, pelado y picado en cubos
1 cucharadita de miel cruda
2 cucharadas aceite de coco, fluidificado
2 tazas de garbanzos cocidos (o 1 lata de 15 oz. [443,6 ml])
2 cucharadas de aceite de oliva virgen extra
3 cucharadas de curry en polvo

Quinoa con mango y menta

Combine la ralladura y el jugo de lima, el cilantro, la sal y la pimienta en un cuenco pequeño.

Cocine la quinoa: combine 1 taza de quinoa seca con 2 tazas de agua y ½ cucharadita de sal. Cuando suelte el hervor, reduzca la flama a fuego lento, tape y cocine por 15 minutos. Remueva del fuego y deje cocer al vapor por 5 minutos más, retire la tapa y esponje la quinoa con un tenedor.

Mientras se cocina la quinoa, parta el pepino, la menta, y el mango. Sazone con miel, sal y pimienta al gusto. Combine con la quinoa cocida y el aceite de coco, revolviendo para combinar.

Disfrútelo con garbanzos sazonados al curry.

Garbanzos sazonados al curry

Precaliente el horno a 300ºF [148,9ºC].

Después de que se hayan enjuagado y escurrido los garbanzos, déjelos que terminen de secar dándoles pequeñas palmadas con una toalla. Combine el aceite de oliva, el curry en polvo, la sal, y la pimienta en un cuenco grande. Después agregue los garbanzos y revuelva hasta que queden completamente cubiertos. Acomode la mezcla en una capa sobre una plancha para hornear recubierta y colóquela en una parrilla en el nivel más bajo del horno.

Hornee durante 20 minutos, sacuda la plancha a la mitad del tiempo de horneado. Deje enfriar antes de disfrutarlos.

Lista de compras

2 tazas de garbanzos cocidos
  (o 1 lata de 15 oz. [443,6 ml])
½ manojo de cilantro
1 pepino
1 lima [limón verde]
1 mango
1 manojo grande de menta

Revise la despensa

Granos de pimienta negra
Aceite de coco
Curry en polvo
Aceite de oliva virgen extra
Miel cruda
Quinoa seca
Sal marina

Cena del martes

Pollo mediterráneo con aceitunas sobre ensalada cocida de espinaca y escarola   Rinde 4–6 porciones

Pollo mediterráneo con aceitunas

¼ de taza de aceite de semilla de uva
1 cebolla amarilla pequeña, picada
5 dientes de ajo, finamente picados
1¼ lb. [567 g] de pechuga de pollo deshuesada y sin piel, partida en rebanadas
  de 1 pulgada [2,54 cm]
1 cucharada de orégano fresco, sin tallo
⅓ de taza de aceitunas kalamata sin hueso, picadas en trozos grandes
1 frasco de alcachofas en agua, picadas en trozos grandes
2 tazas de caldo de verduras o caldo de pollo
2 cucharadas de vino tinto o vinagre de vino tinto
½ cucharadita de sal marina
Pimienta negra recién molida, al gusto
¼ de taza de albahaca fresca, sin tallo y picada en trozos grandes

Precaliente el horno a 375ºF [190,6ºC].

Caliente a fuego medio-alto un sartén grueso que pueda ser metido al horno. Agregue el aceite, la cebolla y el ajo con una pizca de sal. Cocine durante 2–3 minutos, después agregue el pollo y cocine hasta que comience a dorarse, alrededor de 4 minutos.

Añada el resto de los ingredientes, excepto la albahaca fresca, revolviendo para cubrir el pollo. Tape y meta al horno para cocerlo durante 20–25 minutos. Remueva del horno y mezcle con la albahaca picada. Sazone al gusto.

Ensalada cocida de espinaca y escarola
Rinde 4 porciones

2 cucharadas de aceite de oliva virgen extra
½ lb. [226,8 g] de espinaca
1 cabeza de escarola italiana, picada
1 cucharada de miel cruda
¼ de taza de grosella seca
¼ de cucharadita de sal marina

Caliente un sartén a fuego medio-bajo, añada el aceite de oliva. Agregue las espinacas y la escarola en 2 tantos; cuando el primer tanto se haya cocido, entonces agregue el segundo, ya que haya espacio.

Cuando las hojas estén brillantes y ligeramente suaves, añada la miel, las grosellas y la sal. Sofría durante 3–4 minutos, y sazone al gusto. Sirva el pollo encima de la ensalada cocida.

Lista de compras

¼ de taza de albahaca fresca, sin tallo y picada en trozos medianos
1¼ lb. [567 g] de pechuga de pollo deshuesada y sin piel, partida en rebanadas de 1 pulgada [2,54 cm]
1 cabeza de escarola italiana, picada
5 dientes de ajo, finamente picados
1 cucharada de orégano fresco, sin tallos
½ lb. [226,8 g] de espinaca
1 cebolla amarilla pequeña, picada

Revise la despensa

Alcachofas en agua
Granos de pimienta negra
Grosella seca
Aceite de semilla de uva
Aceitunas kalamata sin hueso
Aceite de oliva virgen extra
Miel cruda
Vino tinto o vinagre de vino tinto
Sal marina
Caldo de verduras o caldo de pollo

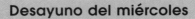

Desayuno del miércoles

Eliminador de grasa de arándano rojo y pepino
Rinde 1 porciones

Un estudio realizado en 2012 encontró que el jugo de los arándonos rojos, los arándanos rojo europeos y las grosellas negras reducen los componentes que provocan la inflamación.

2 peras, Bartlett o asiática
1 pepino, pelado si no es orgánico
½ taza de hojas tiernas de espinaca no muy apretada
½ limón [amarillo], pelado si no es orgánico
2 cucharadas de arándanos rojos, frescos o congelados
1 trozo de una pulgada [2,54 cm] de raíz de jengibre
6 cubos de hielo (opcional)

Pique las peras y el pepino y procéselas en la licuadora hasta obtener un batido. Añada el jugo de limón [amarillo], los arándanos rojos, el jengibre, y el hielo al gusto, licue hasta conseguir una consistencia cremosa.

Lista de compras

½ taza de hojas tiernas de espinaca
1 pepino
1 limón [amarillo]
1 trozo de una pulgada [2,54 cm]
   de raíz de jengibre

2 peras
1 bolsa de arándano rojo frescos o
   congelados

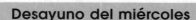

Desayuno del miércoles

Frittatas individuales de salmón ahumado
Rinde 4 porciones

¡Un encantador desayuno de fin de semana que también funciona como un desayuno rápido, para cuando esté de paseo o como un bocadillo para iniciar la semana con el pie derecho!

8 huevos orgánicos grandes
½ taza de leche de coco
2 cucharadas de aceite de oliva virgen extra, más un poco más para los moldes
½ taza de cebolla morada, finamente picada
½ lb. [226,8 g] de salmón ahumado rebanado, partido en trozos pequeños
8 cebolletas, rebanadas finamente
¼ de cucharadita de sal marina
Pimienta negra recién molida, al gusto

Precaliente el horno a 325ºF [162,8ºC].

Bata los huevos con leche de coco hasta que queden completamente homogéneos.

En una olla pequeña a fuego medio, agregue 1 cucharada de aceite de oliva. Sofría en el aceite las cebollas durante 3 minutos con sal y pimienta, al gusto. Apague el fuego. Añada el salmón, las cebolletas y las cebollas sofritas a los huevos y mezcle los ingredientes.

Con la cucharada de aceite de oliva restante, engrase ligeramente 8 moldes para magdalenas (o si usará capacillos, engrase la parte interior de ellos). Distribuya uniformemente la mezcla de modo que rellene ¾ partes de cada molde; si aún le queda mezcla llene otros moldes.

Hornee durante 15 minutos, hasta que esponjen y queden ligeramente dorados. Disfrútelos una vez que se hayan enfriado.

Lista de compras

8 huevos orgánicos grandes
1 cebolla morada pequeña
½ lb. [226,8 g] de salmón ahumado rebanado, partido en trozos pequeños
1 manojo de cebolletas

Revise la despensa

Granos de pimienta negra
Leche de coco
Aceite de oliva virgen extra
Capacillos (si lo desea)
Moldes para magdalenas
Sal marina

Almuerzo del miércoles

Sopa miso tónica con arroz integral y jaroses de manzana y nuez   Rinde 4 porciones

Sopa miso tónica con arroz integral

Este tónico le ayudará a equilibrarse cuando se sienta aletargado o que está a punto de enfermarse. Use el doble de la receta si desea que sobre para un par de días.

4 tazas de caldo de verduras
2 tazas de agua
2 trozos de 2 pulgadas [5,08 cm] de kelp
1 trozo de 1 pulgada [2,54 cm] de jengibre, rebanado y ligeramente machacado
2 tallos de citronela (use el tercio de abajo del tallo, trócelos un poco para liberar el sabor)
4 cebolletas, rebanadas finamente
2 tazas de rúcula
2 tazas de arroz integral cocido
3 cucharadas de miso de garbanzo, mezclado con una pequeña cantidad de agua caliente
2 cucharadas de jugo de limón [amarillo] (el jugo de 1 limón pequeño)
Sal marina, al gusto

Caliente el caldo y el agua con el kelp, el jengibre, la citronela hasta que comience a hervir. Baje el fuego y deje cocinar a fuego lento durante 10 minutos. Saque del agua el kelp, el jengibre, y la citronela, si lo desea. Agregue la cebolleta y la rúcula, y cocine a fuego lento durante 2 minutos más.

Retire del fuego, incorpore el miso, el jugo de limón, y pruébelo. Agregue el arroz cocido, sal, y más limón si lo desea.

Lista de compras

2 tazas de rúcula
1 trozo de 1 pulgada [2,54 cm] de jengibre,
1 limón [amarillo]
2 tallos citronela
1 manojo de cebolletas

Revise la despensa

Arroz integral
Miso de garbanzo
Kelp
Sal marina
Caldo de verduras

Jaroses de manzana y nuez   Rinde 4 porciones

3 manzanas Gala o Fuji medianas, peladas, sin corazón y partidas en cubos
   pequeños
1½ tazas de nueces en mitades, ligeramente tostadas, frías y picadas en trozos
   grandes
¼ de taza de vinagre de manzana
½ taza de menta o cilantro frescos, finamente picados
1 cucharada de miel cruda

En un cuenco grande revuelva todos los ingredientes. Mantenga la mezcla ta-
pada a temperatura ambiente hasta que sean servidos.

Lista de compras	Revise la despensa
3 manzanas 1 manojo de menta o cilantro 1½ tazas de nueces tostadas	Vinagre de manzana Miel cruda

Cena del miércoles

Brochetas asiáticas de pollo con ensalada de fideos de arroz   Rinde 4 porciones

Con anticipación: Remoje las brochetas de bambú durante 1 hora para evitar
que se enciendan al momento de cocinar el pollo. Si usará brochetas de
metal, cúbralas con aceite de oliva y manténgalas aparte hasta que el pollo
está listo para usarlas.

Marinado

2 cucharadas de aceite de ajonjolí
1 cucharada de salsa de pescado libre de gluten
1 cucharada de vinagre de arroz
2 cucharadas de jugo de lima [limón verde]
½ manojo de cilantro, finamente picado
2 cucharadas de miel cruda
2 dientes de ajo, finamente picado
1 trozo de 2 pulgadas [5,08 cm] de jengibre, finamente picado
½ cucharaditas de sal marina
¼ de cucharadita de pimienta negra recién molida
1¼ lb. [567 g] de pechuga de pollo deshuesada, sin piel y limpia. Cada pechuga
   cortada en 8 rebanadas para ser ensartadas en la brochetas

Precaliente el horno a 475ºF [246,1ºC].

Prepare el marinado. Quite la grasa de las pechugas de pollo y rebane. Sumerja el pollo dentro del marinado, cubra con película plástica y deje reposar durante 1½ horas a temperatura ambiente o durante 3 horas dentro de la nevera.

Ensarte las brochetas en el pollo y colóquelas en una plancha para hornear y ase a la parrilla durante 7 minutos o hasta que estén completamente cocidas (el tiempo de cocción dependerá del espesor de las rebanadas de pollo).

Ensalada de fideos de arroz: Siga la receta de la semana dos: Cena del viernes, omita el camarón para hacer una guarnición vegetariana.

Lista de compras

1¼ lb. [567 g] de pechuga de pollo deshuesada, sin piel
1 manojo de cilantro
2 dientes de ajo
1 trozo de 2 pulgadas [5,08 cm] de jengibre
1 lima [limón verde]

Revise la despensa

Granos de pimienta negra
Salsa de pescado libre de gluten
Miel cruda
Vinagre de arroz
Sal marina
Aceite de ajonjolí
Brochetas

Desayuno del jueves

Coctel tiempo de verduras   Rinde 1–2 porciones

Muchos estudios han identificado a los poliacetilenos de la zanahoria como fitonutrientes que ayudan a inhibir el crecimiento de las células del cáncer de colon.

4 zanahorias, bien fregadas, sin hojas o tallos
1 manojo de grelo o cualquier otra verdura de hojas verde oscuro
1 limón [amarillo], pelado si no es orgánico
1 diente de ajo
1 trozo de 2 pulgadas [5,08 cm] de jícama, bien fregada o pelada si no es orgánica
1 manojo de berro

Corte la fruta o la verdura para que quepa en el tubo de alimentación de su extractor de jugos. Procese los ingredientes y revuelva. Vierta en un vaso y beba tan pronto como sea posible.

Lista de compras

4 zanahorias
1 diente de ajo
1 jícama pequeña (use el sobrante
    picado en una ensalada)
1 limón [amarillo]

1 manojo de grelo o de cualquier
    otra verdura de hojas verde
    oscuro
1 manojo de berro

Almuerzo del jueves

Arroz de jengibre y cebolleta con ensalada primavera de col rizada   Rinde 4 porciones

Arroz de jengibre y cebolleta

Remoje en agua 1½ tazas de arroz la noche anterior a la que desee preparar esta receta.

Cocine el arroz por la mañana y déjelo enfriar de manera que pueda saltearlo al estilo chino para la cena. Esta es la manera tradicional de asegurar que su arroz salteado al estilo chino no quede pegajoso o cremoso.

2 cucharadas de aceite de coco
2 tazas de cebolletas finamente picadas (2 manojos)
3 cucharadas de jengibre finamente picado (3–4 pulgadas [7,62–10,16 cm])
⅓ de taza de vinagre de arroz
2 tazas de germinado de frijol
5 tazas de arroz integral cocido, frío y separado suavemente con un tenedor

Salsa

3 cucharadas de caldo de verduras
3 cucharadas de aminoácidos de coco (o salsa de soya)
1½ cucharaditas de aceite de ajonjolí puro
1½ cucharaditas de sal marina
Pimienta negra recién molida, al gusto

Mezcle todos los ingredientes de la salsa y ponga aparte.

Caliente un sartén grande o un wok a fuego alto, una vez que esté muy caliente añada el aceite. Agregue las cebolletas y el jengibre; y saltee al estilo chino durante 20 segundos. Añada el vinagre de arroz, el germinado de frijol y revuelva durante 1 minuto. Incorpore el arroz y saltee al estilo chino durante 2–3 minutos hasta que se caliente. Añada la salsa y mezcle con 2 utensilios hasta cubrir el arroz y las verduras.

Sírvase como guarnición o bien, como un platillo completo salteando al estilo chino el pollo o el pescado con un poco más de salsa (hecha arriba) y sal, y agréguelo al arroz.

Lista de compras

2 tazas de germinados de frijol
3–4 pulgadas [7,62–10,16 cm] de
    jengibre
2 manojos de cebolletas

Revise la despensa

Granos de pimienta negra
Arroz integral
Aminoácidos de coco o salsa de
    soya
Aceite de coco
Aceite de ajonjolí puro
Vinagre de arroz
Sal marina
Caldo de verduras

Ensalada primavera de verduras y col rizada
Rinde 4-6 porciones

Esta receta se mantiene en buen estado por 4–5 días en la nevera, así que haga una porción grande y úsela como una crujiente guarnición o como acompañante de cualquier comida.

1 manojo de rábanos, en rebanadas delgadas
2 manojos de col rizada, sin tallos y picada en pedazos pequeños del tamaño de
    un bocado
2 tazas de arvejas chinas
1 manojo de remolacha con sus hojas; la remolacha rallada y las hojas picadas
2 cebolletas, rebanadas finamente
1 trozo de 2 pulgadas [5,08 cm] de jengibre, finamente picado
¼ de taza de ajonjolí
3 cucharadas de jugo de limón [amarillo]
2 cucharadas de aceite de oliva virgen extra
½ cucharadita de sal marina

Mezcle todos los ingredientes en un cuenco grande. Con las manos limpias estruje las verduras para exprimir el agua que contengan, por lo menos 15 veces.

Después de 10 minutos vuelva a exprimir las verduras. Puede terminar la receta en este punto o repetir el procedimiento una vez más.

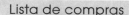

Lista de compras

1 manojo de remolacha
1 trozo de 2 pulgadas [5,08 cm] de
    jengibre
2 manojos de col rizada
1 manojo de rábanos
½ manojo de cebolletas
2 tazas de arvejas chinas

Revise la despensa

Jugo de limón [amarillo] (o 2
    limones [amarillos])
Aceite de oliva virgen extra
Sal marina
Ajonjolí

Cena del jueves

Salmón con cubierta de pacanas al arce con puré de raíz de apio y brócoli al vapor   Rinde 4 porciones

Hagan sonar los tambores por favor. ¡Esta es la receta favorita de mis clientes y de mi familia! Un amigo de mi madre quien era un chef profesional y un bailarín (como yo), creó esta original receta. Yo la he adaptado ligeramente, pero sigue siendo el gran favorito. Espero que usted la disfrute tanto como yo, es muy buena para cenas familiares y ocasiones especiales.

Salmón con cubierta de pacanas al arce

1½ lb. [680,4 g] de filete de salmón sin espinas
Aceite de oliva virgen extra para barnizar el pescado
¼ de cucharadita de sal marina
Pimienta negra recién molida, al gusto

Cubierta

¼ de taza de jarabe de arce
1 taza de pacanas
1 cucharadita de pimienta negra recién molida
½ cucharaditas de sal marina

Precaliente el horno a 325ºF [162,8ºC].

En un procesador de alimentos pique con impulsos breves los ingredientes para la cubierta hasta que obtenga una mezcla fina y homogénea. Coloque el salmón en una plancha para hornear recubierta. Barnice el salmón con el aceite de oliva y sazone con sal y pimienta. Presione la mezcla de maple y pacanas sobre el filete de salmón. Hornee el filete de salmón durante 25–30 minutos, o hasta que esté completamente cocido en el centro.

Parta el salmón en 4 porciones o sírvalo entero como aperitivo acompañado de endivias de Bruselas.

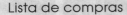

Lista de compras

1½ lb. [680,4 g] de filete de salmón sin espinas

Revise la despensa

Granos de pimienta negra
Aceite de oliva virgen extra
Jarabe de arce
Pacanas
Sal marina

Puré de raíz de apio   Rinde 4 porciones

2 lb. [907,2 gr] de raíz de apio
2 cucharadas de aceite de oliva virgen extra
2 cucharadas de aceite de coco
1 taza leche de coco
¾ de cucharadita de sal marina (o más si lo desea)
Pimienta negra recién molida, al gusto

Pele la raíz de apio y córtela en trozos medianos. Colóquelas en una cacerola grande (4 cuartos [3785 ml]), con agua fría cubriendo las verduras unas 2 pulgadas [5,08 cm]. Coloque la cacerola fuego alto y deje hervir. Continúe cociendo hasta que se traspasen fácilmente con un tenedor, alrededor de 15–20 minutos. Escurra y coloque la raíz de apio en un cuenco grande. Añada los aceites, la leche de coco, la sal y la pimienta. Machaque con un triturador de papas hasta obtener una consistencia cremosa. Agregue un poco más de sal si lo desea.

Para más adelante: Mantenga el puré caliente colocándolo en un cuenco de metal con tapa sobre una cacerola con agua hirviendo a fuego lento hasta por 1 hora (baño maría).

Brócoli al vapor   Rinde 4 porciones

2 lb. [907,2 gr] de brócoli, cortado en pequeños grumos
½ cucharadita de sal marina, para el agua hirviendo

Ponga a hervir 2 pulgadas [5,08 cm] de agua en una olla, y añada ¼ de cucharadita de sal y los grumos de brócoli (puede ser en una vaporera o bien, solo agregándolos al agua).

Con una tapa que ajuste bien, tape y deje al vapor durante 3–4 minutos. Escurra y sírvalos inmediatamente, o enfríe bajo el chorro de agua fría si los servirá después.

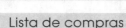

Lista de compras

2 lb. [907,2 g] de brócoli
2 lb. [907,2 g] de raíz de apio

Revise la despensa

Granos de pimienta negra
Leche de coco
Aceite de coco
Aceite de oliva virgen extra
Sal marina

Desayuno del viernes

Renovador batido de almendra y vainilla
Rinde 1–2 porciones

Un cuarto de taza de almendras contiene casi 99 mg de magnesio. Estudios han demostrado que la deficiencia de magnesio está relacionada con los ataques cardiacos, y que carecer de suficiente magnesio inmediatamente después de un ataque cardiaco promueve que los radicales libres dañen el corazón.

1 taza de almendras crudas, remojadas durante la noche
1 taza de leche de almendras
1 taza de moras o frutas del bosque (arándanos azules, frambuesas, o zarzamoras)
½ cucharadita de extracto de vainilla puro
6 cubos de hielo

Remoje las almendras en agua durante toda la noche para que puedan germinar (este proceso permite que las almendras germinen parcialmente, lo cual elimina las enzimas inhibidoras e incrementa el valor nutricional). En una licuadora procese las almendras, la leche de almendras, las moras, la vainilla, y el hielo. Vierta en vasos y sirva tan pronto como sea posible.

Lista de compras

1 taza de almendras crudas
1 pinta de moras de su elección

Revise la despensa

Leche de almendras
Extracto de vainilla puro

Almuerzo del viernes

Ensalada de pollo con curry servida en charolas de lechuga con jaroses de manzana y nuez   Rinde 4 porciones

Una deliciosa ensalada para el almuerzo o para la cena. ¡Una receta de Cherie!

½ taza de mayonesa o aderezo libre de huevo marca Veganaise
1 cucharadita de jugo fresco de limón [amarillo]
2 cucharadas de curry en polvo
2 tazas de pollo cocido, picado
¼ de taza de apio partido en cubos
½ taza de cilantro picado
¼ de taza de almendra fileteada
1 cabeza de lechuga romana o lechuga de hoja verde

Mezcle la mayonesa, el jugo de limón, y el curry en polvo. Coloque el resto de los ingredientes (excepto la lechuga) en un cuenco mediano o grande y revuelva con la mezcla de la mayonesa. Refrigere por lo menos una hora antes de servir.

Sirva la ensalada de pollo en las hojas de lechuga o bien, hágalas tiras y revuélvalas con el resto de la ensalada.

Nota: Las almendras puedes ser sustituidas por nueces. También puede comerse con jaroses de manzana y nuez (Vea la receta en semana cuatro: Almuerzo del miércoles).

Lista de compras

½ penca de apio
2 pechugas de pollo (cocido)
1 manojo de cilantro
1 limón [amarillo]
1 cabeza de lechuga romana

Revise la despensa

Curry en polvo
Almendra fileteada
Mayonesa o Veganaise

Cena del viernes

Hamburguesas de salmón silvestre con ensalada de cardamomo, aguacate y radicchio   Rinde 4 porciones

Hamburguesas de salmón silvestre

1¼ lb. [567 g] de salmón, sin piel, picado
2 dientes de ajo
1 trozo de ½ pulgada [1,27 cm] de jengibre
2 cucharadas de Mostaza Dijon
¼ de taza de estragón, picado
2 cebolletas, finamente picadas
2 cucharadas de miso de garbanzo, disuelto en 1 cucharada de agua tibia
1 huevo, batido
½ taza de migajas de pan libre de gluten o harina de almendra
1 cucharada de linaza molida
Aceite de girasol, para cocinar
Sal marina, al gusto

Coloque el ajo y el jengibre en un procesador de alimentos y pique finamente con impulsos breves. Añada el salmón y procese de nuevo con impulsos breves hasta que estén completamente picados. Remueva la mezcla del procesador de alimentos y colóquela en un cuenco mediano.

Agregue el resto de los ingredientes y mezcle suavemente con la mano hasta que estén completamente incorporados. Forme bolas del tamaño de un taza medidora de ¼, aplánelas para formar pequeñas tortas y refrigérelas por lo menos durante 1 hora o hasta 1 día.

Cocine a la parrilla o en un sartén: Engrase ligeramente con el aceite de girasol. Coloque las tortas en el sartén (o en la parrilla), no coloque demasiadas.

Cocine a fuego medio-alto durante 5 minutos por el primer lado, después voltéelas y cocine por el otro lado durante otros 4–5 minutos.

Una vez cocinadas, colóquelas en un plato y espolvoree sal, repita el procedimiento hasta que todas las hamburguesas queden cocidas.

Cómalas con bollos libre de gluten o solas con lechuga y el aderezo de su elección (¡a mí me encanta la mostaza Dijon!).

Lista de compras	Revise la despensa
½ taza de migajas de pan libre de gluten o de harina de almendra	Miso de garbanzo
1 huevo	Mostaza Dijon
2 dientes de ajo	Linaza
1 trozo de ½ pulgada [1,27 cm] de jengibre	Sal marina
½ manojo de cebolletas	Aceite de girasol
1¼ lb. [567 g] de salmón	
1 manojo de estragón	

Ensalada de cardamomo, aguacate y radicchio
Rinde 6 porciones

Esta es una de mis ensaladas favoritas para preparar en clima frío. A través de calentar ligeramente el aderezo de la ensalada obtenemos una cálida ensalada (no fría) para el invierno. El cardamomo es la "reina de las especias", históricamente es la especia favoritas entre las mujeres.

Aderezo

6 cucharadas de aceite de coco tibio
2 dientes de ajo, finamente picados
1 trozo de 1 pulgada [2,54 cm] de jengibre finamente picado
2 cucharaditas de cardamomo molido
1 cucharadita de cilantro molido
1 cucharadita de vinagre de umeboshi
2 cucharaditas de mostaza Dijon
1 cucharadita de miel cruda
Sal marina, al gusto
Pimienta negra recién molida, al gusto

Ensalada

3 tallos de apio, finamente rebanados de manera sesgada
2 aguacates, picados en trozos de 2 pulgadas [5,08 cm]
6 tazas de rúcula
1 cabeza de radicchio, picado
½ taza de nueces, tostadas
Sal marina, al gusto
Pimienta negra recién molida, al gusto

Caliente el aceite de coco a fuego medio-bajo. Añada el ajo y el jengibre, revuelva durante 15 segundos. Agregue las especias y continúe moviendo durante 15 segundos más. Añada el resto de los ingredientes y continúe revolviendo para que se mezclen los ingredientes y queden ligeramente calientes.

Vierta en un cuenco y mezcle con todos los ingredientes de la ensalada hasta que quede suavemente cocida y completamente cubierta de aderezo.

El aguacate hará la ensalada ligeramente cremosa. Sazone con sal y pimienta y sirva inmediatamente.

Nota: Si desea preparar este aderezo y esperar para servirlo, use aceite de oliva en lugar de aceite de coco ya que este no se solidifica. Si no encuentra vinagre de umeboshi (busque en la sección de alimentos orientales) puede sustituirlo por una cucharada de vinagre balsámico.

Lista de compras

- 6 tazas de rúcula
- 2 aguacates
- 3 tallos de apio
- 2 dientes de ajo
- 1 trozo de 1 pulgada [2,54 cm] de jengibre
- 1 cabeza de radicchio

Revise la despensa

- Granos de pimienta negra
- Aceite de coco (o aceite de oliva virgen extra)
- Mostaza Dijon
- Cardamomo molido
- Cilantro molido
- Miel cruda
- Sal marina
- Vinagre de umeboshi
- Nueces

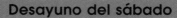

Desayuno del sábado

Manzana yucateca   Rinde 1 porción

Hay evidencia de que algunos aspectos inflamatorios de la obesidad pueden ser alterados a través de los compuestos que contienen azufre del ajo.

2 manzanas
3 hojas de col rizada
1 diente de ajo (no es necesario que se pele)
Una pizca de sal marina celta
Una pizca de pimienta negra recién molida,
Una pizca de pimienta dulce

Corte la fruta o la verdura para que quepa en el tubo de alimentación de su extractor de jugos. Procese las manzanas, la col rizada y el ajo; revuelva con las especias. Vierta en un vaso y beba tan pronto como sea posible.

Lista de compras

2 manzanas
1 manojo de col rizada
1 diente de ajo

Revise la despensa

Pimienta dulce
Granos de pimienta negra
Sal marina celta

Almuerzo del sábado

Wrap de berza con pollo del suroeste y ensalada mexicana de repollo   Rinde 4 porciones

Wrap de berza con pollo del Suroeste

1 lb. [453,6 gr] de pechuga de pollo deshuesada y sin piel (2)
8 hojas grandes de berza, con la mitad del tallo cortado
1 taza de zanahoria, rallada
1 taza de pepino, rebanado finamente
1 taza de cilantro, picado
2 aguacates, rebanados
Pimienta de Cayena, al gusto
Jugo de lima [limón verde], al gusto
Sal marina, al gusto
Pimienta negra recién molida, al gusto
1 taza de salsa de tomatillo (tomate verde) (opcional)

Escalfe o ase la pechuga de pollo durante 12–15 minutos o hasta que esté completamente cocida.

Rebane el pollo y sazone con la sal, la pimienta, la pimienta de Cayena y el jugo de lima [limón verde], al gusto. Deje reposar mientras prepara los ingredientes del wrap de berza.

Remueva los tallos centrales de las hojas de berza y corte las hojas en 2 partes a lo largo de manera que obtenga 4 mitades por persona.

Alinee las 16 mitades y distribuya todos los ingredientes entre el total de hojas. Acomode un poco de cada verdura en el primer tercio de la hoja de berza. Añada el pollo rebanado.

Prepárese para enrollar: Doble la parte inferior de la hoja sobre los ingredientes, y enrolle la hoja hacia afuera (lejos de usted). Asegure con un palillo y repita el procedimiento con el resto de las hojas.

Disfrútelo con salsa de tomatillo o con salsa picante, al gusto.

Lista de compras

2 aguacates
2 zanahorias
1 lb. [453,6 gr] de pechuga de pollo deshuesada y sin piel
1 manojo pequeño de cilantro
1 manojo grande de hojas de berza
1 pepino pequeño
1 taza de salsa de tomatillo (tomate verde) (opcional)

Revise la despensa

Granos de pimienta negra
Pimienta de Cayena
Jugo de lima [limón verde]
Sal marina

Ensalada mexicana de repollo   Rinde 4–6 porciones

1 cabeza de repollo verde, sin centro, finamente rebanada
3 zanahorias, cortadas en juliana
1 manojo de cilantro, finamente picado
1 manojo de cebolletas, finamente picado
2 dientes de ajo, finamente picados
⅓ de taza de jugo de lima [limón verde]
½ cucharadita de sal marina
1 cucharada de aceite de oliva virgen extra
Pimienta negra recién molida o pimienta de Cayena, al gusto (opcional)

Mezcle todos los ingredientes en un cuenco. Con las manos limpias, masajee los ingredientes, estrujándolos por puñados a la vez. Repita este procedimiento 20 veces en total. La ensalada deberá reducirse en volumen y estar completamente cubierta de aderezo. Pruébela y sazone al gusto en caso de ser necesario. Mantenga en refrigeración hasta por 5 días.

Lista de compras

1 cabeza de repollo verde
3 zanahorias
1 manojo de cilantro
2 dientes de ajo
Jugo de lima [limón verde]
1 manojo de cebolletas

Revise la despensa

Granos de pimienta negra
Pimienta de Cayena
Aceite de oliva virgen extra
Sal marina

Cena del sábado

Crepas de garbanzo con relleno de zanahoria y arame con una ensalada simple con semillas de calabaza   Rinde 4–6 porciones

Esta es otra receta que he adaptado de mi escuela de cocina y de la chef Myra Kornfeld. Me gusta lo fácil que es hacer crepas, y el relleno está repleto de asombroso arame, mi verdura del mar favorita. Aventúrese a probar esta interesante receta. ¡Creo que quedará complacido con el resultado! Congele cualquier sobrante de la pasta para crepas.

1 taza de harina de garbanzo
1 taza de harina libre de gluten
1 cucharadita de sal marina
2 cucharadas de aceite de oliva virgen extra o aceite de coco
2 tazas de agua tibia
¼ de taza de cebollín finamente picado
½ taza de arame, seco
1 cebolla morada, en rebanadas delgadas
1 zanahoria grande, rayada
1 cucharadita de aceite de ajonjolí
1 cucharada de jengibre picado
Vinagre de ciruela umeboshi (opcional)
Sal marina, al gusto
Pimienta negra recién molida, al gusto

Fotografía por Polara Studio

En un cuenco, cierna las harinas y mézclalas con la sal. Añada el aceite de oliva o coco y el agua e incorpore completamente hasta tener una mezcla uniforme. Agregue el cebollín y continúe batiendo. Deje reposar a temperatura ambiente durante 30 minutos. Remoje el arame durante 10 minutos, y después escúrralo.

En un sartén, agregue la cebolla, la zanahoria, el aceite de ajonjolí, el jengibre, la sal, la pimienta y un poco de vinagre de umeboshi. Añada agua hasta casi cubrirlo (¾ del volumen de los ingredientes). Cuando comience a hervir, reduzca la flama y permita que se cocine hasta que se evaporen los líquidos, aproximadamente 30 minutos o más.

Mientas tanto prepare las crepas: caliente a fuego medio una crepera pequeña o bien un sartén antiadherente. Engrase ligeramente el sartén con aceite. Vierta aproximadamente un ¼ de taza de la mezcla para crepas en el sartén, y extiéndala en forma circular hasta cubrir totalmente el fondo del sartén. Cuando la superficie comience a burbujear, aproximadamente 1 minuto, deprenda las orillas y voltee. Cocine por ese lado durante 30 segundos.

Para servir rellene cada crepa con un ¼ de taza del relleno de arame y enrolle. Decore con cebollín.

Para la ensalada simple con semillas de calabaza: Combine un ¼ de taza de aceite de oliva y ¼ de taza de vinagre de manzana, y agregue una pizca de sal (puede agregar pimienta de Cayena si lo desea). Añada 4–6 manojos de rúcula o de mezcla de lechugas verdes, revuelva hasta estar completamente cubierta de aderezo. Sazone al gusto y agregue encima ½ taza semillas de calabaza tostadas con sal.

Lista de compras

1 bolsa de arame seco
4–6 manojos de rúcula o mezcla de lechugas verdes
1 zanahoria grande
1 taza de harina de garbanzo
1 manojo de cebollín
1 trozo de 1 pulgada [2,54 cm] de jengibre
Vinagre de Umeboshi (opcional)
1 cebolla morada

Revise la despensa

Vinagre de manzana
Granos de pimienta negra
Aceite de coco
Aceite de oliva virgen extra
Harina libre de gluten
Sal marina
Aceite de ajonjolí

Desayuno del domingo

Perejil vivaz   Rinde 1 porción

El limón [amarillo] ayuda a eliminar el ácido úrico de sus articulaciones, lo que es una de las causas principales de la inflamación de las articulaciones.

½ manojo de perejil
2 tallos de apio
1–2 zanahorias, bien fregadas, sin hojas o tallos y con ambos extremos recortados
½ pepino, pelado si no es orgánico
½ limón [amarillo], pelado

Corte la fruta o la verdura para que quepa en el tubo de alimentación de su extractor de jugos. Beba tan pronto como sea posible.

Lista de compras

1–2 zanahorias
1 manojo de apio
1 pepino

1 limón [amarillo]
1 manojo de perejil

Desayuno-almuerzo del domingo

Pan francés horneado vacacional   Rinde 6 porciones

He aquí un platillo festivo para el desayuno de fin de semana, perfecto para recibir visitas. Comience a prepararlo la noche anterior, de manera que el pan se remoje con todas las especias y sabores. ¡Es delicioso y festivo, además de ser naturalmente libre de gluten y de lácteos!

1–2 cucharadas de aceite de coco, para engrasar los moldes y un poco más para la cubierta
1 hogaza de pan libre de gluten (cortada en rebanadas de 1½ pulgada [3,08 cm])
½ taza de pacanas
½ taza de pasas, arándano rojo o grosellas
3 tazas de leche de coco
3 huevos
2 cucharadas de azúcar de coco
La ralladura de 1 limón [amarillo]
½ cucharadita de sal marina
1 cucharada de extracto de almendras
1 cucharadita de canela
⅛ de cucharadita de nuez moscada
½ taza de jarabe de arce, para la cubierta
1 taza de uvas frescas rebanadas o plátanos rebanados

213

Engrase con aceite de coco un molde para hornear de 9–13 pulgadas [22,8–33,02 cm].

En el molde acomode las rebanadas de pan en capas muy apretadas, espolvoreando las pacanas y la fruta seca entre cada una de las capas.

Bata la leche de coco, los huevos, el azúcar de coco, la ralladura de limón, la sal marina y el extracto de almendras en un cuenco. Vierta sobre el pan. Espolvoree con la cucharadita de canela y el ⅛ de cucharadita de nuez moscada.

Cubra con una película plástica y refrigere durante toda la noche (o por lo menos unas horas).

Retire la película plástica y hornee a 400ºF [204ºC] durante 35–40 minutos, o hasta que dore. Corte en cuadros y bañe con el jarabe de arce y la fruta fresca rebanada.

Lista de compras

1 hogaza de pan libre de gluten (cortado en rebanadas de 1½ pulgada [3,08 cm])
3 huevos
1 taza de uvas frescas rebanadas o plátanos rebanados
1 limón [amarillo]
½ taza de pacanas
½ taza de pasas, arándano rojo, o grosellas

Revise la despensa

Extracto de almendras
Canela
Leche de coco
Aceite de coco
Azúcar de coco
Jarabe de arce
Nuez moscada
Sal marina

Fotografía por Polara Studio

214

Almuerzo del domingo

Sushi vegetariano de calabaza moscada con ensalada primavera de verduras y col rizada
Rinde 8 porciones

Los días festivos son importantes para mi familia. Yo soy la más joven de tres mujeres, y hasta ahora seguimos planeando con anticipación nuestros menús, con mucho entusiasmo y una sana dosis de sentido del humor. ¡Nos encante disfrazarnos! Yo inventé esta versión vegana de sushi crudo para una divertida fiesta de cosecha de otoño. ¡Disfrazado o no, intente preparar está receta para su próxima reunión!

3 tazas de jícama, picada en cubos de 1 pulgada [2,54 cm]
3 tazas de nabo, picado en cubos de 1 pulgada [2,54 cm]
½ taza de nueces de la India crudas
1 cucharada + 1 cucharadita de sal marina
2 cucharadas de vinagre de arroz
1½ tazas de calabaza moscada cocida, pelada y rebanada
1 manojo de cebolletas
1 manojo de hojas de mostaza, sin tallo
Ajonjolí negro
1 paquete de hojas de nori (alga)

Coloque en un procesador de alimentos los cubos de jícama, el nabo, y las nueces de la India con 1 cucharada de sal, procese con impulsos breves hasta tener los ingredientes del tamaño de granos de arroz. Hágalo por partes si es necesario. Presione el "arroz" sobre un colador para eliminar cualquier exceso de humedad. Combine la mezcla de "arroz" con la cucharadita de sal restante y el vinagre y revuelva en el colador para eliminar más humedad.

Extienda las hojas de nori con el lado rugoso hacia arriba. Vierta una cucharada uniforme de la mezcla de "arroz" sobre el tercio inferior de la hoja de nori. Extienda el "arroz" en forma de cuadrado sobre toda la hoja dejando un ¼ de pulgada [0,635 cm] de cada lado. Acomode horizontalmente pequeñas cantidades de cada uno de los ingredientes (1 cebolleta, ½ hoja de mostaza, tiras largas de calabaza moscada, una pizca de ajonjolí negro). Enrolle

Fotografía por Polara Studio

apretadamente desde usted hacia afuera. Colóquelo con el extremo de la hoja hacia abajo y repita con la siguiente hoja. Rebane con un cuchillo para pan (aserrado) y sirva. Humedezca el cuchillo entre cada corte para mejores resultados.

Cómalo acompañado de la Ensalada de verduras y col rizada de primavera (semana cuatro: Almuerzo del jueves).

Lista de compras

3 lb. [1361 g] de calabaza moscada
1 jícama grande
1 manojo de hojas de mostaza
1 paquete de hojas de nori
1 manojo de cebolletas
½ taza de ajonjolí negro
2 nabos grandes

Revise la despensa

Nueces de la India crudas
Vinagre de arroz
Sal marina

Cena del domingo

Shiitake salteado al estilo chino con batatas japonesas asadas y sopa miso tónica   Rinde 4 porciones

Shiitake salteado al estilo chino

¼ de taza de aceite de coco
4 dientes de ajo, rebanados en rodajas
3 tazas de hongo shiitake (completos si son pequeños o bien en mitades si son grandes)
1 cabeza grande de bok choy (o 6 cabezas pequeñas bok choy), rebanado de manera sesgada
3 pulgadas [7,62 cm] de bardana, en rebanadas finas (opcional)
1 cucharada de vinagre balsámico
½ cucharadita de sal marina
½ taza de nueces tostadas o almendras, picadas en trozos grandes con el procesador de alimentos
Pimienta negra recién molida, al gusto

Mis en place (esto significa en francés "puesto en el lugar", nos referimos a tener todo listo en su área de trabajo dentro de la cocina) todos los ingredientes, esta receta es rápida de preparar.

Caliente el aceite de coco en un wok o en un sartén hasta que esté caliente. Añada el ajo y dórelo, aproximadamente durante 30 segundos. Agregue el hongo shiitake, cocine por 3–5 minutos hasta que esté bien dorado. Añada

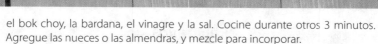

el bok choy, la bardana, el vinagre y la sal. Cocine durante otros 3 minutos. Agregue las nueces o las almendras, y mezcle para incorporar.

Pruebe y sazone con pimienta y sal o vinagre si lo desea.

Batatas japonesas asadas Rinde 4 porciones

Las batatas japonesas tienen una cáscara de color morado y una pulpa de color casi blanco. Son extremadamente dulces y por si solas necesitan de muy poco trabajo para hacerlas ¡deliciosas!

2 batatas japonesas grandes
3 cucharadas de aceite de semilla de uva
½ cucharadita de sal marina

Precaliente el horno a 400ºF [204ºC].

Corte las batatas en cubos de 1 pulgada [2,54 cm]. Mezcle las batatas con el aceite y la sal en un cuenco y después distribúyalas en una plancha para hornear.

Hornee durante 35–40 minutos, o hasta que estén doradas. Deles vuelta durante el tiempo de horneado para dorarlas por ambos lados.

Acompáñelas con la Sopa miso tónica (semana cuatro: Almuerzo del miércoles).

Lista de compras

1 cabeza grande de bok choy (o 6 cabezas pequeñas de bok choy)
3 pulgadas [7,62 cm] de bardana (opcional)
2 batatas japonesas grande
4 dientes de ajo
3 tazas de hongo shiitake

Revise la despensa

Vinagre balsámico
Granos de pimienta negra
Aceite de coco
Aceite de semilla de uva
Sal marina
Nueces o almendras

A la carta

¡Pruebe su receta favorita de las semanas anteriores! Practique para hacerla perfecta, ¡tiene una segunda oportunidad para preparar una cena que le encante!

Refrigerios

Aros de cebolla Rinde 6–8 porciones

4–5 cebollas dulces (amarilla, blanca, Walla Walla)
¼ de taza de vinagre de sidra de manzana o de coco
¼ de taza de jugo fresco de limón [amarillo]
¼ de taza de aceite de oliva virgen extra
2 cucharadas de levadura nutricional
Una pizca de sal marina

Corte las cebollas en rebanadas y apártelas. En una licuadora, agregue el jugo de limón, el vinagre, el aceite de oliva y la pizca de sal, y licue hasta obtener una mezcla homogénea. Vierta sobre las cebollas para marinarlas y deje reposar por varias horas. Antes de colocar los aros de cebolla en una plancha del deshidratador, sacuda los aros para eliminar el exceso de líquido y que no goteen. Espolvoree con levadura nutricional. Deshidrate a 105–115ºF [40,56–46,11ºC] durante 7–8 horas o hasta que estén crujientes.

Lista de compras

1 limón [amarillo]
4–5 cebollas dulces

Revise la despensa

Vinagre de sidra de manzana o de coco
Levadura nutricional
Aceite de oliva virgen extra
Sal marina

Frituras de calabaza italiana deshidratada

2 calabazas italianas
Sal marina, al gusto

Rebane las calabazas italianas en delgadas rodajas y espolvoree un poco de sal marina, si lo desea. Usted puede también espolvorear su sazonador favorito. Coloque las rebanadas de calabaza italiana en la plancha del deshidratador y deshidrate durante 7–8 horas a 105–115ºF [40,56–46,11ºC] o hasta que estén crujientes. Son sorpresivamente dulces y deliciosas.

Lista de compras

2 calabazas italianas

Revise la despensa

Sal marina

Tomates con albahaca deshidratados

3–4 tomates
12–16 hojas de albahaca

Corte los tomates en rebanadas delgadas y coloque una hoja de albahaca fresca encima de cada rebanada una vez que los haya colocado en la plancha del deshidratador. Deshidrátelos aproximadamente durante 12 horas a 105–115ºF [40,56–46,11ºC] o hasta que estén crujientes.

Lista de compras

3–4 tomates   1 paquete de albahaca fresca

Dip de remolacha brillante   Rinde 3 tazas

He aquí una colorida, brillante y nutritiva versión del hummus para usar como dip de verduras. Es también muy bueno para usarse con galletas saladas. Una bienvenida adición a un "crudité" tradicional. Esta es una receta que adapté de mi madre, quien me crió con hermosas comidas caseras y ensaladas frescas todos los días.

2 remolachas rojas medianas, cocidas hasta estar tiernas (1½ tazas)
1 taza de garbanzos cocidos
2 dientes de ajo
¼ de taza de harina de almendras (o almendra fileteada molida)
½ taza de aceite de oliva virgen extra
⅓ de taza de vinagre de vino tinto
½ cucharadita de sal marina

Procese todos los ingredientes juntos en una licuadora o un procesador de alimentos añadiendo un poco de agua si es necesario para adelgazar la mezcla.

Disfrútelo con verduras crudas o una rebanada de pan tostado libre de gluten, con una ensalada de quinoa o pollo cocido.

Lista de compras

2 remolachas rojas medianas
2 dientes de ajo

Revise la despensa

Harina de almendras o almendra
    fileteada
Garbanzos
Aceite de oliva virgen extra
Vinagre de vino tinto
Sal marina

Bolas superpoderosas de semillas   Rinde 40 bolas

Esta receta rinde mucho, así que usted puede congelarlas y tomar unas 4 más o menos cuando necesite un aperitivo durante el día. Vale la pena prepararlas todas en una sola ocasión y congelarlas o mantenerlas en la nevera para después (hasta por 10 días).

1 lb. [453,6 gr] de mantequilla de semillas de calabaza o de mantequilla de
    semillas de girasol
14 oz. [396,9 gr] de miel cruda (casi 2 tazas)
3 tazas de hojuelas de avena
2 tazas de ajonjolí blanco (o hojuelas de coco rallado sin edulcorar)

En un cuenco, mezcle la mantequilla de semillas de calabaza o de semillas de girasol y la miel cruda.

Utilice las hojuelas de avena como están o bien, licúelas para obtener una textura polvosa. Añada el avena a la mezcla de mantequilla con miel y revuelva hasta que se combinen completamente. Ajuste la consistencia si fuera necesario.

Usando las manos, forme pequeñas bolas con la pasta. Humedezca las manos con frecuencia para evitar que se pegue la pasta. Revuelque las bolas sobre ajonjolí o coco rallado. *Refrigere y ¡disfrútelas!*

Lista de compras

1 lb. [453 gr] de mantequilla de
    semillas de calabaza o de
    mantequilla de semillas de girasol

Revise la despensa

Miel cruda
Hojuelas de avena
Ajonjolí blanco (o coco rallado)

Postres

"Tarta de queso" vegana   Rinde 6–8 porciones

3 tazas de nueces de la India crudas
½ taza de jugo fresco de limón [amarillo]
¼ de taza de néctar de coco o de jarabe de arce puro o 1 cucharada de néctar
    de coco con ¼ de cucharadita de stevia líquida
½ taza de aceite de coco, fluidificado
2 cucharaditas de extracto de vainilla puro
Agua, la necesaria

Remoje las nueces de la India por un mínimo de 4 horas, o bien, toda la noche. Coloque en una licuadora de alta velocidad, como la VitaMix, las nueces de la India remojadas, el jugo de limón, el néctar de coco, el aceite de coco y la vainilla; y procese hasta que quede cremosa. Si es necesario añada el agua poco a poco en cantidades pequeñas; usualmente se necesita un ¼ de taza de agua. No permita que quede demasiado líquida. También puede usarse un procesador de alimentos, pero no quedará tan cremosa como cuando se hace en una licuadora de alta velocidad.

Nota: No funciona en una licuadora convencional.

Corteza de pacanas

1 taza de hojuelas de coco sin edulcorar
1 taza de pacanas
½ taza de harina de coco o de almendras
2 cucharaditas de canela molida
2 cucharadas de néctar de coco o jarabe de arce puro
5 cucharadas de aceite de coco

Coloque todos los ingredientes secos en un procesador de alimentos y procese con impulsos breves para conseguir que todos los ingredientes tengan una consistencia semejante a migajas de pan. Agregue el néctar de coco y el aceite de coco, y procese con impulsos breves hasta que la pasta quede homogénea y se comience a desprender de las paredes del procesador. Coloque las pasta en un molde para tarta y, usando los dedos, presiónela suavemente cubriendo el fondo y las paredes del molde. Coloque la costra en el congelador por lo menos durante 30 minutos. Una vez fría la costra, vierta el relleno en ella y refrigere por lo menos durante 1 hora.

Lista de compras

3 tazas de nueces de la India crudas
1 taza de hojuelas de coco sin edulcorar
½ taza de harina de coco o de almendra
1 limón [amarillo]
1 taza de pacanas

Revise la despensa

Canela
Néctar de coco, jarabe de arce puro o stevia líquida
Aceite de coco
Extracto de vainilla

Peras escalfadas con jengibre y avellanas
Rinde 4 porciones

Las peras escalfadas son una saludable y elegante manera de terminar una comida. Reduciendo el líquido donde se escalfaron las peras conseguimos una salsa espesa llena de sabor para bañar las peras.

Corone con avellanas y como una opción añada granillo de cacao para convertirlas en una ¡golosina de chocolate!

Utensilios

Una cacerola mediana o grande
Papel pergamino para cocinar
Tijeras
Cuchara para colar

Ingredientes

6 tazas de agua
⅓ de taza de jarabe de arce (o 1 taza de jugo de manzana)
5 clavos enteros
2–3 rajas de canela
1 cucharadita de extracto de vainilla
1 cucharada de extracto de naranja (o más extracto de vainilla)
Ralladura de 1 limón [amarillo]
¼ de taza de jengibre, picado en trozos grandes
4 peras maduras, peladas, sin corazón
2 cucharadas de avellanas, picadas (decoración)
2 cucharadas de granillo de cacao (decoración opcional)

En una cacerola grande a fuego alto combine el agua, el jarabe de arce, los clavos, la canela en rajas, el extracto de vainilla, el extracto de naranja, la ralladura de limón y el jengibre.

Una vez que haya pelado las peras y les haya quitado el corazón, deslícelas suavemente dentro del agua, asegurándose de que queden completamente cubiertas. Si no cuenta con una herramienta para descorazonar las peras, una vez que estén escalfadas y frías, usted puede simplemente cortarlas en mitades y quitarles las semillas.

Coloque el papel pergamino cubriendo la parte superior de la cacerola (haciendo un orificio del tamaño de una nuez al centro) de manera que las peras se mantengan sumergidas durante el tiempo de cocción.

Deje hervir las peras a fuego medio-bajo alrededor de 30 minutos, hasta que las peras estén tiernas al pincharlas con un tenedor (pero que sigan manteniendo su forma).

Remueva las peras con una cuchara para escurrir y déjelas reposar en la plancha para hornear para que se enfríen rápidamente.

Vierta la mitad del líquido donde se escalfaron las peras en un sartén y redúzcalo aproximadamente a ½ taza, hasta que cubra la parte de atrás de una cuchara.

Sirva las peras enteras o en mitades, empápelas con la salsa reducida y decórelas con avellanas o con el granillo de cacao.

Lista de compras

6 pulgadas [15,24 cm] de jengibre
1 limón [amarillo]
4 peras maduras

Revise la despensa

Canela en rajas
Granillo de cacao
Avellanas
Jarabe de arce (o jugo de manzana)
Extracto de naranja
Extracto de vainilla
Clavos enteros

Fotografía por Polara Studio

223

Barras linzer de frambuesa   Rinde 10 barras

Algunas veces solo necesitamos comer algo dulce. Me gusta usar la miel cruda como el principal edulcorante en postres, aderezos y batidos. Cuando se toma en pequeñas cantidades, armoniza el hígado. La miel es uno de los mejores alimentos que proveen de energía si no usa en exceso ni se procesa en exceso. ¡Disfrútela!

Aceite de coco, para engrasar el molde
1½ tazas de harina libre de gluten
¾ de taza de azúcar de coco
½ taza más 2 cucharadas de nueces picadas, divididas
1 cucharada de cacao en polvo sin edulcorar
2 cucharaditas de ralladura de naranja recién hecha
¼ de cucharadita de polvo para hornear
¼ de cucharadita de bicarbonato de sodio
¼ de cucharadita de sal marina
1 cucharadita de canela molida
¼ de cucharadita de nuez moscada molida
¼ de cucharadita de clavo molido
1 huevo grande (o 1½ cucharaditas de sustituto de huevo marca Ener-G Egg
    Replacer disuelto en 2 cucharadas de agua tibia)
2 cucharadas de aceite de oliva
2 cucharadas de agua
¾ de taza de jalea de frambuesa sin semillas
1 cucharada de jugo de naranja
2 cucharadas de miel cruda

Precaliente el horno a 350ºF [176,7ºC].
    Engrase con aceite de coco un molde para hornear de 9 por 9 pulgadas [22,8 x 22,8 cm] o de 7 por 11½ pulgadas [17,78 x 29,21 cm].

Fotografía por Polara Studio

Coloque el harina, el azúcar, las nueces (dejando las otras 2 cucharadas aparte), el cacao, la ralladura de naranja, el polvo para hornear, el bicarbonato de sodio, la sal y todas las especias en un procesador de alimentos.

Procese con impulsos breves hasta que las nueces estén finamente picadas. Añada el huevo (o el sustituto de huevo), el aceite de oliva y el agua. Procese hasta tener una mezcla húmeda.

Pase la mezcla al molde engrasado y presiónela para conseguir una capa uniforme.

Hornee durante 20–25 minutos, hasta que la corteza quede seca al tacto y esté dorada.

Mezcle la jalea de frambuesa y el jugo de naranja en un cuenco. Esparza uniformemente sobre la corteza. Espolvoree con las nueces picadas restantes.

Hornee las barras hasta que la jalea burbujee, aproximadamente 10-15 minutos más.

Saque del horno y salpíquelas con la miel mientras las barras están aún muy calientes.

Desmolde las barras y colóquelas en una rejilla de metal para que se enfríen completamente antes de cortarlas en barras.

Lista de compras

1 huevo grande (o 1½ cucharaditas de sustituto de huevo Ener-G Egg Replacer
1 naranja pequeña (para la ralladura y el jugo)
¾ de taza de jalea de frambuesa sin semillas

Revise la despensa

Polvo para hornear
Bicarbonato de sodio
Canela
Aceite de coco
Azúcar de coco
Harina libre de gluten
Clavo molido
Nuez moscada molida
Aceite de oliva
Miel cruda
Sal marina
Cacao en polvo sin edulcorar
Nueces

NOTAS

Introducción
Su plan dietético para una salud vibrante

1. Brainyquote.com, "Ralph Waldo Emerson Quotes" [Citas de Ralph Waldo Emerson], www.brainyquote.com/quotes/quotes/r /ralphwaldo105704.html (consultado el 8 de octubre de 2014).

Capítulo 1
La inflamación: amiga o enemiga

1. Como fue citado en P. F. Louis, "Reduce Inflammation Effortlessly by Taking These Top Antioxidants" [Reduzca la inflamación sin esfuerzo tomando los mejores antioxidantes], Naturalnews.com, 21 de julio de 2013, http://www.naturalnews.com/041293_chronic _inflammation_ immune_system_antioxidants.html (consultado el 9 de octubre de 2014).

2. Como fue citado en Jonathan Benson, "Cholesterol Is NOT the Enemy: It's Inflammation That's Making You Fat and Killing You Slowly" [El colesterol NO es su enemigo: La inflamación es lo que lo engorda y lo mata lentamente], 8 de mayo de 2013, Natural news.com, http://www.naturalnews.com/040234_high_cholesterol _heart_disease_medical_myth.html (consultado el 15 de octubre de 2014).

3. Zachary A. Marcum y Joseph T. Hanlon, "Recognizing the Risks of Chronic Nonsteroidal Anti-Inflammatory Drug Use in Older Adults" [El riesgo del uso crónico de antiinflamatorios no esteroides en adultos mayores], *Annals of Long Term Care* [Anales de cuidados a largo plazo] 18, no. 9, septiembre de 2010: 24–27.

4. David R. Hamilton, "5 Beneficial Side Effects of Kindness" [5 efectos secundarios benéficos de la amabilidad], Huffingtonpost .com, 2 de agosto de 2011, http://www.huffingtonpost.com/david-r

-hamilton-phd/kindness-benefits_b_869537.html (consultado el 15 de octubre de 2014).

5. Western Washington University [Universidad de Washington Occidental], "Inflammation" [Inflamación], http://www.wwu.edu/depts /healthyliving/PE511info/infection/Causes.html (consultado el 15 de octubre de 2014).

6. U. N. Das, "Is Obesity an Inflammatory Condition?" [¿Es la obesidad un estado de inflamación?], *Nutrition* [Nutrición] 17, no. 11–12, (noviembre–diciembre de 2001): 953–966; P. Trayhurn and I. S. Wood, "Adipokines: Inflammation and the Pleiotropic Role of White Adipose Tissue"[Adipomioquinas: La inflamación y el papel pleiótico del tejido adiposo blanco], *British Journal of Nutrition* [Revista británica de nutrición] 92, no. 3, (septiembre de 2004): 347–355.

7. H. Florez, S. Castillo-Florez, A. Mendez, et al., "C-Reactive Protein Is Elevated in Obese Patients With the Metabolic Syndrome" [La proteína C-reactiva es elevada en pacientes con síndrome metabólico], *Diabetes Research and Clinical Practice* [Investigación de la diabetes y práctica clínica] 71, no. 1 (enero de 2006): 92–100.

8. A. D. Pradhan, J. E. Manson, J. E. Rossouw, et al., "Inflammatory Biomarkers, Hormone Replacement Therapy, and Incident Coronary Heart Disease: Prospective Analysis From the Women's Health Initiative Observational Study"[Análisis prospectivo del estudio de observación sobre la salud de la mujer], *Journal of the American Medical Association* [Revista de la Asociación Médica Estadounidense] 288, no. 8 (28 de agosto de 2002): 980–987.

9. B. L. Stauffer, G. L. Hoetzer, D. T. Smith, C. A. DeSouza, "Plasma C-Reactive Protein Is Not Elevated in Physically Active Postmenopausal Women Taking Hormone Replacement Therapy" [El plasma de la proteína C-reactiva NO se eleva en mujeres con actividad postmenopáusica que toman sustitutos hormonales], *Journal of Applied Physiology* [Revista de fisiología aplicada] 96, no. 1 (enero de 2004): 143–148.

Capítulo 2
Alimentos y factores que contribuyen con la inflamación

1. Greatest-Inspirational-Quotes.com, "Health Quotes" [Citas saludables], www.greatest-inspirational-quotes.com/health-quotes.html (consultado el 15 de octubre de 2014).

2. Como se hace referencia en Jessica Levine, "The Strange Reason Diet Soda Makes You Fat" [La extraña razón por la que los refrescos de dieta te hacen engordar], Menshealth.com, 21 de junio de 2012, http://www. menshealth.com/weight-loss/diet-soda-fat (consultado el 15 de octubre de 2014).

3. S. Liu, J. E. Manson, J. E. Buring, M. J. Stampfer, W. C. Willett y P. M. Ridker, "Relation Between a Diet With a High Glycemic Load and Plasma Concentrations of High-Sensitivity C-Reactive Protein in Middle-Aged Women" [La relación entre una dieta con alta carga glucémica y las concentraciones de plasma de proteína C-reactiva en mujeres de mediana edad], *American Journal of Clinical Nutrition* [Revista estadounidense de nutrición clínica] 75, no. 2, (marzo de 2002): 492–498.

4. Mark Hyman, "How Diet Soda Makes You Fat (and Other Food and Diet Industry Secrets)" [Cómo los refrescos dietéticos lo hacen engordar (y otros secretos de la industria de alimentos y dietas)], Huffingtonpost.com, 7 de mayo de 2013, http://www.huffingtonpost.com/dr-mark-hyman/diet-soda-health_b_2698494.html (consultado el 15 de octubre de 2014).

5. Datis Kharrazian, *Why Do I Still Have Thyroid Symptoms When My Lab Tests Are Normal: A Revolutionary Breakthrough in Understanding Hashimoto's Disease and Hypothyroidism* [Por qué persisten los síntomas de la tiroides si los estudios de laboratorio registran rangos normales: Un revolucionario avance en el conocimiento del hipotiroidismo y la enfermedad de Hashimoto], (Carlsbad, CA: Elephant Press Books, 2010), 29.

6. Brian Foley, "Hashimoto's Thyroid Auto Immune" [Tiroides autoinmune de Hashimoto], Health and Wellness Center [Centro

de salud y bienestar], http://www.youralternativedoctor.com
/hashimotos-thyroid-auto-immune/ (consultado el 15 de octubre
de 2014).

7. Craig A. Maxwell, "Goitrogens and Your Thyroid—the Surprising
Truth You Need to Know" [Los bociógenos y su tiroides, una sor-
presiva verdad que usted necesita saber], Askdrmaxwell.com, 9
de septiembre de 2013, http://www.askdrmaxwell.com/2013/09
/goitrogens-and-your-thyroid-the-surprising-truth-you-need-to
-know/ (consultado el 15 de octubre de 2014).

8. Como se hace referencia en Mark Hyman, "Milk Is Dangerous for
Your Health" [La leche es dañina para su salud], Drhyman.com,
11 de noviembre de 2013, http://drhyman.com/ blog/2013/10/28
/milk-dangerous-health/#close (consultado el 15 de octubre de
2014).

9. A. Zampelas, D. B. Panagiotakos, C. Pitsavos, C. Chrysohoou y
C. Stefanadis, "Associations Between Coffee Consumption and
Inflammatory Markers in Healthy Persons: The ATTICA Study"
[Asociación entre los consumidores de café y la inflamación en
personas saludables: El estudio ATTICA] *American Journal of
Clinical Nutrition* [Revista de nutrición clínica estadounidense]
80, No. 4, (octubre de 2004): 862–867.

10. Mark Hyman, como se citó en Danielplan.com, "The Liquid
Menace: Alcohol" [La amenaza líquida: el alcohol], http://www
.danielplan.com/healthyhabits/alcohol/ (consultado el 15 de octubre de 2014).

11. Mercola.com, "Engineered Poison Lurking in Your Everyday
Food?" [¿Hay veneno químico asechando diariamente en tu comida?], Dr. Mercola Interview With Jeffrey Smith, 3de abril de
2010, http://articles.mercola.com/sites/articles/archive/2010
/04/03/jef-frey-smith-interview.aspx (consultado el 12 de noviembre de 2014).

12. Tom Philpott, "Longest-Running GMO Safety Study Finds Tumors
in Rats" [El estudio más prolongado de seguridad de los OMG encuentra tumores en ratas], MotherEarthNews.com, abril/mayo de

2013, http://www.motherearthnews.com/natural-health/gmo -safety-zmgz13amzsto.aspx#ixzz3IzXXQD3a (consultado el 14 de noviembre de 2014).

13. Como fue citado en Elisha McFarland, "The Link Between Nightshades, Chronic Pain and Inflammation" [La relación entre las solanáceas, el dolor crónico y la inflamación], Greenmedinfo.com, 21 de abril de 2013, http://www.greenmedinfo.com/blog/link -between-night-shades-chronic-pain-and-inflammation (consultado el 15 de octubre de 2014).

14. PR Newswire, "Researchers Say Tart Cherries Have 'the Highest Anti-Inflammatory Content of Any Food'" [Investigadores aseguran que la cereza ácida es el "alimento con mayor contenido antiinflamatorio"], 30 de mayo de 2012, http:// www.prnewswire.com /news-releases/researchers-say-tart-cherries-have-the-highest-anti -inflammatory-content-of-any-food-155672215.html (consultado el 15 de octubre de 2014); Marco Torres, "How Tart Cherries Reduce Inflammation and Oxidative Stress" [Cómo la cereza ácida reduce la inflamación y el estrés oxidativo], http://healthimpactnews.com /2014/how-tart-cherries-reduce-inflammation-and-oxidative-stress/ (consultado el 15 de octubre de 2014).

15. SweetWater Health, "Bulletproof Food Sense iPhone App First to Detect Food Sensitivities" [Sentido alimenticio blindando: Aplicación para iPhone es la primera en detectar sensibilidad a alimentos], Sweetwaterhrv.com, 16 de julio de 2013, http:// sweetwaterhrv.com/Press/SWH%20BPE%20press%20release %20July%2016%202013.pdf (consultado el 15 de octubre de 2014).

Capítulo 3
¡Cambie su dieta; cambie su vida!

1. Goodreads.com, "Hippocrates Quotes" [Citas de Hipócrates], http://www.goodreads. com/quotes/62262-let-food-be-thy -medicine-and-medicine-be-thy-food (consultado el 15 de octubre de 2014).

2. Mark Hyman, *Ultra-Metabolism* [Ultrametabolismo] (Nueva York: Atria Books, 2006).

3. Federation of American Societies for Experimental Biology [Federación de Sociedades Estadounidenses de biología experimental], "Anti-oxidant Found in Berries [Los antioxidantes que se encuentran en las moras], Other Foods Prevent UV Skin Damage That Leads to Wrinkles" [Otros alimentos que previenen las arrugas causadas por los daños de los rayos UV en la piel], Sciencedaily .com, 23 de abril de 2009, http://www.sciencedaily.com/releases /2009/04/090421154318.htm (consultado el 15 de octubre de 2014).

4. Lindsay Kobayashi, "To Live Longer, Eat 7 Servings of Fruits and Vegetables Per Day" [Para vivir más tiempo, coma 7 porciones de frutas y verduras al día] (blog), Public Health Perspectives, 8 de abril de 2014, http://blogs.plos.org/publichealth/2014/04/08/7 -fruit-veg/ (consultado el 14 de noviembre de 2014).

5. The Nutrition Source, "Vegetables and Fruit: Get Plenty Every Day" [Verduras y frutas: cómalas abundantemente todos los días], Harvard School of Public Health [Escuela de salud pública de Harvard], http://www.hsph.harvard.edu/nutritionsource/vegetables -full-story/ (consultado el 14 de noviembre de 2014).

6. Maureen Callahan, "The Fiftysomething Diet: Should You Be Juicing?" [La dieta de los cincuenta y tantos: ¿Debería estar haciendo jugos?], NextAvenue.org, 30 de junio de 2014, http://www .nextavenue.org/article/2013-03/fiftysomething-diet-should-you -be-juicing (consultado el 14 de noviembre de 2014).

7. Como se hace referencia en Leo Galland, "Cherries for Health: Better Than Aspirin?" [Las cerezas para la salud: ¿Son mejores que la aspirina?], Huffpost.com, 11 de abril de 2011, http://www .huffington post.com/leo-galland-md/cherry-season-fight-pain-_b _844654.html (consultado el 13 de noviembre de 2014).

8. Callahan, "The Fiftysomething Diet: Should You Be Juicing?" [La dieta de los cincuenta y tantos: ¿Debería estar haciendo jugos?].

9. S. V. Joseph, I. Edirisinghe, y B. M. Burton-Freeman, "Berries: Anti-Inflammatory Effects in Humans" [Moras: Su efecto anti-inflamatorio en los seres humanos], Journal of Agricultural and Food Chemistry [Revista de química agrícola y alimentaria] 62, no. 18 (17 de marzo de 2014): 3886–3903.

10. Sally Fallon y Mary G. Enig, "The Oiling of America" [Aceitando a Estados Unidos], Westonaprice.org, 1 de enero de 2000, http://www.westonaprice.org/health-topics/the-oiling-of-america/#rise (consultado el 15 de octubre de 2014).

11. Stephan Guyenet, "The Diet-Heart Hypothesis: Oxidized LDL, Part 1" [Hipótesis de la dieta del corazón: La oxidación de las LDL, Parte 1], Whole Health Source [Fuente de salud integral] (blog), 3 de agosto de 2009, http:// wholehealthsource.blogspot .com/2009/07/diet-heart-hypothesis-oxidized-ldl-part.html (consultado el 14 de noviembre de 2014).

12. Amanda Ruggeri, "Is Your Olive Oil Lying About Its Virginity?" [¿Su aceite de oliva miente acerca de su virginidad?], The Cut [El corte], http://nymag.com/thecut/2014/09/your-olive-oil-lying -about-its-virginity.html (consultado el 14 de noviembre de 2014).

13. DrAxe.com, "Your Olive Oil Extra-Virgin Is Fake!" [¡Su aceite de oliva virgen extra es falso!], http://draxe.com/fake-olive-oil/ (consultado el 14 de noviembre de 2014).

14. MedicalNewsToday.com, "Organic Food Is More Nutritious Say EU Researchers" [Los alimentos orgánicos son más nutritivos aseguran investigadores estadounidenses], 29 de octubre de 2007, http://www.medicalnews-today.com/articles/86972.php (consultado el 13 de noviembre de 2014).

15. Kimberly Gallagher, "A Hearty Burdock Recipe, and Other Burdock Ideas" [Saludables recetas de bardana y otras ideas para usarla], Learningherbs.com, 1 de julio de 2010, http://learning herbs.com/remedies-recipes/burdock-recipe/ (consultado el 15 de octubre de 2014).

16. Botanical Preservation Corps, "Rhodiola Root" [Raíz de rhodiola], botanicalpreservationcorps.com/store/rhodiola-rosea (consultado el 15 de octubre de 2014).

17. Chronic Inflammation: Special Focus: Nutritional Intervention [Inflamación crónica: Enfoque especial: Intervención nutricional], trabajo presentado en septiembre de 2014 por Sally Fisher, MD.

Capítulo 4
Recetas y plan de alimentación de veintiocho días para una salud vibrante

1. Susan Albers, "The 10 Best Healthy Eating Quotes" [Las 10 mejores citas acerca de la alimentación saludable], *Comfort Cravings* [Saciando el apetitito] (blog), *Psychology Today* [Psicología hoy], 13 de julio de 2011, http://psychologytoday.com/blog /comfort-cravings/201107/the-10-best-healthy-eating-quotes (consultado el 7 de noviembre de 2014).

* Suscríbase al Boletín de consejos jugosos [Juicy Tips Newsletter] gratuito de La Dama de los Jugos en www.juiceladyinfo.com.

Sitios web de Cherie

www.juiceladyinfo.com o www.juiceladycherie.com: información para adelgazar y preparar jugos.

www.cheriecalbom.com.

www.gococonuts.com: información sobre el consumo de coco y el aceite de coco.

Los retiros con jugos de salud y bienestar de La Dama de los Jugos

¡Lo invito a que nos acompañe durante una semana que puede cambiar su vida! Nuestros retiros ofrecen alimentos orgánicos de alta cocina crudos con un ayuno de jugos de tres días a media semana. Ofrecemos clases interesantes e informativas en un hermoso y pacífico escenario donde usted podrá experimentar sanidad y restauración del cuerpo y del alma. Para más información, y las fechas de los retiros, llame al 866-843-8935 en los Estados Unidos.

Curso en línea de salud y acondicionamiento físico de La Dama de los Jugos

Para más información, visite www.juiceladycherie.com bajo Weight Loss [Pierda peso] o llame al 866-843-8935 en los Estados Unidos.

Programe una consulta de nutrición con La Dama de los Jugos

Llame al 866-843-8935 en los Estados Unidos.

Para invitar a La Dama de los Jugos a dar una plática para su organización

Llame al 866-843-8935 en los Estados Unidos.

* Esta información es en inglés.

Otros libros de Cherie y John Calbom

Estos libros se pueden pedir en los sitios web arriba mencionados; o bien llamando al 866-8GETWEL (866-843-8935) en los Estados Unidos.

Cherie Calbom, *El gran libro de jugos y batidos verdes* (Casa Creación).

Cherie Calbom, *La dieta turbo de La Dama de los Jugos* (Casa Creación).

Cherie Calbom, *La dieta para perder peso de fin de semana* (Casa Creación).

Cherie Calbom, *Remedios para los desórdenes de la tiroides* (Casa Creación).

Cherie Calbom, *The Juice Lady's Remedies for Asthma and Allergies* [Remedios para el asma y las alergias de La Dama de los Jugos] (Siloam).

Cherie Calbom, *The Juice Lady's Remedies for Stress and Adrenal Fatigue* [Remedios para el estrés y la fatiga suprarrenal de La Dama de los Jugos] (Siloam).

Cherie Calbom, *The Juice Lady's Living Foods Revolution* [La revolución de alimentos vivos de La Dama de los Jugos] (Siloam).

Cherie Calbom, *The Juice Lady's Guide to Juicing for Health* [La guía de La Dama de los Jugos para hacer jugos para recuperar su salud] (Avery).

Cherie Calbom y John Calbom, *Juicing, Fasting, and Detoxing for Life* [Hacer jugos, ayunar y desintoxicarse para vivir] (Wellness Central).

Cherie Calbom, *The Wrinkle Cleanse* [Límpiese de las arrugas] (Avery).

Cherie Calbom y John Calbom, *The Coconut Diet* [La dieta de coco] (Wellness Central).

Cherie Calbom, John Calbom y Michael Mahaffey, *The Complete Cancer Cleanse* [Límpiese completamente del cáncer] (Thomas Nelson).

Cherie Calbom, *The Ultimate Smoothie Book* [El libro definitivo de los batidos] (Wellness Central).

Extractores de jugo

Descubra cuáles son los extractores de jugo recomendados por Cherie. Llame al 866-8GETWEL (866-843-8935) en los Estados Unidos o visite www.juiceladyinfo.com.

Deshidratadores

Encuentre los mejores deshidratadores recomendados por Cherie. Llame al 866-8GETWEL (866-843-8935) en los Estados Unidos o visite www.juiceladyinfo.com.

Estimulante del sistema linfático

Para ver la máquina de oscilación (estimulante del sistema linfático), visite www.juiceladyinfo.com o bien, llame al 866-8GETWEL (866-843-8935) en los Estados Unidos.

Suplementos alimenticios de verduras en polvo

Para comprar o para obtener información sobre Barley Max, Carrot Juice Max y Beet Max, vaya a www.juiceladyinfo.com o bien, llame al 866-8GETWEL (866-843-8935) en los Estados Unidos (estos polvos son ideales cuando usted viaja o cuando no puede hacer jugos).

Aceite de coco virgen

Para más información sobre el aceite de coco virgen, visite www.juiceladyinfo.com o www.gococonuts.com; o bien llame al 866-8GETWEL (866-843-8935) en los Estados Unidos. Para ahorrar dinero, le recomendamos que pida productos en cantidades grandes como galones o cuartos de galón, ya que no los encontrará fácilmente en los almacenes.

Kit de limpieza interna

El kit completo y exhaustivo de limpieza interna contiene dieciocho artículos para un programa de limpieza de veintiún días. Usted obtiene un kit de limpieza de colón gratuito, junto con el rejuvenecedor de hígado y vesícula, el restaurador de bacterias amigables, el limpiador de parásitos, el rejuvenecedor de pulmón, el rejuvenecedor de riñón y vejiga, el rejuvenecedor de sangre y piel y el rejuvenecedor de la linfa. Visite www.juiceladycherie.com para más información. Usted puede pedir los productos de limpieza y obtener 10% de descuento llamando al 866-843-8935.

BerryBreeze™

Mantiene las frutas y las verduras frescas por más tiempo y su nevera con un fresco aroma. Puede ayudarlo a ahorrar hasta $2200 dólares al año mediante evitar el desperdicio de frutas y verduras. Para más información visite www.juiceladycherie.com.

* Regístrese para recibir el boletín de inspiración semanal de la chef Abby. En él encontrará recetas, consejos y otros recursos para cocinar: www.abbys-table.com

Sitio web de la chef Abby, donde encontrará más recetas, un blog semanal de consejos e información sobre eventos: www.abbys-table.com

Escriba a la chef Abby a: info@abbys-table.com.

Para asesorías y clases acerca de alimentación saludable, llame al (503) 828-7662 en los Estados Unidos.

Para clases a grupos y cenas de práctica, póngase en contacto con Abby a info@abbys-table.com o llame al (503) 828-7662 en los Estados Unidos.

Facebook: busque Abby's Table, Portland, OR

Instagram: abbycookswith

Pinterest: Abby's Table

Twitter: #abbystable

* Esta información es en inglés.